The Romance of History

LAWRENCE S. KAPLAN

The Romance
of
History

Essays in Honor
of
Lawrence S. Kaplan

Edited by

Scott L. Bills

&

E. Timothy Smith

The Kent State University Press
Kent, Ohio, and London, England

© 1997 by The Kent State University Press, Kent, Ohio 44242
All rights reserved
Library of Congress Catalog Card Number 96-27660
ISBN 0-87338-563-2
Manufactured in the United States of America

Designed and composed in Trump Mediaeval
by Diana Gordy at The Kent State University Press.
Printed by Braun-Brumfield, Inc.

02 01 00 99 98 97   5 4 3 2 1

Library of Congress Cataloging-in-Publication Data

The romance of history : essays in honor of Lawrence S. Kaplan /
    edited by Scott L. Bills and E. Timothy Smith.
        p. cm.
    Includes bibliographical references and index.
    ISBN 0-87338-563-2 (cloth : alk. paper) ∞
        1. United States—Foreign relations—1945–1989. 2. United States—
    Foreign relations—1801–1809. 3. North Atlantic Treaty Organization—
    History.   4. Cold War. I. Kaplan, Lawrence S. II. Bills, Scott L. III. Smith,
    E. Timothy.
    E840.R58   1997   96-27660
    327.73—dc20

British Library Cataloging-in-Publication data are available.

For Lawrence S. Kaplan,
scholar, mentor, & friend

Contents

Acknowledgments

C ertainly a number of people participated in the genesis of this volume. The initial suggestion for the festschrift came from Bert Zeeman and Cees Wiebes and was then carried forward by Victor Papacosma, the current director of the Lyman L. Lemnitzer Center for NATO and European Community Studies. We then welcomed the opportunity to edit the volume. A number of Kaplan's former students were unable to take part in the project because of conflicting commitments or lapsed research interests. Even so, their enthusiasm for the book was energizing. As the first article drafts began to arrive, we relied upon the expertise of Harry W. Fritz, Richard Immerman, Jeffrey Kimball, Robert McMahon, and Robert Schulzinger as readers. Their comments, always incisive, much improved the quality of the end product. In addition, Carrie Sullivan and Michele Sparks, graduate assistants at Stephen F. Austin State University, helped with the tedious task of transferring text to diskette, thus speeding along the final manuscript. Kenny Hite and Stella Carroll at Barry University assisted with correspondence. We thank all of the above, as well as each contributor, for their efforts toward the completion of this festschrift, so richly deserved by the man it honors as mentor and friend.

Introduction

The measured and careful words of Lawrence S. Kaplan have, over the years, helped probe and define two vital areas of American history: first, the diplomacy of the early republic and, second, the evolution of the North Atlantic Treaty Organization. Both eras were filled with challenges, risks, and policymakers alternately wise and unwise, brash and humble, idealistic and pragmatic. Both periods were punctuated by crises that appeared to threaten the foundations of the nation. And, for Kaplan, both eras were linked by a common thread of reason that patiently shaped an effective diplomacy to shield the republic in a world shadowed by the sway of global rivals. Through a lifetime of teaching and scholarship, Kaplan has given voice to one of the vital tasks of the historians' profession: to tell stories that probe, enlighten, and provoke. As he remarked in an interview in 1986, "It was the romance of history that first attracted me. The stories are filled with excitement."[1] His own excitement remained unabated through forty years of teaching at Kent State University, wooing his undergraduates and challenging his graduate students to pursue the kind of sophisticated, multiarchival research he himself had learned and practiced.

Kaplan knew early on that he intended to be a historian. It was a sentiment that drew upon his own father's love of such historians as Thomas Macaulay and Edward Gibbon (it was Macaulay's book that his father kept in the car's glove compartment) and was nurtured by Kaplan's schooling at Colby College, Maine, where he began attending classes in 1941 at the age of sixteen. Two years later he was drafted into the army and served in the Philippines in the Signal Corps. Here was a true watershed. From battlefields and bivouacs, Kaplan worked on an extension course on the French Revolution offered by the University of Wisconsin. "They sent me Louis Gottschalk's textbook, *Era of the French Revolution,* and I had reports to do; and I was doing them in the rain, in the foxhole." The reports were not very good, admits Kaplan, but the task was meaningful. "As for the course, I never finished it, [only] about ten or twelve lessons . . . it was just too much." Why bother? "Well, I was concerned with keeping alive an intellectual life of sorts even in the service, and that was a way of doing it." He recalls also the important experience of participating in the liberation of a Filipino town on the island of Samar, finding there, on a wall, a copy of the Philippines constitution prepared by the Japanese puppet regime—a document that closely paralleled the American model. However, the constitution seemed to be a poor match to the Filipino situation, a realization that Kaplan credits as having directly stimulated his thoughts about the universality of the U.S. system. On his journey home after the Japanese surrender, Kaplan read the works of such American historians as Charles Beard and Samuel Flagg Bemis. By war's end, he had developed both a desire to work with Bemis (at Yale) and to pursue his interest in the impact abroad of American ideas and institutions. But the Ivy League campus was not easily accessible. Journeying to New Haven, Kaplan found everyone "polite enough" but unwilling to give him much credit for work completed at Colby. For this reason, he finished his undergraduate work in Maine. "Colby gave me credit for physical education (for being in the army); they gave me credit for science for my cryptographic study (which was not scientific)—they cut a lot of corners for a lot of us [veterans]."[2]

It was to be Yale University, of course, for graduate school, where Kaplan and Robert Ferrell became close friends: "We met the first day . . . and the requirement at the university was that you had to pass German and French in order to be enrolled as a doctoral student. We'd both come from smaller schools, and we saw that German exam and each of us knew we weren't going to pass it. I didn't know him that first time. We just sort of greeted each other." But they found themselves together again in their examiner's office after "word got out that no American history major passed the exam. . . . And we looked at each other dolefully." Each failed his first day at Yale—two men from towns called Waterville, one in Maine, the other in Ohio. "We wondered whether we were going back again in disgrace." Both passed the second time, worked successfully with Bemis, and have maintained close personal and professional ties to this day. It is for this reason that Robert Ferrell has been designated as keynoter for the festschrift.

Kaplan's doctoral work focused on the early republic, particularly on the diplomacy of Thomas Jefferson. "Bemis wanted me to do a dissertation to refute the Jeffersonians—do a real Federalist diatribe. Which I didn't. That isn't what I wanted to do. . . . I didn't regard myself as anti-Jefferson [and] . . . had no intention of being a Federalist apologist." Alexander DeConde seconds this judgment in his essay for this volume. Yet, to many other students in the field, no student of Bemis could be a friend to Jefferson. In fact, Bemis felt the final manuscript was "too soft" on the statesman from Monticello, but he accepted the dissertation. It was a rare experience, Kaplan later remembered, to work with a man of such keen intellect. However, Bemis's authoritarian teaching style did not endear him to many students. Years later, Kaplan consciously developed a different style: less antagonistic, more forgiving, more gracious, more open to opposing viewpoints.

Degree in hand, however, there were no jobs. Ferrell, Kaplan, and others appealed for guidance. (Kaplan had married in 1948; his wife, Jan, a psychologist by training, helped to put him through graduate school.) "We all panicked and went up to the graduate office and said we have no jobs and they . . . looked as if we had committed some kind of faux pas even talking about something like jobs—the assumption at Yale was that you worked for love and you married for money. You don't talk about 'jobs.'" But this was a GI generation of scholars without independent means.

Fortunately, the historian Sherman Kent, formerly of the war-time Office of Strategic Services, came to the reserve. Ensconced in Washington, he drew Yale graduates into government positions. Kaplan was recruited for work in the Pentagon, in the Office of the Historian, and assigned to study the North Atlantic Treaty. "I didn't know anything about it," he recounts. "I didn't even pay attention in 1949 [when the treaty was signed]—I was deep into Jefferson." As a junior historian in the office, he "was tapped to do this massive study of the Military Assistance Program, which was the Defense path into NATO, that linked NATO to the Pentagon." Much of the work of Pentagon historians consisted of "writing their semiannual reports, which were dreadful things." But Kaplan had found a new interest. "I conceived at that time something I've stayed with for forty years: that the Atlantic Alliance was the end of something that had begun with the Treaty of Mortefontaine [abrogating the Franco-American Alliance of 1778]. . . . From 1800 to 1949, [there was] almost a hundred and fifty year period [of nonentanglement]—and this [notion] was exciting to me. I cared very little about the Military Assistance Program, but NATO attracted me. So off and on, I did work on it. I was there three years and got about 150 pages done." At that point, he submitted the manuscript to the Office of North Atlantic Treaty Affairs "with the notion that they would profit from this, to help them make policy—this was the whole idea for the office. It was sent down there, and I just waited on tenterhooks, and it was two or three weeks, though it seemed like ten, what would they say about this? And they finally responded, sent back word that this—and I shan't forget this either—this was a wonderful project, a great piece of work, *but we don't have time to read it.* If I would reduce it to one or maybe two pages, they would give it their full attention. And at that point, I figured this is not for me. I've got to get out of here."

This was the spring of 1954. Teaching jobs were scarce. Through the academic grapevine, Kaplan learned of a job at Kent State University. The chair preferred Harvard men but would settle for Yale. Kaplan interviewed for and was offered the position. "And so I made the choice. I was twenty-nine years old and figured if I didn't get into teaching now I may never do it. And I took it." This was still an era when Kent had a semirural setting. As Kaplan recalls, "The main street was narrow with the trees and leaves making an arbor effect. It was just lovely, and the campus was small. It really looked nice to me." And it was supposed to look nice. A 1959 brochure, published by the city's Chamber of Commerce, declared that amid the industrial belt of northeastern Ohio, the town retained its pastoral charm and was "resplendent with attractive houses and beautiful trees."[3]

Lawrence and Jan Kaplan settled into "Tree City" comfortably, if not always contentedly. Initially, the years at Kent were rather quiet. He honed his teaching skills, published several articles on Jefferson and NATO, served on committees, and chaperoned dances. It was in 1958 that Kaplan sat down and outlined, "for myself really, this idea of working in two areas, the early and the late. . . ." It was a propitious moment: a heightened interest in research and publishing coincided with the inauguration of Kent State's history doctoral program in 1961—a program that would require a core of dedicated scholars. Then Bemis came for a visit in 1964. Retired now, a bit more affable, he was systematically touring his former students. He pressed Kaplan to get his dissertation published. The book appeared in 1967 as *Jefferson and France: An Essay on Politics and Political Ideas*, soon followed by *Colonies Into Nation* (1972). It was during a research trip in the early 1960s that Kaplan first met Alexander DeConde, whose contribution to the festschrift analyzes the full thematic range of Kaplan's writings on the early republic.

Thus began an energetic and fruitful career as scholar that would, by the 1970s and 1980s, find Kaplan teaching less and traveling more. However, if he taught less, it was not for want of enthusiasm. Instinctively, Kaplan rejected the cold, imperial style of his mentor at Yale. As he put it, "Bemis was *the* great scholar, a potentate, and he behaved that way." More to the point, he commented, "I don't believe in terrorizing students." Yet, Kaplan "respected the fact that the discipline was there [in Bemis's courses,] and we really learned; and I wanted to be able—if I could do it—to get that sense of excitement and discipline without the authoritarian manner." This was his great achievement in the classroom. As one graduate student recalled, "I remember him as a warm, caring, and concerned teacher. I remember him as an enthralling lecturer able to hold people's interest quite easily.

'Nobody ever cared about Maine,' he would bellow during his lecture on the Aroostock War [1838–39]."[4] In front of his class, Kaplan was ever animated, physically and vocally, pacing, his voice rising and falling, sometimes booming. His blend of anecdotes, historiography, and narrative was masterful. Students remembered his penchant for giving exams in the library, where one could smoke, giving his test-takers the run of the stacks so long as they did not consult their lecture notes.

To his upper-level courses, Kaplan might confide that a few broad axioms were sufficient to allow his survey students to rest easy at night, but for the more sophisticated, he would do better. In doing so, he conveyed the genuine complexity of history, encouraging discussion, meeting outside of class with his graduate students and asking them to "swim" in documentary collections and other primary sources, as well as to read more standard historiographical fare. Acting consciously "contra Bemis" as lecturer, Kaplan also refused to be the same kind of stern shepherd among his graduate flock. He encouraged the expression of opposing viewpoints in his seminars and even rewarded those who, by the 1970s (including the editors of this volume), considered themselves "revisionists" and preferred to read William A. Williams, Joyce and Gabriel Kolko, Lloyd Gardner, and others who challenged established orthodoxy about the origins and character of the cold war.

Though they might joke about it in class, Kaplan and Ferrell were uneasy about the strife in their field during the early 1970s. They both felt "beleaguered." The targeting of older Cold War theories and institutions could hardly fail to strike at the rationale for the North Atlantic Treaty and question not only its efficacy but its purpose. Kaplan's own enduring themes had already been well adumbrated: an American tradition of detachment from political and military obligation to Europe. "When we talk of isolationism, we don't talk about Latin America; we don't talk about Asia. It's the memory of European exploitation of the colonies and later of the early republic; and the whole history of the early republic was an attempt to stay free from control and at the same time profit from whatever relationship that could be made. And this was essentially done by the time of the Monroe Doctrine [followed by continental expansion over the next century]." For decades afterward, American leaders favoring a larger global role garnered little public support for international entanglements. "Here were these distinguished people who were quite ineffectual, would-be Europeans or wannabe Europeans, who were representing the country at a time when no one had much interest in what they were doing. They were disregarded."

Heavy British investment in the burgeoning infrastructure did not result in control of U.S. internal affairs. "That is, the United States really enjoyed—and this is Bemis's point—a relatively free ride in the nineteenth century. And that, of course, comes to a close gradually in the twentieth century, with a lot of the illusions still pretty much intact: we are a superior nation, we have a moral vision, and so forth." For Kaplan, only close involvement with Europe would have counted as an abandonment of isolationism. Economic interaction did not entail the kind of commitments inherent in politico-military ties. No, America pursued a path of nonentanglement, as advised by its Founding Fathers, until the arrival of the Cold War. Then, pushed by a ruthless and expansionist Soviet Union, the United States embarked on a historic and heroic reversal with NATO and succeeding commitments.

This analysis, of course, was anathema to revisionists of all stripes, including the followers of William A. Williams's "open door" thesis as well as (and worse, from Kaplan's perspective) those with assorted leftist ideological agendas. Orthodoxy was more than foolhardy: it was court history that legitimized an American imperium. The Vietnam War caused an intense debate within the historical profession alongside the widespread societal upheaval.[5] "I felt that we were fighting a very defensive war against the aggressive younger generation, fueled by the Vietnam issue, who were after the consensus historians," lamented Kaplan. The proponents of orthodoxy were assailed in a manner that violated what Peter Novick has termed the "comity" of the discipline. "Most historians, to be sure, were not found at the extremes," wrote Novick, "but the center had lost its vitality."[6] It was "really very rough," recalls Kaplan, especially at conferences, those periodic professional gatherings where the atmosphere previously could be relied upon to be dry, sedate, even boring. No longer. Conferences became battlegrounds between opposing historiographical legions.

The fading of the intensity of this intradisciplinary conflict has often been retold. It did force Kaplan and others to rethink many of their earlier assumptions, though not ultimately to reject them. As the essay by Bert Zeeman and Cees Wiebes ably points out, Kaplan was eager to embrace the "postrevisionism" of John Lewis Gaddis when it appeared in 1983 as an effort to revitalize the center.[7] Because of its conservative bent, Kaplan still readily identifies with the thesis. As he said with reference to Gaddis's original presentation: "He's the one who restored the balance, you see, with his postrevisionism, which really is a more sophisticated view of court history—the critics were right about that."[8] Indeed, postrevisionism did mute the generational character of the historiographical dispute, and it did so in a way that allowed Kaplan and others to remain unconvinced by the claims of the revisionist camp. "The main theme of the revisionists is that we were the ones that started the Cold War, that the Soviets were essentially acting defensively; but that isn't the case."

Asked in December 1994 how his ideas had changed over the years, Kaplan felt that he might have "softened" on Jefferson. His ideas on isolationism remained much the same. His views on the Cold War had moderated but were still within reach of the old orthodoxy. Even so, he worried that American globalism had become too much a reflex action: "I feel more now that we've taken on too much. I feel much more inclined toward a John Quincy Adams now than I would have forty years ago. That you can't do everything. One of the things I liked about the Nixon Doctrine, if it were honest, is that it really was saying that the Truman Doctrine was too much. . . . It was phony [in that it was put forward as a new doctrine when in fact it was more designed simply to cover the American retreat from Vietnam], but nonetheless it made a lot of sense. We're drifting between temptations to go back to the shell and the temptation to keep the superpower status and take on the world. We've never resolved that. My information now suggests that we should lean more toward the more modest position than the more extravagant." And NATO? "I think NATO has to survive, for our own sake. . . . Europe needs NATO not just because of Russia but because of Germany." The North Atlantic Treaty Organization "provides a stability and a justification for an American involvement that I think continues to be important." The alliance remains a crucial reminder of a direct U.S. interest in the affairs of the Old World. Due in large part to the pioneering work of Kaplan, the Atlantic Pact remains a vital area of research and publication in the field of American diplomacy. The legacy he leaves the profession is that of dedicated scholar, admirable mentor, and prolific writer. His sustained pursuit of truth carried him further toward the revisionists than he perhaps intended, accompanied by an abiding integrity and stubborn insistence upon themes that remain vibrant and engaging.

Lawrence Kaplan's two fields of scholarship required two separate essays of analysis, such has been his extensive impact in the field. Surely there is no better indicator of success than his tenure, respectively, as president of the Society for the Historians of American Foreign Relations (1981) and, also, the Society for Historians of the Early American Republic (1991–92). In his essay, Alexander DeConde contends that Kaplan's career-long scholarly concerns are revealed in his initial writings about the early national period, that "much of his thinking on the history of the developing republic shows an unusual stability." DeConde emphasizes Kaplan's "balanced judgment" and finds persuasive his emphasis on diplomacy as the key factor both in securing American independence and solidifying Federalist and Jeffersonian factions in the 1790s. Yet, Kaplan's Jefferson is flexible, even pragmatic, despite his long-term affection for France. According to DeConde, three themes dominate Kaplan's scholarship in this area: "They are Jefferson as the commanding figure of the period, the advantages American diplomatists gained through their exploiting of European quarrels [also a Bemis thesis], and the blossoming of nonentanglement, or isolationism, as the bedrock of American foreign policy."

Dutch scholars Cees Wiebes and Bert Zeeman provide an analysis of the principal elements of Kaplan's contributions to NATO scholarship over a forty-year period. They credit Kaplan with drawing the attention of fellow historians toward the study of NATO in its own right, rather than as an appendage to broader Cold War policymaking. Wiebes and Zeeman sketch the evolution in his Cold War views from what they call a traditionalist/ realist model toward a postrevisionist position, specifically, a moderate neorealist. The authors found three main themes in Kaplan's NATO studies. First, they note the importance he places on the beginnings of the alliance, its evolution, and the relationship between NATO and the United States. Second is the theme of isolation/entanglement, stretching from the beginning of the republic through and beyond the North Atlantic Treaty, which is so strongly advanced in our discussion above. Finally, they note that much of Kaplan's work has centered on the continued vitality of the alliance through a series of difficult crises. Wiebes and Zeeman are able to identify in Kaplan's career the official historian, the researcher, and the lecturer: the multilevel scholar and teacher that many of his students have sought to emulate.

Robert Ferrell's "Diplomacy without Armaments, 1945–1950" serves as our keynote article, carrying forward the orthodox view of an America hardly in a position to menace distant lands in the immediate postwar years. Noting Harry Truman's inexperience, Ferrell describes a floundering foreign policy in the months after Franklin Roosevelt's death in April 1945. Although Truman was a quick-study, he was hampered nonetheless by an incompetent Edward Stettinius and an inexperienced James Byrnes, who "was no fit successor to Stettinius, save in comparison to Stettinius." Ferrell portrays a rather dismal process of demobilization, regrouping, and rebudgeting for the postwar military establishment, combined with senior officers preoccupied with interservice rivalries. This state of affairs lent small support to an aggressive diplomacy toward the Soviet Union. The atomic bomb, writes Ferrell, supposedly the mainstay of American deterrence, was not available in significant quantities as a deliverable weapon until 1950. The nuclear shield "was anything but that." Like Kaplan, Ferrell sees the Korean War as the real breath of life for NATO and the start of a genuine American military renaissance.

Ronald L. Hatzenbuehler, one of the few students whom Kaplan found willing to study in the early national period, opens the third section of the book with a discussion of certain themes that have run through American history from Thomas Jefferson to the present, including some developed by Kaplan in his own studies. Noting the efforts of President William Clinton to draw on the Jeffersonian tradition, Hatzenbuehler compares the first inaugural address of both men. He stresses the vast differences in the country over the two hundred years separating the two leaders and points out that Jefferson's address necessarily contained concerns clearly rooted in his era and his personal experiences. However, despite the time span that separates Clinton and Jefferson, Hatzenbuehler argues that there are many common elements in their addresses. In particular, the essay focuses on isolationism. Where Jefferson called for entanglement with no one, Clinton sought to reaffirm a close working relationship with America's allies. This reflects not a rejection of Jefferson's views but rather the belief that the United States had arrived at the place our Founders envisioned, with democracy expanding across the globe.

Lynne K. Dunn focuses her work on issues frequently at the heart of Kaplan's scholarly interest: isolationism and internationalism. Her study centers on the internationalists of the 1920s, who, despite the defeat of U.S. membership in the League of Nations, constituted a significant portion of the opinion makers and attentive public. Yet, even with their numbers and their financial resources, the internationalists failed to have a significant impact on the Republican administrations of the 1920s. In particular, Dunn is interested in those internationalists "marginalized" in the generic histories of the decade. Noting the importance of the prevailing concepts of sovereignty and nationalism, and the divisiveness within dissenters' ranks, she concludes that genuine internationalist ideals were prostituted in pursuit of political victories.

Lawrence Kaplan has recalled that the army made available various reading materials during his service in the Philippines in 1944–45. He sought to sustain an active intellectual life while serving as a private in the forces of "Dugout Doug," as the general was often referred to in lecture (not always fondly). George T. Mazuzan's article describes a process whereby professional historians who remained out of uniform played a direct role in providing informational materials to "citizen-soldiers" of the republic, offering a "knothole through which to view the sometimes difficult interaction between the American military and civilian scholars engaged in what both parties viewed as service to a common patriotic enterprise." It was the American Historical Association that provided the institutional base and human resources for a troop-education campaign designed to produce discussions

"attractive for a broad soldier audience." Mazuzan effectively outlines the operation and the perhaps inevitable problems of a pro-
paganda/educational program that required the active cooperation of a number of wartime agencies. In addition, there were
wrangles over the treatment of sensitive topics, when historical
analyses clashed with army priorities. But in the end, concludes
Mazuzan, the successes of the project outweighed the bureaucratic tangles and marked an advance for what would later be
termed public history, a field that Kaplan explored as well.

Scott L. Bills examines the work of the Council of Foreign Ministers (CFM) outside its usual framework of treaty maker for the
victorious allies and boiler room for early Cold War tensions. Instead, he focuses on the lesser-known task performed by the Council in supervising the disposition of former Italian colonies in
Africa: Libya (with its distinct areas of Cyrenaica, Tripolitania,
and the thinly populated Fezzan), Eritrea, and Italian Somaliland
(Somalia). When the peace treaty of 1947 stripped Rome of its
African empire, it was the CFM that assumed interim responsibility for the colonies. British military administration, established
in all former colonies during the war, remained in place, and the
Council designated a special Four Power Commission of Investigation to travel through the territories to evaluate the socioeconomic conditions and assess the wishes of the local populations.
The long, difficult process bore no fruit in terms of a resolution of
the colonial question, which passed to the United Nations in 1948.
However, the lengthy, often tedious, discussions did much to sustain close Anglo-American cooperation in the Middle East, and
the work of the Commission of Investigation represented the most
thorough analysis of the colonial condition up to that point in
history.

E. Timothy Smith builds upon a foundation introduced in
Lawrence Kaplan's work on the United States and NATO. Smith
explores the pacifist and internationalist opposition to the North
Atlantic Treaty. Rather than focusing on the "isolationists," his
article centers on those who felt that the United States should be
actively involved in the postwar world but opposed a military
alliance. Examining prominent individuals, including Henry
Wallace and James Warburg, and various groups opposed to the
Atlantic Alliance, Smith identifies several shared themes, includ-

ing the pact's threat to the United Nations, the potential for the militarization of U.S. foreign policy, and the danger that lay in supporting the aspirations of colonial nations. Noting the validity points in the critique, Smith concludes, as did Kaplan, that the opposition had no impact in 1949.

Richard F. Grimmett addresses the role of foreign policy in Republican politics in the 1952 presidential election. Noting the division between the Old Guard and the eastern internationalist wing within the party, Grimmett analyzes the effort by the isolationist senator, Robert Taft, to win the presidential nomination, asserting that Taft's ideas set the tone for the 1952 campaign. In doing so, he draws heavily upon the Taft Papers in the Library of Congress. Grimmett notes that while the eventual winner, Dwight Eisenhower, favored U.S. involvement in Europe, Taft worked with Eisenhower and John Foster Dulles to write a party platform they could all accept, and Eisenhower needed Taft's support. Although the Democrats attempted to point out the evident cracks in the Republican coalition, they failed to diminish Eisenhower's credibility. Once elected, Eisenhower was forced to confront such contradictions, and, as Grimmett concludes, did not end containment, but rather expanded its frontiers.

T. Michael Ruddy examines the American response to neutralism during the 1950s, focusing on Finland, "a nation precariously poised on the border of the Soviet Union." Ruddy emphasizes that the Eisenhower administration in truth understood the appeal of nonalignment amid the rigidity of the Cold War order but remained concerned that the Soviets would exploit neutralism in order to generate greater influence in world affairs. The author looks at the role of Finnish leader Juro K. Paasikivi in presiding over a policy that mollified Stalin's worries about a Helsinki regime linked to the West. In this way, Paasikivi preserved Finland's internal autonomy while reassuring U.S. policymakers of his peoples' basic pro-Western allegiance. Ruddy's article shows how an avowedly hard-line anticommunist administration exhibited a "basic pragmatism" and thus finessed the issue by distinguishing between "neutrality" and "neutralism."

J. K. Sweeney, in the final article, explores the unusual relationship between Portugal and the United States during the Salazar years, especially the complex politics engendered by the Second

World War and postwar period, including the Atlantic Alliance. For Washington, the driving force behind sustaining friendly relations with Lisbon was the desire to retain U.S. air bases in the Azores, first established during World War II and viewed as essential in the Cold War era. Sweeney points out that a major problem in the relationship was Portugal's role as a colonial power, first in Southeast Asia during the war, then later in Angola. Despite the frequent disagreements over colonial possessions and strategic priorities—capped by the 1974 revolution—the fact remained that the arrangements between the two nations were a "marriage of convenience": a relationship, Sweeney notes, which remained a useful contractual obligation.

Abbreviations

AAIC	American Association for International Cooperation
AALN	American Association for a League of Nations
ADA	Americans for Democratic Action
AEC	Atomic Energy Commission
AHA	American Historical Association
BMA	British Military Administration
CCAO	Chief Civil Affairs Officer (War Office)
CFM	Council of Foreign Ministers
CIG	Central Intelligence Group
COI	Commission of Investigation
DCA	Director of Civil Affairs, War Office
DDEL	Dwight D. Eisenhower Library
DEPITCOL	Deputies for the Former Italian Colonies
DSNA	Department of State Records, National Archives
EDC	European Defense Community

FNLA	National Liberation Front of Angola
FO	Foreign Office
FOR	Fellowship of Reconciliation
FRELIMO	Mozambican Liberation Movement
FRUS	Department of State, *Foreign Relations of the United States*
HSB	Historical Service Board
JCS	Joint Chiefs of Staff (U.S.)
LEP	League to Enforce the Peace
LFNS	League of Free Nations Society
LNNPA	League of Nations Non-Partisan Association
MRB	Military Reference Branch, National Archives
NA	National Archives, Washington, D.C.
NAACP	National Association for the Advancement of Colored People
NAT	North Atlantic Treaty
NATO	North Atlantic Treaty Organization
NCPW	National Council for Prevention of War
NSC	National Security Council
PCA	Progressive Citizens of America
PRO	Public Record Office, Kew, England
RG	Record Group
SAC	Strategic Air Command
SCPC	Swarthmore College Peace Collection
SACEUR	Supreme Allied Commander, Europe
SHAFR	Society for Historians of American Foreign Relations
SYL	Somali Youth League
UMT	Universal Military Training
UN	United Nations

UNO	United Nations Organization
WHO	White House Office
WILPF	Women's International League for Peace and Freedom
WRL	War Resisters League

Historiography

CHAPTER I

Perspectives on the Early Republic

ALEXANDER DECONDE

Among historians of American diplomacy, Lawrence Kaplan
represents a dwindling breed. A versatile scholar involved
in diverse and wide-ranging intellectual and professional interests, he has nonetheless devoted a significant portion of his career to teaching, studying, and writing about the foreign relations
of the early national period. Few diplomatic historians today spe-
cialize in, or even occasionally focus on, this aspect of the American past. To him, however, it has always been an important part
of his professional commitment.

When, in the late forties, Kaplan began his graduate studies at
Yale, early American diplomacy still attracted considerable scholarly attention. Several of the nation's finest historians devoted
their endeavors to it. His distinguished mentor, Samuel F. Bemis,
for one, acquired his international reputation by examining the
diplomacy of the Founding Fathers and those who immediately
followed. He received two Pulitzer prizes for books on the Jay
Treaty and on John Quincy Adams.[1]

Given this background, Bemis, in a seminar in 1948, logically
steered the young Kaplan into examining the diplomacy of the
early period. Specifically, the established scholar put the new graduate student to work on Thomas Jefferson, a topic that became
the basis for Kaplan's doctoral dissertation on Jefferson and France,

3

and for much of his later research and writing. Shortly after receiving the doctorate, Kaplan began publishing what would become a stream of scholarly essays, starting with a piece on the French philosophes and the American Revolution. A number of his pieces dealt with aspects of early American diplomacy.[2] Within the next decade, Kaplan continued to write and publish important essays while reworking and polishing his dissertation. In 1967 he published the result as his first book, *Jefferson and France: An Essay on Politics and Political Ideas.*[3]

In *Jefferson and France* we can see a kind of model for most of Kaplan's writing—except for important bibliographical pieces—that followed on the foreign relations of the early republic.[4] This study lays out his basic style of scholarship, as well as themes, theses, and interpretive issues that would engage his attention for many years. It also reveals his perspective on significant issues in the politics and diplomacy of the national period he would choose to explore in greater depth in the course of his scholarly career.

In this book, as the title suggests, the seven chapters revolve around Jefferson and his ideas relating to foreign relations, their sources, their influence on policy, and the politics of diplomacy, rather than primarily around the give-and-take of negotiations that form the traditional core of diplomatic history. Throughout, Kaplan analyzes Jefferson's thinking, its international scope, its connection to domestic politics as they affected the developing American nation, and its impact, where appropriate, on foreign policy. Although in later years Kaplan would admit that many of his "initial conceptions have been modified over time," much of his thinking on the history of the developing republic shows an unusual stability. For example, he never abandoned his assessment of Jefferson, implicit in his initial study, as "the dominant figure of his age."[5]

Following this major publication, Kaplan continued to write on specific problems of the early national period in articles for scholarly journals. At the same time he embarked on a larger venture, an interpretive synthesis of the diplomacy of the American Revolution and of the Federalist period, which was published in 1972 and titled, appropriately, *Colonies into Nation.*[6] He grounded this work on the overarching theme of a blossoming American nationalism, evident even in the colonial period, a theme he acknowledges to be associated with the work of the historian Max Savelle.[7] Kaplan, in a sense, goes further than Savelle, averring that, by 1763, "it is simple enough to assert and even to document the facts of colonial autonomy and colonial diplomacy. They existed; they flourished."[8]

Kaplan shows how soon this irrepressible nationalism led to America's revolution. From this point on, he advances several significant theses. As he puts it, "The path of independence led . . . to a political isolation that the next generation was to complete."[9] Several generations of historians have long embraced this interpretation as dogma. Kaplan gives it high priority, examines it, explains it, and demonstrates its validity.

A second thesis, that diplomacy had a major role in the winning of independence from Britain, also has wide acceptance among historians of American foreign relations but provokes challenge from historians who focus on internal affairs. The latter often regard the diplomacy of the Revolution as less important than other factors, such as the outcome on the battlefield and the political conditions in Britain and the colonies. I have always found Kaplan's thesis persuasive, particularly because he offers it with balanced judgment.

He uses the same balance in dealing with other controversial issues. For example, he analyzes from several perspectives France's crucial decision to aid the United States, to recognize it, to conclude an alliance with it in February 1778, and to join it in war against Britain. Then he explains the decision in terms found in most of the literature on the subject but with a spin of his own. France's foreign minister, the Comte de Vergennes, he writes, desired "a psychic recovery from the traumatic losses of 1763." He "wanted revenge upon Britain and the reduction of her status in the world."

Most historians overdo the revenge thesis by citing it as an end in itself. But Kaplan makes more sense of it. He stresses, as do most astute statesmen, that the French leaders sought something tangible for their aid. They wanted the "establishment of France in Britain's place."[10] In another piece, Kaplan points out that to a considerable degree Dutch sympathy for the American cause, too, rested on the anticipation of gain.[11]

This desire for benefit generally oils the engines of diplomacy everywhere. In this instance, the French profit motive appears starkly logical because, as Kaplan points out in a later piece where he deals with the same theme, "the French decision for alliance was also a decision for war" and hence a costly one that had to bring some tangible reward. Moreover, as the superior power, in Kaplan's perspective, France made the American connection an "entangling alliance" to ensure a long-term benefit.[12] He points out that with the alliance, "France gave the United States a remarkable gift—that of a successful conclusion to the Revolution." In another essay he shows that "in the short run the benefits outweighed the debits."[13]

After the Americans, with the aid of France, secured their independence, many of them who also thought in terms of gain and loss came to view the alliance with suspicion. They saw it as no longer capable of conferring solid benefits upon them or the nation as a whole. Indeed, Kaplan concludes, "The treaty lost much of its significance to both parties after the war ended." Even though the alliance would survive for almost two more decades, he maintains that after independence "it lacked vitality."[14]

Yet the alliance had been and remained an important component of Jefferson's Francophilia, or reputed Francophilia. Kaplan explains why in *Jefferson and France*, as he traces the bond to France and analyzes it from beginning to end. This theme of the French connection plays prominently in his other writings.[15] He points out that prior to the American Revolution Jefferson nurtured pride in his Anglo-Saxon heritage and that even when the Revolution came he did not at first realize how crucial the role of France would be in the winning of independence. Only with the "formation of the French alliance with the United States," Kaplan writes, did Jefferson begin to change his opinion of France and embrace her.[16]

In Kaplan's analysis, this "affection for France" was "deep and genuine" but not a blind, emotional, or "boundless" love affair.[17] Jefferson embraced France mainly because he had come to fear and detest Britain. Perceiving France as a potential counterweight to British power, he turned to Paris with a keen awareness of American goals and interests. He came to believe also that a community of interest in "domestic as well as foreign affairs existed between his country and France."[18] Yet in his first two years in the cabinet, Kaplan argues, a consensus "over America's relations with the outside world persisted."[19] It broke down after 1792, when France became a republic.

At that point, in Kaplan's view, "The emotional dimension of Anglophilia dominated the Federalist outlook on the world even as Great Britain's treatment of American commerce took a turn for the worse."[20] In the following years, as France and the United States quarreled over the nature of American neutrality, Jefferson's preference for France remained steadfast.

In dealing with the major foreign policy issues of these years, Kaplan advances two other theses diplomatic historians generally accept but that often arouse dissent from other scholars. He maintains that the diplomacy of the early republic, usually considered as dominated by Jefferson and Alexander Hamilton, had a vital function in the survival of the young nation in a hostile world. Challengers of this thesis perceive internal politics and economic factors as more significant. Kaplan asserts that "Anglophilia and Francophilia were the source of the divisive passions which marked the 1790s rather than agrarianism and mercantilism. A foreign policy still tied to the fortunes of Europe, which neither statesman had desired in 1789, dictated the direction of American politics."[21]

Thus, Kaplan regards the debates over the orientation of foreign policy as producing the great division between Federalist and Jeffersonian politicians. Other historians insist that sectional, economic, and other factors were of greater consequence in begetting the two national political parties.

Again, I find Kaplan's perspective one we cannot ignore. He does not dismiss the importance of the domestic component in the emergence of national political parties because he recognizes that virtually from the beginning of the republic politicians blended domestic concerns with foreign policy issues. His interpretation of national party origins, though, rests on solid ground because the rivalry between Jefferson and Hamilton did not split George Washington's government until Britain went to war with France in 1793.

In assessing the break in unity in Washington's cabinet and hence the transition from "faction," as Federalists would say, to party government, Kaplan generally sides with the Jeffersonian perspective rather then the Federalist. Even though, as in this instance, he generally depicts Jefferson and the policies he espoused in a favorable light, he balances such an appraisal with occasional criticism. For example, he regards the Virginian's conduct toward the Girondin emissary to the United States, Edmond Charles Genêt, as improper because, as secretary of state, Jefferson neglected to inform Genêt, as he should have, of the limits of American aid to France.

Kaplan also accepts the hypothesis, congenial to Federalist thinking, that at this time France's Directory sought to enmesh the United States as an active ally in its war against Britain. He thereby takes issue with other historians who could be regarded as in the Republican camp. Such scholars argue that French leaders saw greater benefit from a United States that remained a nonbelligerent ally rather than one that engaged directly in hostilities against Britain. The French objected, however, to what they regarded as American policies favorable to Britain.

Jefferson agreed with the French position. Indeed, as Kaplan maintains, he "never wavered in his belief that America's prosperity, if not survival, depended on the strength of France." Kaplan also points out that Jefferson was, "above all else, an American seeking America's advantage out of his relations with France."[22]

Jefferson, who did not wish the United States to be drawn into war regardless of its alliance with France, fundamentally espoused a neutrality favorable to France. On this point, Kaplan again expresses a selective criticism of Jeffersonian policy. He writes that "the Jeffersonians deluded themselves in believing they could have both neutrality and the alliance."[23]

Kaplan reserves deeper criticism, however, for the Federalists. "Washington's success in holding France at bay," he writes, "was at the price of a neocolonial status in the British empire. But it was a status that Hamilton considered vital to America's political and economic survival."[24] Jefferson, of course, battled such subservience, imagined or real, to Britain and in 1796 even sought to succeed Washington and change Federalist policy.

On this score Kaplan again criticizes Jefferson, saying that at this point he "was unable to distinguish national interests from his party's interests, or party interests from French interests."

Kaplan also challenges what has long passed as conventional wisdom by pointing out that John Adams's election to the presidency "was more a rebuke to France than it was a testament of Hamiltonian politics."[25]

Yet in assessing the troubles with France, Kaplan, unlike many historians who deal with the subject, maintains that "France had a powerful case for her hostility" toward the United States. In a later piece, he restates this position in stronger terms, saying, "France was right. Its anti-American measures in the face of the American position were not inordinate."[26]

At the same time, Kaplan casts light on the dark side of French politics. He believes that the French pulled back from their hostility to the United States for selfish reasons. They negotiated the Convention of Mortefontaine that in 1800 ended the Quasi-War because they needed a peace that would give them time to occupy and hold Louisiana against a possible American threat.

From this assessment Kaplan proceeds to sum up the Federalist era in terms few historians dispute. In the realm of foreign policy, he asserts, the new American nation had produced a company of sophisticated statesmen and diplomatists that steered it into the new century with a record of remarkable achievement— independence, expanded territory, and peace. Shortly thereafter, when Jefferson entered the presidency, he gladly accepted and benefited from this basically Federalist achievement. He even changed some aspects of his attitude toward France, as in the matter of the Quasi-War, which as vice-president he had opposed. His altered view on the French relationship became evident in his inaugural address, with its call to Americans to shun connections to European politics. Now that the French alliance had been buried, he asked his people to support, as had Washington in his farewell address, a foreign policy of no entanglements.

In Kaplan's view, this "repugnance for political connections with Europe became a vital part of the American isolationist tradition, a fundamental code that made alliances un-American propositions, even into the twentieth century."[27] In all of his pertinent published scholarship, from the beginning to his most recent writings, Kaplan deems Jefferson's isolationist policy the key to his new relationship with France and to his views on international politics in general.

In tracing Jefferson's bond with France through the presidential years, Kaplan asserts that he came to regard France as just one more factor in the European balance of power. For example, when the president learned the truth of France's intentions toward Louisiana, he even backed away from a close relationship devoid of entanglement. He became in many respects a former Francophile.

Jefferson's critics point out that expediency had a hand in this and other reversals of principle. For example, the president dampened his hatred of Britain to the extent of being willing to seek an alliance with it against France. Unlike other interpreters of this episode, Kaplan dismisses the talk of a British alliance as a political gambit. He maintains that Jefferson never saw it as a real possibility because, in his eyes, Britain remained the traditional enemy.

Critics assert also that Jefferson put aside his alleged pacifism, which Kaplan regards as a dominant but limited factor in his policies, to pick up every weapon at his disposal, even war, to thwart France and gain territory at the mouth of the Mississippi River. Some analysts see an even more ruthless streak in the president. They maintain that he stood ready to use force whenever he could do so cheaply or gain decided advantage from it. Kaplan, however, argues that Jefferson genuinely balked at the reality of war.

In obtaining Louisiana, Jefferson even abandoned his commitment to a strict construction of the Constitution, embracing, in effect, the broad interpretation dear to Hamiltonians. Kaplan defends this shift in principle, as well as other concessions to expediency. He argues that Jefferson acted as a loose constructionist in defiance of previous constitutional convictions because he believed the "Republic's survival was at stake" and felt compelled "to avoid loss of a vast empire in the West." The key to "Jefferson's flexibility," he writes, "lies in his early recognition of the importance of the external world in American affairs."[28]

Kaplan also contends that, despite Jefferson's fear of monarchy and despotism and the potential for monarchical abuse of authority in the presidency, he shared Hamilton's belief in a strong executive, primarily in the area of foreign affairs. In an essay published in 1987, Kaplan points out that even while the Founding Fathers were shaping the Constitution, "Jefferson wanted an executive with the power to represent a nation that would be united on foreign relations."[29] In addition, he believes that the Founders at Philadelphia wished to strengthen as well the power of Congress "in every matter relative to foreign affairs." In all, Kaplan concludes, "the success of the Constitution was vital to Jefferson's hopes for American foreign relations."[30]

Many years later, during his second term as president, Jefferson had the opportunity to use executive power as though monarchical. During the *Chesapeake* affair in 1807, public sentiment appeared ready to support him in the use of force against Britain for humiliating the U.S. Navy. Moreover, such retaliation seemed logical in light of Jefferson's attitude toward Britain, which he still regarded as a menace. Kaplan maintains that in this case "Great Britain . . . purposely provoked the Anglophobia of the Jeffersonians to a degree that exceeded the tensions of 1793." The president even "talked about war in his correspondence with French" friends and with the French minister to the United States.[31]

Nonetheless, Jefferson again avoided war. This time he did so because he thought that in the embargo, or the weapon of economic coercion, he had a less costly and more effective means of changing British policy and protecting American property than military violence. While not privy to the president's French correspondence, Federalist critics perceived his general anti-British stance as yet more evidence of his Francophilism. They charged, in Kaplan's words, "that France had a willing tool in its American supporters, who, having followed every directive of their master, were merely forging the last link in a long chain of subservience to that country."[32]

Kaplan refutes this charge as well as the criticism of later historians that, in dealing with Britain over the maritime crisis, "Jefferson pursued or urged a policy that served French interests."[33] He does point out, though, that Jefferson admitted the embargo would not hurt France. Kaplan insists that the president persisted in trying to punish Britain because he viewed it as a greater threat to the United States than France. Yet because the embargo failed to restrain French depredations against Americans or to persuade the British to cease seizures of American shipping and seamen, critics and even friendly historians regard it as Jefferson's major foreign policy failure.

While Kaplan, too, criticizes the embargo policy as revealing "the flaws in Jefferson's understanding of the balance of power in Europe," he does not condemn it.[34] He sides with those who maintain it failed only because it did not last long enough to force concessions from Britain. It should not, therefore, be regarded as a "mistake."[35]

Kaplan also refutes Federalist charges that in 1812 James Madison deliberately led the country into war on the side of France, behaving thereby as a vassal of Napoleon. Kaplan also denies that Napoleon tricked Madison into war or that the president behaved as "an ally, client, or dupe of France." He claims that in deciding on war the Madisonians did not concern themselves with the fate of France, pointing out that "the administration made no alliance with France, received no special benefits from the cobelligerent, and conferred none in return."[36] Kaplan does grant, though, that "Madison and his colleagues consigned to France a prominent if not always acknowledged role in their war against Britain."[37]

All along, and especially during the course of the War of 1812, Jefferson still clung to his view of Britain as America's principal enemy. He claimed, however, that he had never been hostile to the British people. Kaplan characterizes this attitude, as well as that toward France, as "more confused than subtle."[38] After the war, Jefferson's fear of Britain diminished, but his antipathy toward it did not vanish.

In the postwar years, Jefferson's attitude toward France took on some hostility, but to the day of his death he retained an affection for it. His feelings toward Britain became more benign in those years, as well. For instance, in October 1823 he urged President James Monroe to accept Britain's bid for an alliance intended to block possible French and Spanish attacks on the emerging Latin American states. Jefferson abandoned much of his hostility toward Britain because of, in Kaplan's view, "the changing international environment." Jefferson now perceived Britain, "willingly or not," as serving "American interests." He wished "to use that nation to keep America free from Old World entanglements," a familiar theme in much of Kaplan's scholarship.[39]

Whether dealing with France or Britain, Kaplan maintains that Jefferson, and Madison too, acted fundamentally on the thesis taken from Samuel Bemis that "Europe's troubles were America's opportunity." This idea appears again and again in Kaplan's works.[40] When he applies it to Jefferson, Kaplan presents it as part of his effort to seize advantage from the balance of power in Europe. Jefferson may have misunderstood the intricacies of the concept, but, as Kaplan explains, he did see in this policy the basic source of security for the United States.

Kaplan portrays this exploitation of Europe's distresses as considered policy and as a critical factor in Jefferson's success as a statesman. Kaplan even applies this principle to the attitude of U.S. leaders toward the Latin American wars for independence. "For a brief time," he writes, "circumstances permitted a commingling of the destinies of the Americas based on common sentiments." More importantly, however, the leaders in Washington perceived in the new countries to the south "opportunity to be derived from Spain's troubles." They acted favorably toward the revolutionary regimes not out of sentiment but because they saw advantage to be gained from doing so.[41]

This concern for tangible advantage through diplomacy, as well as admiration for Jefferson, remained strong features of Kaplan's thinking on diplomacy and politics throughout his academic career. Indeed, his positive views of the Virginian grew stronger as the years passed. In a study written in the seventies, for example, Kaplan maintains that "no statesman of the revolutionary and early national periods made a more substantial contribution to the development of American foreign policy than Thomas Jefferson." Reflecting the intense interest among diplomatic historians of the period in "realism" versus "moralism" in international politics, Kaplan adds that "no one" blended moralism with the realistic or "practical pursuit of national self-interest more effectively than he [Jefferson]."[42]

In sum, three large themes appear dominant in Kaplan's scholarship on the early republic: Jefferson as the commanding figure of the period; the advantages American diplomatists gained through their exploiting of European quarrels; and the blossoming of nonentanglement, or isolationism, as the bedrock of American foreign policy. Kaplan plays on these and lesser themes with skill and sophistication, demonstrating the qualities that contribute to his reputation as a masterful historian. He writes lucidly, researches thoroughly, does not allow his analyses to outrun his data, yet speculates straightforwardly on controversial issues. For these reasons, among others, his judgments and analyses come together in a balanced, refined, and important assessment of the diplomacy of the early republic. In total, he makes a major contribution to scholarship that stands the test of time with little, if any, tarnish. Subsequent studies have not invalidated his major interpretations. Indeed most, if not all, of his writing in this area remains as interesting and meaningful now as when he published it.

CHAPTER 2

NATO and the United States

An Essay in Kaplanesque History

CEES WIEBES & BERT ZEEMAN

Few will doubt the characterization of Lawrence S. Kaplan as America's preeminent scholar on the history of the North Atlantic Treaty Organization. Kaplan has contributed in an extraordinary fashion to the blossoming of NATO studies: as a writer of numerous books, chapters, and articles; as a commentator; as a supervisor of dissertations; as a member of dissertation committees (in the United States and in Europe); as founder and first director of the Lyman L. Lemnitzer Center for NATO Studies at Kent State University (in 1991 rechristened the Lemnitzer Center for NATO and European Union Studies); as an organizer of and host to conferences; and as a source of inspiration for scholars around the world. Without claiming this to be the final word on the subject, we will try in the five sections of this essay to analyze the principal elements of his scholarly contribution.

I

Kaplan's publications on NATO span a period of forty years. The first one, an instructive bibliographic essay on NATO's first five years, was published in 1954, the most recent one in 1994.

Although it is sometimes difficult to draw a strict line separating some works from others, we have counted forty-seven original contributions dealing specifically with NATO, excluding, for instance, publications with a more general scope, those in which NATO's role is only of secondary importance, and translations.[1] While some of Kaplan's essays have appeared in two different publications (often in slightly different form[2]) or have been included, slightly or considerably revised, in one of his books,[3] the number remains impressive.

It is possible to subdivide the forty-seven publications in a number of ways: by publication date, type of publication, and principal subject. A classification by publication date offers the following result:

TIME SPAN	NUMBER OF PUBLICATIONS
1950–59	2
1960–69	6
1970–79	6
1980–89	23
1990–96	10

Clearly, the eighties were the most important decade in Kaplan's publishing career for his NATO-related research. This fact becomes even more evident when we realize that five of the ten publications since 1989 were contributions to conferences to commemorate NATO's fortieth anniversary. There is no need to dwell at great length on the reason for this state of affairs. Before 1974, the records dealing with NATO were not open to public scrutiny, greatly hampering historical study. From 1974 onward, Kaplan was preoccupied with the updating, revision, and expansion of his manuscript on the origins and early years of the Mutual Assistance Program. Only after the publication in 1980 of *A Community of Interests: NATO and the Military Assistance Program, 1948–1951*, was he able to devote all his attention to NATO and take advantage of newly opened records.

As to the type of publication, we find the following:

monographs	4
edited volumes	8
scholarly articles	31
popular articles	3
encyclopedic entries	1

Three of the monographs were published in the 1980s, the fourth being a revised edition of one of them. The eight edited volumes, which sometimes carry Kaplan's introduction, were often outgrowths of conferences organized by the Lemnitzer Center.[4] Two volumes, *NATO and the Policy of Containment* and *Recent American Foreign Policy: Conflicting Interpretations*, both published in 1968, were readers dealing with American postwar foreign policy. Kaplan's editorship of these volumes marked an early recognition of his stature as an American diplomatic historian. The thirty-one scholarly articles can be subdivided into original contributions, specially commissioned essays, and (revised) conference papers. All three popular articles were published in NATO's own journal, the *NATO Review* (formerly the *NATO Letter*).[5]

As to the principal subjects covered, the classification is somewhat more arbitrary, because not all of Kaplan's publications are easy to categorize:

NATO's history	34
NATO's "current" state	8
NATO historiography	5

This last summary clearly shows Kaplan's principal interest, but there is no doubt that he is not exclusively interested in NATO's past. He also has a keen eye for NATO's ongoing problems and the methodological problems associated with the historical study of an evolving subject.

II

In his writings, Kaplan is forthright but not very prone to making rash, harsh, or radical statements. Although answers, solutions, or judgments are often considered "elliptical," "opaque," or "oblique" by Kaplan, his prose is mostly sober and to the point, sometimes even marred by unnecessary modesty. When he claims in his essay on European revisionism that it is "based for the most part on *my limited encounters* with European scholars at meetings in Western European centers over the past six years,"[6] one must realize that he is, at least according to us, one of the few American historians of the postwar period who is genuinely interested in the insights provided by scholars from the Old World. His frequent participation in European conferences, his numerous invitations extended to European scholars to lecture at Kent State University, and his participation in North Atlantic projects, all lend credence to this assertion. Rather than stress limited contact with Europeans, one should underline Kaplan's openness toward and interest in the European historical scene.

A subject especially dear to him, one which consequently leads to impassioned commentaries, is what Kaplan considers the unjustified neglect of NATO by (American) historians. In 1974, for instance, he castigated his colleagues (to the left and right of the political spectrum) for their paltry contribution to the body of NATO literature. That contribution had been, in Kaplan's words, "minimal to date." The Atlantic Alliance in its first generation deserved "a consideration from historians it has not yet received."[7] In 1980, he repeated this judgment: "The North Atlantic Treaty Organization has been the subject of examination for the past thirty years from almost every possible angle of observation. The one notable exception has been the historical perspective."[8] In Kaplan's opinion, the responsibility for this state of affairs rested upon the lack of primary materials; the fact that NATO was still an ongoing alliance, an open-ended issue historically; and, especially, the view of traditionalists and revisionists alike that NATO was only a minor matter in the evolution of the Cold War. In later years Kaplan time and again questioned and criticized this lack of attention for NATO. It is fair to say that from his first major scholarly publication in 1954 into the 1990s, he has drawn the attention of fellow historians to the need to study NATO in its own right instead of as a mere appendage to Cold War policy-making.

Kaplan has never played a prominent role in the sometimes heated discussions among American diplomatic historians about the origins of the Cold War. Only in 1983, as a member of a panel at a meeting of the Organization of American Historians, did he make some pertinent comments.[9] Nevertheless, it is possible to sketch an evolution in his thinking regarding schools of Cold War historiography. In his early writings, Kaplan no doubt must be termed a traditionalist/realist. In 1954, NATO was simply "the clearest challenge to Soviet expansionism since the end of World War II." Four years later, NATO was "necessary to deter further Soviet expansion after World War II." And in 1971, in more prosaic terms, "Here was the crest of the communist westward wave, whether propelled by the winds of communist doctrine or by a reaction to American measures. What could the United States do to stem the tide?" Washington was only pushed reluctantly into the Cold War.[10]

However, Kaplan was not unaffected by the wave of New Left revisionist analysis. In his 1982 article on Western Europe in "The American Century" (a Society for Historians of American Foreign Relations [SHAFR] presidential address given in 1981), he admitted that in the 1950s and 1960s, when the United States was at the zenith of its power in Europe, he had taken for granted the permanence of the American imperium and the beneficence of its intentions. Now he recognized that the Marshall Plan was an example of Samaritanism as enlightened self-interest, that political as well as economic control accompanied the American presence in Europe, and that the visible political symbol of the Pax Americana was NATO itself.[11] To talk in terms of empire and politico-economic control—and to characterize the first supreme allied commander, Europe (SACEUR), Dwight D. Eisenhower, as "the American proconsul"—is unthinkable without taking into account the publications of William Appleman Williams and Joyce and Gabriel Kolko. A few years earlier, in a paper presented to commemorate the twenty-fifth anniversary of the outbreak of the Korean War, revisionist sentiment was already evident in one of his concluding remarks concerning the long-range impact of the

North Korean invasion. He observed that if there was a long-term impact, "it was in the aggressive American acceptance of the challenge of leadership, particularly executive leadership, with its potential for abuse in domestic and foreign relations."[12]

The SHAFR presidential address is important for still another reason: it showed Kaplan to be an avowed postrevisionist. Having to some extent accepted the imperial verbiage of the hardcore revisionists, he was still eager to stress the intentions with which the United States acquired its empire. In Kaplan's opinion, "The most significant effort to link Europe to an American destiny came not from the Americans but from European leaders." For as long as possible, the United States delayed accepting its new role as one of the world's two superpowers and only concluded a transatlantic alliance to allay European fears. "The consequent domination of Europe was not on the U.S. agenda." In this way, Kaplan clearly foreshadowed Geir Lundestad's empire-by-invitation concept developed in the early eighties.[13]

Reflecting on the fact that postrevisionism has become the generic term for a wide variety of sometimes conflicting interpretations, perhaps, Kaplan now can best be termed a moderate neorealist. To a large extent, Kaplan returned to his initial beliefs after the fall of the Berlin Wall. With the demise of Communism, he confidently claimed that "containment has worked." NATO had fulfilled its primary function: protecting the West against Communist ambitions.[14] The United States and the Western European states had been "faced with an apparently powerful Soviet Union prepared to extend communism" into any vital part of the world. One notable change, however, needs to be recorded here. In his earliest writings on NATO, the Soviet threat is clearly and unequivocally portrayed in military terms; in his most recent writings, Kaplan is more realistic. As he observed in 1990, "The issue was not one of an imminent invasion of Soviet troops, but revival of faith in the future that seemed to have escaped in the fires of the Second World War."[15]

Two other characteristics of "Kaplan, the scholar" need to be stressed here. The first concerns his relationship with the lifeblood of historians, the archives. In his NATO research, Kaplan has been in the forefront of those stressing the need for opening new records and conducting multiarchival research. He has long championed the cause of opening the NATO archives themselves to qualified researchers. For instance, at a conference held on 14–15 October 1982 at the Eisenhower Library in Abilene, Kansas, in the presence of (among others) the then and various former SACEURs, he made an urgent appeal to release early NATO documents with a low order of classification. Careful as always, he stated that his comments were "not intended to be a bill of indictment" against SHAPE or the secretary-general. At the same time, he pointed to the absurdity of the fact that private archives or U.S. presidential libraries contained classified NATO documents that were still unavailable in Brussels.[16] Kaplan was also the first American to use in a fruitful way the records of NATO's predecessor, the Western Union.

The second characteristic of special interest is Kaplan's predilection for historical parallels. The two entangling alliances of 1778 and 1949, the Monroe Doctrine and the Truman Doctrine, and the crises in NATO in the sixties and the eighties have all been the subject of comparative analysis.[17] Kaplan thus exhibits a keen eye for the need "to draw lessons from history" without falling into the trap of asserting that history only repeats itself.

III

Those who are familiar with Lawrence Kaplan's writings about the North Atlantic Treaty Organization will know that several themes are most dear to him. In the first place, there is the early history of NATO itself. Dating from his employment as a member of the Historical Office of the Department of Defense, Kaplan has produced important studies that highlight aspects of the beginnings of the Atlantic Alliance, the evolution of the organization over the years, and the intriguing relationship between NATO and the United States. His three monographs are Kaplan's testament to the importance of NATO as an object of historical study in its own right. Secondly, coupled with his other major field of historical interest, Thomas Jefferson and Jeffersonian politics, Kaplan is intrigued by the relationship between NATO as the ultimate entangling alliance and traditional American isolationism and support for the United Nations. A third major theme in his writings is the vitality of NATO. Declared dead more than any

other postwar international alliance, especially after the demise
of the Warsaw Pact, NATO has outlived all its competitors (with
the exception of the Western European Union). In a number of
publications, Kaplan has tried to apply the generational idea to
the evolution of NATO since 1949.

The monographs on NATO that Kaplan published in the eighties contain most of the essential elements of his contribution to
NATO studies and also illustrate the three faces of Kaplan, the
scholar. *A Community of Interests* is the product of Kaplan, the
official historian. Initiated in the early fifties while he was employed by the Office of the Secretary of Defense, it is a meticu-
lously researched study of the origins, trials, and tribulations of
the Military Assistance Program in the years 1948–51. A first draft
was completed in the 1950s but shelved in the face of more pressing assignments in the Historical Office. Thanks to Alfred
Goldberg, Kaplan was asked in the seventies to update, revise,
and expand this draft with an eye to publication of the manuscript in the newly initiated series published by the Historical
Office.

A Community of Interests is a fine example of administrative
history. Competently arranged, with attention to the larger issues of interagency and interallied rivalry, it combines enormous
detail regarding the conception and management of the military
assistance program. The general reader will probably be put off
by the detailed way in which Kaplan treats his subject, but historians and political scientists alike will make, and have already
made, excellent use of his study. Kaplan traces the origins of the
military assistance program to the Truman Doctrine of March
1947, describes the complex process leading to the creation of
NATO, and recounts the planning for and implementation of the
military aid programs (with emphasis on the Western European
countries) until the February 1952 meeting of the North Atlantic
Council in Lisbon. Kaplan's conclusion is paradoxical: the assistance programs made NATO in this period a true military alliance, inaugurating a mammoth military-industrial complex on
both sides of the Atlantic; yet, the day-to-day record of these years
reflected "the kinds of frustrations which produce a sense of failure."[18]

As most reviewers noted, despite "the community of interests," Kaplan's story is first of all a story of friction and conflict among the interested parties.[19] On the one hand, there was intra-agency rivalry within the Department of Defense, interagency rivalry between this agency and the State Department, and rivalry between the executive branch and Congress. On the other hand, there was the sensitive relationship between the United States and its Western European allies. This makes his tale complex, but also one going beyond a simple official history. Those interested in policy analysis and the decision-making process in the United States will find this study as rewarding as those studying interallied relations in a bipolar world.

The United States and NATO, published in 1984, is the product of Kaplan, the researcher. It is a combination of previously published articles (five of the eight main chapters were published between 1977 and 1982) and original, unpublished material (characterized as "the main body of this volume" by the author[20]). Preceded by a chapter comparing the entangling alliances of 1778 and 1949, and concluded by one assessing the long-range impact of the United States on its European allies, Kaplan traces the diplomatic and political history of the postwar American involvement in Europe. He particularly documents the role of Washington in the negotiations in 1948–49 leading to the signing of the North Atlantic Treaty. In two bibliographic essays, one originally published in 1954 and one specifically written for this volume, Kaplan reviews NATO's early history.

One reviewer characterized this study as a companion volume to A Community of Interests.[21] Indeed, it provides some of the necessary political and diplomatic background to the military assistance programs described in such detail in the latter. One of Kaplan's main assertions is that the American decision to join NATO was not a foregone conclusion. The Truman administration had to break with one of America's cherished traditions, its age-old isolationism; it had to overcome the opposition of those who believed that the United Nations should be the prime instrument of preserving international peace; and it had to convince those in the Defense Department and in Congress who feared that an alliance would drain U.S. economic and military resources.

As in other studies on the origins of NATO, the importance of lower-echelon officials in bringing about this reorientation in American foreign policy—in this case State Department officials John D. Hickerson and Theodore C. Achilles—comes strongly to the fore.

Two other major themes dominate the story. First, there was the problematic relationship between the North American and Western European halves of the Atlantic Alliance. Kaplan makes it clear that the initiative for the alliance was European. He stresses the importance of the Treaty of Brussels (1948) in convincing the Truman administration that close involvement with Western Europe was worth the risk.[22] He also clearly recognizes the delicate relationship between the creation of an Atlantic community and the American insistence on the establishment of a United States of Europe. Another major theme, echoing sentiments expressed in *A Community of Interests,* is NATO's state of unpreparedness until the outbreak of the Korean War. This war transformed the alliance from a paper guarantee into a genuine military organization, making that event, rather than the signing of the treaty in 1949, the watershed of American isolationism.

In 1985 we concluded that *The United States and NATO* was somewhat disappointing given the fact that a large part of the material had been published previously.[23] This observation holds true for those who are interested in NATO's early history and are familiar with Kaplan's other publications. Yet we must add that Kaplan's book is still the most definitive treatment of the American role in the early years of the alliance, even ten years after its publication.

Kaplan's third monograph, *NATO and the United States,* published in 1988, is the product of Kaplan, the lecturer. In just 185 pages, he traces the symbiotic relationship between the United States and its longest-lasting entangling alliance, from 1949 to the mid-1980s. In these four decades, Kaplan distinguishes five milestones in the evolution of the relationship: the Korean War in 1950; the accession of the Federal Republic of Germany in 1955; French withdrawal from the military organization in 1966; the effect of the Harmel-initiative and détente on NATO in the late 1960s and early 1970s; and the dual-track initiative of 1979.[24]

Written in the closing days of the Cold War, Kaplan is keen to stress the importance of NATO in preserving Western democratic values and its resilience in the face of recurring interallied crises. American-European disagreements have indeed been the major threat to NATO's existence; but, aided by the perception of a common foe, the allies have been able to overcome all problems. According to Kaplan, common interests and the promise of a genuine community, rather than its character as a defensive organization coping with a powerful Communist adversary, will determine NATO's place in history.[25]

I V

In 1958, Kaplan for the first time addressed the relationship between American isolationism and its participation in NATO. Noting the erosion of isolationism in the postwar period, he questioned whether the tenets of isolationism had been as overwhelmed by events as the term itself since policies directly opposed to long-lived traditions had to be defended in the name of isolationism. At that time Kaplan considered the longevity of isolationism deserved; it had been a useful aid in the development of nineteenth-century America. The oft-cited talismans of this self-serving isolationism had been George Washington's observations on America's differences from Europe in his farewell address in 1796, Thomas Jefferson's warnings against foreign entanglements in his first inaugural address in 1801, and James Monroe's pronouncement on the inviolability of the Western Hemisphere in 1823.[26]

The conclusion of the North Atlantic Treaty in 1949 required that the Truman administration confront the Congress and the public at large, educated about and familiar with these talismans, with an entangling alliance. Administration officials did so by going out of their way in their testimony "to show that the treaty conformed not only with the spirit but also with the letter of isolationism." In doing so, they first of all proclaimed the elasticity of the boundaries of isolationism itself. The Monroe Doctrine had stretched these borders to cover the entire Western Hemisphere; the North Atlantic Treaty merely extended such borders across the Atlantic Ocean. "It was no longer the Atlantic Ocean but an Iron Curtain that separated the United States from the Old World. The doctrine of the two spheres remained intact." Furthermore, administration representatives stressed the nonmilitary functions of the new treaty, drawing as much distinction as possible between the old European military alliances and this new venture. Thus, "the Government succeeded in invoking the shibboleths of isolationism to win acceptance of a policy that marked a departure from the isolationist traditions."

Afterward, Kaplan time and again returned to the major themes raised in this early article, elaborating, refining, and sometimes reconsidering prior statements. Eleven years later, Kaplan again explicitly addressed the question of isolationism. Acknowledging the fact that the United States had never turned its back on the world, had never had been isolationist in the purest sense, he stressed that "isolationism in the American tradition is specifically identified with Europe, notably with England and France, and is equated with revulsion from political connections with Europe."[27] Ties other than commercial had been systematically, and successfully, avoided; and after 1945, the sentiment was still the same. The United States expected the United Nations ("a surrogate foreign office of the United States") to take care of postwar international affairs; behind the cover of that organization, Americans could withdraw and deal with more important domestic matters. However, this involvement without responsibility lasted only a few years. Soviet behavior educated Americans to the realities of world power. Washington accepted the balance of power as a rule of international life and subsequently assumed the leadership in maintaining that balance. American isolationism was traded for the Pax Americana.[28]

Kaplan also recognized the importance of the resistance of internationalists who would oppose an organization that might cripple the United Nations. He stressed the sensitive relationship between the North Atlantic Treaty and the UN Charter. The language of the treaty conformed as closely as possible to the letter of the charter without making the clear claim that the treaty was a regional arrangement within the limits of the charter. The Truman administration thus "invited charges of duplicity for suggesting functions which the new treaty could not possibly have included." Yet, dire circumstances forced the administration to act as it did. NATO was necessary to deter further Soviet expansionism, and it signified the formal U.S. break with isolationism.[29]

In 1982, Kaplan even concluded that "this form of internationalism, rather than familiar isolationism, appeared to be the major stumbling block preventing the Truman administration from moving more quickly to cope with Soviet expansionism in the late 1940s through traditional alliances." He wrote, "The trouble was less over a revived isolationism than over the acceptance by most of the foreign policy elites of the United Nations as the way of the future. A military alliance, bilateral or multilateral, it was feared, would undermine the foundations of the new world order."[30]

V

NATO's vitality is another theme running through Kaplan's writings. With obvious pleasure he often recounts the innumerable instances that the coming death of NATO has been proclaimed. Already in 1961, Kaplan had observed that the character of the alliance in 1949–50 was "largely a paper affair." There was no real leadership in its first two years. NATO's existence rested simply upon an American commitment to Europe, based on Article 5 of the North Atlantic Treaty.[31] Ten years later he repeated these observations in identical terms, asserting that NATO was an organization "with no organs to implement a co-ordinated defense system . . . more shell than substance. The flurry of activity in the wake of these acts of establishment appeared more significant than it actually was."[32] The outbreak of the Korean War in June 1950 marked a turning point in NATO's history. The North Korean invasion of the South "forced the United States either to transform NATO or to abandon it." The Truman administration chose the former course, reorganizing NATO's structure, the most obvious expressions being the appointment of a supreme allied commander and the presence of American troops alongside Europeans; reassessing the geographical boundaries of the alliance leading to the inclusion of Greece and Turkey and, ultimately, Germany; and forcing the issue of German rearmament.[33]

According to Kaplan, the rearmament debate nearly killed the emerging alliance.[34] Luckily, the French government made a pretense of responding to the conditions the United States placed on continued assistance and association with Europe. The elaborate Pleven Plan of October 1950, proposing a European Defense Community (EDC), haunted the alliance for the next four years. Kaplan is clear in his evaluation of this plan: the French had "proposed the [EDC] treaty and signed it to deflect American plans from something even less palatable, and had managed to stall the proceedings for almost three years."[35]

Nevertheless, despite this and many other crises, NATO survived. Kaplan, therefore, rightfully concluded in 1961 that "pessimism over the future of the alliance is not wholly warranted."[36] Thirty years later he confidently observed, "Even if the more extravagant hopes of 1989 should come to pass and the Cold War between East and West should be permanently terminated, NATO will still have functions to perform." Or, in Kaplanian terms, there will be a "NATO in the Third Generation."

Kaplan used the generational idea for the first time in 1970 in a short contribution to the *NATO Letter* and expanded upon a year later in a major assessment of NATO's first twenty years of existence.[37] Given the fact that the signatories to the treaty were entitled to end their membership in 1969, according to Article 13, he observed that NATO had "survived for a generation, and it has thereby fulfilled, at least, the minimal expectations of its founding fathers."[38] A year later he coined the phrase "the first generation of NATO" to denote the period in which NATO primarily had been a military alliance dominated by the United States, the 1947 Truman Doctrine providing its frame.

On its twentieth anniversary, NATO entered its "second generation," a term Kaplan used for the first time in 1980.[39] As he observed that year, "There are identifiable milestones . . . that mark stages of NATO's growth, and the one that most clearly stamps the end of one generation and the beginning of another was the election of Richard Nixon and the ushering in of a Nixon-Kissinger era in American foreign policy."[40] The redefinition of containment, as exemplified by the Nixon Doctrine, reinstated Europe as America's top priority.

However, Washington won little credit from its European NATO partners, who were suspicious of the unilateral détente with the Soviet Union practiced by the Nixon-Kissinger team. Charles de Gaulle's 1960s-era cry that the United States would never sacrifice its own security for the sake of Europe continued to reverberate. West-West relations grew even more sour because of continued U.S. criticism of Europe's unwillingness to make greater sacrifices in building the military strength of NATO. The "desertion" of Washington by its European allies (with the exception of the Netherlands) during the 1973 October War in the Middle East merely reinforced the fact that "Europe and America were as far apart in mutual trust as they had ever been in the past."[41]

Yet, NATO survived even the malaise of 1974 and did not fade out in subsequent years in the same manner as the South East Asian Treaty Organization (SEATO) in 1977 or the Central Treaty Organization (CENTO) in 1979. The mutual dependency of the United States and Western Europe was strong enough to overcome all friction. There was simply no alternative, although NATO had to find a way to accommodate the changing relationship between the United States and a maturing European Community. Kaplan saw in 1980 a reinvigorated and unified NATO, in which both authority and responsibility were more widely shared than in the past, as the solution for the future. Otherwise, the many centrifugal forces at work in the alliance might neutralize, or even eclipse, the centripetal force of the shared perception of a Communist threat.[42]

Thus, NATO in the second generation adjusted to new challenges, paying tribute time and again to Kaplan's 1954 observation that NATO's "responsiveness to changing circumstances had been a major source of strength."[43] In 1983, NATO experienced its "year of decision" in the second generation, but the alliance again passed the test.[44] Soviet efforts to intimidate Western European public opinion failed as legislatures accepted the deployment of Pershing and cruise missiles. The fall of the Berlin Wall must be considered the milestone that marks the end of this generation and the beginning of the third.

Taking the generational idea a little further, one might conclude that after some serious birth pangs in 1948–49, NATO was born on 4 April 1949. In the first generation, the organization slowly matured, despite some cases of childish squabbles (e.g., American anger at Britain and France during the Suez Crisis) and a serious period of puberty (France's withdrawal from the military organization). In 1969, NATO came of age. In the second generation, the organization developed a love-hate relationship with its Communist counterpart. As it happened, NATO cuddled its friend and foe to death. Consequently, in the third generation, NATO is facing a serious midlife crisis, which is dealt with in Kaplan's 1994 contribution to NATO studies, the updated edition of *NATO and the United States.*[45]

Kaplan brings forward several political factors to support his contention that NATO again will survive. First of all, the containment of Germany is an unspoken but genuine factor in the maintenance of Europe's links to America. Furthermore, the uncertainties in Eastern Europe provide another stimulus to the continuance of the alliance. In particular, instability in the former Soviet Union remains a primary motive for the continued existence of NATO. The immediate result could even be, according to Kaplan, to reenergize the alliance.

What about America's role with respect to NATO's future? Kaplan acknowledges that pressures for the dissolution of the alliance and the withdrawal of U.S. forces from Europe may be found more in the United States than in Europe. However, he considers them to be the "inevitable by-products of the end of the Cold War," because even NATO in the post–Cold War era is accepted as a part of American foreign policy in the way that "abstention from alliances had been in the 1930s."

Nevertheless, even Kaplan must acknowledge that, in view of all the complex obstacles, prospects for survival in the mid-1990s are rather dim. But if NATO continues to survive, it will only be because "Europe has failed to come up with any viable alternative." Ethnic conflicts in the Balkans and elsewhere, the upsurge of Russian nationalism, and the fears of a too-powerful Germany all leave NATO, "as flawed as it is, as the only stabilizing multinational instrument in the world." The North Atlantic Treaty Organization will also remain in place because it is, according to Kaplan, the only vehicle legitimizing the U.S. presence in Europe and the only organization with the means to act in a crisis. In an ideal situation, it could even be the military arm of the United Nations, which actually took place in former Yugoslavia with the stationing of troops from the multinational Implementation Force (IFOR). For Kaplan, with this potential in mind, NATO still has a future, even when the will to act is missing. Therefore, he remains convinced that the organization will overcome this crisis, as it has done so many times in earlier generations, leaving NATO the prospect of a well-deserved old age. The future, and Larry Kaplan, will tell.

Keynote

CHAPTER 3

Diplomacy without Armaments, 1945–1950

Robert H. Ferrell

"Diplomacy without armaments," Frederick the Great once said, "is like music without instruments." The thought bears repetition when one looks back over American diplomacy in the twentieth century, and especially when one thinks of the early postwar years, the half-decade from the end of the Pacific War in 1945 until the beginning of the Korean War in 1950. Here was a dangerous time in world affairs, if ever such might have been discerned in all the half-decades, decades, and even centuries since the rise of nation states at the beginning of the modern era. Here was a time when American officials, finding themselves in trouble with the Soviet Union, did not have the military wherewithal to back up what they said and sometimes did. We must remind ourselves that during the years when the United States tried to arrive at a modus vivendi with the Soviet Union, and passed through successive crises attempting the task, the forces and armaments with which the country confronted the USSR were far from adequate.

In setting out what the United States did against its Soviet opponents, observers and later historians tended to write as if America's good intentions should have persuaded the country's antagonists in Moscow. Seldom does one read that the military forces with which the American side sought to oppose the Soviets were not at all impressive, that the Americans were dealing from a terribly weak hand, that both in conventional and nuclear power the American side was incapable, if its full dimensions had been known, of impressing Joseph Stalin. Had there been a full disclosure of the nation's military power, we might now assume, many of the conversations and meetings in faraway places and debates in the United Nations Organization and elsewhere, the pourparlers that sometimes failed but sometimes succeeded, would have failed promptly and irrevocably.

I

In 1945, the immediate difficulty in relations between the United States and the Soviet Union stemmed from the inexperience of both President Harry S. Truman and the American people. When leadership passed from the failing hands of President Franklin D. Roosevelt to Truman on 12 April, Truman remarked to a group of reporters that he felt as if the sun, moon, and stars had all fallen upon him and, in a touching addition to these confessional words, asked the reporters to pray for him. This, then, was the initial awkwardness in American foreign policy, the fact that the ex-vice-president was woefully unprepared for his new duties.

Truman had been told nothing by Roosevelt. The president, for twelve years and not quite three months, did not have a high estimate of his successor and had chosen him as his running mate in the summer of 1944 only because a group of Democratic party leaders, observing FDR's physical decline and anticipating his death, had foisted him on the president.[1] The fact that Roosevelt did not anticipate his own death meant that it would be quite reasonable to ignore Truman, as FDR had ignored before him Henry A. Wallace and John N. Garner. Truman learned little or nothing from Roosevelt, save for a few domestic problems, such as when he arranged for Wallace early in 1945 to become secretary of commerce despite the opposition of almost the entire membership of the Senate. Other than this, FDR gave Truman almost no attention. He did tell him about the nuclear program and the possibility of nuclear weapons (when the two met under a magnolia tree on the south lawn behind the White House in

August 1944, after the convention in Chicago gave Truman the vice-presidential nomination). Beyond that meeting Truman met Roosevelt only once or twice in private and saw him three or four times in meetings with other people. They communicated on a few occasions through letters or memos, but that was all.

The result was that when Truman became president, espied the next morning swiveling uncertainly in the presidential chair behind the big desk, he was bereft of information about policy. In foreign relations he had to begin at the beginning. Truman's entire experience in politics was in domestic affairs. He knew no more about the course of the war, not to mention diplomacy, than did the man or woman in the street. In domestic matters he had spent ten years in Missouri county politics, and he understood the meaning of power in such political equations as the machine then dominated by Boss Thomas J. Pendergast. The new president had received other instruction in the politics of power during his ten years in the Senate, beginning in 1935. But in foreign matters he remained remarkably untutored. In 1941, when Hitler's Germany attacked Stalin's Soviet Union, Truman made the later-famous remark, surely offhand, that America's best course was to watch while the two European behemoths fought each other, and to aid whatever side began to weaken. From this perception of truth he had gone on to address, through his Senate investigatory committee, the immense problems of mobilization, and he knew a great deal about how the war effort was proceeding. On this particular subject he again beheld the equations of power, as President Roosevelt announced various goals and then almost nonchalantly announced overarching agencies that would translate the goals into reality. When one agency failed, FDR announced that a new agency would take over.

During the war era, Truman often tired of Roosevelt's slowness with the mobilization as well as the president's compromises, which, though they came because of the need to placate industrial and labor leaders (and hence partook of the equations of power), did not move in the straight direction that Truman preferred. Once in a while Truman said what he thought, and on one special occasion, when he allowed an article to be written and appear under his name in *American* magazine, was so forthright that he believed it undermined his position with the White House.

As months passed he discovered otherwise. He was not involved, however, in problems of military strategy, not to mention diplomacy; and when the time came for decision-making in strategy and diplomacy, he did not know much. He told his first postmaster general, Frank C. Walker, "I know nothing of foreign affairs, and I must acquaint myself with them at once."[2]

By the time of the Potsdam Conference, which began in mid-July 1945, the new president had learned something about his diplomatic problems. He had taken papers home each night as he left the Oval Office and went upstairs to the White House's private quarters on the second floor. He liked to say afterward that he read a stack of papers six-feet high—and the remark is believable, though in the manner of all busy executives, he did not literally read the stack but leafed through it, fastening on the gist of arguments, concentrating on summaries and conclusions, all in the attempt to understand what he would be up against at Potsdam and afterward, perhaps into a full term in his own right.

It was an unfortunate fact that the new president then found himself with a totally inadequate secretary of state, Edward R. Stettinius, Jr. In one of his first acts he had to get Stettinius out of office, whereupon he appointed another totally inadequate man (at least in terms of knowledge of foreign affairs) to the same position.

The inadequacies of Stettinius were almost legendary and certainly had become a subject for gossip by the time Truman became president. The best explanation of Stettinius's appointment late in 1944—when Cordell Hull, suffering from tuberculosis, suddenly resigned—was that Roosevelt wanted to continue (as had been the case under Hull) to be his own secretary of state. Stettinius looked like a leader and was most affable; he was in the department at the moment, and in that sense his appointment was reasonable. In no other way, however, was it reasonable, for he was superficial to a fault, could only float on the surface of affairs, and needed constant briefing. The almost crude manner in which Truman got him out of office perhaps showed the contempt for Stettinius held by all knowledgeable Washington insiders. The new president sent the secretary of the Democratic party, George E. Allen, out to San Francisco, where Stettinius was presiding over the conference that was drawing up the UN Charter. Allen, in effect, asked what the secretary's price would be for departure from office. At first Stettinius was irate, as he should have been, quite apart from his incompetence in office. It gradually became apparent that Stettinius's price was three arrangements: In addition to the honorific appointment that Truman offered as first American representative to the UNO, with the rank of ambassador, Stettinius asked for a four-motor airplane and an office in the White House, in either the east or west wing. Without these signs of authority, Stettinius told the president, it would appear to the public as if he had received "a kick in the pants." The president assured him he had not received a kick in the pants.[3]

But when the secretaryship of state passed from such an innocent into the hands of the man who under Roosevelt had been "assistant president" for domestic affairs, a man who knew thoroughly the domestic equations of power, it was not a good transition. James F. Byrnes, like Truman, had utterly no experience with diplomacy. Robert L. Messer, in his hostile account of Byrnes's tenure as secretary of state, has made this point well.[4] Byrnes, of course, had attended the Yalta Conference in February 1945 and came back home ahead of Roosevelt, held press conferences, and became known as the expert on Yalta. In fact, Byrnes's presence at Yalta had been a charade on Roosevelt's part, for Byrnes had been furious, with good reason, over the president's putting him up, one might say, for the vice-presidency just prior to the Chicago convention, and then putting him down, dissimulating (lying, Byrnes said privately) as he did it, all in favor of Senator Truman. Byrnes had quit his job as assistant president, and Roosevelt took him to Yalta as a consolation prize. The wartime president included Byrnes in the group of advisers going to Yalta almost in the flippant way he included the Bronx political leader, Edward J. Flynn. Once at Yalta, Byrnes had virtually nothing to do, though he did sit at the round table with the leaders and principal assistants of the Big Three. Excluded from one meeting because it was nominally a military meeting, Byrnes threatened not to attend a dinner that evening, and only with reluctance did he finally attend: this may have been one reason why Roosevelt sent him home early. It was a squalid business, really, and does not deserve large recital save for the fact that Byrnes was no foreign policy expert and hence no fit successor to Stettinius, save in comparison with Stettinius.

And then, in surveying the lack of understanding of what political scientists describe mistakenly as power politics (which always are equations of power), there was the inadequate foreign education of the American people. When U.S.-Soviet relations began to cool, in the last months of the European war, there was little time for the ill Roosevelt to instruct his countrymen in the problems that were about to arise with America's principal ally. The American people perhaps had understood the need to accept the Soviet Union as an ally, even before entrance into the war in December 1941, when Roosevelt, upon the German attack into Russia, offered lend-lease to the USSR. But as the years passed, they forgot the awkwardness of close ties with a regime that had killed almost all its leader's enemies during the 1930s. The president himself "had a hunch," to use the phrase of William C. Bullitt, that he could get along with Stalin, and he played the hunch until nearly the end of the war. Within the upper reaches of the administration it was well known that the Russian lend-lease protocols were almost without conditions; although the president believed this fact could not easily be changed, he went along with it because of his larger hunch that time would resolve problems with the Soviets. When time ran out early in 1945, when Yalta proved a difficult negotiation and there followed the virtual Soviet explosion concerning negotiations in Switzerland over surrender of German forces in Italy, Roosevelt had no time to prepare public opinion for a different policy. President Truman momentarily attempted to turn things around when Foreign Minister Vyacheslav Molotov passed through Washington en route to the San Francisco Conference, but he backed away from his own forcefulness and then, to Prime Minister Winston Churchill's intense displeasure, arranged to have American troops withdraw from the Russian zone of Germany. All this, again, was essentially withheld from public notice, and the American people, as was true of their new leaders, Truman and Byrnes, were unprepared for what was to follow.

II

The conventional military strength of the United States in the half-decade 1945–50 was deplorable. The favorite general of American GIs, Omar N. Bradley, appears to have told the collaborator on his autobiography, published posthumously, that in the immediate postwar years the U.S. Army could not have fought its way out of a paper bag.[5] The root administrative cause of this predicament was the point system, with which the army, and to some extent the navy, began the enormous task of demobilization. The system has almost been forgotten, although it was well known to soldiers and sailors of the time. The idea was to allow for an orderly demobilization and at the same time permit real veterans, compared with soldiers who had only completed a few weeks or months of service, to get out of the military first. After World War I, demobilization had been chaotic, leading to much ill will, principally because the American Navy in 1918–19 did not have enough ships to bring the two million troops home immediately from France. This was not the problem after World War II (there were delays in the Pacific theater because of the enormous distances). And the point system in itself, with some exceptions, was not the problem, for the system gave points for being in the army or navy, for serving abroad, and for serving in combat zones, though it also gave points for possessing a wife and children, which, to single veterans, seemed grossly unfair. The trouble with the point system was that as veterans passed into the depots and then to ships for the voyage home, a sort of game of musical chairs developed within the units that remained abroad, or, for that matter, such units at home that included veterans. As each slot in a unit opened, it had to be filled, and each filler in turn required a substitute. It produced chaos within the companies, battalions, regiments, divisions, and all supporting organizations. In its working out, the point system became the best possible device for ruining the efficiency of the U.S. Army and Navy.

A much less important reason for the organizational chaos that beset the armed services after the war was the decision by military planners in 1945 and thereafter to try to hold experienced men and women, if necessary, by maintaining the wartime ranks. The services soon found themselves with an enormous number of highly ranked individuals, both enlisted and officer— especially officer. To measure the result in terms of inefficiency would require a skilled sociologist, or a team of sociologists, but suffice it to say that the surfeit of ranks turned in on itself. Matters soon came to a place where there was a general for approximately every one thousand enlisted ranks, each general required assistants, and administrative confusion was pervasive.

Domestic American politics entered into the decision, thoroughly understandable at first in terms of the need to keep an infrastructure for mobilization, to hold most of the "forts" and posts and cantonments that the services maintained during the war. The army thus required an immense force simply to garrison its possessions in the United States and abroad.

As if these obstructions to a lithe, smooth military organization were not enough, there was the decision, which was inevitable, to create a third military service. Such was done de facto during the war through the practical independence of the U.S. Army Air Forces. But in 1947 the air force achieved its formal independence, with all the duplication that followed, including new blue uniforms. The institutionalizing of this change, which of course required an air force academy, absorbed the energies of ranking officers who might have concentrated on organizing their new service in an efficient way.

The enlisted members of the postwar army, navy, and air force were mostly volunteers. The services themselves wanted to try to attract men, rather than force them, and the humors of the many former conscripts were such that they celebrated this arrangement. The inefficiencies of voluntarism need hardly be addressed. There were too few volunteers for the army, and to fill its ranks, it was necessary to go over to a draft. Meanwhile, the public relations people took money from the services to advertise their attractiveness, an enterprise that may not have increased national preparedness.

During 1945–50, the successor to Franklin Roosevelt did his very best to hold down the budget requests of the military services, which gave rise to problems almost without number. Let it be added that Truman had excellent reason to hold down the budgets. He was greatly concerned that the national budget be balanced and, if possible, wanted to produce surpluses so as to retire the wartime debt, which was ten times the dollar amount of the debt after World War I. Despite all the political talk that Truman was another loose-spending Democrat, garnished by stories of how he was naught but a failed haberdasher, Truman was a fiscal conservative. Surprisingly, too, during the eight national budgets of his time, four were in deficit, and four in surplus.

The president's firm control of the national budget gave rise to rebellions within the defense establishment, which further subtracted from military readiness. Now almost forgotten, the rebellions were serious and, it sometimes seemed, interminable. The shoe-horning necessary to create the air force and to bring the three services together in what was at first described as an establishment and, later, as the Department of Defense, required negotiations of months, even years. Then the air force immediately wanted more money, and the navy, fearful for the retirement of its wartime fleet (which itself was larger than all the navies of the world put together), soon was fighting for what it considered its life. Indeed, the entire postwar half-decade was marked by ferocious interservice rivalries that naturally drained many energies.

The result was a conventional force that was grossly inefficient for support of the diplomacy of the Truman administration vis-à-vis the Soviet Union. A specific testimony to that fact appeared very early in the administration, in the question of what to do concerning the Palestine problem, the proposed division of the British mandate into Arab and Jewish portions. There was constant concern among the Americans and the British that the Soviets might attempt to intervene. Perhaps it was the Truman Doctrine that kept them out, or maybe it was the 1946 UN controversy concerning the Soviet failure to leave Azerbaijan in northern Iran. For whatever reason, the Soviets largely kept out of the Palestine question. The Americans, however, to the chagrin of the British, were very much involved because of intense pressure on the Democratic administration by the Jewish lobby, whose strength centered in New York City. Secretary of Defense James V. Forrestal, concerned about Arab displeasure and the threat to the U.S. Navy's oil supplies in Saudi Arabia, liked to talk in cabinet meetings and elsewhere of how the hapless British could not keep peace in Palestine with sixty thousand troops and that it would require twice that number of UN troops, presumably American, to enforce any UN resolution. The U.S. Army could not have provided that many troops. Fortunately the whole issue was determined, largely in the way the Truman administration desired, by the preponderance of force exercised by the Jews in Palestine. But it was an embarrassment not to be able to underwrite UN arrangements in a postage stamp–sized area such as Palestine.

A more serious situation regarding America's lack of military force arose in relation to the Berlin blockade of 1948–49, produced by Soviet antipathy toward the London recommendations of June 1948, allowing an essentially independent West German government in Bonn. General Lucius D. Clay, the military governor of the U.S. zone, together with Ambassador Robert D. Murphy, favored sending an armed convoy by rail to Berlin. Truman's other advisers did not want to do that, for, in case of a shoot-out or even a stalemate (if, say, the Soviets had routed the convoy to a siding, letting it sit there without supplies of any sort), the advancing force would have to fight or retreat ignominiously, and they saw no real course except the latter. Troops available within West Germany, in the American and British zones, were not good enough to oppose the Red Army. A fortuitous event, the institution of an airlift, removed the administration from what otherwise surely would have been a withdrawal from Berlin and, therefore, a defeat. The U.S. Army was incapable of defending the American position, and diplomacy could have done nothing.

Throughout the negotiation of the Treaty of Dunkirk, then the Brussels Pact, and finally the North Atlantic Treaty, the unspoken fact (which at times was openly spoken, at least in private meetings) was that Western troops were incapable of resisting the Soviet army. Strategic plans, as they were called, all were plans for withdrawal, with the words carefully chosen as to how the troops would move backward, some to the Channel ports and others to Spain and Portugal. The very idea of holding any line at all was confined to the Rhine, which was hardly a defense of West Germany, and that was a most tentative confinement, with explanations of what would happen when that line collapsed. The British and other continental nations in NATO did not have any equipment and could not afford any. The French, unsure that they even wished to send a military contingent, were always looking sideways to their imperial responsibilities in Algeria and Indochina. There never was any serious military force available to NATO until after the opening of the Korean War, when in 1951 the United States sent four divisions to reinforce the two already there, and especially when, years later, West Germany entered NATO and undertook to furnish twelve divisions. Before the Korean War changed worldwide equations, Western forces opposing Russian forces in Europe were hardly worthy of the name. It was a well-known remark of that era, 1945–50, that if the Soviet troops desired to conquer Western Europe, all they needed were shoes.

Testimony to this truth of military defenselessness in terms of conventional forces came years later in the posthumous Bradley book, in which Bradley or his literary collaborator not only referred to the paper bag but remarked that in those dangerous early postwar years, half of the 552,000 officers and men of the U.S. Army "were overseas on occupation duty, serving as policemen or clerks. The other half were in the States performing various administrative chores."[6] General George C. Marshall, back in the Pentagon in 1950 as secretary of defense, told a small audience that he had been almost helpless in 1947–49 when he was secretary of state.

> I remember, when I was Secretary of State, I was being pressed constantly, particularly when in Moscow [the Moscow Conference of foreign ministers, 1947], by radio message after radio message to give the Russians hell. . . . When I got back I was getting the same appeal in relation to the Far East and China. At that time, my facilities for giving them hell—and I am a soldier and know something about the ability to give hell—was 1 1/3 divisions over the entire United States. This is quite a proposition when you deal with somebody with over 260 and you have 1 1/3 . We had nothing in Alaska. We did not have enough to defend the air strip at Fairbanks.[7]

III

But was not the United States protected by nuclear weapons during this entire period? Whatever the limitations of conventional forces, could not the supply of atomic bombs suffice to keep the Soviet Union out of Western Europe? Churchill, whose speeches had moved Britons and Americans during the dark days of war, and who enjoyed turning phrases, liked to say during the immediate postwar years that only the bomb stood between civilization and chaos—that, mirabile dictu, by a quirk of fate, the bad had preserved the good, the very threat had made straight the way to safety. It was a paradoxical thing, the very stuff of speech making, and Churchill could turn the logic a bit by pointing out the fragile nature of the arrangement and how it was also necessary to rearm in a conventional way. In early 1947, he stirred Western Europeans and some Americans with this oratory, and the result was the Council of Europe, where there was a forum but, frankly, not much more. That was another issue. Meanwhile, the atomic bomb preserved everything. Or did it?

As the years have passed, more information has become available. Scholars have worked over the information, and some disquieting facts have emerged. One of them is the lack of U.S. nuclear power in 1945–50. When U.S. Army control of nuclear weapons, including their manufacture, came to an end in January 1947 with the organization of the Atomic Energy Commission, the bomb assembly teams that the army had brought together and trained were thrown to the winds, dispersed. As David A. Rosenberg has shown, throughout the remainder of that year the AEC had no assembly teams. To put together a bomb was a complicated operation, one which required twenty-four men and nearly two days; then, because of the need to recharge a weapon's batteries, the bomb could not remain in a plane, ready for dropping, for more than forty-eight hours. Moreover, a vital part of the bomb, the polonium initiators necessary to ready a critical mass, had a half-life of 138 days and were in short supply in 1947. What would have happened in an emergency during 1947? This was the year of decision for American foreign policy toward the Soviet Union, with announcement of the Truman Doctrine and the Marshall Plan. During that time the United States effectively possessed no nuclear weapons.[8]

At the outset of that dismal year, 1947, there might have been, after assembly, a single available bomb. Truman, in a horrendous breach of security told White House staffers in 1946 that the United States had six bombs. In another security breach, he told one of his World War I lieutenants, visiting at the White House the next year, that the country had eleven bombs. But in 1947 the effective count apparently was one. Years later, Gregg Herken talked to David E. Lilienthal, the first chairman of the AEC, and the conversation was quite illuminating. Lilienthal spoke of when he had gone to Los Alamos in January 1947 to look over the weapons laboratory and its storage facilities. "Probably one of the saddest days of my life was to walk down in that chicken-wire enclosure," he said. "They weren't even protected, what gimmicks there were. . . . I was shocked when I found out. . . . Actually we had one [bomb] that was probably operable when I first went off to Los Alamos; one that had a good chance of being operable."[9]

The encouraging side of things was that, beginning in 1948, bomb production rose rapidly. An arrangement with Britain and Canada, concluded in January 1948, gave the United States the entire production of uranium mines in the Belgian Congo. Fat Boy plutonium bombs, known as Mark III weapons, were being replaced by Mark IV bombs that used only half the plutonium and weapons-grade uranium. Mark III weapons required artisans; they were tailor-made. Mark IV bombs meant assembly lines. All the while, the AEC recruited assembly teams, and presumably the problem of the initiators was solved. But the discouraging news was that the British physicist Klaus Fuchs, whom the FBI discovered was a spy, might have revealed to the Soviets the nature of the radar fusing mechanisms of the Fat Boy plutonium bombs. Until AEC scientists could replace the Fat Boys with Mark IVs, the Soviets could have jammed the aiming mechanisms of the bombs—all of the U.S. arsenal from 1945 until 1948. The Soviets were fascinated during this period with radar jamming, perhaps with good reason.[10]

Nor is even this possibility everything that needs to be said about America's vaunted nuclear power in 1945–50, for until the time of the Korean War the planes of the Strategic Air Command (SAC) were incapable of dropping bombs on targets, even if the

Soviets had not compromised the radar fusing devices. The demobilization of 1945–46 gravely affected the readiness of SAC,
crews of which carried the nuclear bombs. During the next two
years the command was under the nominal guidance of Gen.
George C. Kenney, a well-known figure during World War II, but
the effective commander was Maj. Gen. Clements McMullen, who
reduced SAC's readiness to a shambles through a program known
as cross-training, which required pilots to be competent in
nonflying duties and crew members to learn alternate aircrew
positions. McMullen trained his crews on targets that were easy
compared with what would occur under combat conditions. Planes
flew at low altitudes of ten or fifteen thousand feet. In January
1949, SAC's new commander, the vigorous Gen. Curtis E. LeMay,
sent all his bomb groups over Dayton, Ohio, near Wright Field, in
a simulated attack. He gave the crews maps of Dayton dated from
1938, required them to make passes at high altitude, and sent
them in at night. The weather was poor, with thunderstorms.
The result was a fiasco. Not a single plane fulfilled its mission.
LeMay was so shaken by the bomb runs that he described that
night as the darkest in air force history. During the next months
he worked over his command, changed everything, and gradually matters came under control, but it is safe to say that not
until 1950 was SAC able to do anything near what it was supposed to do.[11]

IV

For more than forty years, enormous numbers of books and articles have appeared about the Cold War, especially its beginnings
in 1945–50. Most of them relate the inadequacies, though not
always in detail, of President Truman and Secretaries Stettinius
and Byrnes and occasionally remark on the confusion of the
American people. Not many of them mention the lack of conventional force behind that era's diplomacy, and few remark on
the possibility that the nuclear shield was anything but that.
During this time, American military authorities were drawing
up war plans, arranging how conventional and nuclear forces were
to perform their allotted tasks. The Pentagon was full of ranking

officers, rotated in and out, who drew up plans with such names as Pincher, Makefast, Broiler, Halfmoon, and Offtackle. Behind their projections was not very much—maybe nothing. On the Soviet side a good deal of this weakness must have been known. Verne W. Newton has shown the extraordinary successes of the British diplomat Donald Maclean, who penetrated the State Department and the AEC while his colleague Kim Philby did the same with the CIA.[12] What held off the Soviets, persuaded them not to move while the advantage was on their side, is at present difficult to say.

Articles

CHAPTER 4

"Answering the Call"

The First Inaugural Addresses of
Thomas Jefferson and
William Jefferson Clinton

RONALD L. HATZENBUEHLER

Three days before he took the oath of office as the forty-second president of the United States, Bill Clinton visited Monticello, the home of America's third president, Thomas Jefferson. The day started off with clouds and a few snowflakes, but when the president-elect arrived, "an almost blinding sunlight" welcomed him to the oft-photographed west lawn. There, before approximately three thousand people (including 750 Charlottesville-area school children who won their spots in the crowd through a lottery), Clinton paid homage to Jefferson as a "man of the people" and pledged during his presidency "to stay in touch with America."[1]

In his inaugural address, Clinton again referred to Jefferson as a man who "believed that to preserve the very foundation of our nation, we would need dramatic change from time to time. Well my fellow Americans, this is our time. Let us embrace it."[2] Earlier in the speech, there was an indirect reference to Jefferson as well, when Clinton said that the nation's Founders had declared independence in order "to preserve America's ideals—life, liberty, and the pursuit of happiness." Including Jefferson in the address worked well for the new president because the references introduced the primary theme: that Americans needed to embrace change in order to renew themselves and their nation to face the challenges of the future. "Profound and powerful forces are shaking and remaking our world, and the urgent question of our time is whether we can make change our friend and not our enemy."

It is hardly surprising that William Jefferson Clinton mentioned his namesake in his inaugural address. Presidents often borrow Jefferson's words or name, hoping to gain public support for their programs. Franklin Roosevelt, who leaned more toward the Hamiltonian view of government, kept trays of quotes from Jefferson to be worked into his speeches. But it would be a mistake to conclude that Clinton used Jefferson in his inaugural remarks simply for political effect. With Monticello as the backdrop, Clinton hinted at the major commonalities between the two administrations. He admired Jefferson, he said, as "one . . . [who] believed in the power of ideas which have made this country great."[3]

I

Perhaps because the interval between the two presidencies is so large, most commentators compared Clinton's speech to those of more contemporary chief executives. Change, hope, and renewal were also the primary themes of Franklin Roosevelt's first inaugural, Clinton's only other direct reference to a Democratic president.[4] Philip Hamburger, who as a youth heard Roosevelt's speech in 1933, noted, in his report for *The New Yorker*, parallels between the events he witnessed sixty years apart. Hamburger was especially impressed by the good spirits among people who tried and failed to get close to the Lincoln Memorial for the extravaganza three nights before inauguration. "Thousands of black faces, yellow faces, white faces. No pushing, no shoving. Cynics don't buy this, but there are times when hope is palpable."[5]

Marshall Ingwerson, writing for *The Christian Science Monitor*, also found apt the comparison with FDR, noting that both Roosevelt and Clinton "ousted a sitting president who was perceived as too passive for times that demanded change."[6] But Ingwerson did not stop with Roosevelt. Like most other commentators, Ingwerson linked Clinton's address more closely with those of two presidents Clinton did not mention—John Kennedy and Ronald Reagan—rather than the two he did.

Ingwerson characterized the tone of Roosevelt's, Reagan's, and Clinton's addresses as that of a Jeremiad, a style of sermon rooted in the warning that "a people with a special covenant . . . have strayed from it and need to return to the fold."[7] "Clinton borrowed some style and phrasing from Kennedy this week," Ingwerson concluded, "[but his] inaugural symbolism could not have been more different," especially the "'communitarian' . . . emphasis—an outlook that differs from both liberalism, based on individual and group rights, and conservative individualism." Indeed, Ingwerson reported that the model Clinton's aides embraced "for a tightly focused presidential agenda" was President Reagan's first term.[8]

Evoking Kennedy was easy. As an editorial in *The New Yorker* indicated, candidate Clinton encouraged comparison between the two men with his "Kennedyish mannerisms (the thumb-topped fist jab, the stiff slouch with hand in jacket pocket); and a black-and-white clip of a glowing sixteen-year-old Clinton meeting Kennedy in a Rose Garden reception line . . . [as] the climax of Clinton's Convention film." But having made the comparison, the editorial emphasized how different the two speeches were. Kennedy focused almost entirely on foreign affairs; Clinton recalled the domestic agenda that was the basis of his run for the presidency.[9]

Writing for *The Wall Street Journal,* Jeffrey H. Birnbaum and Michael K. Frisby agreed that the speech reprised the language of Kennedy but also "bore similarities" to Reagan's 1981 oration because of its "anti-government" language; because it was filled with optimism (compared with Jimmy Carter's pessimism); and because it "dealt with taking over the presidency from the opposing party." This final emphasis was necessary, they hinted, because of Clinton's transition to the presidency, "a transition that has often seemed bogged down in Washington business as usual[,] . . . highlighted by close relations with Congress and the appointment of many Washington insiders to high government posts. . . . Washington's streets have been lined with stretch limousines for days."[10] Christopher Hitchens made the same point, with anger, in *The Nation:*

> There were fewer public spaces available on the bleachers than there had been even at Bush's inaugural; a third fewer by one count. Wall Street and K Street and "the donor community" took care of

the rest. If it had been a Republican approaching the throne through this pelting storm of laurels and plaudits, surely some liberal cynic would have reminded us that January 21 was the bicentennial of the execution of Louis XVI. . . . I was reminded, while watching the ease with which baptized-again William Jefferson Clinton performed, of an old film about Huey Long. The master gathered the acolytes of business around him at the start of the campaign and said: Those of you who come in with me now will get big pieces of the pie. Those of you who wait until later will get smaller pieces of pie. Those of you who delay too long will get—Good Government.[11]

Such comments amount to a stinging indictment: sounding like Kennedy, but without the flourishes; hopeful like FDR, but without the fanfare; triumphant like Reagan, but lacking his specifics.

Perhaps there's no surprise, then, that former Reagan speech writer William Safire was among the few who gave it high marks. He rated the speech "a B, but because his delivery was so good and the day was sunny and hope contagious, I gave it a B+." Still, Safire faulted the president for subject-verb and pronoun-antecedent disagreement; for confusion between "raised" and "reared"; and for using a double negative. "I am all for reducing the size of the White House staff by 25 percent, as candidate Clinton promised," Safire concluded, "but maybe he should leave unfilled a couple of national security slots and hire one good copy editor."[12]

Safire's jab points up an important difference between the "Man from Monticello" and the "Boy from Hope [Arkansas]." No one ever suggested that Thomas Jefferson needed a copy editor. Still, a survey of period newspapers reveals that acclaim for Jefferson's first inaugural was limited to Republican newspapers. The *Independent Chronicle & Universal Advertiser* (Boston), for example, printed the speech in its March 12–16, 1801, edition and granted it effusive praise the following week. "Old South" contrasted the derision Federalists heaped upon Thomas Jefferson the presidential candidate with the conciliation preached by Thomas Jefferson as president. Although Jefferson had been denounced as a person intent on destroying government and religion, the president revealed himself instead to be a patriot and a Christian—"an enemy to the persecuting spirit of bigotry, but a friend to that be-

nign temper, which secures the happiness of society, and estab-
lishes the sacred doctrines of the Gospel on a foundation too permanent to be shaken by zealots, or sanguinary fanatics." Therefore, the author offered the speech as an American classic:

> The great principles of our government are brought within the com-
> prehension of every individual; it is . . . a PERFECT SYSTEM, so
> completely condensed, that it exhibits in one view all the vital or-
> gans of its existence. The man who studies this speech cannot be
> ignorant of the essential qualities of a free government; it is a lesson
> which should be early learnt to our children, as containing those
> rudiments, which ought to direct not only the statesman in his du-
> ties, but instruct each citizen in the preservation of his rights.[13]

Federalist newspapers also frequently reprinted Jefferson's address,[14] but comments on it took a far different bent. Perhaps the
most stinging series of indictments appeared in the *Connecticut
Courant* (Hartford), where, beginning in late August 1801 and
continuing through November, the paper published no less than
seven satirical rebuttals of Jefferson's words. In the first,
"HYPERION" related a dream in which he was transported to
hell, where a new "Chief Magistrate" had just delivered his inaugural speech. HYPERION praised the oration for its "infinite merit
in the composition," but faulted it for containing "many parts,
too sublime, for any earthly imagination to conceive its imagery,
and too profound, for any human understanding to comprehend
its meaning."[15]

One portion of Jefferson's speech came under special attack
from the Federalist newspaper. Immediately preceding the section of the address containing his famous statement, "we are all
republicans—we are all federalists," Jefferson reflected that "the
throes and convulsions of the ancient world, . . . [had produced]
agonizing spasms [in] infuriated man, seeking through blood and
slaughter his long-lost liberty." "Merciful genius of letters and
philosophy," the Federalist critic observed, "'Aliquando dormitat
Homerus.' *Even Homer sometimes sleeps.* Whatever doubts men
may have entertained of the soundness of your political creed, it
is presumed no man in future will deny you the palm of supremacy
in the art of *sinking* and confounding metaphors."[16]

Most of Jefferson's biographers view such criticism as partisan hyperbole and have universally praised Jefferson's phraseology in his first inaugural. Dumas Malone suggests that the speech "wrote a notable chapter in the history of the American presidency . . . [and] established his historic claim to the title of father of American political democracy." In addition to its "verbal felicity," Jefferson succeeded in mixing his plans for his time with his hopes for all times. His words, according to Malone, "were both timely *and* timeless."[17] Merrill Peterson emphasizes the care that Jefferson put into writing the address (three drafts), which in style and content "bore the personal insignia of its author. Never had he soared to higher or lovelier peaks of republican ideality. Never was his happy faculty of condensing whole chapters into aphorisms more brilliantly displayed."[18]

No wonder Bill Clinton, who, according to one account, wrote "most" of his address,[19] suffers by comparison. But then, so have the addresses of most presidents.

I I

In comparing the words of the two men, one is struck first by how different are the worlds they lived in and the many changes American society has undergone since the turn of the nineteenth century. Early in his speech, Clinton compared the world of horseback and travel abroad by ship with the modern world of instantaneous global communications and commerce. "Technology," he marveled, "is almost magical." Politically, American society has also expanded since Jefferson's time to include people, notably women and blacks, who could not be citizens in 1801. In recognizing George Bush for his service to the United States, Clinton also thanked "the millions of men *and women* whose steadfastness and sacrifice triumphed over depression, fascism, and communism" (emphasis added). He also mentioned the civil rights movement and at the end of his address paraphrased Dr. Martin Luther King, Jr.'s "I Have a Dream" speech by saying, "From this joyful mountain top of celebration, we hear a call to service in the valley." Most notable in this regard, however, was the fact that Clinton mentioned children or young Americans four times in his text, families three.

Not only has the size of the body politic expanded since 1801, so has the size of the "Washington community."[20] Jefferson talked of creating "a wise and frugal government, which shall restrain men from injuring one another, [and] which shall leave them otherwise free to regulate their own pursuits of industry and improvement"; Clinton promised to curb "powerful people [who] maneuver for position and worry endlessly about who is in and who is out, who is up and who is down. . . . Let us give this capital back to the people to whom it belongs."

If these were some of the differences Clinton saw from a distance of almost two hundred years, Jefferson's inaugural contains other concerns clearly rooted in his day and in his personal experiences. Religion appears in Jefferson's address five times. He first broached the subject in the negative context of differing political opinions: "Having banished from our land that religious intolerance under which mankind so long bled and suffered, we have yet gained little if we countenance a political intolerance as despotic, as wicked, and capable of as bitter and bloody persecutions." Later, in a similar context, he promised "equal and exact justice to all men, of whatever state or persuasion, religious or political."[21]

Two positive contexts of religion reinforce such views. Toward the middle of his address, Jefferson expressed his belief that God intended for religion to help people, not to hurt them, because in America people were "enlightened by a benign religion, professed, indeed, and practiced in various forms, yet all of them including honesty, truth, temperance, gratitude, and the love of man; acknowledging and adoring an overruling Providence which by its dispensations proves that it delights in the happiness of man here and his greater happiness hereafter." At the very end of the speech, he developed this theme further: "May that Infinite Power which rules the destinies of the universe, lead our councils to what is best, and give them a favorable issue for your peace and prosperity."[22]

Because Jefferson believed that God intended for people to be happy, peaceful, and prosperous, he might have argued (as John Kennedy did in 1961) that government was his agent on earth for accomplishing these goals. He did not. Integral to Jefferson's view of good government was his belief that people's opinions, especially their religious beliefs, were completely outside of government's control. In his "Bill for Establishing Religious Freedom" (1777), Jefferson argued "that the opinions of men are not the objects of civil government nor under its jurisdiction."[23] Later, in *Notes on the State of Virginia* (1787), he wrote, "The legitimate powers of government extend to such acts only as are injurious to others. But it does me no injury for my neighbor to say there are twenty gods, or no god."[24]

In addition to Jefferson's views regarding religion, his inaugural address sought to dispel ideas that democracy was a weak form of government. "I know . . . that some honest men fear that a republican government cannot be strong; that this government is not strong enough. . . . I believe this, on the contrary, the strongest government on earth." Key to the nation's strength were its industrious people and the bounteous riches of the land itself. Two years prior to his acquisition of the Louisiana Territory, Jefferson spoke in his inaugural of "a wide and fruitful land . . . with room enough for our descendants to the thousandth and thousandth generation."

Almost two hundred years later, religious views are still a divisive force in the nation on many issues of public policy, but these divisions seem less fundamental than in Jefferson's day. Clinton quoted from Galatians in his address: "And let us not be weary in well-doing, for in due season we shall reap if we faint not."[25] Following his quotation from scripture, however, he ended his address with the caveat that people would hear the words "in [their] own way." In other words, God would help people to serve their country, but each person might well hear a different message of how to render that service.

I I I

Although time does separate the two men and their eras, there are many common elements in their addresses. First, both men came into office following twelve years of control by the opposition political party. Each president had to promise a break with prior policies, and each sounded conciliatory and promised to promote national unity. However, because he was the first president to come into office through a peaceful transfer of power, Jefferson's task was far harder than Clinton's. The third president emphasized that his election proved the power of the Constitution to bind people "under the will of the law, and unite [them] in common efforts for the common good." Because of this unanimity, it was possible for all citizens to "unite with one heart and one mind. . . . Let us then, with courage and confidence pursue our . . . attachment to union and representative government."[26] In short, Jefferson believed that it was his job to put the majority back in control of the nation. Twice in his address, he spoke of the right of the majority to rule the country, based upon "the right of election by the people." Later in his life, Jefferson spoke of "the revolution of 1800," a fundamental change in the *principles* of government.[27]

Concerning the strength of republican government, Clinton began his address by noting the transition from the "shadows of the Cold War . . . [to] a world warmed by the sunshine of freedom." Later, he mentioned the collapse of communism and the continuing challenge for Americans "to lead the world we did so much to make." Clearly, there were no longer doubts about the form of government, only continuing differences about how best to make it function.

For his part, Clinton focused attention on "the era of deadlock and drift" through which the nation had passed, but he asked Americans to "reform our politics . . . so that we can feel the pain and see the promise of America." Clinton felt what Jefferson had in 1801, that the people had wanted a change in leadership: "The American people have summoned the change we celebrate today. You have raised your voices in an unmistakable chorus. You have cast your votes in historic numbers. And you have changed the face of the Congress, the presidency, and the political process itself." Therefore, Clinton first asked the Congress to join with him in answering the people's request for change, and then he asked the people to join him also: "We must do what America does best: offer more opportunity to all and demand more responsibility from all. It is time to break the bad habit of expecting something for nothing, from our government or from each other. Let us all take more responsibility, not only for ourselves and our families but for our communities and our country."

Because this section of the inaugural sounds so much like John Kennedy's "Ask not what your country can do for you; ask what you can do for your country," it is easy to forget that Jefferson also emphasized that the people would have to play their part in accomplishing the goals he outlined in his inaugural address. Because he believed so strongly in republican government, and because he believed that many Federalists were monarchists who wanted to reestablish hereditary rights in America, Jefferson emphasized that the hard work of the people was building the nation, not the government. In America, Jefferson believed, people possessed "a due sense of our equal right to the use of our own faculties, to the acquisitions of our industry, to honor and confidence from our fellow citizens, resulting not from birth but from our actions and their sense of them."

The theme of hard-working, independent, virtuous citizens was a favorite of Jefferson's, and he seldom missed an opportunity to repeat it. In *A Summary View of the Rights of British America* (1774), Jefferson reminded the king that "America was conquered, and her settlements made and firmly established, at the expence of individuals, and not of the British public. Their own blood was spilt in acquiring lands for their settlement, their own fortunes expended in making that settlement effectual. For themselves they fought, for themselves they conquered, and for themselves alone they have a right to hold."[28] Twenty years later, in *Notes*, he praised farmers as "the chosen people of God, if ever he had a chosen people, whose breasts he has made his peculiar deposit for substantial and genuine virtue. . . . Corruption of morals in the mass of cultivators is a phenomenon of which no age or nation has furnished an example."[29]

Based upon these ideas, he promised in his first inaugural "encouragement of agriculture, and of commerce as its handmaid." As Drew McCoy has delineated so masterfully in *The Elusive Republic*, Jefferson believed that the further a country moved from agriculture and the closer it came to manufacturing, the more misery and stagnation it attracted. By expanding across space and by providing markets for the surpluses produced by farmers, the nation's "most virtuous and independent citizens," Jefferson hoped to forestall movement through time from agriculture to commerce to industry.[30]

Hand-in-hand with these views was Jefferson's promise to reward farmers for their industry by curbing the size of government, which had grown in size and cost under Alexander Hamilton's plan for the national debt and John Adams's Quasi-War with France. A "wise and frugal government," Jefferson asserted at the beginning of his speech, would leave people "free to regulate their own pursuits of industry and improvement, and shall not take from labor the bread it has earned. This is the sum of good government." Toward the end of his address, he made the same point, promising "economy in the public expense, that labor may be lightly burdened [and] the honest payment of our debts."

In the same context, Jefferson included his plans for foreign affairs: "peace, commerce, and honest friendship with all nations—entangling alliances with none." There would be no more preference for England over France as under Washington and Adams; no more expensive navies; no more personal, standing armies to be led by Hamilton, a would-be Caesar. And to carry into effect these beliefs, Jefferson ratified the Convention of Mortefontaine, which Adams's emissaries had negotiated.[31]

Clinton used surprisingly similar ideas during his inaugural address. The national government, he said, had become filled with people who had forgotten "those people whose toil and sweat sends us here and pays our way." Although he mentioned the national debt only once ("We must invest more in our own people—in their jobs and in their future—and at the same time cut our massive debt"), Clinton alluded to it several times: "An economy that is still the world's strongest . . . is weakened by business failures, stagnant wages, increasing inequality, and deep divisions among our own people"; "We know we have to face hard truths and take strong steps[, but] we have not done so"; and "Drifting has eroded our resources, fractured our economy, and shaken our confidence."

Also like Jefferson, Clinton moved from the nation's financial problems to an examination of foreign affairs:

> To renew America, we must meet challenges abroad as well as at home. There is no longer clear division between what is foreign and what is domestic—the world economy, the world environment,

the world AIDS crisis, the world arms race—they affect us all. . . .
While America rebuilds at home, we will not shrink from the challenges, nor fail to seize the opportunities, of this new world. Together with our friends and allies, we will work to shape change,
lest it engulf us. When our vital interests are challenged, or the
will and conscience of the international community is defied, we
will act—with peaceful diplomacy whenever possible, with force
when necessary.

Obviously, there are important differences between the two men
and their eras. Jefferson emphasized physical isolation from Europe ("kindly separated by nature and a wide ocean from the ex-
terminating havoc of one quarter of the globe"); Clinton stressed
connectedness through telecommunications and business.
Jefferson promised "entangling alliances with none," and Clinton
stressed working with "our friends and allies."

Despite such differences, reflecting the rise of the United States
to a position of world leadership, an important similarity deserves
underscoring. As Lawrence S. Kaplan has argued so persuasively,
most of Jefferson's "isolationism" stemmed from his beliefs that
European countries operated under governmental systems different from, and antithetical to, that of the United States—"nations
who feel power and forget right, advancing rapidly to destinies
beyond the reach of mortal eye."[32] Because Americans lived by
different values and different principles, the basis of which
Jefferson carefully delineated in his inaugural address, he suggested
that it would be foolish to focus attention on foreign nations rather
than on ourselves. Whatever the differences between Jefferson
and George Washington concerning Hamilton's financial plans and
attachment to Great Britain, Jefferson agreed with Washington's
farewell address and his "Great rule of conduct," especially that
portion which said, "Europe has a set of primary interests, which
to us have none, or a very remote relation. . . . Under an efficient
government, the period is not far off, when we may defy material
injury from external annoyance; . . . when we may choose peace
or war, as our interest guided by justice shall counsel."[33]

    Seen in this light, Clinton's unmistakable message on foreign
affairs was that the United States had at length arrived at the
place the Founders envisioned. "Our greatest strength," Clinton
said, "is in the power of our ideas, which are still new in many

lands. Across the world, we see them embraced—and we rejoice. Our hopes, our hearts, our hands, are with those on every continent who are building democracy and freedom. Their cause is America's cause." Once in the minority, Americans now stood with the majority because others around the world had embraced our ideas.

Clinton developed this theme more fully in a speech to members of the diplomatic corps at Georgetown University two days before his inaugural.[34] "There is an essential continuity in American foreign policy," he said. "Our relations and actions abroad are rooted in enduring interests, alliances, friendships and principles." He mentioned commitments to peace in the Middle East, reductions in nuclear arms, suffering in Somalia, and changes within the Soviet Union. Then, he stated that under his administration U.S. foreign policy would rest on three pillars: "economic security, . . . a restructuring of our Armed Forces to meet new and continuing threats to our nation's security and international peace, [and] . . . democratic principles and institutions which unite our country and to which so many people around the world aspire." Following up on the last of these points, he promised

> whenever possible . . . [to] support those who share our democratic values because it is in the concrete interests of America and the world at large. History has borne out these enduring truths: democracies do not wage war against one another; they make better partners in trade and diplomacy; and democracies, despite their inherent problems, offer the best guarantee for the protection of human rights.[35]

The message was clear: As the world is comprised more and more of democracies, international trade will be the focal point of nations' foreign policies. Therefore, each nation, including the United States, "cannot prosper at home without engagement abroad. We will therefore seek economic strength at home through increased productivity—while we seek to ensure that global commerce is rooted in principles of openness, fairness, and reciprocity."[36]

Three hundred days into Clinton's administration, the Congress passed the North American Free Trade Agreement (NAFTA). This pact, begun prior to Clinton and endorsed by all the living presidents, was Clinton's first step toward international trade based on "openness, fairness, and reciprocity," goals that have motivated American presidents throughout the twentieth century, especially Woodrow Wilson.[37] The genesis of such ideas belongs not in the twentieth century but rather in the period of America's founding. No president better expressed these ideas as forming the basis of the nation's foreign policy than Thomas Jefferson, when in March 1801 he promised "peace, commerce, and honest friendship, with all nations." He articulated other American ideals that day—freedom from governmental interference in people's lives, democratic control of the nation's institutions, the rule of law—but he told Americans forcefully that domestic and foreign policy cannot be separated, that who we are at home determines who we are abroad.

IV

It is important to note, in conclusion, that many have faulted Jefferson's performance as president based upon the words he used in his first inaugural address. Federalist newspapers called him to task within four months of his taking office for failing to live up to the conciliatory spirit of his oration. In July 1801, the *Trenton Federalist* calculated that over thirty Federalists had been removed from their offices simply because they belonged to the opposite party from the president. "We will still believe," the editorial concluded, "that at the time Mr. Jefferson made his speech he was *sincere,* really intended 'equal justice' to the federalists; but that he is now compelled, by the *imperious* voice of *party,* to abandon his promise." At the time of the inaugural address, the editorial continued, Federalists universally trusted the president, and Republicans hoped he was lying: "In solemn, conclave met such was their language:—'Can this really be the speech of Mr. Jefferson? Can the man of the people so basely have deceived us? Can he truly intend that the despised federalist shall enjoy *equal privileges*? Shall this our servant dare to say, "We are all federalists, we are all republicans?" What! has he not been elected by *our party,* and shall he not be a *party* President?'"[38]

Among recent writers, none has more stridently criticized Jefferson for failure to match words and actions than Fawn Brodie. In her book, *Thomas Jefferson: An Intimate History,* Brodie called the speech "one of the great seminal papers in American political history, . . . [with] an almost Biblical impact," but she disparaged the speech for setting a standard too high for its author to achieve:

> Here, as in the Declaration of Independence when he wrote that all men were created equal and entitled to life, liberty, and the pursuit of happiness, he was enunciating an ideal as if it were a reality. This was one of Jefferson's special qualities as a revolutionary statesman, that he could define the visionary future as if it were the living present, and this without any sense of contradiction. . . . In this respect it can be said that Jefferson dwelt in a fantasy world . . . [where] his fantasy of the just world was so intertwined with the real world that it blurred the contradictions in his own behavior, a total consciousness of which might have served to destroy his faith in his own destiny.[39]

Brodie is right, at least in part. The longer Jefferson stayed in office, the less able he was to accomplish the goals he outlined in his inaugural. The Napoleonic Wars trapped the United States between the British shark and the French tiger; both countries trampled on "neutral rights." Even the Louisiana Purchase, arguably Jefferson's greatest accomplishment as president, cannot be made to fit neatly within the plans he outlined on March 4, 1801, because of its ambiguous constitutionality and its cost.[40]

The *New York Times* reacted similarly to Clinton's speech. In the address, the newspaper editorialized, the new president said he would reform politics in the nation, but "his record as Governor and candidate show that he occasionally confuses mere assertion with real accomplishment. . . . [W]ith the uncancellable promises of his own speech, William Jefferson Clinton has proclaimed a new dispensation for this nation and its capital. As it was spoken, so let it be."[41]

In devoting their first speeches as president to the theme that ideas can promote change, both men opened themselves to the criticism of falling far short of their intentions. Almost two hundred years after Thomas Jefferson's first inaugural address, it is clear that he accomplished less than he promised, but the verdict is still out on William Jefferson Clinton. It will be for some time.

CHAPTER 5

Internationalism and the Republican Era

LYNNE K. DUNN

Henry Cabot Lodge was triumphant. "We have won the fight. We have destroyed Mr. Wilson's League of Nations and . . . we have torn up Wilsonism by the roots." William E. Borah was equally jubilant as he asserted that the Republican victory in the presidential election signified "an absolute rejection of all political alliances or leagues with foreign powers" and "the dedication of this nation to the foreign policy of George Washington and James Monroe, undiluted and unemasculated." With these comments, reported in the *New York Times* on 4 November 1920, the two Republican senators claimed victory in the struggle over postwar foreign policy. The people had spoken, and the dangerous, emasculating Wilsonism was eradicated.[1]

Despite the fact that many of the senators' contemporaries immediately denied the assertions that the 1920 election had served as "a solemn referendum" on the League of Nations—and analysts have confirmed that domestic issues really accounted for the Harding landslide—the sentiments expressed by Borah and Lodge were enshrined in the consensual interpretation of the era. Diplomatic historians, focusing on the rejection of the League and the pursuit of an "unentangled course," concluded that internationalism, both as an ideology and as a policy, was defeated in 1920: isolationism prevailed during the Republican era. This analysis determined not only the evaluation of the decade for the next forty years, it continues to restrict the context in which the period is studied today.

Beginning in the 1960s, revisionist historians, led by William A. Williams, challenged the consensus interpretation. They produced a body of work that attacked the isolationist framework, asserting that the failure to consider economic activity produced an analysis far too narrow to explain U.S. foreign policy. Subsequent studies of the 1920s by Joan Hoff, Carl Parini, Michael Hogan, Melvin Leffler, Frank Costigliola, and Emily Rosenberg built on this foundation as they examined specific elements of interwar policy and thoroughly rejected the internationalist-isolationist dichotomy. Some accepted the "open door" thesis while others moved to "independent internationalism" and "liberal-developmentalism" and then on toward a corporatist analysis of private-public cooperation and aggressive international activity.[2]

This revisionism has been supplemented by research that approached the issue from another perspective. Work by Warren Kuehl, Charles Chatfield, Sondra Hermann, Charles DeBenedetti, and Robert Divine focused on the 1920s as a period during which a highly self-conscious foreign policy elite (who called themselves internationalists) participated in an intense ideological battle over the nature and conduct of American foreign policy.[3] Unfortunately, this work has remained somewhat marginalized, largely ignored in effecting an overview of foreign policy priorities.[4]

The failure to weave this debate into the tapestry of the decade, to produce an integrated, multidimensional picture, is at least partially attributable to the fact that the internationalists were largely ineffectual. Poll after poll showed public support for some type of revised League, and even more compelling evidence existed of public support for membership in the World Court.[5] And yet, despite the fact that the internationalists constituted a significant portion of the opinion makers and attentive public and that they had impressive financial resources at their disposal, they were unable to bring this public opinion to bear on successive Republican administrations and appreciably affect policy.[6] Clearly the internationalists failed. Nevertheless, they should neither be ignored nor dismissed, for, as Lawrence S. Kaplan and Morrell Heald have reminded us, "If there is a distinctive pattern in the American diplomatic experience, it emerges from the fact that the cultural setting is less a backdrop than a vital cog in the workings of foreign affairs."[7]

Why did the internationalists fail? This question remains central to any integrated analysis of the Republican era. This chapter will posit that the answer can be found in study of the internationalist elite. Prior to 1919, the commitment of such activists to a stable, peaceful world order created a sense of "community." Despite differences in approach, the internationalists were largely united by their opposition to the prevailing world order. The overall label had meaning.[8] However, members of this group had arrived at only the most superficial ideological consensus. With the creation of the League of Nations as the strongest expression of internationalist ideals, differences between factions were thrown into bold relief.

To mask this disagreement and keep their ideals alive after the defeat of the League, internationalist organizations emphasized global cooperation, heightened general support for the League of Nations as a European institution, and worked to create "an internationalist mind." This approach produced a variety of groups with impressive membership rolls, generating large attendance at lectures and providing favorable poll responses, but the success obscured the central issue. Internationalist objectives would only be achieved when U.S. policymakers were willing to sacrifice a degree of national autonomy and accept the spirit of collective action and security.[9] Since the activists, whose roots lay in nineteenth-century internationalism, did not agree on this themselves, their programs avoided addressing the problem. Subsequently, their failure came neither at the hands of an apathetic and lethargic public nor from a unified isolationist block in opposition, but rather from their own inability to agree upon and articulate a coherent alternative to nationalism and unilateralism.

Had the internationalists confronted well-defined groups in opposition to their ideals, their task would have been easier and their differences less apparent. However, their opponents were far from a political monolith.[10] Contemporaries noted this diversity even among the anti-League "irreconcilables," many of whom had considerable interest in world affairs.[11] Indeed, Senator Borah and his supporters often defended their role in defeating the League by claiming to favor increased cooperation as long as they could avoid entangling alliances. Even Arthur Sweetser, noted American internationalist and League of Nations official, found it difficult to characterize Borah as "an absolute isolationist."[12] This was, at heart, the most difficult problem for the internationalists. Their opponents did not advance an argument in favor of isolationism but rather relied on subtle attacks on the League, as established by the covenant, to defend their course.

Claims abounded that the covenant had been written in secret, that the League was a superstate designed to dominate the world, and (reflecting efforts to win converts among hyphenates, farmers, and workers) that the organization was originally conceived as the instrument of Wall Street and was now dominated by Great Britain. All of these arguments were buttressed by the traditional appeal to George Washington's admonition against permanent alliances.[13] Although such criticisms would have been relatively easy to counter, League supporters rarely responded.

The opposition of prewar reformers, liberals who had heretofore maintained close links to the internationalist community, posed a more serious challenge. Frederick C. Howe, a widely known Progressive reformer, argued that Americans could not resolve the problems of Europe and it would be best to concentrate on the ones at home.[14] Many liberals complained about decisions regarding territories and colonies, reparation terms, and a peace treaty that showed only a limited concern for social and economic justice. The problem clearly lay in their association of the League with an unjust settlement that maintained a capitalistic-imperialistic system and preserved the political status quo. American socialists, wary of the League, argued for nearly a decade about whether or not to endorse it. They finally made a reluctant commitment in 1928, which thereafter they applied in principle but not in practice. This delayed and qualified endorsement reflected fears of imperialism, which struck a responsive chord in the hearts of many Americans.[15] In this sense, liberals disappointed in the 1919 Versailles settlement proved to be a more troublesome group of doubters than those irreconcilably opposed to the League.

Opposition also flowed from individuals who professed to be friendly toward the League and the World Court but who expressed doubts about the actual efficacy of U.S. membership. Such people praised the League, claiming that it was a splendid institution for Europe.[16] They conceded the importance of the international organization and often argued for limited American cooperation until circumstances favored membership. Republican senator George W. Pepper of Pennsylvania argued that the League should admit that it was only an administrative body. Once the League abandoned any pretense that it had the power to avert war, the United States could readily join.[17] This approach proved to be insidious, as a number of internationalists contended that continued agitation for League membership merely stiffened the opposition. They maintained that the advocacy of membership should be dropped in favor of an emphasis on cooperation.[18]

Finally, internationalists faced a divisive threat from opponents who argued more subtly still, combining their criticisms of the League with attacks on specific internationalist positions and tactics. Critics noted that the internationalists displayed an excessive reliance on "machinery," the actual organizational structure, as if that in itself would solve problems. The League existed, but was it capable of doing much? Skeptics also questioned some of the analogies of the pro-League activists. The example of the United States as the model for a confederation or federation seemed especially vulnerable to challenge: the thirteen states had much more in common than did nations in the diverse world of the 1920s. Others questioned what they saw as an almost mystical confidence vested in international law.[19] As confidence in judicial processes eroded during the 1920s, buttressing opposition arguments, evidence of League impotence reinvigorated arguments in defense of the status quo. Critics consistently denied the allegation made by the internationalists that U.S. membership in the League would make it a more successful instrument. Most of the major postwar problems, they argued, did not affect the United States, and thus it could not contribute to their solution.

Although certainly confronted with a difficult task if they had only to counter such arguments, internationalists had an even more difficult time dealing with divisions within their own ranks.

The League of Free Nations Society (LFNS) is particularly illustrative of this dilemma. Founded in 1918 by such liberal activists as Herbert Croly, John Dewey, and Charles and Mary Beard, LFNS members were not pleased with the covenant, especially those provisions which repudiated the principles of self-determination and social justice. Under the chairmanship of James G. McDonald, the society initially urged ratification without reservations if "accompanied by a declaration of liberal principles." After March 1920, recognizing the need for a presidential-senatorial compromise, the society's members agreed to petition President Wilson to resubmit the treaty and to consent to any reservations the Senate desired. Thereafter the group did little until it reorganized in 1921 as the Foreign Policy Association.[20]

Members of the liberal ecumenical community who traditionally supported internationalist objectives were even more critical. *World Tomorrow*, expressing the views of this group, declared that "Only a spiritual and economic revolution will save mankind and make possible a genuine association of free peoples." This theme appeared in other articles, which insisted that loyalty to internationalism sprang from an emotional attachment: there could be no temporizing. "Leagues, Pacts, Associations, Conferences are just as peaceful, unselfish, and high-minded as the governments that compose them." The League could never operate on liberal or enlightened grounds; it was a deceitful union of imperialists. As long as nations resorted to their old ways, they were essentially undermining international organizations.[21]

Members of the peace movement also posed problems for League supporters. Traditionally, pacifists favored some form of world organization. However, they now voiced concern over the covenant, particularly Article 10, with its reliance on military force. While they favored peace and global cooperation, they showed little sympathy for the machinery designed to prevent war. Although many pacifists sided with the reservationists during the Senate's debates, after March 1920 they divided over the question of whether to abandon League membership, promote it with acceptable limits, or seek an acceptable alternative. Thus, as one observer noted, they adopted the advice of the mother to her daughter who wished to learn to swim. "Hang your clothes on a hickory limb, but don't go near the water."[22]

Peace advocates, as distinct from pacifists, were even more difficult to deal with because of the wide diversity of views and positions they adopted. They defined themselves as internationalists, stating that their differences with League supporters were primarily ones of emphasis: internationalist stands were secondary to antiwar activity. Subsequently, peace activists straddled the subject of commitments and advocated policies of general cooperation rather than obligation. Ultimately, their deep-seated opposition to sanction-based collective security, expressed through a willingness to propose and accept alternatives to the League, made their support half-hearted, at best, and dangerously divisive, at worst.

Given the divisions within the internationalist community, Woodrow Wilson's declaration that the election of 1920 should be "a solemn referendum" appears all the more damaging. Clearly internationalists were split over the League and, as Wilson was well aware, they were equally divided by party. At their conventions, both Republicans and Democrats wrestled with the League issue, convinced that the foreign policy debate would play a significant role in the electoral campaign. Henry Cabot Lodge, evermindful of the 1912 split that had given the presidency to a Democrat, carefully maneuvered himself into the position of temporary chairman of the convention so that he might present in his keynote address a moderate position on the League.

Ultimately, the Republican plank, carefully crafted by Elihu Root, had to be masterfully noncommittal to avoid wholesale defections among the party faithful. The plank endorsed peace and "an international association . . . based on justice" which would "provide methods which shall maintain the rule of public right by development of law and decision of impartial courts, and which shall secure instant and general conference whenever peace shall be threatened by political action, so that the nations pledged to do and insist upon what is just and fair may exercise their influence and power for the prevention of war."

Although the plank was worded to pacify the irreconcilables, avoiding mention of the League, the pledge to play a constructive role in world affairs through "an international association," with emphasis on courts, was the bare minimum required to appease the internationalist wing of the party. That wing, led by men like former president William Howard Taft, Harvard University president Abbott Lawrence Lowell, influential editor Hamilton Holt, leader of the New York State Republican party Herbert Parsons, noted Yale economist Irving Fisher, and prominent businessman Theodore Marburg, could not be safely ignored.

The attempt to mask the tensions within the Republican party, however, was largely unsuccessful. The ambiguity of the platform became apparent with publication of the "Statement of the 31." Released to the press on 14 October 1920, this public declaration interpreted the plank and the position of presidential candidate Warren G. Harding in the broadest possible way, finding proof of an internationalist inclination. The statement affirmed a commitment to "a true course to bring America into an effective league to preserve peace" and went on to insist that Harding had promised to "combine all that is good and excise all that is bad" to achieve the "highest conception of helpful cooperation." Ultimately, fifty-six very prominent Republicans endorsed this interpretation, not only committing the party to a course more friendly to the League of Nations than Borah or Lodge favored, but also indicating that there was a powerful cadre within the party determined to influence Harding once he was in office.[23]

As the Republican factions struggled over their platform, the Democrats convened in San Francisco. They, too, had to wrestle with the League question. Charges that Wilson's obstinacy had killed the treaty would embarrass them in the campaign, but they could not renounce his role or ignore him. When Democratic National Chairman Homer S. Cummings delivered the keynote address at the convention, he commended the covenant as the one constructive achievement of the war and called for a clear statement favoring membership in the League. The statement officially adopted by the party was less wholehearted in its support. The plank praised Wilson's role in the creation of the League and endorsed affiliation but with suitable limitations. "We do not oppose the acceptance of any reservations," it declared, "making clearer or more specific the obligations of the United States to the League associates."[24]

By the eve of the election, it was clear that, although neither party had enthusiastically embraced the League of Nations as constituted in 1920, neither had completely rejected internationalist ideals. As a result, the election returns, far from the "absolute rejection" and "destruction" spoken of by Borah and Lodge, indicated that the foreign policy debate would continue.

Early in January 1921, representatives of the World Peace Foundation, the Carnegie Endowment for International Peace, the League of Free Nations Association, the Pro-League Independents, the Church Peace Union, and the League to Enforce Peace (LEP) assembled to discuss a new organization to promote League membership. The majority of these representatives were Republicans. They shared the optimism of the signatories of the Statement of the 31 about their ability to influence President-elect Harding, particularly if they could mobilize a public campaign. Coming together under the banner of American Association for a League of Nations (AALN), they decided to focus their efforts on drafting a list of changes to make the covenant acceptable to the public. Yet, from the outset, their efforts were stymied. The AALN founders had hoped that either the venerable Elihu Root or the popular Herbert Hoover would accept the presidency of the new organization. Both declined. The organization was dealt a second blow when Taft, president of the LEP, insisted that its members withdraw from the American Association. In the months after the election, the management committee of the LEP was committed to a cautious approach. Although many of the members were pushing Taft to act more vigorously, he resisted the pressure, arguing that the organization might lose everything by being too aggressive. He believed that if League members would agree to satisfactory revisions in the covenant, then the Senate could be persuaded to join. Given this view, he opposed any move that would alienate the new president. The committee bowed to Taft's arguments, agreeing not to press Harding until he had talked "with prominent friends of the League."[25]

By March 1921, some LEP members, led by A. Lawrence Lowell, began expressing doubts about this strategy in the face of Harding's ambiguous inaugural address. At this point, however, their critique was undercut by the president's selection of a secretary of state. Harding appointed Charles Evans Hughes, who had endorsed membership in the League and signed the Statement of the 31.[26]

The wavering among the LEP leadership about the proper amount and type of pressure to exert on Harding cloaked a deeper, organizational division. Executive Secretary William H. Short had joined Lowell in advocating a more vigorous role for the organization, a position that evoked criticism from Taft and the more cautious members. When Harding, in a special message to Congress on 12 April, suggested that the Treaty of Versailles be ratified without the covenant, dissension in the LEP forced Lowell and Taft to call a meeting of the executive committee. Competing resolutions resulted in a compromise statement issued on 30 April, which reaffirmed support for the Harding administration's efforts to achieve "any effective organization" that would preserve "peace and justice" through "a Court of International Justice, with appropriate sanctions for securing a resort thereto and machinery for conference and cooperation . . . ."[27] When dissenters failed in their attempt to include some expression of support for the existing League of Nations, Theodore Marburg could not understand such faith in an administration with a hostile record toward the international organization. The protest stimulated additional debate, revealing a wide range of views within the League to Enforce Peace.[28]

Professor John Bates Clark of Columbia University believed that cooperation between nations would lead gradually to a new "informal association which, if long continued ought to ripen into a league." Taft argued that practical considerations should determine the group's course even if they did not lead to the most desirable result: the irreconcilables and Harding would soon part company, thus leaving the president free to act. Lowell agreed and extended the argument. The covenant had never included the most essential LEP proposal, which called for "the employment of military force against a member which goes to war without previous resort to judicial and arbitral tribunals." Since they had already abandoned a great deal, they should gamble on the Harding administration and at least gain something. Marburg responded that the existing League represented reality and must be supported. By endorsing Harding's undefined association, he said, Taft and Lowell were betraying the cause. Herbert Parsons responded more bluntly. He considered "talk about an Association of Nations as bunk." Realists should admit that the irreconcilables dominated the new administration. Yet Taft and Lowell could not accept that assessment. They believed that they would still prevail over irreconcilables in their party and that Hughes would lead the nation into accepting the Versailles Treaty.[29]

Torn by internal differences, the League to Enforce Peace lost members and financial support. A staff that had been as large as seventy in November 1919 dwindled to five by April 1921. Treasurer Herbert S. Houston raised sufficient funds to pay a $9,500 debt and accumulate $4,000 for a "next campaign," but no one could decide when that would develop.[30] Marburg suggested that they send League publications to all senators, but Lowell feared that such a move might alienate supporters. Short proposed an innocuous "World-Our-Neighbor" educational program that could include discussion of the "League of Nations as an association of neighbors for making a rational and peaceful world," but that idea elicited only limited support. Lowell then asked Hughes for suggestions and received a warning not to mount any demonstrations.[31] Hughes preyed on fears that any agitation might upset his plans as he prepared for the forthcoming Washington Naval Conference.

In fact, the Washington Conference, which assembled on 12 November 1921, did momentarily distract the internationalists. On several occasions, Harding had coupled the idea of disarmament discussions with his association of nations proposal, although he was purposefully vague about how this might unfold. For this reason, the July call for disarmament discussions has been characterized as a ploy by the Harding administration to demonstrate its commitment to world peace "while ignoring the League of Nations." Indeed, throughout October 1921, LEP leaders stopped debating how they might pressure Harding and focused on how they could best support the Washington Conference.[32]

During the interim, the LEP lost Taft, who resigned in July 1921 to become chief justice of the Supreme Court. Lowell assumed the presidency, and former attorney general George Wickersham accepted the executive committee chair. The group decided in December to wait until the disarmament conference ended before launching any new programs. The organization never really revived. In 1922, the LEP mounted an unsuccessful drive for funds, but its leaders eventually acknowledged the irreparable

divisions within the organization and formally ended its existence in September 1923.[33]

Meanwhile, the attempt to create the American Association
for a League of Nations had foundered. Wickersham had issued a
call for representatives of internationalist groups to come together.
On 23 April 1921 at the Century Club in New York City, this
gathering heard reports that Secretary Hughes favored League
membership, that he was thinking of resubmitting the treaty to
the Senate, and that the Harding administration wanted no outside agitation for the moment. During the ensuing spring months,
however, optimism faded about the Harding-Hughes commitment
to these positions. Members from fourteen peace and internationalist groups gathered on 10 May, this time at Lowell's urging.
There was agreement on three points: they condemned the Knox
resolution for a separate peace with Germany; endorsed the
Harding administration, provided it continue to work for U.S.
participation in some type of international organization; and called
for initiatives toward disarmament.

A final attempt to create a permanent organization committed
to supporting the League occurred in mid-July 1921. Raymond
Fosdick and Hamilton Holt issued the call, and delegates from a
number of women's organizations seemed eager for action. However, no permanent body emerged from these efforts, as respon-
dents agreed to a delay until the League to Enforce Peace elected
a new president following Taft's resignation.[34]

As the congressional elections of 1922 approached, Republican
internationalists determined that they must form an organization capable of influencing the party. They faced a difficult dilemma, as they could not actively attack their own incumbents
without creating bitter intraparty factionalism. The participants
decided to reorganize as the American Association for International Cooperation (AAIC). Wickersham, who served as chairman,
conferred with Lowell, Straus, and other signers of the Statement
of the 31, and they agreed to lend their support.

Democrats, recovering from their defeat in the 1920 election,
also began an organizing drive. Not surprisingly, they centered
their appeals around Wilson's name, hoping to attract both partisan and nonpartisan constituents. For the firmly partisan, there
was the image of "Wilson as Fallen Democratic Party Leader."

For attracting nonpartisan, independent, or Republican internationalists, the image became "Wilson as Symbol of an Ideal." The
latter emphasis was reflected in the Woodrow Wilson Foundation, founded in March 1921, as enthusiasts created an agency
designed to honor the former president and perpetuate his liberal
and democratic ideals through awards or grants. A second attempt
to keep his name before the public appeared in the form of the
Woodrow Wilson clubs, which began at Harvard University when
students, led by Robert C. Stuart, invited Holt to speak. By December 1921, fifty-four chapters had been organized on campuses,
and a national council began a campaign for funds to foster an
exchange of foreign students and promote research on Wilson and
the Versailles conference.[35]

Yet another venture emerged in May 1921 in the form of the
Woodrow Wilson Democracy, the most clearly partisan of the
groups using Wilson's name. The Woodrow Wilson Democracy
hoped to force the Democratic party to adhere to "popular, progressive, and humanitarian ideals" associated with Wilson, to seek
candidates in the 1922 and 1924 congressional campaigns who
were dedicated to those ends, and to gain a pro-League plank in
the 1924 platform.[36]

Ultimately, internationalists in both parties met with failure.
As the campaigns began, Wilson approached Democratic National
Chairman Cordell Hull and insisted that the program of the
Woodrow Wilson Democracy group deserved attention. The Democracy platform stated that the United States should join the
League, send representatives to a European commission dealing
with economic and reparation questions, and face issues related
to tariff, labor, and trade. Former presidential candidate James
Cox called for a special meeting to formalize a program for the
congressional campaign in the fall of 1922, but nothing came of
these efforts. A decision was made to keep issues simple and ambiguous.[37] Party leaders ignored the Woodrow Wilson Democracy.
The subject appeared so rarely during the autumn that some
irreconcilables boasted that the Democrats had abandoned the
League.[38]

The Republican AAIC was equally unsuccessful. In late October they had launched full-scale agitation for membership in the
League on the basis of the elimination of Article 10. This effort

was so wholly unsuccessful that the group agreed to modify its goals. The focus instead would be to educate the public so that voters would support membership in the World Court and participation in the economic and social commissions of the League. For the moment, campaigns for membership would be set aside.[39]

Certainly part of the difficulty experienced by League supporters in both parties stemmed from their inability to claim that they spoke for the entire internationalist segment of the public. Journals like the *New Republic, The Nation,* and *World Tomorrow* continued to articulate the liberal perspective expressed during the treaty debate. The *New Republic* left no doubt about its position. Cooperation with the League and other organizations could be tolerated, but because of its origins the League could never be trusted, especially since European political leaders continued to dominate it. A satisfactory resolution of postwar problems could not be realized through the League.[40] The National Council for Prevention of War (NCPW), organized in 1921, headed by Frederick Libby and representing over thirty organizations, provided a voice for the peace contingency. Its threefold platform called for "Progressive World Organization, Worldwide Reduction of Armaments by International Agreement, and Worldwide Education for Peace." The NCPW remained noncommittal regarding League membership.[41]

Following the 1922 congressional elections, internationalists were forced to recognize the failure of the partisan, political approach. They had failed to influence either party's position; and liberal criticism, groups like the NCPW, and the looming demise of the League to Enforce Peace made it apparent that they were in total disarray. When Justice John H. Clarke announced his retirement from the Supreme Court, coupled with a statement that he planned to devote his life to work on behalf of the League along nonpartisan lines, the favorable public response encouraged many internationalists to believe that Clarke could provide the leadership their movement needed. The AAIC, chaired by Wickersham, moved to unite with Clarke's League of Nations Non-Partisan Committee to form the League of Nations Non-Partisan Association (LNNPA). After some months of maneuvering and negotiation, Clarke prepared a statement broad enough to appeal to nearly everyone. He invited citizens to participate in "an independent, nonpartisan" effort designed to cultivate a public mood that would induce the administration to join the League under whatever terms seemed wise, consistent with the Constitution, "and consonant with the dignity and honor, the moral responsibility and power of our Republic."[42]

This statement became the "creed" of the new LNNPA on 5 December 1922.[43] At a gala dinner for 750 guests on 10 January 1923, the LNNPA united diverse groups and began its labors.[44] The League to Enforce Peace provided the names of its members, the World Peace Foundation committed money, the Pro-League Independents joined, and Fosdick turned over the files and library of his news bureau. Substantial gifts amounting to twenty thousand dollars arrived from Chicago philanthropist Anita McCormick Blaine, Clarke, Fisher, and industrialist Cleveland Dodge.[45]

Holt and Short also assumed positions of leadership. The former chaired the finance committee and devoted his time to speaking and fund-raising. He and Colby organized a lecture series for areas where Senate elections would be held in 1924. Local chapters were to be organized in these areas.[46] Short, who had been executive secretary of the League to Enforce Peace, served in the same capacity for the new organization. Initially, the Holt-Short collaboration was extremely successful. The association received $54,075.26 in its first six months. After Holt and Short took charge, operations expanded. By 1924, with a staff of over a dozen, the association was spending ten thousand dollars a month.[47]

Despite some hesitation, efforts proceeded to obtain pro-League planks in both party platforms in 1924. A subcommittee of Clarke, Wickersham, Harriet Lees (Mrs. James) Laidlaw, Narcissa Cox (Mrs. Frank) Vanderlip, Stephen Duggan, Fosdick, Strong, and Bainbridge Colby prepared drafts, which they presented to delegates at the conventions. Their goal was to prevent the Republicans from denouncing the League and to block any Democratic tendency to water down its endorsement. A secondary priority was apparent in efforts to solicit the views of senatorial candidates on World Court membership and to obtain public statements of their support.[48]

The Democrats responded coolly to representatives of the Non-Partisan Association. The party's plank observed that "there is no substitute for the League of Nations as an agency working for peace," but it then avoided the issue by calling for a national referendum on membership.[49] The Republican plank was equally innocuous, stating only that no peace agreement should violate the independence or rights of the United States.

Observers that year were well aware that both parties deliberately avoided any commitment to the League. This was especially true of the Democrats. The conditions associated with a referendum, with no deadlines and with Congress designated as the initiator, meant that no popular vote would ever be taken. Even if held, Democratic attorney David Hunter Miller argued, a referendum would have no constitutional weight and only confuse the issues. As one writer concluded, the Republicans "[have] abandoned the League idea, while the Democrats are not willing even to go as far as Mr. Lodge and the Republican Senators went in 1919."[50]

Calvin Coolidge's election surprised few people, and LNNPA officials drew few conclusions from the results.[51] Voters cast their ballots on the basis of domestic concerns, and pro-League citizens supported both Coolidge and John W. Davis. A few arch-isolationist senators like Republican Joseph Medill McCormick of Illinois and Democrat James Shields of Tennessee were defeated, but that marked no trend. The (at best) inconclusive results should have made League advocates wary. Yet they maintained their optimism. The supporters of the LNNPA apparently agreed with Fosdick when he concluded that more "long, hard work" would "be necessary before America sees the light."[52]

And work they did. In 1925, a new and energetic branch of the Non-Partisan Association emerged in Chicago, where it enjoyed substantial support from Anita McCormick Blaine and Congressman Morton D. Hull. Within two years the branch hired Clark M. Eichelberger, who displayed youthful enthusiasm and amazing organizational talents. He saw the League as "the greatest cause in the world for which I am perfectly willing to devote my life." He assisted in creating chapters throughout the Midwest that distributed printed materials, held hundreds of meetings each

year, and started a journal in March 1928 called the *League of
Nations Chronicle*. In a few months it had a circulation of over
five thousand. By 1930, Chicago served as the Midwest office of
the association, overseeing activities in thirteen states.[53]

There can be no doubt that the League of Nations Non-Partisan Association did move constructively in one area: Everyone
agreed that educational campaigns should "sell" the League to
the American people, and various committees did this effectively.
Newspapers published by the LNNPA (under varying titles) reported on developments in Geneva, pending legislation, major
international events, and programs of the association. They also
contained book reviews, summaries of speeches and articles, and
essays on the value of the League and the World Court. Miscellaneous broadsides and pamphlets appeared, with over 800,000 distributed in the first eighteen months; in 1926 a movie, "Hell and
the Way Out," glorified the League of Nations.[54] A Speakers Bureau of 300 in 1923 grew to 475 by 1924. Fisher, Holt, Colby,
Lucia Ames Mead, and Nehemiah Boynton, pastor of the Clinton
Avenue Church in Brooklyn, went on national tours that lasted
for months. Public forums, luncheons, and dinners reached other
listeners.[55]

Association speakers in the schools invited students to write
essays based on their reading of "Survey of the League of Nations" published by the LNNPA secretariat. By 1928, an annual
examination on the League involved 5,000 students in 950 schools.
A college division organized branches on campuses, with sixty-
five operational by the middle of 1924. A Model League of Nations Assembly program also proved to be popular. By 1928, the
association needed a staff of six persons to supervise its school
activities. To reach the general public, the LNNPA provided a
"clip sheet" of news releases to journals and daily newspapers; by
1926, this organ had a distribution of six thousand.[56]

A Committee on Church and Religion headed by MacFarland
reached another constituency, and Harriet Laidlaw established
contact with national women's organizations. After the association began a hospitality operation in Geneva, it organized a
travel club to promote visits.[57] In 1929 and 1930, all activity
focused on the tenth anniversary of the League of Nations, a
campaign to rally support for the pending London disarmament

conference and to promote Senate approval of the World Court protocols.[58]

In an effort to attract broader support, the LNNPA began endorsing projects that supplemented its primary objective. It cooperated with publisher Edward W. Bok when he sponsored a peace prize in 1923; it called for greater cooperation with League commissions; it endorsed participation in disarmament discussions; and it supported the ratification of treaties on obscenity, child labor, and white slavery. As the so-called "outlawry" movement gained headway, the association reluctantly rallied behind it and the Kellogg-Briand Pact. In the late twenties, the LNNPA endorsed treaties of arbitration "of the New Type, exemplified by Locarno," and called for a neutrality policy under which the United States would not trade with any treaty-breaking country. Although these issues were in keeping with internationalist goals and beliefs, they were a step back from a commitment to League membership.[59]

By the late twenties, the LNNPA was beginning to experience financial difficulties. The clearest indication of declining fortunes and influence, and the failure of dreams, came in the electoral campaign of 1928. Despite four years of intensive educational work, neither the Democratic nor the Republican party paid any attention to the association. During the campaign, even Newton Baker and other stalwarts decided to focus on Court membership and avoid the issue of the League. They lost even on that more modest objective. The Republican platform proclaimed the advantages of "freedom from entangling alliance" and a high tariff. Herbert Hoover shifted markedly away from his previous support for the League. Nor did Democratic internationalists have any influence on their presidential candidate, Alfred E. Smith of New York, who avoided the issue entirely.[60]

At least partial recognition of their failure in the political arena was reflected in the decision, coming in late 1928, to change the name of the LNNPA to the League of Nations Association. At the same time, a simplified statement of purpose deleted the qualification that membership "be consistent with the Constitution, . . . the moral honor, dignity, and responsibility of the United States."[61] The change in name implied more than the loss of the group's nonpartisan character. In fact, it represented recognition

that League of Nations membership was no longer a viable political issue.

This reality is all the more startling when other internationalist activity is taken into consideration. During the 1920s, more
than fifty organizations—some newly created, others longer lived
—committed themselves to "internationalist ideals." Their programs ranged from support for the League of Nations and the World
Court, through broad general efforts to promote creation of an
"international mind."[62] Groups like the Foreign Policy Association and the Council of Foreign Relations promoted discussion
and debate of international issues and provided the clearest bridge
to the constituency studied by revisionist historians. Other groups
committed themselves to equally broad perspectives, ranging from
ecumenicism to creation of a universal language. Despite the depth
and breadth of all this internationalist activity, the organizations
formed were impotent. How and why, then, should this activity
be granted meaning and significance?

Ultimately, a new synthesis will arise when historians begin to
look at the point at which internationalists came into conflict
with their opponents. The chief obstacles to the attainment of
internationalist goals were nationalism and issues of sovereignty.
Traditional opponents of internationalism (typically, albeit erro-
neously, labeled isolationists) accepted the fundamental soundness of a world system in which the nation-state expressed the
will of humanity. Any collective action had to be based on the
willingness of states to collaborate, and little should be done to
undermine the independence and autonomy of the actors. Internationalists, although extraordinarily diverse in terms of the
amount of sovereignty they were willing to compromise, tended
to accept a denigration of nation-state autonomy to a degree that
would bind nations to cooperative, collaborative action in pursuit of humanistic aspirations, the ultimate goal being the end of
war and a rising standard of living and economic security for all
people.

During the 1920s, internationalists failed to address this basic
issue that separated them from their opponents. They compromised at every turn, settling for "cooperation" rather than commitment and emphasizing education, which ultimately sancti-

fied the continued existence of autonomous nation-states. They offered ambiguous positions based on a revised League, disemboweled by revision of Article 10. This was their failure. They did not fail to generate debate; they failed to clarify the debate in a way that made it meaningful. This failure—the prostitution of genuine internationalist ideals in pursuit of political victories— meant that little or no progress was made during the interwar years. Although the creation and rapid acceptance of the United Nations after World War II was heralded as a result of internationalist efforts, this was a hollow victory. The United Nations enshrined great-power autonomy in the Security Council and, as E. Timothy Smith points out in his article in this volume, even this minimal commitment to collective action gave way to a Cold War consensus which returned to reliance on traditional regional alliances. Today the world is beset with conflicts that have their origins in nationalism. Around the globe people are fighting to create new states as the symbol of their identity and the vehicle through which they will express their aspirations. Perhaps a renewed study of alternatives is in order.

CHAPTER 6

Public History Serves the Nation

The Historical Service Board, 1943–1945

George T. Mazuzan

In the late 1970s historians entered the field of public history in full force. Today the label "public historian" is a well-known term within the profession. Although they initially emerged with an identity problem, public historians discovered their roots actually went back several generations. The best-known early practitioners were combat historians, who researched and wrote about the exploits of the American armed forces during the Second World War. Others served less conspicuous roles in the intelligence services, where their research abilities were valuable assets. But historians and social scientists also played another generally unrecognized role during that war. Because of its desire to take advantage of several factors particular to the field of history and its organization, the War Department made a contract with the American Historical Association (AHA). The AHA agreed to provide written materials for informal educational purposes that would be used with the citizen-soldiers in the armed forces.[1] This episode is a knothole through which to view the sometimes difficult interaction between the American military and civilian scholars engaged in what both parties viewed as service to a common patriotic enterprise.

Informal Education in the U.S. Army

A variety of functions were assigned to the Army Service Forces (ASF), a major command within the military establishment. Tasks ranged from carrying out important supply activities, publishing *Yank* magazine, selecting sites for prisoner-of-war camps, to producing motion pictures. Units within the Service Forces also assumed a large responsibility for soldier morale. To accomplish this part of its mission, the ASF provided educational opportunities designed to maintain troop morale in camp as well as to give GIs, most of whom were draftees, something to anticipate when they returned to civilian status at the conclusion of hostilities.[2]

Even before the Pearl Harbor attack, the War Department wanted to introduce servicemen to the issues involved in the European and Asian wars. The department tried experimental orientation courses that dealt with the daily events of the foreign conflicts. The program gave little attention, however, to national and domestic problems arising out of the war that might directly affect American troops. After the United States entered the conflict, the department broadened its educational approach by ordering unit commanders to provide time once a week for open discussion on any subjects that might interest their soldiers. Most officers in charge of troop units, however, concerned more with the military aspects of their training programs, gave low priority to the discussion idea. The program floundered.[3]

The Special Service Division within the Army Service Forces, involved with the off-duty time of soldiers, assumed the responsibility for filling this apparent void. General Frederick Osborn, a prominent New York banker who had been appointed a brigadier in 1941, headed the division. Osborn's civilian background included the prewar chairmanship of the Joint Army and Navy Committee on Welfare and Recreation. That experience provided him familiarity with some of the special problems associated with soldier education. Through several army reorganizations in 1942 and 1943, Osborn eventually led the ASF Morale Services Branch and subsequently became director of the Information and Education Division, with overall responsibility for troop education.

Colonel Francis Spaulding assisted Osborn as the chief of the education branch. A Harvard-educated Ed.D., and dean of that university's graduate school of education, Spaulding took a leave of absence in 1942 to join the Army Service Forces. He spent his first year in the group studying ways to initiate an educational program that would meet two criteria: promote discussion of a range of problems that army leaders thought were or should be the concern of its citizen-soldiers; and avoid using a significant amount of the precious training time of unit commanders.[4]

The GI Roundtable Series

In the context of the army's primary mission of training men for military pursuits, Spaulding and his staff appreciated that it was not the service's main responsibility to educate personnel about civilian affairs. That was a desirable objective, nonetheless, and both Osborn and Spaulding believed that the army could be a vehicle to furnish troops with unbiased information on current issues and problems. The troops could then use the provided materials for self-education. After experimenting with and reviewing several formats, Spaulding's education branch, with the full support of General Osborn, launched the "GI Roundtable Series."[5]

The main idea for the series can be traced to a project attempted earlier. *Reader's Digest* had published and distributed pamphlets to civilians for use in the discussion of current affairs. In 1942, the army contracted with the popular magazine to make available reprints of the articles for a special publication, *Camp Talk*, that the army distributed on an experimental basis to selected troop units. The soldiers used *Camp Talk* (only one issue was ever published) as core reading material around which to organize off-duty discussion groups. Favorable response greeted the experiment. Aware of that endeavor, Spaulding developed it into the proposed armywide roundtable discussion group idea.

Studies had revealed that the average soldier's educational level was the tenth grade.[6] The army developed a tentative bibliography of twenty pamphlets, written in interesting and succinct language and geared to this tenth-grade-level audience. Army personnel as well as outside consultants would furnish the topics for the pamphlets. Osborn and Spaulding believed they could achieve both readability and objectivity with the assistance of a scholarly organization. So the army turned to the American Historical Association.

The Historical Service Board

In the summer of 1943, Spaulding approached Guy Stanton Ford, executive secretary of the AHA, with the idea of troop discussion forums. Ford arranged for Spaulding to present the army's proposal to a special AHA Executive Council meeting. Spaulding told the assembled historians that the army had considered several organizations for the task. His list had also included the Social Science Research Council, the American Council of Learned Societies, and the American Council on Education. For several reasons, however, the historians ranked first. A historical approach to the series was an important consideration, as were the AHA's reputation for impartiality and independence and the fact that the organization's charter had been incorporated under an act of Congress. Spaulding assured the council that if the AHA took on the task, the assigned writers would have total freedom in preparing the material. The council authorized Ford to proceed with a formal arrangement.[7]

Ford subsequently organized the Historical Service Board (HSB) as an advisory committee to work exclusively with a small staff on the GI Roundtable series. Ford coaxed Theodore C. Blegen, dean of the graduate school at the University of Minnesota, to direct the project starting in October 1943. At the AHA's Capitol Hill headquarters in the John Adams Building of the Library of Congress (better known at that time as the Library of Congress Annex), Ford arranged space for Blegen and his staff. The ten-member board guided Blegen. The interdisciplinary fields of the HSB membership reflected the variety of the subject matter that would be proposed: Shepard B. Clough, economic historian at Columbia; Robert B. Cushman, political scientist at Cornell; Dixon Ryan Fox, historian and president of Union College; Waldo G. Leland, director of the American Council of Learned Societies; Edwin G. Nourse, an economist at the Brookings Institution; historian J. Salwyn Schapiro of the City College of New York; Arthur M. Schlesinger, historian at Harvard University;

Robert R. Wilson, Duke University political scientist; and Donald R. Young, sociologist at the University of Pennsylvania. Ford served ex officio and also chaired the HSB. The board's work was more than perfunctory; two members served as referees for each manuscript and all were consulted often as the program moved ahead.[8]

A contract between the War Department and the Historical Service Board established the essentials of the program. Its term ran initially from 1 September 1943 to 30 June 1944. The agreement required the HSB to provide the army three manuscripts a month beginning in December. The board had to maintain "high standards of completeness, accuracy, objectivity, and English style" as well as receive the "advice and aid of such military personnel as may be provided." Initial compensation amounted to thirty-five hundred dollars each month with a proviso for revision of the sum once the project had been launched.[9]

Organizing the Mission

To produce the final manuscripts, Blegen used an evaluation procedure similar to the process used by academic publishing houses and scholarly journals. He sought out and contracted with individual authors to write the articles on particular topics. Selected board members read the manuscripts. Occasionally, outside readers were used, but only if a board member felt unqualified to act as a critic. Since the HSB accepted responsibility for the manuscripts, it was free to scrutinize them to eliminate bias and argumentation. The authors then revised their pieces, and a second reading and editing took place before a finished product was forwarded to the army education branch. Further reading and criticism occurred there, sometimes by more than one government agency, if the topic fell under the purviews of multiple agencies. The army then returned the manuscript to the HSB staffers who reviewed and incorporated the commentary of government readers. In most cases, Blegen required the author to make a final revision, and for this work the author received a stipend of three hundred dollars.[10]

Blegen dispatched an instructional memo to the authors, underscoring the scope of the program. Maximum length for a pamphlet was twelve thousand words. Blegen emphasized the army's belief that the pamphlets should be "attractive for a broad soldier audience." He told his authors, "Make writing easy, clear, popular, interesting. Do not use footnotes. Avoid expressions (like 'current,' 'recent,' 'this year,' etc.) that tend to date the pamphlet. Use short sentences and short paragraphs." He reminded them of the average educational level of their audience but noted that one soldier in eight had some education beyond high school. So, he wrote, "avoid any touch of 'writing down' to or patronizing our audience." Blegen was aware of the value the army placed on materials free of bias and propaganda. He warned his authors: "The need of maintaining a high level of objectivity thus cannot be too strongly emphasized. We want to be careful to do justice to both sides of an argument, to avoid tendential writing, to keep personal judgments and ready-made conclusions out."[11]

Developing Manuscripts

The army produced the first pamphlet—actually a manual for the roundtable leaders who would use the pamphlets to initiate discussions. Quite informative, the "Guide for Discussion Leaders" included information on how to stimulate interest, select the right subjects, and lead a discussion. The manual gave details on whether to choose an informal discussion group, a panel, or a single-speaker forum. It also suggested how to develop dialogue, debate, and ask questions to get at the heart of the subject. A list of reference materials was appended, indicating additional pamphlets that were forthcoming. Each pamphlet, the guide noted, would be written in a popular style and would include factual material about some question of interest to the soldiers. Undoubtedly to calm any fears among prospective discussion leaders, the manual also explained that each pamphlet would contain suggestions to the leader on how to handle the particular issue and noted that the subjects were chosen after careful analysis of recent studies done on the interests of army personnel.[12]

With the program outlined, Blegen and his staff went to work. They sent three manuscripts to the Morale Services Branch in December 1943, and regular submissions followed in subsequent months. Pamphlet topics covered wide subject areas. Some were international and political—for example: "Is the Good Neighbor Policy a Success?" "What Shall be Done About Germany After the War?" "What Future for the Islands of the Pacific?" "What Shall be Done About Japan After Victory?" Others dealt with the wartime alliance. There were pamphlets on "Our British Ally," "Our Chinese Ally," "Our Russian Ally," "Canada: Our Northern Neighbor," and "Lend-Lease." Moreover, some of the most interesting ones covered mundane subjects which nonetheless concerned the average soldier: "Can War Marriages Be Made to Work?" "Do You Want Your Wife to Work After the War?" "Shall I Build a House After the War?" "What Will Your Town be Like?" "Does It Pay to Borrow?" Such booklets were directed at those very frustrating questions to which many GIs probably gave much thought and undoubtedly discussed in their off-duty bull sessions. Other topics, for example, "What is Propaganda?" and "Can We Avoid a Postwar Crime Wave?" were ones the army thought important to be addressed.[13]

Generally, the HSB completed the manuscripts on schedule, but Blegen often encountered a considerable delay both in getting approval from the Morale Services Branch and in seeing the works through to a final printing. Blegen's relationships with Osborn, Spaulding, and Maj. Donald Goodrich, another army liaison officer, were excellent; but he often found that his military counterparts had very little influence in obtaining timely approval of the manuscripts from nonmilitary agencies and sometimes even from other military offices. Goodrich admitted the problems to Blegen and noted that practically every question that arose had to be cleared through a half-dozen offices. In all projects relating specifically to foreign nations, for example, the Office of Strategic Services had been requested to read the manuscripts. In some instances, the manuscripts were sent also to the Division of Military Intelligence. Papers about Allies were read by the embassies of the countries concerned, and the War Department called on the State Department for its judgment about certain booklets that touched questions of foreign policy. According to Blegen, all this took excessive and, he thought, unnecessary time.[14]

Theodore Blegen was a taskmaster. He wanted the program to move on schedule, so he pressured his authors and his critical readers. Despite his prodding and striving for perfection, the HSB and the staff devoted a large amount of time to criticism and revision before they believed any manuscript was ready to be dispatched to Goodrich for the military round of approvals. With his firsthand knowledge of the HSB's painstaking efforts to produce solid manuscripts, Blegen was annoyed by the "lively apprehensions in the minds of some [military] officers of public criticism of the final product." These delays aroused the director enough that by June 1944 Blegen asked for a special meeting of the AHA Executive Committee to consider discontinuing the program once the association satisfied the initial contract. He cited the fact that the army had launched the discussion program but then delayed completion of the necessary materials.[15]

In spite of Blegen's misgivings about the military response, the army and the AHA renewed the contract. It provided an increase in monthly compensation from $3,500 to $5,000 with no increase in the monthly quota of manuscripts. When the war ended in 1945, a balance had accrued so that another renewal for 1945–46 specified a reduction in payment to $1,000 each month to complete the remainder of the program.[16]

A constant and major concern throughout the program was the writing style of many authors. Most scholars, accustomed to writing for specialized audiences, had difficulty placing the contents of their assigned topics at an approximate tenth-grade level. Osborn wrote Blegen about this problem early in the program and asked him specifically to review all ongoing work for a "too heavy" treatment. Blegen concluded in his final report to the board that "scholars generally have too seldom learned to write clearly and interestingly no matter how vital and fascinating their subjects." For this reason, Blegen considered having some pamphlets written by popular writers and using scholarly experts as critics and revisers. The cost estimates, however, proved prohibitive, so Blegen solved the problem by employing special rewrite editors on a part-time basis.[17]

Some of the academic authors approved of the rewriting; others did not. Columbia University economist Theodore Taylor, whose manuscript on Lend-Lease was thoroughly revised, wrote to Blegen: "I can only say that your 'rewrite man' possesses a remarkable gift for popularization." On the other hand, Guy Stanton Ford warned Prof. Kenneth Colegrove of Northwestern,

"Don't be surprised that your brainchild has been put through a course of sprouts. It's a great game if you don't weaken." Colegrove was not amused: "I am disappointed at the mutilation of my original copy. What a low opinion of the intellectual level of our boys in uniform is entertained by your rewritemen!!" Ever the smooth administrator, Ford attempted to mollify Colegrove by responding, "I suggested you as choice among the names proposed [to write the manuscript] because I knew of your good sportsmanship." After receiving the printed pamphlet, Colegrove remained less than impressed. "You indicate that I am the author of this little pamphlet," he wrote Ford, "but I need a microscope in order to find a few sentences which I recognize as my own." He nonetheless accepted the changes, saying, "I fully realize how the Historical Service Board was handicapped by official views."

Colegrove was not alone in needing appeasement. To Theodore Sellin, editor of *The Annals,* who submitted an unsuitable manuscript on the possibility of a postwar crime wave, Ford observed tactfully, "When your manuscript first arrived, we felt it would need some popularization for our soldier audience. We submitted the paper to an expert rewriter who has worked with us during the past year. He has a gift for turning material into popular form and the War Department has accepted his style as well suited to our GI readers."[18]

Universal Military Training: A Divisive Topic

In addition to the problems of delay and writing styles, there were debates on what was appropriate for publication. The manuscript on universal military training (UMT) is a good example. At the start of the program, Blegen contracted with Columbia University professor of government Grayson Kirk to write the pamphlet "Shall We Have Universal Military Training?" Kirk returned his twenty-six-page manuscript in December 1943. The introductory part of the article covered the theoretical pros and cons of this controversial subject. Then Kirk turned to the practical problems that UMT implementation would present in the postwar period. Specifically, he emphasized international political considerations.

Kirk essentially questioned the amount of military force the United States would need in peacetime. Given the prospects of postwar collaboration in an international peacekeeping organization, as declared by the Big Three foreign ministers in their 1943 Moscow Declaration, Kirk speculated on the kind of agreements that would be necessary to keep peace in the world. He cited the possibilities of individual national forces, regional forces, or some independent separate military group. In raising these points, valid in the context for any critical, objective discussion of UMT, Kirk concluded that all options would have a distinct affect on military policies, especially obligatory training, that might be adopted by the United States as well as by its allies. Kirk's considerations, in retrospect touching on a crucial issue of the future Cold War, became the nub of a disagreement over the manuscript between the army and the Historical Service Board.[19]

Board member Robert Wilson's initial comment on reading Kirk's manuscript anticipated the problem. Concerned about public opinion, Wilson suggested delaying issuance of the pamphlet until a clearer idea about where the nation stood on the issue could be ascertained. Blegen and Kirk disagreed, although they suggested some minor revision of the manuscript. In late February 1944, Blegen dispatched it to his army contacts.[20]

The army returned the manuscript with the suggestion that the last section on the practical application of UMT be deleted. There was no longer any certainty that UMT could be included in the GI Roundtable series. Earlier, the army had surveyed the attitude of troops toward UMT; on every occasion, between 60 and 70 percent of those questioned favored UMT over the prewar system of taking volunteers only. But the international and political ramifications of the suggested policy were not nearly as clear. The army reviewers asserted that the submitted material unnecessarily broadened the issue. After reading this criticism, Blegen wrote to Ford that "this kind of change, if it were carried through, would defeat the progress of open, candid discussion in the GI Roundtable." In turn, Ford noted that "in the last place, it's up to us (author, Board, and staff) to decide on matters of scope." He concluded that "the Army's 'suggestion' at least insofar as it concerns deleting the final pages, should be flatly rejected."[21]

Blegen soon discussed the dispute with Major Goodrich, stating that the suggested revision fell "within the scope of a pamphlet on UMT." Any discussion of Universal Military Training, he argued, had to indicate its relationship to larger issues and problems. Omission of that discussion would eliminate virtually everything that touched upon the practical realities. Consequently, he told Goodrich that the HSB could not "meet with the wish of the War Department that it should omit the final pages."[22]

There the issue stood. In a later off-the-record conversation, Colonel Spaulding told Blegen that the War Department was absolutely unwilling "to raise any question in an official publication as to the possibilities that the commitments made . . . by the allied leaders would not be faithfully carried out." Blegen reported to Professor Kirk that "we are in kind of a stalemate on the matter." The army felt that publication would appear "to endorse statements which by some persons may be adjudged interpretations of actual diplomatic or legislative policies that are at present in the formative stage." But Blegen would not be muzzled in that way. He informed Kirk that he was "not willing to bring out with our [HSB] approval an incomplete consideration of the question."[23]

Thus was the paper set aside until the summer of 1944. At that time the army again brought up the question of using the manuscript. Blegen renewed the issue with Kirk but maintained his position that the paper could not be published without the disputed section. Kirk agreed, updated the manuscript, and the army sent it to the printer. The pamphlet, however, was not distributed.[24]

This unfortunate disagreement raised the ugly question of censorship. Promised a virtual free hand to develop topics for the program, the Historical Service Board utilized the resources it could provide best: scholars devoting as full and objective a treatment as possible to selected topics. When the HSB's collective ideas on objective analysis of a topic conflicted with the army's view, the two groups were destined to be at loggerheads. True, the army did print the UMT pamphlet. But it was a hollow victory for Ford, Blegen, and the HSB because the military ultimately imposed its own form of censorship by withholding the piece.

Completing the Mission

In resolving the potentially divisive issue as it did, the army avoided a rupture with the HSB and its ongoing program. At the end of the first year of operation in September 1944, Blegen returned to the University of Minnesota and Guy Stanton Ford assumed the directorship in addition to his AHA responsibilities. His son, Thomas K. Ford, who had been assistant director of the project, handled most of the routine business throughout the remaining life of the HSB.

Once it was evident that the war would soon end, plans were developed to end the project. By November 1945, the work of the board had dwindled so that Ford wrote to Spaulding that the office would be open only one day a week to handle any final details. The project officially ended with the disbanding of the board on 31 December 1945.[25]

From the available records, it is difficult to assess this civilian-military attempt at mass informal voluntary education. As of 1 July 1945, the War Department had published twenty-five titles in its pamphlets series, originally printing fifty-five thousand copies of each pamphlet. Later in the program the print run increased to two hundred thousand. And in mid-1945, the pamphlets were made available to the general public (with the exception of the UMT pamphlet).[26]

The army soldier survey records provide some insight into the educational programs conducted during the war. While none of the questionnaires directly surveyed the use of HSB pamphlets, there is circumstantial evidence that the effort met with some success. In a survey of soldier discussions in the European theater, it was found that the sessions usually lasted between thirty minutes and an hour. Most soldiers believed the duration of the meetings was about right. Most of those surveyed also said that they preferred to read the pamphlets before the meetings. One question in the survey indicated that the level of education did not have an important bearing on a soldier's opinions about the discussions. Not surprisingly, there was a tendency for troops with some college education to participate more in the discussions than those with only a high school or grade school education. In addition, the survey disclosed that 52 percent of those attending the discussions found them "very much worthwhile." When asked how many soldiers in their units "get any good out of the . . . meetings," over 60 percent responded that at least half of them did. In a later survey among a smaller group of soldiers in the

Army Air Transport Division, the percentage of troops answering that they got "a lot" or "some" out of the meetings was even higher: 71 percent. This compared favorably with an 83 percent among infantry troops stationed in the United States who were asked the same question.[27]

Topics covered by the HSB pamphlets appeared to correspond to the concerns of soldiers. In another survey conducted in the European theater of operations in January 1944, troops listed the topics they would most like to hear discussed. The bulk of the answers fell into a broad category labeled "Post War Problems." Included were subjects such as education, employment, demobilization, postwar living, taxes, and industry. Regarding the postwar international scene, topics cited most often included: "Can the German people be reeducated?" "Dealing with Hitler," "Total annihilation of the Japanese," "Disarmament," "Avoidance of future wars," and "Length of stay in occupied countries." Many HSB pamphlets addressed these issues.[28]

What is the significance, if any, of all this effort on the part of both civilian and military groups to provide readable material to the thousands of GIs stationed in many parts of the world? The fact that the program went forward with such industry from 1943 to 1945 suggests that it was considered an important part of the war effort by leaders of both the AHA and the Army Service Forces. In this segment of military history, there are no victories or defeats to tally, no heroes or villains to cite, but only the chronicle of a project that adds a part to the already vast portrayal of the United States in the Second World War. That is the special province of history.

If the AHA's contribution to the war effort is not well known, the fact that the Historical Service Board corralled a group of academics to perform a public service can also make a case for the story's inclusion in the chronicle of public history. It was not an easy match. The record amply demonstrates the differences between the research-oriented academic culture and the everyday world of the soldier. But the common cause of fighting a war most believed to be just brought the parties together and smoothed over apparent differences.

No group of historians was identified as public historians during the period under discussion in this essay. Nonetheless, the academics involved in this enterprise, by lending their expertise to a public organization, practiced what today is considered public history. The booklets produced under the HSB connected the practice of history to the real world. The army wanted to provide its troops with a broad context in which they could understand the real issues American citizen-soldiers faced. Calling on the American Historical Association for assistance, the army was among the first institutions to recognize the contributions of what later became known as public history.[29]

CHAPTER 7

The African Sojourn of the Council of Foreign Ministers

Transnational Planning and Anglo-American Diplomacy, 1945–1948

SCOTT L. BILLS

After the Second World War, empire was still a way of life, formal or informal. Spheres of influence were quite specific, porous or nonporous. The hurriedly refurbished Livadia Palace at Yalta was an appropriate setting for a meeting of rough humor and hard bargaining that represented something more than a summit, a bit less than a new world order. Out on the patio, posing for the famous photographs, the Big Three looked calm and civil, if not brotherly, properly sober as their discussions ranged over wide fields of discourse. They were trolling, fly-fishing, and casting nets. They were alternately cajoling, assertive, and even frank. They were alert, friendly, aloof, and sinister. They were clever and rueful. Together, the Yalta Conference of February 1945 and the subsequent session at Potsdam reinforced the image of distant arbiters with vast collective power. Was the image merely, to borrow phrases from Lenin, "falseness and humbug," concealing the coalescence of another set of "imperialist freebooters"?[1] How long before rivalries would cause the Grand Alliance to splinter, to explode into the frenzied Cold War competition that so marked the postwar era? Names, faces, and headlines became the thematic milestones of an elegiac litany. Two new international agencies bore the brunt of rising expectations and tensions: the United Nations Organization (UNO) and the Council of Foreign Ministers (CFM). The UNO survived, while the CFM perished.

It has long been simplest to measure East-West discord with reference to the European heartland, and the work of the CFM conformed to that model. It was, after all, established in 1945 through a U.S. initiative at Potsdam as the vehicle for negotiating peace treaties for Axis allies in Europe: Bulgaria, Hungary, Italy, and Rumania. The Council of Foreign Ministers was transnational in purpose, redolent of wartime trade-offs, clearly intended to function as a big-power broker. Thus, it coexisted uneasily alongside the newly formed UNO's explicit multilateralism and new-world rhetoric. The CFM was a useful forum despite its storied procedural wrangling and tedious sorties (see Table 7.1). The ministers' work also ably illustrated a lesser-known

Table 7.1

MEETINGS OF THE COUNCIL OF FOREIGN MINISTERS

MEETING	DATES
1st session, London	11 September–2 October 1945
Moscow meeting (tripartite)	16–26 December 1945
2d session, part 1, Paris	25 April–16 May 1946
2d session, part 2, Paris	15 June–12 July 1946
Paris Peace Conference	29 July–15 October 1946
3d session, New York, concurrent with UN session	4 November–12 December 1946
Signing of Italian Peace Treaty	10 February 1947
4th session, Moscow	10 March–24 April 1947
5th session, London	25 November–15 December 1947
CFM Deputies for the Italian Colonies	
1st London round	3 October–22 November 1947
2d London round	2 February–31 August 1948
Final session, Paris	13–15 September 1948

factor in the development of the Cold War, quite effectively revealing the pericentric forces at work in the postwar world.[2] The
final months of the Council's activity focused upon Africa, and
the group's agenda was shaped in part by indigenous nationalist
forces, however inchoate, in the ex-Italian colonies and elsewhere
in neighboring regions, as well as by strategic concerns in Europe
and the Mediterranean. In addition to its obvious role as a harbin-
ger of rising Soviet-American antipathy, the Council for several
years held temporary sovereignty over three ex-Italian colonies
in Africa—Libya, Eritrea, and Italian Somaliland (Somalia)—with
the express purpose of investigating local conditions and determining the ultimate disposition of the territories. This task was
not fully completed, and the matter was passed on to the United
Nations in September 1948; however, in the process, the CFM's
efforts demonstrated convincingly the depth of local nationalist
sentiment and the extent to which the policies of the big powers
were influenced by indigenous elements.

The Italian Peace Treaty

If only the Allies could "pry the world out of its present blood-
soaked rut," wrote one American citizen in a letter of January
1945, then the "experts" could be put to work to resolve the left-
over problems. State Department planners, naturally, already had
discussed and shuffled reams of paper regarding the postwar era.
Overall, their analyses reflected a view of Italy as an opportunist
power whose colonial empire had never been viable (or profitable). Italian antifascist exile Luigi Sturzo was annoyed by such
sentiments—first, by the embedded ethnocentrism and the concomitant faith in what he termed the "sociologists of American
democracy." His country, said Sturzo, did not need lessons in
governance. Second, he had written extensively during 1944–45
of the need to redeem Italy's pluralistic past and to reintegrate its
people and culture into Western Europe. This process would necessarily include a return of Italy's African colonies (except for
Ethiopia).[3] But Italian pleas for colonial restoration, whether from
wartime exiles or postwar officials, ran afoul of several larger processes already in motion. American policymakers did not believe
that impoverished Italy realistically could administer a desert

empire in Africa. The heavy subsidization of such colonies during the fascist era could not be continued if the domestic economy were to be effectively reconstructed. Further, State Department discussions about the status of dependent territories included passionate calls for international trusteeship, and the colonies of defeated nations offered the best political opening for such experiments.

Controlling the Italian colonies at war's end, British officials, both civilian and military, were close observers of rising nationalist sentiment in the region. A splintered polity in Eritrea promised difficulties ahead: the barren lands of Somalia were a prize for no one. British military administrations (BMAs) provided regular intelligence on native aspirations and local socioeconomic

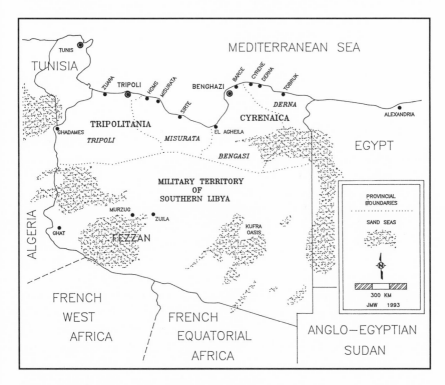

Map 1. Italian Libya, 1939. Adapted from OSS-A-3567-A, RG 226, Cartographic and Architectural Branch, National Archives, and from a map of Libya contained in Box 3, Lot File: Division of African Affairs, RG 59, National Archives. Prepared by Jeffrey M. Williams.

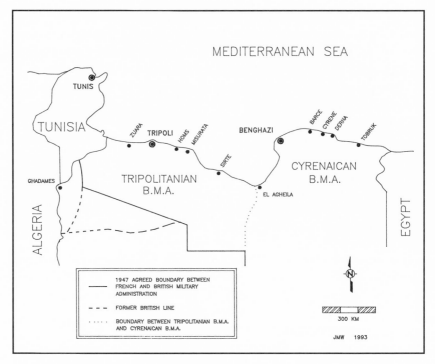

Map 2. Boundaries of the British Military Administrations in Cyrenaica and Tripolitania. Adapted from a map of Libya prepared within the British War Office, Boxes 3-4, Lot File: Records of the Division of African Affairs, RG 59, National Archives. Prepared by Jeffrey M. Williams.

conditions. Particularly important were the reports from Tripolitania and Cyrenaica in northern Libya (see Maps 1 and 2). Labour Foreign Minister Ernest Bevin was determined to retain British influence in Cyrenaica, where the local politico-religious leader, Sayyid Idris, a wartime friend, was a strong advocate of close ties with London. Indeed, in January 1942, Foreign Minister Anthony Eden had stated in the House of Commons that after Axis defeat "the Senussis in Cyrenaica will in no circumstances again fall under Italian determination." Bevin was willing to lend his voice to grander schemes for Italy's overseas territories, including plans for a "Greater Somalia," but it was strategically placed Libya that mattered most.[4]

Once the Council of Foreign Ministers had begun meeting in mid-September 1945, France and the USSR weighed in as key arbiters. The initial presence of China was a folly soon rectified. While Paris officials tended to support Italian claims (in order to sustain the legitimacy of the French African sphere), Soviet negotiators had little use for any Western empires. As it happened, Foreign Minister V. M. Molotov sought at the start to enhance Moscow's strategic position in the region and, later, to appease Italian public opinion during the political turmoil of 1947–48. Of course, the Soviets were not the only power actively to enter the fray of Italian domestic politics. More to the point, however, was the fact that the CFM's loose jurisdiction and endemic infighting only made it more difficult for Italy to find a sympathetic forum for its colonial claims. In other ways, Rome was ultimately more successful, as with Trieste, once heightened East-West discord became the defining current.

Regarding the Italian colonies, the foreign ministers confronted a complex problem. Even a general agreement that trusteeships could be imposed on the territories did not generate easy compromise. There were, after all, several options. The American secretary of state, James F. Byrnes, boldly proposed collective trusteeship regimes supervised by the United Nations, despite opposition from within his own State Department. Other representatives to the Council suggested instead joint trusteeships or alternative multipower arrangements outside UN purview. Should Italy be included in the ranks of prospective trustees? Would the restoration of an Italian administrative role stir local insurgencies, or was this threat exaggerated by ensconced humbug BMAs? Should Libya be treated as a single, unified territory or be divided into three zones (as it was then being administered, with the French controlling parts of the Fezzan, the southern desert)? Where did idealism end and foolishness begin? Who were the freebooters, the liberators, the enlightened entrepreneurs of the status quo?

The on-off-on character of CFM sessions during 1945–46 did little to produce accord on the colonies. There were angry exchanges between Bevin and Molotov. Byrnes raged privately about Russian duplicity. Early on, the Soviets had put forward a claim for trusteeship over Tripolitania, which, though rejected by the other powers, remained a stumbling block. But there were differences as well within the Western camp. French Foreign Minister Georges Bidault preferred a weak, docile neighbor in Tripolitania, alongside Tunisia; Bevin feared that any sort of Italian restoration would provoke Arab uprisings against his thinly manned BMAs; and Byrnes remained wedded to his plan for UN trusteeship. There was no consistent support for genuine independence for any of the Italian colonies. Two-track diplomacy, begun during the CFM's second session, in Paris, at French initiative, signaled the scheduling of informal private meetings in addition to the public plenaries. Tirades were not ended, but progress was made toward compromise solutions and the calling of a general peace conference. The gridlock regarding colonies was broken by mid-summer 1946. Italy would renounce all claims to its colonies; the territories would remain under interim British occupation; final disposition of the colonies would be made by the four CFM powers within one year of the coming into force of an Italian peace treaty. If the Council could not reach agreement in the allotted time, then the matter would pass to the United Nations Organization.[5]

To be sure, there was reason to distinguish Mussolini's Italy from both its predecessor and successor regimes. It was Carlo Sforza, the antifascist spokesperson and postwar Italian foreign minister, who lectured Americans in 1942 about the need for big powers to abandon the "colonialistic idea" in the Near East. "The colonial field," he said, "has been filled even more than any other political field with illusions, prides, resentments, anachronistic hatreds." Yet, Sforza also captured the key ambivalence of Italian policymaking when he averred that his country had been as good a colonizer as any other Western power and therefore deserved to continue that role if other nations intended to maintain their imperial spheres.[6] On VE Day, Italy's interim prime minister had reminded President Truman of Italian sacrifices for the Allied cause after the 1943 armistice. By August 1945, Italian officials were actively lobbying for a lenient peace. A harsh treaty might tug Italy away from its Western orbit. Foreign Minister (later prime minister) Alcide de Gasperi wrote to Secretary Byrnes on 22 August 1945, contrasting the benign colonization efforts of his country with the more exploitive imperialism of "the Anglo-Saxon system." A note of 4 September from the Italian Embassy in Washington argued that Italy had carried out the "great work of civilization" in its colonies, in the process sowing large, productive settler communities.[7]

The reality was quite different. Only in Tripolitania were Italian settlers still a significant part of the population, and only there were Italo-Arab relations reasonably good. Settlers had been evacuated from Cyrenaica during the warfare of 1942–43. Many Italians in Eritrea and Somalia either had been forcibly relocated by the British or had become refugees in swollen cities like Asmara or Mogadishu, where they were employed primarily by the occupation authorities. There was no empire to restore. It was in this vein that Byrnes had written to De Gasperi, shortly before the beginning of the first CFM session, advising that Italy approach the "forthcoming negotiations" with a "realistic awareness" of what might be achieved.[8] The verdict of State Department and Foreign Office analysts was clear: prewar Italy had for reasons of prestige sought to gather together the crumbs left over from the "scramble" of the late 1800s, and the few colonies that Italy did administer constituted a sizable drain on a perennially weak economy. Such judgments also reflected typical State Department thinking on European empires—that their days were numbered, that the imperial powers must recognize and accept this inexorable destiny.

Signed in February 1947, the Italian Peace Treaty formally stripped Italy of its overseas territories. There would be no final decision on disposition of the former dependencies until a special commission had visited each colony, conducted a systematic survey of the respective societies, and reported back to the CFM deputies, who would then make detailed recommendations to their ministers.[9] When the peace treaty went into effect in mid-September 1947, the Council was given one year to complete its investigation. The process began in a workmanlike manner, with the Commission of Investigation (COI) officially constituted in October 1947 and en route to Eritrea before the end of the year. During their seven-month sojourn, the commissioners found themselves walking, driving, and flying over some of the most desolate terrain in Africa, interviewing hundreds of townspeople, peasant farmers, and roadside travelers in an effort to fathom popular wishes. Naturally, other considerations interfered, both strategic and political. Anglo-French rivalry in the region remained palpable. American interest flared, died down, then was rekindled by Cold War anxieties. Soviet delegates talked and balked, complaining about delays even as their pedantic attention to procedural matters slowed the pace of discussions. The meeting minutes of the Commission of Investigation and the Deputies are laced with wry humor as well as suspicion and frustration.

Before the COI began its task, however, the Foreign Office launched its own survey effort. The respective British military administrations had been operating as caretakers, largely eschewing reform and investment as per the appropriate international codes. However, this was not a policy that endeared the authorities to the native peoples, who suffered shortages of many kinds. Depressed economies and unhappy Arabs would not provide a very impressive backdrop to the four-power investigation required by the Italian Peace Treaty. At the close of 1947, Libya remained divided into three distinct zones: (1) an embryonic amirate in Cyrenaica, rooted in the Muslim fundamentalist doctrines of the Sanusi (Sanusiya) Order, its Arab peasantry fiercely loyal to Sayyid Idris, who had led from exile a long struggle against Italian overlordship; (2) a more urbanized and ethnically volatile society in Tripolitania, where the Sanusis claimed few adherents; (3) and the French-controlled oases in the Fezzan. There was little reason to assume that a unified Libya would emerge, given the following facts:

1. British officials intended to retain close ties with Cyrenaica but were loathe to take on the task of overseeing Tripolitania, and could see little likelihood of dislodging the French from the Fezzan;

2. The American secretary of state was unwilling to accept any administrative responsibilities in Africa and promoted a collective trusteeship plan that was ideologically appealing but never won much affection from the Europeanist-dominated State Department or the Joint Chiefs of Staff;

3. The French were determined to see Italy restored in Tripolitania, to retain control of the Fezzan (or earmark various parts of it for incorporation into already-existing French colonies), and to sponsor Italian restoration in other colonies, if possible; and

4. Soviet leaders were determined to use the colonial issue to better their bargaining position on European questions and, where possible, to bolster their appeal to the Italian public.

The British Working Party

All was not well in Cyrenaica, the focal point of London's interest in the former Italian colonies. There had been a troubling missive from Sayyid Idris in July 1946, asserting that "public opinion is disturbed." He warned that the lack of progress toward self-rule and economic recovery would undercut British prestige in the territory. Both military and civilian leaders worried that the aging Sanusi leader might feel compelled by younger, hot-headed nationalists to take a harder line toward Britain. Christopher Warner advised his Foreign Office colleagues to "clear our own minds" before expediting the arrival of the CFM inquiry. Brigadier Duncan C. Cumming, chief civil affairs officer for the British occupation forces in Africa, visited Libya in August 1946 and reported that the situation, while confused, was not as "brittle" as he had feared. "Many of the political expressions are mock heroics but the danger of fanatical outbursts remains." Libyans were indeed uncertain about their future and believed that the BMAs could do more for them.[10]

Bevin responded to such developments by seeking what he called a "partial *fait accompli.*" That is, the Commission of Investigation must find a solid British-Sanusi partnership, with Cyrenaica already on its way toward some sort of home rule under Sayyid Idris. Tripolitania might well become an international trusteeship—this was negotiable. There were advantages to sending in a survey team before the CFM's commission touched ground. Britain should have the opportunity to "tidy up matters and present as good a picture as possible as Occupying Power."[11] Overall, the length and expense of the occupation of the ex-Italian colonies was proving to be both a burden and a blessing. Admittedly, London had important leverage. On the other hand, the BMAs placed a strain on military resources; commanders were unhappy about the declining quality of available personnel as demobilization proceeded; and officers wondered about their ability to maintain control as native political agitation increased. The Treasury complained about the expenditure. Delays in the

Council of Foreign Ministers meant that Foreign Office analysts
continued to debate the correct policy, frustrated by their inability to devise a lasting formula. Even so, a consensus had been
reached among civilian and military planners that rated control
of Cyrenaica as the highest priority, followed by various proposals to ease the other ex-colonies into friendly hands.[12]

In the words of David Scott Fox of the Egyptian Department,
the program now was to "predispose" Sayyid Idris and his brethren to support British trusteeship; thus, certain reforms were necessary. An interdepartmental British "Working Party" could "review the existing causes of discontent in the territories" and
develop a "comprehensive plan for the execution of the new progressive policy." Scott Fox wrote, "The urgency of the matter lies
in the desirability of the reforms having time to bear fruit before
that [CFM] Commission arrives." For instance, the sooner a
Cyrenaican advisory council could be set up, giving Idris the sem-
blance of a quasi-constitutional regime, the better.[13]

Bernard R. Reilly of the Colonial Office, former governor of
Aden, was chosen as the head of the Working Party. The group
was scheduled to tour all territories, anticipating a fourteen-week
trip. While Reilly later reported that his party had gained "first
hand" knowledge of local problems, the general conclusions were
not surprising and could have been drawn from the growing stack
of War Office telegrams and memorandums from all parts of the
ex-Italian realm.[14] The Working Party verified, for instance, that
in Cyrenaica the British had inherited a "wreck" of a colony, one
"necessitating a long period of conval[esc]ence." Much reconstruction was yet needed—a rekindling of the human spirit as well as
repair of the damaged physical plant. The territory was by nature
a poor one, and without imperial largesse was "dependent on the
meagre and depleted resources of a mainly pastoral community."
Still, Cyrenaica had "modest assets" for economic recovery, and,
politically, there was strong support for a regime guided by Sayyid
Idris.

However, the Working Party had not been sent out to Benghazi
and surrounding areas simply to catalog problems but also to
suggest reforms that would restore confidence in the occupation
authority and improve living conditions for the inhabitants. Obviously, programs like expanding the educational system or redi-

recting agricultural production would require long-term planning. The committee tried to balance, then, what might be done immediately and bear fruit quickly, and those efforts which could only gradually change the quality of life in the territory. To this end, the Working Party proposed a three-stage process: continued British control as temporary overseer; followed by an Arab state "under close tutelage within some form of [British] trusteeship" for ten years, perhaps longer; followed by a "fully independent Arab state, possibly in treaty alliance with a major power." Britain should "now work openly" toward this ultimate goal.

Economic reform was vital. For this purpose, the Working Party offered several far-reaching suggestions: (1) a more ambitious program of public works, (2) a major effort to revitalize agriculture, and (3) a systematic stimulation of trade. There seemed little likelihood of any significant industrial growth, but an aggressive public works program would absorb surplus labor in the town and countryside. Further, a greater effort toward "Libyanisation" would bring more Arabs into positions of administrative authority.

The Working Party reported that demands for independence did not at all conflict with a desire on the part of "influential people" for close ties with England. Nevertheless, it was "unwise" to count on this friendship to continue "unless a more dynamic policy is adopted, and the measures we advocate put into operation as soon as possible." The party advised, "It is essential that provision be made for immediate spending if our proposals are to have an early effect upon Arab opinion or to influence in any way the conclusions of the Four Power Commission." By April 1947, the War Office had approved recommendations pointing toward a greater Arab role in the Cyrenaican BMA and more effective rehabilitation of the territory. The appointment of an advisory council was put on hold. The Treasury had agreed that the proposed costs were not prohibitive given the important political and strategic issues at stake.[15]

From the opening section of the Working Party's report on Tripolitania, it was plain that the committee had visited two very different territories. Arriving on 5 February 1947, the group spent three weeks consulting with BMA officials and touring the occupation zone. The report on local conditions emphasized that a more thorough analysis was required to describe adequately the imprint of Italian colonization as measured, for example, by the settler farming communities from the fascist era; the character of a heterogeneous society, defined by the interaction of Arabs, Italians, Jews, and other ethnic groups; a more urbanized culture, centered on Tripoli, previously integrated into an autarchic Italian economic zone; and the growth of Arab nationalist spirit. The most pressing problem at the time of the party's visit was crippling drought, which intensified unrest in the hinterland.

Further, there were no plans for British trusteeship. Here there was no Sanusi pillar upon which to build a protectorate. Tripolitania was developed by and for Italians. Severing the link with Rome naturally deprived Tripolitania of its assured market and capital inflow. Nor for various reasons could Britain replace Italy as a prime trading partner. Therefore, the Working Party recommended forging new economic ties between Tripolitania and Italy that would recreate past commercial links outside the context of colonial control. Importantly, as revealed in numerous military analyses and Foreign Office minutes, Britain did not have a strong politico-strategic stake in Tripolitania. Fortunately, the local economy was "comparatively unscathed" by the war, and BMA monopolies had yielded a surplus for the occupation regime during the 1944–45 fiscal year. But the drought cast a lengthening shadow over the territory. As elsewhere in the Italian colonies, the CFM initiative had sparked increased nationalist agitation as Tripolitania's future became entangled in protracted international discussions.[16]

As William Roger Louis has noted, British policy toward Libyan territories "fluctuated" during 1945–47, but the goal of gaining strategic rights in Cyrenaica remained constant. "The case of Libya," Louis observed, "reveals the classic themes of British imperialism recast in a postwar mould: the search for indigenous collaboration and the reconstruction of an administrative framework; the drain on British resources by the continued military occupation; and the attempt to gain the co-operation of the United States in order to secure British strategic rights."[17] From the beginning, Cyrenaica and Tripolitania reflected differing priorities. Military reports emphasized the centrality of Cyrenaica and the secondary stature of Tripolitania. Political analysts saw in Cyrenaica a homogeneous population whose politico-religious leader had successfully linked his destiny with that of Britain's during the war. Economists saw in Cyrenaica the virtue of small-ness, relatively speaking, when compared to massive outlays for development in nearby countries of the Middle East or Africa.

There were problems, of course. Sayyid Idris was a genuine exponent of independence and understandably sought stronger guarantees from Britain as international discussions delayed dis-position of the former Italian colonies. He sought to use the obvi-ous British strategic stake in Cyrenaica to his advantage. Also, he responded to pressures from younger nationalists at home and Arab League officials in Cairo who did not share his basic trust of London policymakers. In truth, Idris did represent a generation of exiles less and less able to comprehend the more impatient na-tionalist spirit of the postwar era. Yet, he remained the central figure. Bevin required his active cooperation to achieve privileged access to strategic facilities. Sayyid Idris, on the other hand, could afford, after long years in comfortable exile, to await an interna-tional judgment that would almost certainly give him consider-able power in his Sanusi realm and possibly beyond.

For Tripolitania, several solutions would do. Effective planning could alleviate the worst effects of drought.[18] More to the point, Tripolitanians had only to tolerate the British Military Adminis-tration, not favor it. What the BMA had to worry about in Tripolitania was maintaining social order, avoiding economic cataclysm, keeping the people adequately clothed, and holding down the fort until other friendly hands took over. Hearts and minds could be put on the back burner.

Not surprisingly, the strongest arguments (from British offi-cials) for Italian restoration, fully or partially, came from the embassy in Rome. Ambassador Noel Charles (later the British CFM Deputy) wrote to Bevin on 12 February 1947 about the "all-out propaganda campaign of the [Italian] Communist Party against Great Britain, the British 'Empire' and the British colonies." The Right, Left, and "the mass of the general population" were all much agitated by the colonial issue. Unfavorable action on the African territories "is well capable of estranging the Italians from us in the future ad infinitum." Charles agreed with those who pointed out that Italian politicians had an unrealistic view of their past imperial mission and the present-day problems involved in

resuming administration of any ex-colony. But it made no difference. "Whether the Italians deserve to lose their possessions or
not is of minor importance," Charles contended. "The way the
disposal of these possessions is handled is a matter of the greatest
importance to future Anglo-Italian co-operation. It is fundamentally a psychological matter."[19] This was not simply the view of
an unabashed Italophile. Charles could be quite blunt in lectur-
ing Italian officials on the futility of their aspirations for overseas
empire and the unfairness of their anti-British remarks. It was,
however, the characteristic view from the Rome embassy, where
exposure to repeated government entreaties and numerous press
reports heightened sensitivity to the colonial issue.

In response, Prime Minister Clement Attlee cautioned Charles
to use every available means to prime Italians with the "true light"
of things, to prick the bubble of "unreality" that pervaded official
circles. There would not be, said Attlee, any Italian restoration in
Libyan territories, and it was most likely that Eritrea would be
linked with Ethiopia. There was some possibility of an Italian
trusteeship in Somalia, but even here London would not take the
lead. Britain could only accept other solutions if done within the
framework of the Council of Foreign Ministers. Here was an important thrust of Attlee's letter: the findings of the Commission
of Investigation would be a welcome buttress to Britain's claims
and affirm the admirable record of its BMAs, and, for that reason,
would serve to quiet Italian grumbling about the whole matter.
British policymakers did not want to be seen as excluding Italy
from Africa; hence, the work of the four-power investigation was
deemed quite necessary, *whether or not the assigned task was
actually accomplished.* Frederick Hoyer Millar of the Western
Department (a reliably pro-Italian voice) similarly commented
on the importance of placing all final decisions about the colonies within the context of CFM diplomacy. However, he worried
that Britain might be isolated as other powers rushed to placate
Italy. Who knew what the Americans had promised in private
meetings with Italian officials? The French were not to be trusted.
And the Soviets, he said, "will lose no opportunity of fishing in
troubled waters" in order to improve their standing among the
Italian populace and damage British prestige.[20]

Constituting the Commission of Investigation

John Utter, adviser to the American CFM delegation in Paris, arranged a brief visit to Tripoli in May 1946. Afterward, he stressed the certainty of indigenous insurrection following unfavorable Council action. Reporting that "it is a common sight to see the Arabs circulating about town and country with guns slung over their shoulders," Utter wrote, "I firmly believe that some gesture should be made to these people to show them some consideration, for they as well as the whole Arab world are increasingly sensitive about being treated as inferiors in a cavalier fashion by Europeans."[21] Two months earlier, Utter had met with Sayyid Idris at the Sanusi leader's exile home in Cairo. Physically, Idris was not imposing. "He is a slight man of medium height and scarcely looks his fifty-six years. A black beard frames his face and accentuates his pallor." The sayyid had a "rather ascetic appearance" and "meditative yet keen eyes behind tortoise-shell rimmed glasses." He was "frail" and worried about his health. "His voice is high-pitched and tends to be monotonous," commented Utter. The sayyid might not seem charismatic, but his popularity in Cyrenaica was undeniable.[22]

Tripolitanians, said Idris, could join a political union under his leadership if they so wished. In any case, he told Utter, Cyrenaica would need a strong ally and benefactor. For this reason, air bases and other concessions would be traded for economic aid, and Britain was the preferred partner. Idris envisaged an autonomous amirate leading to a constitutional regime with a representative parliament. "While the interview produced nothing new," wrote Utter, ". . . it confirmed what I had learned from both British and Arabs in Cyrenaica; namely, the feeling that these people and their leader believe that self-government is their inalienable right, particularly after their conduct as loyal allies and after the sufferings they endured during the war."[23]

Having toured both Tripolitania and Cyrenaica, John Utter was, by summer 1946, well on his way toward becoming the State Department's expert on Libyan affairs. In Tripoli, he found the British performing "ably." True, he acknowledged, there were some Arab complaints, but the attitude of BMA officials was quite logical, given the uncertainty about the territory's future. "Their primary concerns have been to keep order, continue the administration, and feed the population. In this they have succeeded." Only in the city of Tripoli, reported Utter, was there any sort of political "awakening"; even so, it was "incontestable" that the peoples did not want a return to Italian governance. France, Italy, and the USSR were all disliked for predictable reasons (bad colonizers or godless ideology), and the United States was considered pro-Zionist. Hence, none were favored for the administration of the territory.[24]

The indeterminate status of the ex-Italian colonies did not please any of the constituencies involved—British, Italian, Tripolitanian, Cyrenaican, Eritrean, Ethiopian, or Somali. Further delay only accentuated the overriding strategic implications of the final disposition of the territories. As C. Grove Haines pointed out in 1947, the Second World War had demonstrated the clear importance of the "Tripoli-Benghazi-Sicily triangle" and the Red Sea region. Soviet designs on the ex-colonies created a "novel and explosive" situation at the same time as the Truman Doctrine made the United States "one of the principal contestants in the Mediterranean." Moreover, disposition of the territories came amid such trends as French decline as an Eastern Mediterranean power, the fading of British influence throughout the Middle East, the new tide of Zionism, the pan-Arabism of the Arab League, and the surge of local nationalist sentiment. The wishes of native peoples could hardly be ignored, nor could Italy's desire for full or partial restoration be easily discounted. "At all events," remarked Haines, "it now seems a practical certainty that any agreement regarding the colonies will be, in the first instance, a measure of the discord which has risen since World War II rather than the concord which many had hopefully been given to expect."[25]

The problem with awaiting the coming into force of the Italian Peace Treaty, already addressed sotto voce, was that the work of the deputies could not likely be finished in the time allotted. The State Department had initially suggested seven months for the COI's field work, three months for the deputies' deliberations, and two months for the Council's decision making. This 7-3-2 formula would only have worked if the investigatory commission had set out on 15 September 1947, the day the peace treaty went into effect, rather than two months later. In mid-August, Utter was told that the Foreign Office did not foresee a solution of the colonial issue within the CFM, that the matter would pass to the United Nations General Assembly. Ernest Bevin told Dominion officials the same thing in late September, urging them to save their fire for UN sessions. In Washington, Loy Henderson, head of the Office of Near Eastern and African Affairs, also believed that there was little chance the Council would resolve the colonial issue.[26]

The CFM deputies began meeting on 3 October 1947 in London. The appointees were Noel Charles, Britain; Ambassador Lewis Douglas, with Waldemar J. Gallman (embassy counselor) as his alternate, United States; Ambassador René Massigli, France; and Ambassador Georgiy N. Zarubin, USSR. From the start, the deputies' sessions mirrored the meetings of the parent Council in several ways: (1) the procedural rules of the CFM served as guidelines; (2) a similar sense of tiresome, cranky exchange crept into the discourse; (3) the Soviets launched unpredictable procedural sorties; and (4) things nevertheless got done. Agreed terms of reference for the four-power team were promulgated on 21 October. Members of a single Commission of Investigation would "collect and supply" the deputies with the "necessary data" regarding disposition of the colonies "and . . . ascertain the views of the local population." Thus, there would be an analysis of the political, economic, and social conditions in each colony as well as indigenous aspirations. The COI would visit and prepare a separate report for each colony. The commission, however, would make no recommendations concerning final disposition of the territories.[27]

The Commission of Investigation was officially constituted on 20 October 1947, and "other interested governments" were invited to submit their viewpoints. While the commission carried out its field work, the deputies would hear the views of such governments and deal with any issues that arose during the investigation. All four powers agreed that no other nations would be directly involved with the investigative team. The deputies would circulate copies of the COI's reports immediately after completion, giving the interested parties the opportunity to present supplementary opinions if they so desired. John Utter became the U.S. commissioner, and Frank Stafford was his British opposite number. The French commissioner was career diplomat Etienne Burin des Roziers; and the Soviets, after some delay, appointed Artemy Feodorov.

For some months previously, Utter and Stafford had met frequently to forge common ground for the upcoming discussions. In addition, there were ongoing Anglo-French talks on colonial issues (through 1947) that led to a more generally cooperative relationship between the two powers, though this did not initially prove fruitful for the African "safari." David Scott Fox of the Egyptian Department typified his colleagues' thinking in favoring a commission that would be kept on a "short rein" in Cyrenaica. This was also Stafford's view. A superficial survey of the population, relying upon rural shaykhs and a few urban politicians, would best serve British interests.[28] However, limiting the COI's actions *in situ* was difficult. The French as well as the Soviets sought to broaden the scope of the commission's inquiry in order to enhance the case for Italian restoration.

American interest in collective trusteeships had flagged in direct proportion to growing fears of Communist subversion. In July 1947, the Joint Chiefs of Staff advised against any kind of Soviet role in administering the former Italian colonies, even within the framework of a UN trusteeship. It was also contrary to U.S. interests to restore Italy's control of any former territory unless the continued tenure of a noncommunist government in Rome could be assured.[29] A report on 25 July, from the Central Intelligence Group (the immediate precursor to the CIA), neatly summarized the dilemma posed by the colonies, noting that their disposition was "interdependent with developments in Italy." This connection became more evident as the Italian elections of April 1948 drew closer. The CIG paper reiterated the strategic importance of both the Libyan and Red Sea territories and offered what were fast becoming routine judgments about Soviet purpose; these were so standardized that staffers could sit down in virtually any branch of the policymaking bureaucracy and produce, for top-secret consumption, carbon-copy phraseology about the red menace. But it was not clear to CIG analysts whether the Kremlin would try to twist the debate over Italian colonies to its advantage by posing

"as a champion of the native peoples in non-self-governing territories" and befriending the pan-Arab cause, or posing as a champion of Italian restoration and thereby boosting the electoral
strength of the Italian Communist Party.[30]

American policy toward colonial dependencies, read the CIG
brief, was based on the notion of the "orderly recognition of the
legitimate aspirations of native elements." This might have been
the most succinct explanation available: *orderly* in the sense that
U.S. recognition would come after native governments showed
themselves to be nonviolent proponents of self-rule, patiently
negotiating with their respective metropoles, *legitimate* in the
sense that new regimes must not be Communist or any other
leftist variant that, by U.S. definition, could never genuinely represent popular aspirations. Again and again, through the late 1940s
and two ensuing decades, State Department analysts would try
to finesse this dictum in such a way that emergent countries would
find in the United States a model and a friend. As Michael H.
Hunt has shown in his analysis of American foreign policy, distrust of class warfare and violence as the leitmotifs of sociopolitical
change much predated Cold War rivalry. The emphasis on order-
liness was essential. The enthronement of reason and practical-
ity meant a concomitant decline in the value and validity of radical passion and armed insurrection. Such sentiments well
expressed the thinking that underlay the Truman Doctrine and
its logical outgrowths. In June 1947, the London *Economist*
pointed out that Libya was the most problematic of the Italian
colonies "because it is nearest the shadow-line between East and
West. Indeed, since President Truman inaugurated his Greek-
Turkish policy it has been uncomfortably close to that line."[31] As
it happened, American and British policymakers were thinking
alike. Their parallel interests in the Middle East were reified by a
series of discussions in Washington, held inside the Pentagon to
guarantee secrecy, from 16 October to 7 November 1947.

Eritrea and Italian Somaliland

John Utter's early reports from Asmara, Eritrea, were upbeat. He
remarked, "The Commission has resembled pretty much a traveling circus and the people of Eritrea have responded to our visit

with great excitement and much flag-waving." He praised the BMA's efforts to maintain order, though there had been "some minor scuffles between political parties and a few broken bones." Within the commission, said Utter, the Soviets thus far had been "remarkably cooperative" on most issues, while the French delegation moved from "difficult" to obstructive.[32] After the commission had completed its work in Eritrea by mid-December and begun its first draft report, Utter remained wary of the French and became more critical of the Soviets.[33] His cables revealed a rising contentiousness that did not block the group's field work but did threaten the prospect of producing agreed summary reports, and a close Anglo-American collaboration countered by a Franco-Soviet entente trying to embarrass the BMAs, inflate pro-Italian sentiment in the colonies, and prove that local peoples were too unschooled to administer themselves. Paris diplomats had said openly for two years that they desired an Italian admin-

Table 7.2

FOUR POWER COMMISSION OF INVESTIGATION

VISIT	DATES
Eritrea	12 November 1947–3 January 1948
Italian Somaliland (Somalia)	6 January–3 March 1948
Tripolitania	6 March–15 April 1948
Fezzan	15 April–25 April 1948
Cyrenaica	25 April–20 May 1948
Rome, interviews with former Italian settlers	20–23 May 1948

COMMISSION REPORTS	DATE COMPLETED
Eritrea	19 June 1948
Italian Somaliland	19 June 1948
Libya	5 July 1948

istration in Tripolitania. "Their attitude in regard to Libya could not be worse from our point of view than it is at present," minuted D. W. Lascelles of the Egyptian Department on 25 November 1947.[34] (See Table 7.2 for the commission's travel schedule.)

The commission's visit to Italian Somaliland encountered some rough weather. There was a bloody riot on 11 January 1948 that left fifty-two Italians dead in the streets of Mogadishu. Many more were injured. It was, read one report, a two-hour battle "with bullets, arrows, broken bottles and knives," instigated, said the BMA, by pro-Italian troublemakers who disrupted a parade by the Somali Youth League (SYL).[35] The violence left its mark. The War Office immediately began planning to avoid a "similar rumpus" in Libyan territories. The Commission of Investigation subsequently opted, in Utter's words, "to accept as an experiment [a] French proposal of embarking upon [an] unheralded tour of [the] country visiting towns, villages, encampments and chatting with passersby." While Utter and others disliked this "amateur Gallup Poll" style of inquiry, it became a standard feature of COI activity throughout Tripolitania and Cyrenaica and produced interesting results.[36]

Italian officials quickly took advantage of the Mogadishu riot to press their case with the Western powers. From Rome, British Ambassador Victor Mallet reported that Somaliland events had much raised the "temperature" of public discussion of colonial issues.[37] United States Ambassador James Dunn confirmed that the matter now garnered more attention. Had Italy come full circle from a weak, disparaged Axis ally, through the halfway-house armistice and gently punitive peace treaty, to a new position of real strength, with valuable chips to place on the table? A sense of born-again national importance seemed to animate Italian leaders as they insisted that in Somalia, and everywhere in the former colonies, Rome would be welcomed as an old and trusted friend. Italian demands ballooned. Foreign Minister Carlo Sforza wrote directly to Ernest Bevin, assuring the foreign secretary that he did not personally believe the British had shown bad faith in Somalia. But, he said, Italian public opinion was not so kind; the Mogadishu killings had had an intense psychological impact. A friendly gesture from London would reassure the Italian people that there could be effective collaboration between the two countries. If Italy fell to the Communists, Bevin would bear the blame. Sforza warned that there were no more "tight compartments" in Europe. "We are, in the Continent, like a house of cards and if the Italian card falls, the French one will fall, and so on."[38]

Tripolitania and Cyrenaica

"Most of the flora of the country is more conspicuous for its thorns than for its flowers or fruit," wrote Brigadier D. C. Cumming in a pamphlet about Cyrenaica penned for British troops during the war.[39] Metaphorically, he had captured the appropriate image for the postwar discussions of Libya. Bevin's tenure as foreign secretary was marked by a determination to reshape and reform the structure of empire but not to eliminate all the bonds of dependency. Thus had his ambition to retain a military foothold in northeastern Libya done much to define the CFM's playing field. However, it was ironic that Labour ministers, champions of the working class and the industrial ethos of social democracy, found themselves relying upon the support of the conservative, tribal elements of the Libyan hinterland. If the countryside would overbear the cities, the status quo could be preserved.[40]

By their own admission, 1947 was a difficult year for the Tripolitanian and Cyrenaican BMAs. From Benghazi, the chief administrator reported the peoples' "increasing irritation and impatience" with the occupation. Happily for the British, the people continued to support a Sanusi amirate for the "Cyrenaican nation," as stated, for instance, in a declaration of 7 May 1946 signed by notables of the territory.[41] The war had given the Sanusi a powerful patron. However, that link accentuated a historical division between Cyrenaica and Tripolitania, as the sayyid and his followers sought an autonomy that might embrace other Libyans but not be imperiled by them. Majid Khadduri has detailed the delicate negotiations that opened in Cairo in June 1946 between Idris and Tripolitanian nationalists. The basis for a unified state, under the sayyid, seemed to be taking shape. But in January 1947, a Benghazi meeting of leaders from both territories failed to produce an agreed program. As Khadduri explained, there was a deadlock over the matter of whether to press against all odds for a united Libya. Even the younger, more aggressive Cyrenaican nationalists insisted that the supremacy of Idris must be "accepted by all." Whether or not there should be union under the Sanusi banner remained a point to frustrate Tripolitanian activists as their parties were rent by factional struggles. Meanwhile, from Benghazi, Chief Administrator A. L. Kirkbride reported that, following the sayyid's return, "we have continued to make use of his influence in keeping the country quiet and in guiding local political ambition in the direction most suitable to ourselves."[42]

The most influential Tripolitanian leader by the time of the commission's arrival was an exile, Bashir al-Sadawi, who had been a resistance leader during the Italian conquest in the early 1920s. Afterward, he served as adviser to King Ibn Saud until renewing his contacts with Libyan nationalists in 1946. In March 1947 he organized what was formally called the National Council for the Liberation of Libya, though more often referred to as the Libya Liberation Committee. Unable to secure formal cooperation from Cyrenaican leaders, his group remained only a limited venture. Even so, Tripolitanian parties rallied to Sadawi's three-point program of independence, a unified Libya, and membership in the Arab League. Emissaries to the countryside distributed pamphlets to villagers explaining how they should respond to the four-power commission. The Liberation Committee opposed Rome's restoration under any guise, including trusteeship. In late March 1948, Foreign Office adviser J. C. Penney reported from Cairo that Sadawi appeared to be "scoring a very considerable success" in unifying Tripolitanian political opinion, even having "squared the Jews" and some antifascist Italian groups.[43]

The COI's official communiqué upon arriving in Tripoli stressed that "the work of the Commission will be restricted to the collection of facts." As part of this process, the COI would visit "centres where the population can most easily be congregated" to "hear individuals and communities, both native and European, representative of all inhabitants of Tripolitania." As elsewhere, the commission prepared sets of questions to be asked during its hearings:

1. How were you selected by the people in your [town] quarter?
2. If in a meeting, when was it held?
3. How many people were present at the meeting?

4. If not a meeting, how were you chosen?
5. Did you consult with all the people in your quarter to obtain their views regarding the future of Tripolitania?
6. Were there any among them who had other opinions than those which you have expressed here?[44]

While commissioners did not in every case ask exactly the above questions in the specified order, they showed a remarkable determination to pursue such points. In part this was a product of the difficulty, already encountered in Eritrea and Somalia, of evaluating the legitimacy of local nationalist groups whose leaders inevitably claimed wide appeal. Whatever could not be quantified in the "battle of statistics"[45] being waged within the commission could be downplayed or possibly ignored. Thus, first in Tripoli and next in Benghazi, the commissioners pecked away at what seemed trivial matters. For instance, when the Cyrenaican National Congress claimed to represent the aspirations of all people in the territory, the Soviet delegate asked, "I would like to be precise, has the Congress at its disposal exact documentary evidence that the whole population wants independence . . . ?" Questions of this nature were common.[46]

It was during the commission's hearings in Tripoli, beginning 17 March 1948, that the four-power delegations had their best opportunity to hear firsthand the views of Arab party leaders. Salim al-Muntasir of the United National Front pointed to the Atlantic Charter as a pledge that must be redeemed. A spokesman for the National Party told the commissioners that Italian rule had impoverished his land, but that the lack of local resources should not discourage the commission: "With independence poverty will be borne. We prefer independence to anything else." His views were seconded by another speaker.[47] "We are a nation which has history behind our back," said Bashir al-Sadawi. "I could stand up and talk for ten years to express all I have to say." Asked by Soviet Commissioner Feodorov if the Libya Liberation Committee wanted "immediate independence without a period of gradual development," Sadawi replied, "Tonight please." Asked by Burin des Roziers how the COI should best measure popular sentiment, Sadawi answered, "We can gather for you the whole people together in one square and they will shout independence. That will settle it then."[48]

At best, what emerged during the hearings were fuzzy federal schemes to bind the two territories. Still, Utter was sufficiently impressed to offer, later, the following analysis: "Cyrenaica and Tripolitania are in much the same position as American states during [the] years of [the] formation of [the] Republic. Each is jealous of the other, and Cyrenaicans are not ready to jeopardize their own privileged position. . . . Thinking people [of] both territories, however, appear to realize [the] necessity of unity to make [a] viable state and desire to achieve this object despite local difference."[49] But *how* would this be done? The commissioners remained skeptical—the British because they were unsure how union might affect their plans for Cyrenaican bases; the French because they feared any démarche that would agitate their neighboring colonial sphere; the Soviets because they saw no orthodox revolutionary group from which they might gain advantage; the Americans because they feared that fragile new Middle Eastern states would collapse in chaos and fall prey to disciplined leftists.

Looming over the COI's work had been the Italian general election scheduled for 18 April 1948. As James E. Miller has pointed out, this vote became "an apocalyptic test of strength between communism and democracy for the leaders of the U.S. government."[50] Without a doubt, the April elections changed Anglo-American strategy in the deputies' meetings. On the other hand, events in Italy had little impact on the work of the Commission of Investigation as it snaked through Libya during the spring of 1948. As before, the fact-finding tour reflected the differing agendas of the two camps, Anglo-American versus Franco-Soviet, although the latter entente began to fray. Moreover, in addition to the obvious national and ideological rivalries, the COI's Libya hearings represented, in another way, a truncated discourse common to the "colonial situation." The commissioners, while hardly in agreement among themselves about matters of grand strategy, nonetheless shared certain assumptions about the legitimacy and organization of local parties and provisional regimes. Even the Soviets, who had no sympathy for the trappings of bourgeois democracy, were high structuralists when it came to the seizure and exercise of political power. The commissioners asked their questions and did not receive answers that suggested to them a mature indigenous leadership.

The Libya Report

The commissioners had decided upon a three-part report for Libya, based on the logistics of their seventy-five-day tour and the need to begin drafting sections as quickly as possible. There was never any doubt that the report would feature discord expressed via such textual tools as brackets (alternate versions), reservations (showing a delegation's refusal to approve a certain passage), and footnotes (registering a brief comment on the character of some part of the text). However, beginning with Tripolitania, the commissioners jointly stated these conclusions:

1. There had been definite improvements in the physical plant and living standards of native peoples as a result of Italian rule;
2. The colony nonetheless had represented a major financial drain upon Italy, the venture only sustained by massive subsidies;
3. The territory remained an agricultural and pastoral economy unable to meet at present its "elementary requirements";
4. Local nationalists groups did not "embrace the mass of the population . . . and the people as a rule do not have a clear understanding of the implications of the party programmes"; and
5. Therefore, the people were not ready for independence.

Beyond this, there was room for considerable disagreement. The section on the "wishes of the population" of Tripolitania contained two separate texts. The French-U.S.-U.K. version noted that the commission as a whole had interviewed about one thousand people, half having applied to be heard and the "remainder being chosen at random." Many shaykhs and notables were accorded only "courtesy interviews without record" so as not to bias the result toward one class over others. This pattern of questioning showed that while a small group of people understood the "implications" of their views, most did not. Bashir al-Sadawi's National Council had preceded the COI in much of its travels, although the American and British insert claimed, "No appreciable difference was detected in the wishes of people who had attended the Council's meetings, those who lived at places not visited by the Council, or, in some instances, those who had never heard of the Council or its leaders." The French commissioner was unwilling to concede this point; hence, there were brackets even among friends. The separate Soviet text asserted that a significant portion of the people preferred Italian tutelage during a "transitional period," there being little genuine understanding of the tasks posed by independence.[51]

Having spent only ten days in the Fezzan, the commission admitted that its tour was "less thorough than was to be desired." Here was a territory with no large towns, a tribal population that was nomadic and seminomadic with nearly 75 percent of the people living a very spartan life. An upper class, consisting of 4 percent of the population, controlled nearly all the cultivated land and commerce of the region. There were no political parties, no newspapers, no public telephones, and no organized transport services. The French administered the territory in a tripartite arrangement: one part supervised by Tunisian authorities, another ruled by a military governor, and a third handled by the commandant of the Southern Territories of Algeria. Separate texts for the wishes of the population did not produce remarkably different results. The agreed conclusions stated that the people were "politically underdeveloped and . . . under strong religious influences" and generally content with French rule.[52]

The commissioners spent twenty-five days in Cyrenaica before leaving on 20 May for Rome in order to interview Italian refugees. Approximately six hundred people were interviewed directly by the four-power delegations. The nationalist program was simple: immediate independence and constitutional government under a Sanusi amirate, rejecting cooperation with Italy and the return of any settlers. According to the COI report, Cyrenaica showed little chance of "establishing an economic equilibrium for many years to come." Without local industries, agriculture and animal husbandry would remain the principal way of life for the Arab population. Regarding local views, the four powers agreed that "most of the people interviewed had little comprehension of the political issues involved." As expected, people deferred to their shaykhs, and the latter uniformly looked to Sayyid Idris for guidance. The French-U.S.-U.K. text made clear that the vast majority of those interviewed did ask for independence under the sayyid's leadership, though few asked for the unity of Libya. A "sizeable body of opinion" preferred outside assistance to come from Britain. There was strong anti-Italian sentiment. The Soviet text only grudgingly admitted that most Arabs favored independence under a Sanusi regime, charging that the commission had mostly talked with shaykhs and notables aligned with the British Military Administration.[53]

Once back in London, the commissioners struggled to finish their report. The deputies expressed dismay at the delay, but this was largely mock criticism. The U.S. and British delegations knew that the State Department had ordered Utter and his colleagues discreetly to slow the process. Zarubin was quite aware that Soviet protests had often delayed COI progress. As chair of the twenty-eighth meeting of the deputies on 16 June 1948, Utter told the group that the commissioners were behind schedule but denied that he and his colleagues were "loafing." The Soviet alternate, Georgiy F. Saksin, insisted that the COI must adhere to the timetable. "It is very strange," he said, "that now the Commission [of Investigation] is giving instructions to the Deputies. It is very strange." As always, the Soviets were the captains of procedure. Utter responded, "There is no use fooling ourselves." The report would not be done on time. In truth, he said, the matter *was* out of the hands of the deputies. Saksin complained that such delays would not allow sufficient time for the interested governments to study the report. Utter answered, "I think we all realize this very well."[54]

The Deputies

While the Commission of Investigation completed its rounds, the CFM deputies continued their London sessions, shadowed by a mounting sense of futility. The group had little to do but compile the views of what the Italian Peace Treaty termed "other interested governments," while awaiting the COI's final reports. Collecting the viewpoints of the other governments was essentially pro forma since the nations involved had already made clear their respective positions at the Paris Peace Conference. Indeed, the more directly concerned any government had become, the more often it had reiterated its opinion publicly and privately.

What made this process problematic for the Western powers was the timing of the Italian elections. The Soviets had weighed in early, announcing in mid-February 1948 that they favored Italian trusteeship over all former colonies. It was a political ploy to which Moscow adhered steadfastly. The irony of the USSR posing as a global champion of anti-imperialist movements coupled with its spirited defense of Italian colonialism (and debunking of Arab nationalism) was not lost on U.S. and British officials; still, the Soviet tactic was troublesome. For this reason, while the deputies idled, the Truman administration launched a full-scale political offensive in Italy. Private assurances of flexibility on the colonies were combined with public Marshall Plan assistance and covert CIA-managed influence peddling.

At the same time, Bevin was authoring a series of memorandums warning that the Soviet advance in Eastern Europe threatened the fabric of Western civilization. Let there be no mistake, he wrote, the Kremlin aimed at nothing less than "physical control of the Eurasian land mass and eventual control of the whole World Island." It was in this context that Bevin cast his net wider in contemplating a new security arrangement for the West. He also considered a more forgiving stance toward Italian claims in Africa, despite the continued hard-line attitude of his military chiefs of staff.[55] Yet, Italy was only one front in the European vortex, and Anglo-American policy regarding the ex-colonies reflected a big picture, which included fears that a Communist victory in Italy would transform any new trusteeship network into a Mediterranean–Red Sea zone for the USSR.[56]

The Italian elections came and went, affirming that the De Gasperi–Sforza regime could withstand the Communist challenge when sufficiently bolstered by external aid. There was no need to accede to the Italian demands for trusteeships over each former colony. Now it remained only to play out the affair in the deputies: to hear statements and collect position papers, accept the COI reports, hear supplementary views, and then fashion a package of final recommendations. On 30 April 1948, the State Department made it clear that the U.S. deputy should take those positions best calculated to gather support when the colonial issue reached the UN General Assembly. It would be unwise for any Western power to initiate a "break-down" of the deputies' session and, for this reason, "reasonable compromises" could be accepted on procedures.[57] There would be no more East-West com-

Table 7.3

VIEWS OF THE DEPUTIES ON THE ITALIAN COLONIES,

AUGUST 1948

	ERITREA	SOMALIA	LIBYA
France	Long-term Italian trusteeship.	Long-term Italian trusteeship.	Support for British trusteeship for Cyrenaica; prefer to see whole Libyan issue postponed.
United Kingdom	Ethiopian trusteeship with an advisory board including Pakistan, Italy, and Eritreans.	Italian trusteeship on condition that U.K. proposal on Eritrea adopted.	British trusteeship for Cyrenaica; support for U.S. proposal to postpone decision on Tripolitania (though no return to Italy).
United States	Cession of Danakil coast and part of plateau (excluding Asmara) to Ethiopia; postpone decision for remainder.	Italian trusteeship.	British trusteeship for Cyrenaica; postpone consideration of Fezzan & Tripolitania for one year.
USSR	Italian trusteeship.	Italian trusteeship.	Italian trusteeship over unified Libya.

Source: U.K. verbatim minutes, 34th and 35th meetings, DEPITCOL, 10–11 August 1948, FO 1086/127, PRO; U.S. verbatim minutes, same meetings, Box 235, Lot File: Deputies, RG 43, National Archives.

promises, however, on matters of substance. Those days were over, obliterated by the drumbeat of incidents, confusion, and Cold War mobilization epitomized by crackling tension over Berlin and the fate of Germany. The views of the other governments were of interest, certainly, when anticipating the UN debate, but they had little bearing on the deputies' work in the summer of 1948.

Secret U.S.-U.K.-French discussions in July failed to produce a consummate common front but did set the stage for greater tripartite agreement within the deputies, as that body finally and formally began consideration of the Italian colonies on 9 August 1948. In secret session through 31 August, the deputies delivered a series of prepared remarks explaining each nation's stance on the Italian colonies. The men spoke to the official record. The major points of agreement and disagreement were already known; even so, there were a few sparks along the East-West divide.[58] The respective positions of the four powers are outlined in Table 7.3.

Some new themes had emerged during the final substantive meetings of the deputies. There was an Anglo-French reconciliation of sorts. For this reason, René Massigli openly recognized Britain's hegemony in Cyrenaica and backed away from his previous insistence upon an Italian regime in Tripolitania. In return, Noel Charles did not contest French control of the Fezzan and revealed London's willingness to accept an Italian return to Somalia (but not Eritrea). Douglas played no decisive role, but the close Anglo-American ties established within the Commission of Investigation bled into the deputies' sessions once John Utter and Frank Stafford returned to London. (The last COI meeting was its 179th, on 20 July.) It was the British rather than the Americans who continued to invest real energy in the CFM structure. However, as with the work on the Libya report, there was no reason to suppose that conflicting views could be reconciled, and there was no real effort to do so. Hence, the deputies' final recommendations, presented on 31 August 1948, were so studded with brackets that, while the peace treaty terms technically were met, subsequent labors obviously had been in vain.[59] But the affair was not over. Uncertainty reigned as to whether there would be, or should be, a formal CFM gathering to ratify the deputies' failure to reach a settlement.

The Final Session of the Council of Foreign Ministers

Foreign Office analysts wondered as early as May 1948 if the next CFM session could be avoided, but there seemed little doubt that it was the intent of the Italian Peace Treaty that the meeting take place. Two months later, Bevin told his staffers that it would be "injudicious" to try to avoid the CFM; in fact, perhaps an agreement could be reached for Somalia and Eritrea.[60] On 8 July, however, Secretary George Marshall informed Ambassador Douglas that the department was "definitely of [the] opinion" that a personal meeting of the ministers was not required. Only the Soviets "would benefit from such [a] meeting as far as [the] Italian Colonies are concerned and even more important it would probably be impossible [to] limit [the] agenda solely to [the] Italian Colonies, thus leading into [a] discussion of Germany through [the] back door." It was hoped that Britain and France would support this position. If necessary that the Council meet, then the best course was to delay the session as long as possible.[61]

Nonetheless, Bevin continued to believe that the peace treaty required a Council meeting and explained this to Douglas. "My own view," wrote Bevin, "was that, if the CFM met, no agreement would be possible and the meeting would be a short one." The matter would then shift to the United Nations, which the four powers had already foreseen. Trying to bypass the CFM, advised Bevin, could lead to a lengthy "procedural wrangle" with the Soviets that might delay reference to the UNO and impair British chances of getting their Cyrenaican trusteeship and withdrawing military forces from Eritrea and Somalia. Douglas reported to Washington that he would be hard-pressed to change Bevin's mind. In response, Marshall confided that the department's opposition was weakening in the face of continued Anglo-American (and French) preconference planning and signs that the German question could be kept off the CFM agenda.[62]

Bevin had good reason to prefer a CFM meeting. Libyan affairs remained potentially disruptive despite reports that the flurry of local political activity had quieted after the departure of the four-power commission.[63] In the same way that Bevin had sought, via the British Working Party in 1947, to establish a "partial *fait ac-*

compli" for the COI and the deputies, he now wanted the option of sponsoring an independent (but allied) Sanusi amirate in the event of UN opposition. Then came a Soviet note of 4 September that forced the issue, and, with mixed emotions, the four powers agreed to assemble in Paris on the thirteenth. Designated representatives were Lewis Douglas for the United States; Hector McNeil, veteran diplomat and minister of state, for Britain; and Andrey Vyshinsky, deputy foreign minister, for the Soviets. French Foreign Minister Robert Schuman would open the proceedings, while Maurice Couve de Murville would represent the foreign ministry during the sessions.

When the officials gathered at the conference table, on 13 September 1948, Vyshinsky notified them that the USSR could not consider this a meeting of the Council of Foreign Ministers, simply a conference of the four powers. Tempers flared quickly. After the storm, Vyshinsky calmly told the other delegates that he had no objection to the conferees taking up the matter of the Italian colonies.[64] The next day, at a morning session, the ministers agreed that they would work until noon of the fifteenth, Paris time, at which point the matter would pass to the United Nations. Vyshinsky then presented the quite familiar Soviet proposal of Italian trusteeship for a "definite period" over each former colony. Douglas was the first to respond, urging the representatives toward a discussion of Italian Somaliland—the one area of agreement in the deputies' recommendations. He believed that "a colony in the hand is worth three in the bush." But the pattern of past deliberations soon drifted much to the fore as the officials trolled the CFM's murky waters for precedents, points, and counterpoints.[65]

The afternoon session of 14 September produced a fit climax to the long months of CFM work on the Italian colonies. Vyshinsky chaired what was surely the most fascinating meeting of them all—one drawing fully upon the dense negotiating record, thrusting virtually all of the disorderly array of accumulated propositions back into the limelight, the chronological lump sum of three years' worth of mind-numbing debate. The meeting began with a U.S.-French proposal for a simple statement approving Italian trusteeship for Somalia, under UN supervision. Hector McNeil assented. Vyshinsky objected, saying (as he had before) that the group could not consider Somalia in isolation. He suggested that the group next discuss the situation in Libya. McNeil refused, asking, "Is it true that all Four Powers are willing now to record their willingness to create an Italian trusteeship for Italian Somaliland?"

Vyshinsky's response created a kind of intellectual pandemonium. Further discussion, he said, would be a waste of time. The Soviet proposal for Italian trusteeships was apparently rejected; in turn, he unfortunately must veto all other current proposals. He then offered a new plan for consideration—placing all three colonies under a UN trusteeship, with an administration responsible directly to the Trusteeship Council, assisted by an advisory board that included the four CFM powers. "I must add," said Vyshinsky, "that for those who are familiar with the history of the work of the Council of Foreign Ministers' Deputies and the various committees and commissions, this proposal . . . will be familiar for the reason that it reproduces almost word for word the proposal made on September 15th, 1945 by . . . Mr. Byrnes."

And indeed he was correct. It was a wonderfully ironic moment. The Council had returned to its starting point. Couve de Murville led the assault against Vyshinsky. The French delegation, he said, was the only one that had remained consistent throughout the Council's deliberations. Since 1945, France had supported a single trustee for the territories and favored Italy for such a role. Both then and now, international trusteeship was impractical. McNeil followed, "disappointed and slightly bewildered by the plight which we now have reached." But for the first time in months, a British representative in four-power talks was able to enter the fray as a champion of Italy, asserting that its people would certainly prefer "a partial restoration of . . . their legitimate aspirations" over none at all. As had Couve de Murville, McNeil termed the proposed UN trusteeship impractical. He was able to cite Molotov's arguments from April 1946 that multipower regimes were clumsy and "that if a child has seven nurses it won't be looked after at all." Thus, he used Molotov to refute Vyshinsky, who had used Byrnes to rebut Western criticism. McNeil again, as had Douglas, asked that the conferees address the matter of Somalia, their single point of light.

Vyshinsky first attacked Douglas's reluctance to take up the proposal for collective trusteeship, then turned to Britain's position. If London were so "favourably disposed" toward Italy, why did McNeil make his firm claim to Cyrenaica? Further, he said, the British were trying to chisel off territory from Ethiopia and Italian Somaliland. Vyshinsky mocked McNeil's lament for Italy. "All this is put into very tragic form—that the last shred is being taken from Italy. But Italy is naked already, and one small shred will never cover her. . . ." He then urged adjournment.[66] As the men reassembled at 11:30 that night, the mood was subdued. Douglas as chair announced that there were only a few procedural matters to resolve. McNeil suggested that, as a matter of "adult tidiness," the group should draft a letter to the UN secretary-general, formally transferring responsibility for the colonies. It was agreed there would be no joint protocol and that each nation would issue its own press releases. At noon on 15 September, the delegates signed the letter, and the Council of Foreign Ministers lumbered off the global stage.[67]

This final CFM session was great political theater, at least to anyone who had been a steady observer of the deliberations of the Council and its ancillaries from 1945–48. At the final session, the United States conceded leadership to its Western partners, primarily out of disinterest. Douglas also lacked the experience with colonial issues that both McNeil and Couve de Murville brought to the conference table. It was left to the British and French representatives to act and sound very much like peers again in a big-power parley. Here at last, in a council whose importance had faded completely, the British and French could trade quips and diatribes with the Russians, almost as if the Cold War had not relegated their nations to such a junior status in Europe.

Conclusion

The years 1947–48 revealed ever stronger ties of mutual interest between the United States and Britain. The disposition of Eritrea, Somalia, and Libya had clear implications for the balance of power in the eastern Mediterranean and Red Sea regions. The controversy that evolved played a significant role in shaping Anglo-American relations during that period. Such matters as Soviet control of Eastern Europe or East-West sparring over Germany have been well looked after, as have other crises that marked the emergence of the Cold War. Events in the Northern Tier, as pointed out by William Roger Louis and Bruce R. Kuniholm, were quite important. Successful antiguerrilla efforts in Greece, wrote Lawrence S. Wittner, legitimized subsequent interventionist campaigns.[68] In addition, much of the history of the Council of Foreign Ministers has focused on what it failed to do, or what it did painstakingly and unsatisfactorily with regard to the peace treaties in Europe. The graven images of the Red Menace, Prostrate Europe, and Muscular America were at the heart of the Western mobilization that can be traced through the Truman Doctrine, the Marshall Plan, the North Atlantic Treaty, and beyond.

However, the underlying congruence of U.S. and British interests in the Middle East was best revealed through the process of repeated consultation on the Italian colonies, establishing a baseline of mutual interest—one that helped override controversies like Palestinian partition and shrinking British military commitments in the Mediterranean. Joint planning for the Middle East, exemplified by the Pentagon Talks of October 1947, was the necessary accompaniment to collaborative efforts in Western Europe. Cooperation on the disposition of Italy's former colonies provided the means for seeing and asserting a common U.S.-British policy that spilled over into close partnership everywhere— assisting the transition from the cramped relations of 1945–46 to the full-blown alliance of 1948–49. It was the British fixation on Cyrenaica, seconded by American military planners, that shaped American policy within the deputies. The State Department chose to follow London's lead. Byrnes had dismissed British planning, but George Marshall did not.

In this way, as in others, the colonial situation impinged upon, in a rather persistent way, the more public spectacle of battleground Europe. Big-power deliberations were influenced by indigenous developments (the rise of nationalist groups and parties) as well as by more standard geopolitical considerations. Armed guerrilla movements in current or former colonies, or the threat of such, were already a potent factor in the new world order of the late 1940s. Hence, the CFM included a field of discourse well beyond the Eurocentric treaty-making with which it is so easily and inevitably associated. The British could not play a "single handed game" in Cyrenaica because of what Benjamin Rivlin called the "Sanusi factor."[69] London had to come to terms with Sayyid Idris, who represented a people to be accorded more than titular respect. Sanusi influence also delayed a movement toward Libyan unity and in that way kept open the option of dividing the colony into separate domains. The blending of grand strategy and Bedouin religious nationalism is necessary to evoke the full story of the Council of Foreign Ministers and the Italian colonies. True, the Council was an early casualty of Cold War rivalry, but it was nevertheless a significant transnational actor, creating the requisite pool of opinions and data upon which subsequent UN negotiations were built.

One need not read H. W. Brand's description of fractals to see "complexity within complexity within complexity"[70] in the story of the Council's African sojourn. It was through the Four Power Commission of Investigation that the Council of Foreign Ministers outlived itself. The CFM persisted as a three-tiered bureaucratic entity engaged in important diplomatic activity beyond its initial treatise. What unfolded was the most systematic effort of the century (up to that point) to discover what kind of governance was desired by colonized peoples, and to do so amid a general survey of the economy and social structure of the territories involved. The work of the Commission of Investigation went far beyond anything conceived by the League of Nations and its mandate system. Certainly there were other investigative groups at war's end—to measure European relief needs, for example, or to inquire into the Palestine situation—but nothing quite like the survey of Eritrea, Somalia, and Libya. It was no easy task. There were searching (and cynical and ethnocentric) questions asked about what made a viable nation. How well could peasant farmers and seminomadic herders understand the ramifications of trusteeship or independence? By what standard could people be judged ready or not ready for self-government? Analysts would continue to underestimate the depth of nationalist spirit among Third World peoples; but events in the ex-Italian colonies, as well as in Indonesia and Indochina, should have been fair warning that such populations, despite harsh conditions, were willing to make great sacrifices for self-determination. The COI hearings and interviews showed that illiterate and semiliterate masses had a voice and history that could be articulated for the world community.

The Commission of Investigation assembled an impressive survey of colonial populations. The commissioners revised their methods as they traveled through Massawa, Mogadishu, and Tripoli. Conflicts within the group guaranteed a more thorough survey than would otherwise have been the case. French and Soviet delegations pressed for expanded on-the-spot surveys in a vain search for pro-Italian sentiment among the Arab population. As policymakers in London, Washington, and elsewhere abandoned their hopes of resolving the colonial question in the CFM realm, the COI delegations continued doggedly to visit waterholes, question people by the roadside, tour town quarters, and then thrash out three major reports. Even at the end, when the commissioners fully realized that their seven-month effort would produce no reward, they still labored long hours to finish the Libya account. While the COI's venture is rarely featured in any summary history of the early Cold War era, it is important for at least three reasons: (1) the commission's internal commentary, as well as the subsequent remarks by the deputies, demonstrated the collapse of support for collective trusteeship, despite extensive wartime planning for this contingency in the State Department; (2) the commission established useful precedents in its survey of colonial territories; and (3) the commission demonstrated the depth of indigenous nationalism, however inchoate, at a time when calls for independence elsewhere were being resisted by the imperial powers.

As the Cold War expanded, its corona flared throughout the colonial rimlands. The powerful imagery of a worldwide confrontation with apocalyptic overtones—given the strategic prizes, the frantic drive for such raw materials as petroleum and uranium, and the ideological satisfaction of winning hearts and minds—was much shaped by rivalry in the Third World. As did Iran in 1946, Libya became an arena for the interplay of big-power rivalry that both predated and was exacerbated by the onset of the Cold War. Even more so than Iran or any other rimland controversy in the immediate postwar years, Libya remained persistently poised at the "shadow-line between East and West." "Had the unity of the Four Powers survived their victory," wrote British official G. K. N. Trevaskis, "they might well have resolved the problem [of Italian colonies] within the short time at their disposal. . . ."[71] But they could not. Libya was the initial African arena for U.S.-Soviet competition, and the ensuing complications generated an early parade of the political frustrations and debris that could be left in the wake of clashing titans.

CHAPTER 8

Beyond the Water's Edge

Liberal Internationalist and
Pacifist Opposition to NATO

E. Timothy Smith

With the announcement of the Truman Doctrine in March 1947, the foreign policy of the United States actively aimed at stopping the expansion of the Soviet Union. Assuming that Moscow sought the establishment of a Communist world, U.S. leadership rallied public opinion behind an increasingly confrontational policy. Viewing America as the world's preeminent power, a consensus took shape based on the belief that the United States had to take an active role in maintaining world order, threatened by Soviet aggression. Until the development of opposition to the Vietnam War, this foreign policy consensus met with little dissent from the public, from within the government, or from within the major political parties. Although the bipartisanship initially associated with this policy weakened after the 1948 election, this Cold War consensus supporting the containment of the Soviet Union remained substantially unchallenged until the mid-1950s, when opposition to nuclear testing created a "ban the bomb" peace movement. Even so, the consensus survived into the 1960s, when the anti-Vietnam War movement shattered it for the moment.[1]

An important element of containment was the North Atlantic Treaty (NAT), signed and ratified in 1949. At the time, the strong domestic support for containment meant that there would be little opposition to the alliance with the nations of Western Europe. Yet, in addition to isolationists, there were groups who continued to oppose the confrontational approach U.S. policy had been taking toward the Soviets. Lawrence Kaplan has noted that historians have operated "on the assumption that the passage of the treaty was a foregone conclusion" because the Truman Doctrine cleared the way. The Senate vote of 82-13 seemed to indicate that there was overwhelming support for the pact. However, considering that the Truman Doctrine was a unilateral action along the lines of the Monroe Doctrine, the administration, according to Kaplan, expected to face significant opposition to treaty ratification. It expected opposition to come from three very different groups: (1) the military establishment, which feared the overextension of U.S. military power; (2) the traditional isolationists who would oppose any alliance with the Europeans; and (3) the advocates of a new international order.[2]

Much has been written about the views of the military and the isolationists toward the treaty. The third group, a collection of diverse and colorful personae, has been given less attention. Included here were anti-imperialists, members of the Progressive party and the noncommunist Left, supporters of the United Nations, and antimilitarists and pacifists who felt that U.S. policy was becoming dangerously militarized. However, this third group posed very little threat to the ratification of the NAT because, as noted by Thomas Paterson, their dissent often marked them in the public mind as "ignoramuses, deluded citizens, conscious troublemakers, irrational misfits, or dangerous traitors."[3] Nonetheless, many of the points raised in opposition by left-liberal internationalists and pacifists were used later by the stronger and more active peace movement of the late 1950s and 1960s and ultimately contributed ideas to the historiographical revision of the causes of the Cold War. Therefore, who they were, why they opposed the Truman foreign policy, especially the NAT, and what they proposed instead deserve historical attention.[4]

The Cold War Consensus

The consensus that emerged in the 1940s in support of an internationalist policy began with efforts by President Franklin D.

Roosevelt to involve the United States in the Second World War. Pearl Harbor shattered the illusion that America was safe from foreign attack and converted many so-called isolationists into internationalists willing to accept U.S. membership in an international organization. Included in this group was Senator Arthur Vandenberg, who came to be associated with what he called an "unpartisan" foreign policy that united Americans "at the water's edge."[5] During the war, internationalists engaged in a determined campaign to assure U.S. involvement in a postwar international organization. Although there was much debate over what form such an agency would take, the United Nations Organization (UNO) gained the support of the U.S. Senate and held the hope for a peaceful future.[6]

The hopes that the UNO could guarantee the peace were shattered by the onset of the Cold War. The Truman administration viewed various Soviet actions at the end of the war as threats to U.S. security. The veto power of the Big Five in the UN Security Council prevented Washington from using that institution to thwart Soviet ambitions. The result was the containment policy, which attempted to restrain Moscow by setting limits to expansion. Washington formally launched containment with the Truman Doctrine and aid to Greece and Turkey in 1947. The Marshall Plan of 1948, among other goals, aimed at stabilizing the economies of Western Europe to prevent their collapse and devolution into Communist regimes. Then, by 1949, convinced that economic assistance was not enough, the Truman administration completed the negotiations for the North Atlantic Treaty, in which the United States guaranteed the security of Western Europe against a Soviet attack.

Although isolationists naturally would oppose the NAT, and formed the bulk of Senate opposition, some liberal internationalists also objected to the pact. As the Truman foreign policy evolved in the first years after the war, there was a struggle in liberal circles and in the noncommunist left of American politics over U.S. policy toward the Soviet Union and domestic Communists. This struggle reached its peak with the presidential candidacy of former vice-president Henry Wallace in 1948 on the Progressive party ticket.[7] Wallace, who had lost his position as secretary of commerce for speaking out against Truman's foreign policy, advocated negotiations and cooperation, rather than confrontation with the Soviet Union. Truman overcame the challenge from the Left; Wallace, hurt by Communist support for the Progressive party, received less than 3 percent of the popular vote. One of the significant results of the 1948 campaign was a division in American liberalism and the emergence of a Cold War liberal consensus that supported containment.

However, some left-liberals, including Wallace, continued to speak out against the administration's policies. They were joined by a variety of other groups in their opposition to the NAT. The basis of such objections has been debated by historians. Kaplan called them "new internationalists" who looked for guidance to the charter of the UNO. Although they were not isolationists, he wrote, the two "shared a dislike for anything resembling entangling alliances or engagement in the balance of power."[8] Other scholars have argued that instead of internationalism, the Truman administration committed the United States to a policy of unilateralism and globalism. While such a policy was promoted as an effort to prevent a return to isolationism, it was also aimed at retaining freedom of action for the United States.[9]

Kaplan was right in noting that the left-liberal opponents of the North Atlantic Treaty were not isolationists. Many were "new internationalists." However, the group also included avowed anti-imperialists who advocated disengagement from empire and those who simply wanted less reliance on military force.[10] Among this latter group were a number of pacifists who did not fit neatly into any isolationist or internationalist category. As the UNO was being constructed, pacifists argued that the organization made no attempt to deal with the causes of war and that it simply ratified the existing power structure.[11] Nonetheless, most pacifists, along with other opponents of containment, viewed the United Nations as a means of global cooperation to be built upon, not ignored.[12]

At the beginning of the Cold War, most people who viewed themselves as internationalists, including most liberals, concluded that force was necessary for peace. They identified peace with the use of the military and economic power of the noncommunist world to contain the USSR. The consensus liberals, including most of organized labor, viewed their opponents with suspicion.[13] Advocates of cooperation with the Soviet Union, civil rights groups, and pacifists were seen as Communist fronts or dupes. By 1949, "[t]o be leftist was to be suspect."[14] The major point of division between the consensus Americans for Democratic Action (ADA) and the Wallace-led Progressive Citizens of America (PCA) centered on the Communist issue. The ADA emphasized the totalitarian and expansive nature of the Russian regime, while the PCA viewed the Soviet Union as an ally in the war against fascism, which now was intent on its own reconstruction. The ADA desired a liberalism free of Communist ties.[15] In fact, most groups opposed to Truman's foreign policy condemned Stalinist repression but rejected the claim that the Soviets were bent on world domination. While some peace advocates continued to work in united fronts with Communists, most were leery of such participation. However, the result was that they, as one historian wrote, had to "walk two fine lines," condemning totalitarianism while encouraging great-power cooperation and defending Communist activism while avoiding collaboration.[16] Such efforts were complicated. For example, one of the leading critics of U.S. policy was the Women's International League for Peace and Freedom (WILPF), which presented itself as noncommunist, yet it was anti-anticommunist, continuous in its support of the right of Communist party members to exercise freedom of speech.[17]

Nevertheless, when the Senate began hearings on the Atlantic Pact, the noncommunists found themselves often linked with the Communists. Frederick Libby, the executive secretary of the National Council for the Prevention of War (NCPW), wrote to the chair of the Senate Foreign Relations Committee, Senator Tom Connally, questioning the fairness in placing Communist party leader Eugene Dennis among the first opposition witnesses. At the time, Dennis was under indictment on charges of conspiracy to overthrow the government. Libby noted, "By giving primary position among opponents of the Pact to this reputed enemy of our form of government, are you not by implication casting aspersions on the patriotism of the witnesses that will follow and by innuendo attempting to smear them as participants in a Communist Front against their will?"[18] Senator Glen Taylor, Wallace's 1948 running mate, noted sarcastically that anyone "who did not agree to this bipartisan coalition on foreign policy had to be following the Communist Party line, because the Communists disagreed with it. I happen to differ with it, so therefore I am following the Communist Party line."[19]

Opposition to the North Atlantic Treaty

Outside of Communists, isolationists, and some doubters in the military, critics of the NAT can be placed in at least five categories (see Table 8.1). Although each group emphasized a different point, opposition had many points in common. The first of these broad categories consisted of those who viewed postwar European problems as political, rather than military, in nature. On the fringe of this group were the United World Federalists, represented at the Senate hearings on the treaty by Cass Canfield, chair of their executive committee. The United World Federalists, however, did not represent a true opposition. Although they did not see the treaty as a program to ensure a permanent peace, they did view it "as a temporary measure necessary for the defense" of the United States. Canfield encouraged the committee to make it clear "that the pact is an emergency measure."[20] A better example of this point of view was James Warburg, a banker, a former financial adviser to President Roosevelt in the early New Deal, and coordinator of U.S. propaganda in Europe during World War II. He did not believe that the USSR was a military threat to the United States, nor did he feel that its leaders sought world domination. He felt that the United States should be less concerned about Moscow and "concentrate upon developing and carrying out a worldwide positive program of reconstruction and reform." If that were done, he believed, America would soon find that it had overcome the Soviet challenge.[21] Warburg's belief that the Soviet threat was not a military one led him to oppose the North Atlantic Treaty.

A second group consisted of congressional internationalists who opposed many of the Truman administration's foreign policy initiatives. Of particular note were Senators Claude Pepper of Florida and Glen Taylor of Idaho. Although Pepper ultimately supported the pact, he was a harsh critic of Truman's foreign policy and had strongly opposed the 1948 Vandenberg Resolution, which had

Table 8.1

OPPOSITION TO THE NORTH ATLANTIC TREATY

GROUPS IN OPPOSITION	GROUPS/INDIVIDUALS
1. Groups/individuals viewing postwar problems as political, not military in nature	Warburg, UWF
2. Congressional critics	Senators Taylor and Pepper
3. Noncommunist Left	Wallace, CAA
4. Secular antiwar groups	WILPF, WRL, NCPW
5. Religious pacifists	PC, FOR

CRITICISMS	GROUPS/INDIVIDUALS
1. Weakens UNO	Taylor, Wallace, WILPF, WRL, PC, FOR, NCPW
2. Militarizes foreign policy	Warburg, FOR, Wallace, NCPW, RG
3. Ignores economic needs for arms sales	Taylor, RG, PC, Warburg
4. Militarizes U.S. society	PC, WILPF, WRL, RG
5. Strengthens colonialism	CAA, UCIA, RG

KEY:

CAA	Council on African Affairs
FOR	Fellowship of Reconciliation
NCPW	National Council for the Prevention of War
PC	Peace Churches (Brethren, Friends, Menonnites)
RG	Religious groups (various denominations)
UCIA	United Congo Improvement Association
UWF	United World Federalists
WILPF	Women's International League for Peace and Freedom
WRL	War Resisters League

paved the way for the NAT.[22] Taylor's opposition to the treaty was based on his strong support of the United Nations. He felt that colonialism and imperialism were the main threats to peace and he hoped that international organizations could bring an end to such economic rivalries. The Idaho senator viewed U.S.-Soviet cooperation as essential to maintain the peace.[23]

Members of the third category, the most diverse, included the noncommunist Left, members of the Progressive party, and anticolonial organizations. Some of these groups admitted Communists as members, but most were not controlled by them. Here, the most outspoken NAT critic was Henry Wallace, who advocated continuation of the wartime cooperation between the United States and the Soviet Union. Since breaking with the Truman administration in 1946, he had opposed both the aid to Greece and Turkey and the Marshall Plan. Also included in the noncommunist Left were African-American organizations concerned about U.S. support for the European colonial powers. Initially the National Association for the Advancement of Colored People (NAACP) emphasized the importance of the anticolonial struggle. However, by 1948, the organization was supporting containment and became increasingly anticommunist. As the NAACP moved to support the foreign policy consensus, it ousted founder W. E. B. Du Bois for his leftist politics. Du Bois then became active in the socialist-oriented Council on African Affairs, which sought to gain support in the United States for anticolonial struggles and favored a Soviet role in Africa to stimulate competition among the great powers.[24]

A fourth opposition category included a variety of secular antiwar groups, some of whom had cooperated with isolationists in the 1930s but, in general, were strong supporters of the United Nations. One organization, the Committee for Peaceful Alternatives to the North Atlantic Pact, was founded specifically to oppose the NAT and included Communist participation. This group, after the ratification of the treaty, changed its name to the Committee for Peaceful Alternatives and sponsored a series of Conferences for Peace.[25] However, the most significant groups in this category were the well-established WILPF; the War Resisters League (WRL), established in 1923 and dedicated to absolute opposition to war; and the National Council for the Prevention of

War. The three organizations actively fought against many components of Truman's foreign policy.

The final category consisted of religious pacifists who opposed all wars. Individuals and organizations in this division often worked closely with other antiwar groups. Included here were representatives of the historic peace churches—Church of the Brethren, Mennonites, and Quakers (Friends)—who frequently made their opinions known on Capitol Hill. The Fellowship of Reconciliation (FOR), led by A. J. Muste, was the most active of these groups. Muste and the FOR, which was founded in 1915 to apply Christian principles and nonviolent change to social issues, were opposed to totalitarianism and believed that the United States could best stop communism by creating a model of economic and racial justice at home.[26] Well aware that their ideas were not accepted by the majority, pacifists continued their efforts to eliminate war. In a letter to Muste, the leaders of the WRL noted that they "must keep trying, even if immediate success is not in sight." They wrote that "[m]eanwhile we can . . . use every issue that is raised by the vicissitudes of power politics to urge our policy and oppose war making measures."[27] Against the odds, the pacifists opposed a foreign policy that they felt would lead to conflict.

The Critiques

Clearly, the groups in the above categories were quite diverse in their background and approaches to foreign policy. Nonetheless, there were several criticisms of the NAT frequently repeated during hearings of the Senate Foreign Relations Committee. One of the most comprehensive lists, although not agreed upon by all the opposition, was published by James Finucane of the National Council for the Prevention of War in that organization's newsletter, *Peace Action.* Finucane cited forty flaws in the pact. Among these were the globalization of the "failed" Truman Doctrine, the recasting of the United States as a gun-toting Caesar imposing a Pax Americana, the support for the four leading colonial powers, the fattening of the military, the commitment to freezing the status quo, the two-camp division of Europe, the encirclement of Russia, the creation of an ascending spiral of arms competition, the mocking of the UN Charter, and the idea that the pact "would attempt to treat the symptoms of world disorder by repression, rather than remove the causes by negotiation."[28]

The War Resisters League, in its criticism of the pact, asserted that it "greatly accelerates the alarming drift toward war and that . . . fact alone is sufficient reason for opposing it." Further, the group listed ten specific reasons for their concern. These included the violation of the purpose of the UNO, the retardation of economic recovery through emphasis on "guns over butter," the potential benefits for the Communists who gained from wartime destruction throughout the century, the increase in hatred and suspicion that poisoned international relations, the additional tax burden that "threatens eventual bankruptcy for both America and Western Europe," the placement of the question of peace or war in the hands of foreigners, and the seizure from Congress of its constitutional prerogative of declaring war.[29] While the WRL and NCPW struggled to defeat the treaty, others accepted the fact that the Senate would ratify the pact. At a National Peace Conference held in April 1949, there was much debate on the points of opposition. In order to avoid some of the "worse consequences" of the treaty's implementation, some called for opposing appropriations for armaments and stressing economic recovery over an arms buildup. At this meeting, it was agreed that the NAT "ought to be modified to make it open to all those who wish to join it, to make sure that it does not become a tool for preserving the status quo in Europe, or colonial domination abroad."[30]

Looking back at these arguments from the post–Cold War perspective, it is obvious that some of the critics' greatest concerns did not materialize. The North Atlantic Treaty did not lead to war. Many of the arguments raised in opposition to the pact had little long-term validity. However, as a general critique of Truman's foreign policy, there were some accurate points. In order to make sense out of the wide-ranging criticism raised during the debate over ratification, the most important opposition points can be arranged into five broad categories: that the NAT (1) weakened the UNO or violated its charter; (2) strengthened the dangerous military focus of the containment policy; (3) emphasized arms sales to Europe over policies favoring economic recovery; (4) strengthened the development of militarism and military decision-making in U.S. society; and (5) lent support to European colonialism. Such were the arguments of the left-liberal internationalists and the peace organizations opposed to the pact.

Although the isolationists also opposed support for European colonialism, they raised additional issues, including the constitutional prerogatives of the Congress and the issue of U.S. entanglement. However, the internationalist opponents of the treaty did not fear entanglement. Speaking on the floor of the Senate, Glen Taylor noted that the press had referred to opponents of the pact as isolationists. He denounced isolationism and indicated his belief that "seeking to bypass, undermine, and destroy the United Nations is not internationalism" and that opposition to "alliances of a military nature" outside of the UNO "which tend to weaken that organization certainly is not isolationism."[31] In fact, common to almost all left-liberal internationalist and pacifist groups in opposition to the treaty was their desire to strengthen the United Nations through a greater U.S. commitment to that organization.

Much of the debate over the NAT focused on its relationship to the United Nations, which is mentioned in several places in the treaty. In the Preamble, the parties "reaffirm their faith in the purposes and principles of the Charter of the United Nations." In Article 1, the pact members pledge to attempt to settle international disputes by peaceful means "as set forth in the Charter of the United Nations." In Article 5, the collective defense of the North Atlantic area is justified by noting that Article 51 of the UN Charter gives nations the right of individual or collective self-defense.[32] The idea that the UNO had failed and that the Atlantic Alliance was necessary to strengthen Western security was a common view held by the treaty's supporters. Secretary of State Dean Acheson, UN representative Warren Austin, Chair of the Senate Foreign Relations Committee Tom Connally, and leading administration officials defended the NAT, stating that the United Nations was still important and that the pact did not bypass it.[33]

Scholars have disagreed over the UN-NAT relationship. Alan K. Henrikson argued that nothing in the treaty violated the UN Charter. He wrote that "[f]ar from intending to subvert the United Nations, substituting partisan collective defense for impartial collective security, the founders of NATO appear to have believed that they were doing what they could to strengthen the UN organization." On the other hand, Roland Stromberg wrote that "by extracting" certain words from Article 52 and ignoring others, "American officials erected a rationalization of the NATO alliance" that did "violence to the letter as well as the spirit of the original [UN] Charter." Stromberg noted the tremendous effort to make it clear that the North Atlantic Treaty was not an old-fashioned military alliance; instead, it was a collective security arrangement consistent with the UN Charter. Lawrence Kaplan wrote that the administration had to assure the nation that the policy of containment and the NAT fit into "the image of the world" that had replaced isolationism. This new image was one based on the notion of collective security "implicit in the existence of the United Nations." He stated that the administration sought to avoid "a direct conflict between a treaty of military alliance and a charter of collective security. To accept one meant to deny the other." Kaplan noted, however, that their effort failed.[34]

During the debate over treaty ratification in 1949, some critics eventually agreed with the administration, hoping that something more could evolve from the NAT to strengthen the UNO. They did so despite doubts. As Senator Claude Pepper noted, when it became apparent that the UNO was not yet able to keep the peace, Washington sought other alternatives. If the United States entered the pact, it "would find an acceleration in the peaceful progress being made in the present cold war." He did express the hope, however, that this was not "going to be the substitute for an effective United Nations."[35]

Most who expressed concern about bypassing the UNO opposed the treaty. E. Raymond Wilson and Barbara Grant, writing for the Friends Committee on National Legislation, argued that the "treaty tends to overshadow and circumvent the UN" in its procedures and expenditures. They noted that under Article 5, the signatories became the judges in their own case, deciding on how to deal with the problem of aggression without any defined procedures or standards. Wilson and Grant wrote, "They are free to act without mediation, and become the judges of the adequacy of the United Nations Security Council actions." They warned that the "size and importance of the nations signing this [North Atlantic] agreement cause it to overshadow the United Nations because it includes three of the five permanent members of the Security Council, all of the major colonial powers, and represents more that 50 percent of the world's industrial capacity." They also challenged the validity of the use of Article 52 of the UN Charter. That article did allow for regional security arrangements, they noted, but Article 53 stated that no enforcement was to be implemented under regional agreements without Security Council authorization.[36]

Rather than focusing on such legalistic issues, most critics emphasized their conviction that the treaty weakened the UNO. Annalee Stewart, president of the U.S. section of the Women's International League for Peace and Freedom, told the Senate Foreign Relations Committee that her organization believed that the inadequacy of the United Nations was due in part to the climate of fear and distrust in international affairs. The task, as WILPF viewed it, was to create a climate of cooperation among the member nations. Stewart argued that the pact was a blow to the health of the UNO because it deepened the divisions between the United States and the Soviet Union and was a return to old-style balance-of-power diplomacy. She noted that it was "never the real intent of the UN Charter to arm nations within the UN against each other."[37]

Charles F. Boss, Jr., executive secretary of the Methodist Church's Commission on World Peace, testified that his organization viewed the United Nations as "the keystone of our national policy." Boss indicated that the commission felt that the NAT weakened the UNO because it was directed against a member nation. He explained that rather than opposing the pact in May 1949, the commission was withholding its support. However, he later noted that if members had known the pact was moving in the direction of rearmament, "they might have taken a position in opposition."[38]

On the Senate floor, the most outspoken internationalist critic of the treaty was Glen Taylor. Although his criticisms were wide-ranging, his most serious concerns related to the role of the UNO. Taylor stated that he had been elected to the Senate on his promise to the voters that he would support an organization to maintain peace and "that organization was the United Nations." He was determined "to oppose everything" that seemed "to have the effect of weakening the United Nations." The Idaho senator believed that the pact would lead to an armaments race that could hasten a war instead of preventing one. He told the Senate that his "principal reason" for opposition to the NAT was that "[d]espite all the assurances to the contrary, I am still convinced that this pact will . . . bypass, undermine, and weaken the United Nations."[39]

Such dissent had little impact on the administration. Although high-level policymakers couched their arguments for regional security agreements in the language of the UN Charter, Washington viewed the UNO as being of little use in conducting a foreign policy aimed at the containment of the Soviet Union. The North Atlantic Treaty Organization, rather than the United Nations Organization, came to be the focus of U.S. diplomacy during the remainder of the Cold War.

Opposition to containment, specifically its military component, made up a second group of criticisms aimed at the Atlantic Pact. In the committee hearings and in other public statements in opposition to the treaty, critics charged that U.S. foreign policy was leading the nation in the wrong direction. The Fellowship of Reconciliation issued a statement that emphasized its opposition to the spread of totalitarian communism, but noted that the United States had increasingly "come to depend upon military power" to accomplish that goal. The FOR argued that war had not ended totalitarianism or brought security, stating that, in fact, America was "less secure than ever."[40] FOR leader John Nevin Sayre, in a letter to Senator Robert Wagner, noted that, with the atomic bomb and biological weapons, the methods of warfare had undergone such a revolutionary change that "former strategies of defense which were based on preponderance of power in old fashioned military weapons" were "totally obsolete."[41]

Many with similar views testified before the Senate Committee on Foreign Relations. Henry Wallace stated flatly that containment was not an American doctrine. First advocated by former British prime minister Winston Churchill in the struggle against Bolshevism, containment would only end in war. Wallace felt that it would militarize the U.S. domestic economy and lead "to national insolvency, the surrender of our traditional freedoms, war, a possible military disaster, and the certain sacrifice not only of life and treasure but of the very system of government which it is supposed to preserve." To Wallace, the North Atlantic Treaty represented the failure of Truman's foreign policy, especially the Marshall Plan, which had aimed at "precluding the need for a military program in Europe."[42]

The theme that the NAT was a "war pact" was quite common among those who testified in opposition. Edward Richards of the WRL noted that the pact was "in reality a war measure, and would, if ratified, make for war and not for peace." Frederick Libby from the NCPW stated that "the Atlantic pact is a war pact because it heightens the tension between the United States and Russia." The Reverend Dudley Burr, chairman of the People's Party of Connecticut, stated that the NAT would "bring war instead of peace because it is basically founded on a war philosophy." Richard Morford, the executive director of the National Council of American-Soviet Friendship and a Presbyterian clergyman, told the committee that he believed "the implications of this pact and building up resistance for attack . . . will in effect be establishing a very tangible threat of war." The Reverend Lee Howe, president of the Northern Baptist Pacifist Fellowship, argued that such methods of containment would fail. He told the committee, "We cannot stop communism or the spread of communistic ideas by a military alliance or the threat of the use of military power."[43] Instead of the NAT, such critics favored increased support for the United Nations and efforts to resolve U.S.-Soviet differences through negotiations.

A third theme common to most pact opponents, and of particular concern to Congress, was the character of the military commitment in the North Atlantic Treaty. Article 3 of the pact called upon members to give mutual assistance to alliance members. Most critics correctly believed that the United States would undertake the rearmament of Western Europe. Testimony before the Senate Foreign Relations Committee and debates on the floor of the Senate articulated the belief that European rearmament was unnecessary and harmful. It was unnecessary because the Soviet Union was not a military threat to the West. It was harmful because it would threaten the economic recovery of Western Europe. Mrs. Clifford Bender, representing the executive committee of the Women's Division of Christian Service of the Method-

ist Church, noted that her organization opposed a policy committed to foreign military aid. It viewed such aid as a hindrance
to economic recovery by "diverting manpower, machines, and
materials for defense purposes." Dr. Henry Cadbury, representing the Friends Committee on National Legislation and chair of
the American Friends Service Committee, stated that the NAT
"creates major competition in American foreign policy by setting up rearmament against recovery and makes our foreign policy
increasingly subservient to military policy."[44]

On the floor of the Senate, Glen Taylor again led the opposition, pointing out that if the treaty were approved, "the arms
will automatically follow . . . [causing] greater and greater defi-
cits . . . by unlimited spending for an endless stream of armaments." He warned that the United States could not hope to
arm its European allies sufficiently to withstand the Russian
army. In this point Taylor was joined by others, including traditional isolationists. Senator Kenneth Wherry of Nebraska noted
that if the NAT were simply a statement like a "keep-off-the-
grass policy," practically everyone could go along with it. However, if the treaty involved "an absolute commitment that we
are to provide arms . . . then the question before us is an entirely
different one."[45] Yet most senators recognized and accepted the
fact that the NAT would mean that more U.S. arms would be
sent to Europe.

James Warburg was one of the most articulate and well-known
critics of the Atlantic Pact. Being a former government official and
the member of a leading northeastern banking family, Warburg had
friends in the Truman administration. He was not opposed completely to the treaty. In fact, he told Secretary Acheson that he
favored the general idea of such an alliance "provided that our commitment would not tie the United States to any predetermined
strategy of defense or theater of action in the event of war." Warburg
felt that he could support the treaty if it did not take "our eyes off
the real danger—which is now not military but political."[46] However, he believed that the NAT as negotiated did just that. Not
only did Warburg reject containment, he believed that the
administration's position was filled with dangerous contradictions.

Prior to his testimony before the Foreign Relations Committee, Warburg sent memos to members of Congress and senators

explaining his objections to the pact. In a 2 February 1949 memorandum, he wrote that the rearmament of Western Europe would not be adequate unless Germany was remilitarized or large numbers of U.S. troops were stationed in Europe. But in either case, he argued, it would "provoke the very attack which it is designed to deter." He believed that the primary threat to Europe was through Communist subversion. In that case, the best defense would be "the rapid rebuilding of its [Western European] economic health and political stability." Hence, he felt that the NAT was not the right solution. It created an ineffective defense against a secondary danger, that of military aggression, at the price of weakening the defense "against the primary danger of political penetration." In his memo, Warburg questioned the entire basis of the containment policy. In a second memorandum, dated 17 February, he stated that an adequate defense force in Western Europe would require a mobilization of manpower "sufficient to disrupt the present efforts to achieve economic recovery."[47]

In his testimony before the Senate committee, Warburg continued his emphasis on these themes. He noted that the NAT represented a "negative approach" to peace, while programs such as the Marshall Plan were a "positive approach," since they attacked the causes of mass discontent. Senator Tom Connally, the committee chair, asked Warburg if he favored giving military aid to allies in Europe. In responding, Warburg elaborated on his position, stating that he believed it "extremely dangerous to divert them from recovery to rearmament." He would send allies limited armed assistance for domestic use only in order to maintain stability, but "not to put them in a position to hold the Oder or the Elbe or the Rhine." He indicated that if we did intend to put them in a position to hold those positions, "then by all means let's do what it takes to hold those lines. We are not going to do that with the present plans." But again, he made it clear that he did not believe it possible to "create a force in Europe capable of holding the frontiers of western Europe against invasion without halting the entire recovery program." He believed that it was not clear to the American people or those in Europe what the "sum total" of the treaty and the arms program meant.[48]

Closely related to the points raised by the critics of rearmament and the containment policy were concerns about the growth of militarism in the United States. The view that America was becoming more militaristic was based on the belief that, because of the Cold War, Washington remained in the grip of wartime thinking. With increasing commitments and responsibilities, military influence in foreign policy also had grown. Critics charged that this extension of military power threatened civilian supremacy and contributed to the ability of the military to sway public and congressional opinion.[49]

Historically opposed to militarism, pacifist groups and churches were outspoken in their belief that the treaty strengthened military influence. Leaders of the War Resisters League noted that they were "profoundly concerned that our Federal Republic has tended to make war its main business." They felt that preparation for war and later payment for its costs constituted the "leading items on the agenda of the national government." In his testimony before the Foreign Relations Committee, Edward Richards decried what the WRL viewed as "the progress of the militarization" of the United States and "the growth of the influence of military minded men" in determining U.S. foreign policy. Richards said that the NAT was "the crowning folly" of this militarization. The Women's International League for Peace and Freedom, in a resolution passed at their annual meeting in May 1949, cited several reasons for its opposition to the pact, including the extension of "military control over foreign policy."[50]

Religious groups stated similar reservations. The Church of the Brethren Service Commission issued a press release in March 1949 expressing alarm over recent developments, including an increase in the control of public thought through military propaganda. Speaking for the service commission before the Foreign Relations Committee, A. Stauffer Curry presented several reasons for the church's opposition to the pact. Although he emphasized his belief that it would encourage aggression, Curry also expressed concern that the pact would intensify "the military domination of American life and thought."[51] The *Christian Century* editorialized that the Atlantic Pact was "conceived by military minds" and represented "the sort of foreign policy whose wisdom seems self-evident to military minds." The editor's concern was that "it will hand over to the military services actual control" of U.S. foreign policy.[52]

Such arguments had virtually no impact in the Senate. Only Senator Taylor expressed sympathy with this view. He told his colleagues in April 1949, "We are moving along toward militarism . . . and it is getting so it is almost a traitorous act to criticize any of the policies which are taking us down the road toward militarism."[53] Although other senators expressed some concern over the growth of executive power, there was no concern about the growth of what President Dwight Eisenhower would label the "military-industrial complex" or what C. Wright Mills called the "power elite." Only later in the Cold War did those worried about the development of militarism in the United States gain a significant audience.

Another group of critics warned of U.S. involvement in support of the European imperial powers. Over the course of the Cold War, emerging nationalism in colonial nations caused a variety of problems for U.S. foreign policy, with Washington frequently supporting the colonial powers. Despite statements from treaty supporters, such as Senator Connally, that the alliance had nothing to do with empire, Scott L. Bills has noted that the NAT contained clauses that "might pull the United States into colonial affairs." For example, in terms later popularized in the administration of Ronald Reagan, State Department officials defended the Portuguese empire in Africa, calling it "authoritarian" rather than "totalitarian." The Portuguese control of the strategic Azores Islands led the U.S. to weigh more favorably the desires of the Portuguese government than demands for African independence.[54] In fact, until Algerian independence in 1962, part of the French empire was to be defended by NATO. The Algerian departments of France were included in Article 6 of the NAT as territories to be covered by the pact.[55]

Critics were concerned that the pact, supported by American arms and men, would be used to protect access to raw materials in the colonies, suppress nationalist uprisings, and exploit cheap labor for the colonial powers. Farrell Dobbs, national chair of the Trotskyist Socialist Workers Party, criticized the inclusion of the Antonio Salazar government of Portugal and the potential for the inclusion of Francisco Franco's Spain. He also criticized the Dutch government for its suppression of Indonesian independence with the aid of U.S. dollars and arms, followed by the arrogant statement, after the signing of the NAT, that "Indonesia is outside the spirit of the pact."[56]

The Truman administration, and, indeed, all of the Cold War administrations, viewed world events through their impact on the East-West conflict. Anticolonial groups, and many African Americans who became more vocal in the postwar era, viewed U.S. priorities differently. Although some of their charges were invalid, they reflected the fact that the world was far more complex than Washington chose to view it. An example of criticism with little validity, but yet an important concern, was the statement by Dr. Joe Thomas, president of the United Congo Improvement Association, to the Foreign Relations Committee. Thomas, in explaining his opposition to the pact, charged that because of the alliance with Belgium, the United States would be compelled "to go to war to defend Belgian slavery in the Belgian Congo." Also, the Council on African Affairs' William A. Hunton indicated that he understood that revolts in Africa against the colonial powers could be interpreted by London and Washington "as a threat to Britain's territorial integrity and security, and all of the parties to the treaty would . . . be called upon to take joint action in crushing the revolt of these peoples by force of arms."[57] In fact, none of the powers intended the pact to be used in this manner.

However, some criticisms relating to colonialism were valid and significant. Carolyn Hill Stewart, in her testimony, questioned the peaceful intent of the colonial powers and worried that U.S. arms would be used against native insurgents. She wondered if the "entanglement and identification" that came with the treaty would force colonial peoples to turn to communism for support. Bishop William J. Walls of the African Methodist Episcopal Zion Church feared that the pact would indicate approval of the situation in the colonies, "bad as it is," and make it permanent. He feared that American arms and boys would be used to suppress "the democratic stirrings of peoples" seeking independence. Such a prospect, he said, "is not a pleasant one to Negro Americans." Aware that most of the colonial world was outside of the treaty's jurisdiction, the Bishop warned, "The colonial powers which have signed the pact are notorious for their disregard for written commitments." Hunton likewise voiced a distrust for the European states, noting that they held hundreds of millions of peoples in subjugation. The NAT governments committed to live in peace, he noted, "are in fact today engaged in wars to maintain their domination over peoples of Burma, Malaya, Indonesia, Madagascar and Viet-Nam."[58]

The North Atlantic Treaty, often given credit for contributing to peace and stability in Europe, ignored the brutal colonial policies of the European states. As Washington viewed the world through the lenses of Cold War anticommunism and its NAT allies, it sacrificed opportunities to encourage development in the emerging nations, and often found itself defending colonial or undemocratic regimes solely to prevent procommunist nationalists from gaining control. This deepened an American association with colonialism and contributed to U.S. involvement in the Vietnam War and other Third World conflicts.

The Alternatives

Most opponents of ratification were not opposed simply to the North Atlantic Treaty. Many of these groups represented individuals who opposed the containment doctrine. They had an alternative view of the world and an active American role in it. Often it was this view that led to their opposition. As James Warburg noted in a 10 March 1949 speech, "In ordinary circumstances, I do not think it is incumbent upon one, who criticizes a proposal to offer a substitute. If you see a man about to walk off a precipice, it is enough to shout a warning." However, in this case, he noted "these are not ordinary circumstances." He went on to state his belief that the Russians did not intend militarily to conquer Western Europe and that the United States should continue its efforts to prevent the political conquest of Europe through economic recovery.[59] While Warburg worried that Washington was so deeply committed to the NAT that a reversal would be out of the question, many others felt that a reversal was essential.

One of the problems facing the advocates of a peaceful approach to the Russians was the question of how to deal with Joseph Stalin's brutal dictatorship. How does one trust what was later called "an evil empire"?[60] In answering that challenge, James Finucane of the National Council for the Prevention of War noted that even if one accepted the argument that the Soviets were the devil incarnate, peace advocates such as himself still believed that "there is something of the divine spark in even the worst of humans." He noted that tradition has the devil as a fallen angel with many of the insights and graces of the heavenly variety. He also reminded his readers of the American legend of Daniel Webster and the devil, when Satan was argued out of the soul of a good New Hampshire farmer. All of this was to point out that the devil cannot be shot or destroyed with a hydrogen bomb; instead, mankind had to learn to solve problems without resorting to war.[61]

Many proposals were offered to avoid warfare. Henry Wallace had been speaking out on cooperative alternatives to containment since 1946. Instead of the NAT, he favored the conclusion of a different treaty, one to establish a unified and democratic Germany stripped of its war potential. He wanted both blocs to agree to refrain from interference in the internal affairs of other nations, to give up military bases in other UN nations and halt arms exports, to resume unrestricted trade and allow the free movement of citizens and ideas, to reduce arms, and to establish a World Reconstruction and Development Agency within the UNO to rebuild Europe and assist developing nations.[62] Wallace's 1948 running mate, Glen Taylor, held that an all-out effort had to be made to build up the UNO and reach agreements on disarmament. He remarked that the Truman administration should "quit this business of even entertaining the thought that we should not negotiate with the Russians." If all possible measures were taken and failed, then he said that the United States "should look to ourselves for our own defense."[63] Many of these ideas had validity, especially those focusing on economic reconstruction. However, in 1949 it appeared unlikely that the UNO was capable of defusing Soviet-American tensions.

Support for the strengthening of the United Nations, disarmament, economic reconstruction, and serious efforts to negotiate differences with the Russians were the main themes proposed by the NAT's opponents. Wilson and Grant, in their critique of the pact for the Friends Committee on National Legislation, called for persistent attempts to end the Cold War through negotiation, expansion of a genuine third party role for the UNO, the reduction of armaments, and the availability of resources for recovery. Wilson, in a letter to Senator Frank Graham, clarified what was meant by negotiation. He explained that he was talking neither about "surrender or appeasement" nor "the abandonment of fundamental principles of liberty and freedom." As an example, he noted that, while the Baruch proposal for international control of atomic energy was generous, the United States had not made a proposal for general disarmament. Wilson wrote that the First World War unleashed communism in Russia, while the second had vastly spread its grip. The idea that it could be contained by military force had to be replaced by an emphasis on investment in the health and well-being of countries "in the process of making up their minds between democracy and communism."[64] The Committee for Peaceful Alternatives to the North Atlantic Treaty proposed more support for the UNO, "whose primary business it is to settle differences among all nations and to maintain peace." The committee also advocated peaceful negotiations, asserting that "[d]ifferent political and economic systems can exist together in peace." Leaders of WILPF, supporting the above ideas, defined reconstruction to mean building democracy through adequate housing, education, and health efforts, as well as protecting civil rights and liberties.[65]

The most far-reaching of the alternative proposals came from the pacifist A. J. Muste, who developed a program to stop communism without war. He favored a domestic reform program, which would create a democratic society that would fill others with a desire to be like the United States. He advocated a foreign policy aimed at supporting "democratic tendencies and forces everywhere." Third, Muste called for a foreign policy that was imaginative and friendly, built on a cooperative economic program aimed at raising living standards and stabilizing economic life. In order to accomplish that, the FOR leader argued, the United States "would have to be willing to put [in] something like the money, effort and brains" it had put into war. Fourth, he indicated that such a program must include the readiness to join in universal disarmament and world government, and even the willingness to set an example by unilateral disarmament. Such a program was aimed at overturning the status quo upheld by the United States. Muste wrote that the world was undergoing a revolution—economic, technological, social, political, and spiritual. This revolution was not launched by the Communists. In fact, he noted, the United States, with its technology and its gospel of human freedom and equality, "had a good deal to do with putting ideas into the heads of Asiatics and Africans." This was a revolution that neither the United States nor the Soviets could stop.[66]

The Fellowship of Reconciliation summed up much of the concern of the opposition and its hope for a different future. The group addressed the belief of most treaty supporters that Soviet peace proposals were not genuine, pointing out that to ignore them was to turn one's back on peace and accept war as inevitable. Instead, such peace offensives should be confronted; if in fact they were phony, the only way to counter them was "with a genuine and all-out peace offensive." When the United States stopped spending all its money and labor on instruments of war, "we shall be forced to build a society of equals" that could give adequate help to lift the weight of poverty and ignorance "from the children of all peoples." Then the "[v]ast multitudes of . . . colored peoples of the earth will be our friends. . . . The multitudes of earth's needy will no longer be moved to envy or hostility against us or constitute an easy prey for totalitarian Communism."[67]

Conclusion

The various alternatives to containment developed between 1946–49 by Cold War critics had some validity. Ideas aimed at world reconstruction, support for democracy, and the elimination of poverty and colonialism would have set an example for the world to follow. Of course, such ideas as stated by various groups and individuals were ignored or never heard by the Truman administration and the Congress. Peace advocates expressed an alternative vision of the world. Truman and Congress saw no use for those ideals and by 1949 the two viewpoints were incompatible. Lawrence Kaplan has indicated that what was remarkable about the critics was not that they failed to exploit the vulnerabilities of the administration's positions, but that their constituencies were remarkably small, that "[t]hey lacked an audience."[68] Those who opposed the NAT were given very little time to make their arguments before the Senate Committee on Foreign Relations. With the exception of Henry Wallace and James Warburg, the senators paid very little attention to what the critics said about the pact. Nonetheless, the vision of the world presented by peace advocates, even if it was not possible to achieve in 1949, was a stirring one and should not be ignored. Over time, their emphasis on strengthening the economic foundation of the world, negotiating a settlement with the Soviet Union, developing the United Nations into an effective world organization, reducing armaments, and the importance of the Third World did contribute to reducing the tensions of the Cold War.

Unfortunately, these ideas were buried for several years by the events in Korea and by the anticommunist hysteria at home. Lawrence Wittner has argued that the Korean War dealt the final blow to the weak postwar peace movement, leaving only pacifists, Communists, and isolationists to oppose U.S. policy. Yet peace advocates continued to struggle against war, formulating alternatives to U.S. military policies "and serving as prophets in the Cold War wilderness."[69] As a result, however, many critics lost credibility and political relevance because they stood for views that challenged the prevailing consensus and, for this reason, they had little impact on policymaking.[70] Yet, as Charles DeBenedetti pointed out, the peace movement of the late 1950s emerged from the liberal internationalist and radical pacifist organizations such as the Fellowship of Reconciliation and War Resisters League.[71]

The presence of these critics points out to us that the United States did have options and that its policy could have progressed along different lines. As Richard Falk observed, such a policy "might have been dedicated to the avoidance of a Cold War or to disentangling responses to Third World nationalism from the dynamics of East-West rivalries." Of course, whether that would have been successful is a matter of speculation. What was evident, Falk noted, was that through the Cold War period forces did work to erode the effectiveness of the postwar consensus. Decolonization, the economic recovery of Europe and Japan, and the proliferation of nuclear weapons all weakened U.S. diplomatic leadership.[72] Disarmament, a strong United Nations, peaceful negotiations, and world economic reconstruction were the options raised by the left-liberal internationalist, anticolonial, and pacifist critics of the North Atlantic Treaty and containment at the beginning of the Cold War. Important in 1949, perhaps they are even more relevant today as the world looks to the construction of a post–Cold War world order.

CHAPTER 9

Republican Party Politics, Foreign Policy, and the Election of 1952

RICHARD F. GRIMMETT

In view of the partisan bitterness that had developed over the Far Eastern policy of the United States during President Truman's second term, the election of 1952 was certain to have significant implications for subsequent American foreign relations, not only in Asia, but in the world generally. Given the American public's disillusionment with the stalemated war in Korea, the Republican party was confronted with a superb opportunity to regain control of the White House for the first time in twenty years. Yet like most political parties, the Republican party was an organization composed of contending factions with a variety of views on the best approaches to take in foreign as well as domestic affairs. On the specific question of what the proper role of the United States should be in the world, the GOP was divided into two major wings: the Eastern branch, which tended to support the principles of collective security and direct U.S. involvement in various projects around the world to resist the spread of communism; and the Old Guard from the Midwest, South, and Far West, which tended to favor limited American involvement in world affairs and a more unilateral approach in the attempt to undermine the Communist threat.

The differences between the two wings on foreign policy questions were generally paralleled by differences on domestic issues, with the Old Guard favoring a limited role for the federal government in economic and social policies, while the Eastern wing was more willing to accept the social and economic changes wrought by the New Deal. Because such divisions of opinion existed within the party, the question of selecting a nominee for the presidency acquired heightened significance in 1952. It seemed obvious that if a representative of the Old Guard were chosen, the political alternative that would be offered to the American people would be greater fiscal economy in government and a substantial contraction of U.S. involvement in world affairs. On the other hand, if a member of the Eastern wing were selected, that fact was likely to portend a continuance of the general thrust of current policies, both foreign and domestic, under Republican management.[1]

As the campaign for the Republican nomination developed in the early months of 1952, it was clear that the person who had the overwhelming support of the Old Guard was Senator Robert A. Taft of Ohio. This was hardly surprising. For some time, Senator Taft had been the *beau ideal* of this wing of his party due to his role as leader of the opposition to most of the social programs of the New and Fair Deals. His more recent rise to ascendancy in the Senate as key spokesman for his party on foreign policy issues, after Senator Arthur Vandenberg's health began to fail in 1949, also augmented his standing with the Old Guard, for Taft generally took a dim view of massive outlays of money for foreign military and economic assistance programs. Although he voted a solid isolationist line on foreign policy questions in the Senate after 1948, Taft generally avoided making the bitter personal attacks associated with the more reactionary isolationists such as Republican senators William Jenner, James Kem, and Kenneth Wherry. Thus, the senator from Ohio—while the major advocate for the interests of the isolationist group in the Senate—was widely regarded as a man of integrity on both sides of the aisle.[2]

This did not mean that Taft lacked partisan political instincts or was unwilling to capitalize on issues for partisan gain. His handling of the questions raised by Senator Joseph McCarthy illustrates that this was not the case. While he conceded privately that the senator from Wisconsin did not "check his statements very carefully" and was "not disposed to take any advice," making him "a hard man for anyone to work with, or restrain," Taft still asserted publicly as well as privately that McCarthy had "performed a great service" to the nation by "arousing" the American people to "the dangers of communist influence in the government." Taft himself strongly believed that the issue of stopping the spread of communism both at home and abroad would be an important one in the general elections in 1952. Thus, he was willing to tolerate the excesses of the man who had popularized this question.[3]

To an important degree Senator Taft set the tone for the campaign of 1952 and focused attention on the issues that would subsequently be the basis for the Republican party's case against the Truman administration. As he pushed his candidacy in earnest during the first months of the election year, Taft stressed that his party could surely win if it emphasized such key questions as corruption and communism in Washington, the trend toward socialism in domestic policies, and the foreign policy debacles in China and Korea. He charged that for years the Federal Bureau of Investigation had sufficient evidence on Communist activities in the federal government to warrant corrective action, but that a "soft" attitude toward this question in the executive branch had prevented the use of appropriate measures to remove Communists from public office. On matters such as these the Truman administration had been "dominated by a strange communist sympathy, by a complete absence of consistency and principle, and by the worst of judgment." Taft further denounced the record of political "immorality" within the administration, "the unlimited spending and taxing and bureaucratic regulation of the Fair Deal," and the "disastrous foreign policy," which had "led to Russian power and unnecessary war [in Korea]." He suggested that because the American people were disturbed by these matters it would be possible to win their support by offering them an honest alternative.[4]

Taft's alternative was the election of a president dedicated to Republican principles which, in his view, presented a clear alternative to those of the Democrats. These principles included "a reduction of Government spending and activity to avoid heavy taxation and a constant slide toward socialism; the restoration of honesty and integrity in government; a foreign policy designed to protect the liberty of the American people without destroying our freedom and economic strength at home." The senator was very much opposed to what was called derisively a "me-too" campaign—one where the Republican party and its candidates said essentially, "we approve the objectives of the New Deal but we can do it better; we approve Mr. Truman's foreign policy but we can do it better." He was convinced that to follow such an approach again, as had been done in 1948 by New York governor Thomas E. Dewey, would ensure another defeat. To achieve success in 1952, Taft sought an all-out attack on the Truman administration and its policies, and he was fully prepared to lead it.[5]

Throughout his quest for the nomination, Senator Taft frequently raised the issue of how the Truman administration's handling of foreign policy had placed the American people in a perilous position. At the same time, he spelled out his answers to deal with the dangers that had arisen. "A foreign policy for Americans," he said, would indicate that "as a good neighbor" it was our desire "to help the rest of the world in every reasonable way." At the same time, it would recognize that such an interest could not be considered "a primary object of foreign policy, or an excuse either for the wrecking of our economy at home or for the terrible tragedy of war." Since the "overriding purpose" of American foreign policy was the "maintenance of the liberty and peace of the American people," it stood to reason that "we should not engage in war unless it" was "essential" for the preservation of peace and the freedom of our nation.[6]

Taft was greatly concerned that American efforts to resist communism abroad would destroy the economy at home, and he frequently referred to this possibility when he discussed foreign policy problems. Although he was in favor of firm opposition to the spread of communism, he was also convinced that we could not "meet the Communist threat all around the fringes of the far-flung Chinese and Russian empires." This was because the United States had to operate within its limited economic capacity. To attempt to "fight the Russians on the continent of Europe or on the continent of Asia" was "an impossible thing," a burden we could not possibly endure. Any effort to do so would lead us "to destroy at home by that expense the very liberty, the very productive system" that had been "the basis of our strength and success in two past World Wars" and that would be "the basis of the defense of the entire free world" should World War III ever come. What was necessary instead was a defense program based primarily on an all-powerful air force "capable of dropping the atom bomb on Russia to deter Russia from starting a third World War."[7]

Because he believed that air power was the key to achieving fiscal solvency at home while maintaining an adequate defense against communism abroad, Taft was never very enthusiastic about the concept of collective security. Although he stated that it was desirable to have as allies nations like France and Germany and that we should be prepared to give them military assistance, such a program, in his view, should not be "the primary basis of our policy." Indeed, at one point Taft went so far as to say that he would be "unwilling to admit that the loss of Europe would make this country unsafe." He was willing, however, to support a limited number of American divisions in the NATO army as "a morale proposition." Even so, he believed that they should be withdrawn as soon as possible and that we should rely on air power to protect the security of Europe until the Europeans could assume responsibility for their own defense.[8]

Yet, it was for the Far Eastern policy of the United States that Taft reserved his sharpest criticisms. He charged that from the beginning of 1950, Secretary of State Dean Acheson had wished "to see Formosa liquidated" and "overrun" by the Chinese Communists. In Taft's view, the secretary's attitude on this matter and his refusal to defend the island were ultimately responsible for the North Korean offensive. He also ridiculed the fact that certain presidential advisers had referred to the Chinese Communists as "agrarian reformers—a kind of Chinese New Deal." Such mistakes in judgment, said Taft, had destroyed the right of the Truman administration to expect the American people to permit its continued control of the nation's foreign affairs. Not only had the administration failed to follow a bipartisan approach after 1948, but it had "lost the peace after we had won the war." Taft believed that the Republican party should confront the Democrats with these blunders during the campaign debate to come.[9]

Although Senator Taft ably articulated the views and concerns of the Republican Old Guard, his orthodox approach to winning the election in 1952 made it certain that he would be strongly opposed by the Eastern wing of his party. To make their opposition effective, it was necessary for the Eastern Republicans to secure a candidate who would have a more broadly based national appeal than Taft and, at the same time, have the capability of holding the party together. The man who had twice before attempted to play this role, Thomas Dewey, was clearly no longer acceptable to the Old Guard. Indeed, the governor had become anathema to his party's conservative wing for his failure to win an almost certain victory in 1948. But Dewey had no intention of seeking nomination for the third time in 1952 and stated so explicitly on 15 October 1950. Dewey's candidate, and thus the favorite of the Eastern wing, was General of the Army Dwight D. Eisenhower.[10]

General Eisenhower had been asked before to run for president by members of both major parties, but had always refused to do so. The pressures that were placed upon him in 1951 and 1952, however, surpassed all that he had previously experienced. Throughout the summer and fall of 1951, Eisenhower spoke to several Republican officials, who came to see him in Paris at NATO headquarters. The message that all of these men brought to the general was effectively summarized by the Republican senator from Massachusetts, Henry Cabot Lodge, Jr. It was essential for the Republicans to win the presidency in 1952, said Lodge, or the nation would be threatened with the elimination of the two-party system. Unfortunately, the senator continued, the Republican party and many of its orthodox leaders had developed a negative public image during the years of opposition. The fact that the Old Guard had opposed sending troops to Europe to serve in the NATO military command strengthened the public belief that the party was unwilling to accept the realities of the atomic age. To counter this perception, Lodge asserted, it was imperative for Eisenhower to permit his name to be entered in the presidential primaries that were soon to come, for only the general could appeal to all groups in America. Only he could win the election and "achieve at least a partial reversal of the trend toward centralization in government, irresponsible spending," the special treat-

ment of pressure groups, while avoiding "the fatal errors of isolationism."[11]

The general told Lodge, after hearing his argument, that he
would "think the matter over." But Eisenhower, in fact, had already become concerned about American politics, particularly as
they related to the North Atlantic Treaty Organization and its
mission in international affairs. Early in his tour of duty as supreme commander, the general had accepted a request to return
to Washington to give his views on the needs of the alliance. He
had reached the conclusion that the assignment of American
troops to Europe and the unreserved support of that decision by
every level of government was mandatory if the Atlantic Alliance was to succeed, and he so informed the Congress. Key members of the Republican party in the Senate, however, were opposed to this action. The most notable individual in this opposition
group was Senator Taft. During his stay in Washington at this
time, General Eisenhower phoned Taft and asked him for a meeting to discuss all aspects of the NATO question. The senator
readily agreed to such a conference but requested that it be held
in private at Eisenhower's office in the Pentagon to avoid undue
publicity. This suggestion met with the general's approval, and
arrangements were made.[12]

Eisenhower hoped that the meeting with Taft would serve two
major purposes: to reassure the general that the Republican leadership, and particularly the Ohio senator, could be counted on to
support the concept of collective security; and to enable Eisenhower to remove his name permanently from future consideration as a presidential candidate. The general was prepared to issue a statement that would have ended any possible political career
if only he received positive assurances from Taft that the senator
would support, in a bipartisan fashion, the idea of collective security as it applied to NATO in Western Europe. When Taft evaded
this issue several times during the meeting and insisted only on
debating the question of the specific number of American divisions to be sent to Europe, Eisenhower concluded that perhaps
"isolationism was stronger in the Congress" than he had earlier
believed to be the case. Because the meeting concluded without
the requisite assurances from Senator Taft on the collective security issue, Eisenhower destroyed the Shermanesque statement

concerning his presidential ambitions that he had written prior to the senator's arrival. Under the circumstances, Eisenhower saw no reason why he should "neutralize" himself completely while members of the party he identified with sought to implement policies to which he was utterly opposed. Had Taft given the proper responses to the general's question, Eisenhower would have eliminated himself from further consideration for the presidency and the course of American political history might have been altered. Instead, the two leaders ultimately found themselves locked in a struggle for the nomination that Taft had dreamed of much of his life and Eisenhower had hoped to avoid.[13]

By January 1952, Eisenhower had confirmed that he was a Republican and allowed his name to be entered in that party's presidential primary in New Hampshire. But beyond these actions Eisenhower refused to go. He still considered his primary responsibility to be the establishment of a viable NATO command and did not believe that he should devote any time to partisan politics. Nonetheless, the pressures upon him to return to the United States and actively campaign mounted daily, and Eisenhower gradually began to see the futility of resisting the draft movement as evidence continued to filter in that he was the favorite candidate of a significant number of his fellow citizens.[14]

In February, the general's strongest backers concluded that if Eisenhower was going to be successful as a candidate for the nomination, the time had come for him to commit himself publicly to seek the position. In order to press this fact upon him, Gen. Lucius D. Clay, a close personal friend, was sent to talk confidentially with the NATO chief, who was in London attending the funeral of King George VI. The meeting between the two men took place on 16 February, and Clay told Eisenhower that it was necessary for his U.S. supporters to know three things: "that he would run if nominated, . . . that he would run for the nomination," and that he would "come home before the convention." After "considerable discussion" and "some reluctance" on the part of the general, he finally agreed to "do all three." In the following month he won two important primary elections, one in New Hampshire and the other in Minnesota. Soon after the latter victory, he took the definitive step. During the first week of April, Eisenhower asked Truman to relieve him of his duties as NATO commander on 1 June and to place him on the retired list without compensation. On 11 April, Truman announced his approval of the general's request. Eisenhower was now openly committed to the race for the nomination.[15]

Eisenhower's decision to return to the United States and stand for the nomination did not mean that he would immediately involve himself in a direct campaign role. Until he was formally relieved of his duties, he had no intention of engaging in overt political activities. This position ultimately served the interests of his candidacy, for he was able to avoid until early June the bitter charges and countercharges that are part of every hard-fought political contest. General Clay believed in February that the struggle for convention delegates had reached a standoff, with nine hundred of them split between Taft and Eisenhower and the other three hundred remaining uncommitted. Nothing could be done now, in his view, that would alter significantly this breakdown. But in June, "when the heat [was] on for the other 300 delegates," the general would "be a fresh figure, untouched by all the campaigning" that had previously transpired and would be "a certain Republican winner." Thus Senator Taft was forced to contend with a "phantom" candidate during the spring of 1952, one whose views on a number of important issues were not publicly known, yet a man who by his reputation as a military hero alone was certain to be the most serious competitor for the nomination.[16]

Although his attitudes on a series of public questions were yet to be presented openly, Eisenhower had expressed a number of political opinions in private to friends and professional associates. During a luncheon held in March 1951, he told C. L. Sulzberger of the *New York Times* that he had a "far greater community of views than disparity of views" with both Senator Taft and former President Herbert Hoover, "despite their vigorous disagreements on the subject of NATO." He also believed that the "most disastrous decision" ever made by American policymakers was to "abandon Chiang Kai-shek because he refused to allow any Communists in his government." Eisenhower later extended this observation by stating that "the greatest disaster in American foreign policy was the fumbling which resulted in handing China over to the Russians and giving them 400,000,000 people to use as they saw fit."

By the end of the year, however, the general had become much more critical of the opinions of Senator Taft. He noted, for example, that a pledge from the senator to support NATO did not "strike him as being worth very much"—a remark that indicated how far Eisenhower had come from the position he had held prior to and during his private Pentagon meeting with Taft. Indeed, Taft's standard views on foreign policy questions were now viewed with contempt by the general. Eisenhower told Sulzberger privately on 11 December 1951 that he believed that "Taft was a very stupid man . . . that he had no intellectual ability, nor any comprehension of the issues of the world." The senator, he said, had a very difficult time grasping the "basic problems." He recognized that Taft had indicated that he was willing to support the "principle that six American divisions should be stationed in Europe and that even this amount could be increased" in a gradual manner. But Eisenhower stated categorically that he "would not place his trust in Taft as a man," for "Taft's own record showed how weak and confused he was."[17]

Eisenhower's primary concern, of course, was always the welfare of NATO, for he believed that its success was "mandatory to our country's security." But he also held opinions on other matters. In January 1952, he commented:

> The real issue of today's political life is human freedom against bureaucracy and regimentation; it is a healthy two-party system against an overwhelming single party; it is clean efficiency and complete honesty in all echelons of government as opposed to bureaucratic bungling; it is justice and fairness for all as opposed to special favors for pressure groups; it is sensible cooperation in a world in which our own balance in spiritual, economic, and military strength must be preserved as opposed to stupid isolation or attempts to *buy* safety.

Most of these points were in strong accord with views later publicly embraced by Senator Taft, and they strengthen the conclusion that the only significant difference between the two of them was on the Atlantic Alliance and its role in American foreign policy. This is further confirmed by Eisenhower's observation that the American people shared his desire for an "acknowledgment that the resources of even such a country as ours have limits" and "that reckless and excessive spending and taxation can, in the long run, be as dangerous to our way of life as are external threats"—a theme that Taft had dwelt upon for some time.[18]

Perhaps the most novel among the general's views on policy issues was his blunt acknowledgment of U.S. globalism. He believed that American foreign policy was, "or should be, based primarily upon one consideration." "That consideration" was "the need for the United States to obtain certain raw materials to sustain its economy and, when possible, to preserve profitable foreign markets for our surpluses." He stated that from this need came the necessity of ensuring that "those areas of the world in which essential raw materials are produced are not only accessible to us," but that "their populations and governments" would be "willing to trade with us on a friendly basis." In his view, "this simple need, with all the short and long term arrangements necessary to assure its fulfillment," were "the things that should concern us in the international field." To Taft the overriding purpose of our foreign policy was to protect the liberty of the American people. To Eisenhower it was to ensure American access to foreign markets and facilitate international trade.[19]

Because the major differences in opinion between Taft and Eisenhower rested in the area of foreign relations, the plank dealing with this subject in the Republican platform was of signal importance. It was possible that substantial controversy over the foreign policy elements in the platform might guarantee the defeat of any candidate who ultimately received the nomination. Eisenhower made it clear to his key supporters that he would not accept the nomination if the Republican party "adopted a platform that leaned toward the isolationist point of view." Nor is it likely in such a case that he or his supporters would have actively campaigned for a candidate who subscribed to that perspective. Such a circumstance was avoided, however, by the efforts of John Foster Dulles, who while privately supporting General Eisenhower, had managed to maintain good relations with both wings of the Republican party.[20]

From March 1952 through the convention in July, Dulles was in touch with Eisenhower, either by correspondence or in person, and discussed several foreign policy questions with him. Although the general did not accept every aspect of Dulles's views, he found himself in agreement on most things of substance. Because of the sensitivity of the foreign policy plank issue, however, Dulles could not actively campaign for the general for fear of alienating the Taft partisans. Thus, Dulles was given the sole responsibility of seeing that a plank on foreign affairs would be written that would most certainly be acceptable to Eisenhower, and, if possible, to Taft as well. This task he readily accepted.[21]

The foreign policy plank that ultimately emerged from the Republican platform committee did serve the purpose of accommodating the views of both wings of the party. Neither Eisenhower nor Taft found any great difficulty in embracing it. As expected, the plank was highly critical of the Truman administration, repeating nearly every charge made by the China lobby regarding the shortcomings of U.S. Far Eastern policies. The document also asserted that the Korean War could have been avoided and that the wartime conferences at Potsdam, Tehran, and Yalta were "tragic blunders." It further echoed the contention that Truman had denied to the Nationalist Chinese government the military assistance necessary to prevent a Communist victory. While Russia had followed an "Asia First" policy, Truman's policy had been "Asia Last." Containment had been a failure. Thus, the question at hand was whether the American people wished to retain in office the leaders who "in seven years, [had] squandered the unprecedented power and prestige" that the United States had held at the end of the Second World War.[22]

The foreign affairs plank did commit the Republican party to the continuation of the policies that had been viable in the past. The United States would, for example, continue to "encourage and aid the development of collective security forces" in Western Europe and elsewhere "so as to end the Soviet power to intimidate directly or by satellites, and so that the free governments will be sturdy to resist Communist inroads." But it would also "end neglect of the Far East," and the United States would make it clear that it had no plans "to sacrifice the East to gain time for the West." Washington would "repudiate all commitments contained in secret understandings such as those of Yalta which aid Communist enslavements." In addition, U.S. policy, "as one of its peaceful purposes," looked "happily forward to the genuine independence of those captive peoples." America would once again "make liberty into a beacon light of hope that will penetrate the dark places." The plank further called for an "end of the negative, futile and immoral policy of 'containment'" that had abandoned "countless human beings to a despotism and godless terrorism." Such an approach would "revive the contagious, liberating influences" that were "inherent in freedom." It would "inevitably set up strains and stresses within the captive world" that would "make the rulers impotent to continue in their monstrous ways and mark the beginning of their end." In the final analysis, the document stated, the Republican party would "always measure our foreign commitments so that they [could be] borne without endangering the economic health or sound finances of the United States." It would not permit this country "to be isolated and economically strangled," nor would it allow the nation to "go bankrupt."[23]

As the party platform was under preparation, General Eisenhower and Senator Taft engaged in a last frantic scramble for delegate support. Eisenhower returned to Abilene, Kansas, on 4 June 1952 to make his maiden political address, and on that occasion he stressed many of the same things that Taft had emphasized earlier in the year. He complained about the problems of inflation and high taxation and warned of the inherent dangers involved in allowing one party to rule for too long. He also deplored the centralization of political power in the federal government. In the area of foreign policy, Eisenhower asserted that the free world's loss of China was "one of the greatest international disasters of our times." Although he supported military assistance to our allies in Europe and would continue to do so, he believed that the United States should take steps to ensure that aid programs did not "bring about an economic chaos that would defeat us all." For a "bankrupt America would mean the loss of all we hold dear and leave much of the world almost naked in front of the Kremlin menace." Yet, despite the fact that he believed that "our entire arms program" had to be "under constant scrutiny," Eisenhower added that he was convinced that the United States could "look forward to decreasing future costs" stemming from NATO and other European aid programs without sacrificing essential goals. It was clearly possible, he said, to obtain "reasonable security with national solvency." He was also certain that the nation could obtain "peace with honor" in Korea.[24]

In the following weeks before the Republican convention, the general would return to these themes time and again. But because his apparent strength among many of the delegates was based upon his military experience and the differences of opinion he had with Taft on foreign policy matters, he discussed these latter questions more frequently than others. He supported the Korean War as an attempt to resist Communist aggression; but he added that had the government been "less trustful" and "less soft and weak" in dealing with world communism, it might have been possible to avoid that war. The true test of any foreign policy in the future, he emphasized, was whether it served "the enlightened self-interest of our own country." The North Atlantic Treaty Organization clearly served this end, and he reiterated that it was vital to our security to continue to support it as well as our allies in Western Europe. A retreat into isolationism by the United States by adopting the viewpoint that we had "little or no stake in the rest of the world" and that "we had no need for friends to share in the defense of freedom," would threaten us with "eventual self-destruction." By following a policy of collective security, however, we could assure our freedom as well as that of our allies.[25]

Eisenhower constantly emphasized that adopting a policy based upon the concept of collective security did not mean that the United States could afford to be reckless in its expenditures or that it would have to assume the burden of defending its allies on a permanent basis. Washington had to be certain to obtain "the maximum return on every dollar spent for defense," for "a bankrupt America [was] a defenseless America." The general also stated his strong conviction that the United States could not "station its troops all over the world to protect every area in which we have a vital interest." In his view, "the essence of collective security" was "as rapidly as possible to lodge the defense of those areas upon their own populations."[26]

In responding to Eisenhower's challenge, Senator Taft referred repeatedly to the fact that he saw no substantial difference between his basic views and those of the general. He pointed out that Eisenhower had subscribed to the Republican statement of principles of 1950, which was largely written by Taft himself.

Thus there could hardly be any "tremendous differences on principle" in either foreign or domestic policies between the two of
them. Taft did say, however, that Eisenhower had displayed an
unwillingness to attack the "complete failure" of the Truman
administration's foreign policy and that the general placed "more
emphasis on Europe." The senator added that he would emphasize "building Air Force strength more and Europe less" if he were
elected president. But even so, he believed that in the last analysis this fact represented merely "a difference in methods, not in
principle."[27]

As the Republican convention convened, however, another
question was uppermost in the minds of a large number of the
delegates. Which man seemed most likely to lead the party to
victory in November? Although Taft was a more appropriate representative of the political views of the bulk of the delegates than
was Eisenhower, a substantial number of them had become convinced that the senator from Ohio could not win in the general
election. At the same time, they were fairly certain that Eisenhower could be victorious. For members of a party that had been
denied control of the White House for twenty years because they
lacked a sufficiently popular candidate, nominating a winner was
more important than nominating a purist, regardless of his service to the party. In the end, this consideration more than any
other explains why the general, and not Taft, won the position as
the Republican standard-bearer in 1952.[28]

The fact that Eisenhower's nomination was facilitated by the
success of his forces in a series of procedural challenges prior to
the presidential balloting made it easy for the die-hard Taft partisans to convince themselves that the nomination had been sto-
len from their candidate. But the evidence does not support this
claim. The senator never had a majority of the delegates even if
all of the challenges had been resolved in his favor. By the time
the roll call vote took place, the outcome was scarcely in doubt.
Perhaps it could have taken more than one ballot to achieve the
final result, but by the night of 10 July, Eisenhower was clearly
the convention's choice.[29]

Eisenhower's victory was quickly followed by his selection of
a vice-presidential nominee, Senator Richard M. Nixon of California. Senator Nixon appealed to the general because of his youth,

the harmony of their political views, and his reputation gained as a result of the highly publicized investigation of Alger Hiss. Since the issue of "Communist infiltration and proper methods for defeating it" in the United States "had become a burning and widespread issue," Eisenhower reasoned that Nixon, who had a "special talent, an ability to ferret out any kind of subversive influence," would be a clear asset to the Republican ticket in 1952. This was particularly true if he were an individual, as Eisenhower believed Nixon was, who had never "overstepped the limits prescribed by the American sense of fair play" in the course of his investigations.[30]

Having won the nomination, Eisenhower's next task was to organize a campaign strategy that would not only capitalize on the weaknesses of the Truman administration but would also gain the enthusiastic support of both wings of the Republican party. This task was rendered more difficult because of the bitter contest the general had to wage against the Taft forces at the convention. Thus securing a prompt reconciliation with the Ohio senator was one of Eisenhower's most immediate concerns. It was a matter of some interest to Taft as well. At the conclusion of the convention, the senator departed from Chicago for an extended vacation at the home of close friends in Murray Bay, Quebec. During his stay there he was the recipient of a number of letters and telegrams from his recent supporters reflecting their strong displeasure with the convention's outcome. The Ohioan told Senator H. Alexander Smith, who was also vacationing at Murray Bay that summer, that the advice his correspondents had given him fell into three distinct categories: he should form a third party that was based on the principles that had been rejected at Chicago, sit out the election and do nothing on behalf of the ticket, or "go all-out and back Eisenhower." Taft told Smith that he intended to endorse the ticket, but that while doing so he intended to "stand by his principles and his friends," and in those instances in which he held different views from Eisenhower, he intended to express them. Furthermore, before he embarked on a campaign on the general's behalf, Taft wanted to have a "preliminary sounding out of Eisenhower's views" and the views of those who supported him on the questions of finance and spending and U.S.

security policy. He wanted an indication that the general was not planning to conduct a "me-too" campaign.[31]

In an effort to enlist the senator's active support in the campaign, Eisenhower sent a wire to Taft on 17 July stating his interest in a personal meeting. The senator agreed to do so, but the exact date for the conference remained unspecified. In the meantime, Taft gave considerable thought to what he hoped to accomplish when the meeting finally occurred. In private notes and memoranda he constantly reiterated the point that he had to take care not to give the impression that he was surrendering his principles or his followers in order to support the Republican ticket. Taft expressed concern that the election of Eisenhower might result in the ascendancy of a "New Deal Republican Administration, perhaps dominated by Dewey," forcing him into a "position more or less antagonistic" to it. He believed that in view of this possibility he needed assurances from Eisenhower that his supporters would not be "purged" from state and national parties and that they be considered for "positions in the new Administration" on an equitable basis. While he recognized that it might be very difficult for the general to provide such assurances, Taft felt that he had to make the attempt to obtain them.[32]

Taft believed that "the real issue" in the campaign was the need to stress the elements of a proper policy at home and abroad. These elements included a "sound fiscal policy" and a reduction of expenses and taxes, as well as the elimination of our "obsession with Europe and European spending," while promoting the concept of air power in our defense policy. He intended to oppose any budget in excess of $60 billion during the second year of the administration and to defend the Taft-Hartley Act as it stood except for justifiable perfecting amendments. He also expected that a "reasonably conservative farm policy" would be followed. When he met with Eisenhower, he planned to state his "certain intention of attacking Truman and Acheson and the whole foreign policy of the Administration on the basis of Yalta, Tehran, Potsdam and Manchuria." Further, if some assurances were not given that made it clear that he did not "have to surrender questions of principle, or abandon his supporters," Taft believed that he would have to issue a press statement that "it was impossible" for him to conclude an agreement with Eisenhower. Although in those circumstances, Taft intended to "support the ticket," he "could not ask others to do so." He did not relish that prospect but was prepared to take such an action if it proved to be necessary.[33]

To facilitate the arrangements for the personal meeting with Eisenhower, Taft wrote to Senator Everett Dirksen of Illinois and asked him to "sound out" Senator Frank Carlson of Kansas, a key spokesman for the general. As noted above, Taft's list of concerns included a commitment from Eisenhower to cut the budget and to reduce taxes. He further desired a statement from the general that "no spender like Paul Hoffman be appointed Secretary of State and that Dewey not be appointed Secretary of State." In addition, Taft wanted a statement of support for the Taft-Hartley Act and the acceptance in principle that "there should be a representation on approximately equal terms in the Cabinet of Taft supporters." The senator did indicate that he did not like asking "for specific assurances on foreign policy" because they were "difficult to give" and "primarily an executive matter." However, he did feel that it was proper to ask that expenses "not be so great as to destroy a free system here at home." Should such an arrangement be worked out, Taft "would be glad to campaign vigorously for the ticket, and urge everyone to go along." Otherwise, the senator would back the ticket but would confine his campaigning to the congressional races in which he was most interested. He concluded by adding that if Senator Carlson was receptive to this general proposal for the terms of a conference, "the exact points" that Taft made were "of course open to discussion."[34]

As Taft waited for final confirmation of the meeting with Eisenhower, he expressed to various supporters his concern about the upcoming campaign. He found it hard to "understand the position of the businessmen and editors" who seemed so interested in the establishment of a "Republican New Deal Administration." He could not see how it was possible "to spend the money they want to spend abroad without spending somewhat comparable sums at home and bringing about the very socialism they say they deplore." The principal interest of such individuals, to Taft, seemed to have been his defeat and thus the prevention of the establishment of a "real Conservative Administration." After the general's nomination, and the subsequent selection of Illinois governor Adlai E. Stevenson by the Democrats, these people had not displayed nearly the degree of "interest in electing Eisenhower as they did in nominating him." Nonetheless, Taft had hopes that Eisenhower would prove to be "reasonably conservative."[35]

After final negotiations were completed between Senators Carlson and Taft in early September, Taft flew to New York on 11 September and met with Eisenhower the following morning from 7:30 to 9:30. At the meeting's conclusion, the senator held a press conference during which he endorsed the general and read a statement of principles prepared by him and agreed to by Eisenhower. While settling the question of whether or not Taft would campaign for his party's ticket in 1952, the "Morningside Heights Agreement" at the same time suggested, by its content and tone, that Eisenhower may have "surrendered" to Taft on major issues in order to obtain his support. Governor Stevenson, the Democratic nominee, was quick to state that that was indeed what had occurred. A close examination of the views of Taft and Eisenhower and the pertinent documents relating to the Morningside Heights conference, however, suggests a contrary conclusion.[36]

Taft's notes used during his discussion with Eisenhower indicate that he was primarily concerned with domestic issues and Republican party politics along the lines he had expressed to Senator Dirksen earlier in the summer. He wanted to know if the Republican minority in the Congress that had "supported the New Deal" and the expansion of the federal government was going to have a predominant influence in an Eisenhower administration. In short, was "the minority tail going to wag the dog?" If that happened to be the case, the senator felt that he would be in no better position to further his views than with a Democratic administration. He reaffirmed the necessity for him to uphold his principles and his supporters if he was to "be of any value," for not having control of the "so-called Taft followers," he could lose them. Taft complimented the general for his positions on the Tidelands controversy and the Fair Employment Practices Commission. But he expressed concern at the tendency in Eisenhower's speeches to accept the New Deal's "social gains" of the last twenty years. To Taft there was "no middle way" on such a main issue. He was also disturbed by the statement of Governor Sherman

Adams of New Hampshire, adviser to the general, that suggested that Eisenhower would make his own platform as president.[37]

Although Taft later stated at his press conference that he did not raise the issue of Governor Dewey or Paul Hoffman serving in the cabinet, or the question of Taft supporters receiving equal representation in it, his private notes indicate that this was not the case at all. Taft apparently not only asked that Dewey and Hoffman be excluded from the cabinet, but that Taft men most certainly be included so that they would "have some influence" with Eisenhower. It further appears that Taft did not dwell on foreign policy to any great extent, but did express his opinion that the "point four" program embodied "grandiose ideas." The senator also emphasized the need for significant cuts in the federal budget so that taxes could be reduced in 1954.[38]

The statement that ultimately emerged from the Taft-Eisenhower meeting reflected many of these points as well as others. When it was released, Senator Taft stated that he had drafted the portion dealing with his own views. "Eisenhower's views," meanwhile, "were roughly sketched in and then written in during and after" the conference. An analysis of a private copy of the statement, with the senator's additions and deletions, indicates that the changes made in the document prior to its release, if anything, were changes toward the positions taken by Eisenhower before and after the Republican convention. Most noteworthy among the revisions made by Taft were the elimination of phrases that specifically associated General Eisenhower with Taft's attacks on Republican New Dealers, that specifically required Eisenhower to repudiate Truman's assertion that he could "begin wars . . . without constitutional authority," and that specifically committed the general to oppose the "further extension of Federal power or spending, in agriculture, in labor and in industry." In the cases where remarks similar to these were retained, they were retained in a much more generalized form. At the same time, Taft *added* a specific commitment to "speak on a national broadcast or at any point throughout the country" on behalf of the Republican ticket.[39]

An examination of the final document reveals that Eisenhower had agreed with Taft to seek a drastic reduction in overall expenses of government, with the level of $70 billion the goal for fiscal year 1954 and $60 billion the goal for fiscal year 1955. But these were goals to be sought, not absolute commitments on budget cuts to be made. The general had also stated his strong belief in the American system's "constitutional limitations on Government power," including his abhorrence of the "left wing theory" that the chief executive had "unlimited powers"—such as President Truman's claim that he could seize steel mills and "usurp other powers generally without constitutional authority." Eisenhower gave Taft assurances that he believed in the "basic principles of the Taft-Hartley Law" and that he would not discriminate against anyone in the making of appointments because they had supported the senator for the presidential nomination. Eisenhower also expressed his determination "to maintain the unity of the entire party by taking counsel with all factions and points of view."[40]

Taft indicated in the statement that he was convinced that Eisenhower supported the "words and spirit" of the Republican statement of principles of 1950 and would "carry out the pledges of the Republican platform." The senator recognized, however, that the general had to be given "the right to develop the details of the program within the general spirit of the platform." Although Taft conceded that he could not state that he agreed "with all of General Eisenhower's views on the foreign policy to be followed in Europe and the rest of the world," he nonetheless believed it was accurate to characterize their differences as "differences of degree." Both men were committed to "battle Communism throughout the world and in the United States." From Taft's viewpoint, the essential thing to do now was to limit expenditures for foreign aid and armament, except in time of general war, to a percentage of our overall income that would "not destroy our free economy at home" and further increase inflation and the national debt. Eisenhower himself, however, made no further comment relating to foreign economic and military aid in the document, apart from his proposal to seek a reduction in overall federal expenditures.[41]

Considered in its entirety, the Taft press statement of 12 September added nothing new to the political debate that had been developing between the two major parties. When Taft observed after his meeting with Eisenhower that the two of them agreed

"100 per cent" on domestic policy, his remark was probably close to the truth. Since the convention, Eisenhower had stressed his opposition to a strong federal government; to waste, extravagance, and inefficiency in Washington; and to corruption in public office. He emphasized the need to ensure that our military expenditures did not undermine our economic system. He also pledged to clean up the "mess" in Washington, reject what he termed "the Left wingish, pinkish influence in our life," and "get back to Americanism." In short, he subscribed to a conservative view of the role of government in domestic affairs that was very similar to that of Taft, although he tended to express his criticisms of the Truman administration in more general terms than the senator and was more reluctant to name the individuals that he criticized.[42]

On questions of foreign policy, substantive "differences of degree" between the two Republicans still remained. This is not to say that Taft and Eisenhower lacked a common perspective on spending questions related to foreign affairs. Both men hoped ultimately to reduce U.S. expenditures for military and economic assistance in Europe as well as in Asia. But the question that effectively divided them was *when* it would be safe to do so. Lacking Eisenhower's personal commitment to NATO, as well as his experience in European affairs, Senator Taft was much more willing to press for immediate cutbacks in American military and economic obligations to the organization on the grounds that it could be done without serious danger to our security or that of the members of the alliance.

But in order to serve the interests of the Republican campaign in 1952, Senator Taft had decided by September to minimize his concern with this question and stress his concordance with Eisenhower's views on domestic issues. This was no minor concession by Taft, for he had a following in his own party sufficient to threaten Eisenhower with defeat if the senator chose to run against him on the ticket of a conservative third party. Instead, he all but guaranteed the election of his former rival by vigorously supporting his party's ticket. This constitutes the true significance of the Taft-Eisenhower meeting at Morningside Heights. It provided the necessary basis for unity in the Republican party for the campaign to come. By courting the senator's favor, Eisenhower displayed a remarkable degree of political acumen. By emphasizing the views of the general with which he agreed, Taft showed that he was willing to be flexible on matters about which he felt deeply in order to further the larger goal of party victory. Thus, Eisenhower emerged from his conference with Taft committed to nothing of substance that he had not been committed to previously. The only concession granted publicly by the general was to give fair treatment to all Republicans when he made political appointments, no matter whom they had supported for the nomination, and this was hardly an extraordinary promise for any presidential nominee to make.

With the support of Taft assured, Eisenhower returned to active campaigning, stressing the themes he had been developing before and after the Republican convention. Because the Democrats had nominated a presidential candidate who was dedicated to the maintenance and extension of the basic policies and programs of the New Deal and Fair Deal, it was easy for the general and other Republican spokesmen to attack the alleged errors of omission and commission of Democratic party leaders during the previous twenty years. For many Republicans, the area of foreign affairs was clearly one where serious mistakes had been made, and where strong criticisms were in order. In early August, John Foster Dulles stated that he, Eisenhower, and Nixon had agreed that it was essential to make foreign policy "the major issue" of the campaign. Dulles asserted at that time that if the Republican candidates were elected they would establish a balanced foreign policy that would view the Far East to be as important to the free world as any other region. Furthermore, as the party platform indicated, said Dulles, the new administration would "abandon the policy of mere containment" and seek actively to foster "hope and a resistive spirit within the captive peoples" in the hope of achieving their ultimate "liberation."[43]

This policy of seeking "liberation" for the Communist satellite nations was one of the few novelties to come out of the Republican platform. And it was a clear illustration of how far the party was willing to go to capitalize on the disillusionment of various voting groups with Truman's foreign policy. Dulles privately admitted that the purpose of advocating the policy was to secure the support of central European ethnic groups, such as the

Poles and the Slavs. Publicly, however, the policy was fervently advocated by Dulles and Eisenhower as a positive and moral alternative to Truman's negative and static policy of containment. "Liberation," of course, would be sought "only by peaceful means." But that significant limit on the new liberation policy did not deter the Republicans from suggesting that it was a notable change from the status quo, or check the rhetorical zeal with which it was touted. As General Eisenhower put it, "the American conscience" could "never know peace" until the captive peoples were once again "masters of their own fate."[44]

This attack on containment and the advocacy of "liberation" by Eisenhower and Dulles were coupled with an emphasis by the general on economy in military spending at home and abroad. Although Eisenhower believed that the United States had to have mobile "security forces whose destructive and retaliatory power" was "so great that it [caused] nightmares in the Kremlin," he also maintained that America had to build its "defense with wisdom and efficiency." It was necessary to "achieve security and solvency." It was clear to the general that we could not build a Roman wall around the globe and man it. To the contrary, the United States needed "more defense for less money." We had to take a "new look" at our foreign economic program.[45]

To do so, said Eisenhower, it was necessary to remove the present administration from power. No longer could the American people trust leaders who had "abandoned China to the Communists," "delivered" seven hundred million people into a slavery worse than Nazism, and permitted the "drift into the Korean war." If such individuals were permitted to remain in power, there was a strong possibility that they might bungle the United States into an even greater conflict.[46]

The general also believed it essential to remove proven Communists and Communist sympathizers from public office. He pledged that if he were elected he would make certain that the men he chose to serve the public trust would not permit "subversion" or "disloyalty" to exist within government. He would do everything necessary under the law to remove the "persistent, gnawing threat of Communist treason" from our country. The American people expected nothing less from its national leadership, said Eisenhower, and he was dedicated to bringing these changes to pass.[47]

The communism-in-government theme was especially stressed by the Republican vice-presidential nominee, Richard Nixon, who charged that the Truman administration had failed to deal effectively with "a dangerous fifth column" of Communists within the nation. It had permitted Communists "to steal our atom bomb secrets, crack our diplomatic codes and honeycomb our secret agencies with treachery." Adlai Stevenson, said Nixon, had "no conception of the danger, scope or strategy" of the Communists presently operating in the country. Nor did Stevenson have the vision, experience, or "backbone" necessary to deal with the Communists on the international scene. His record clearly indicated, asserted Nixon, that he should be called "Adlai the Appeaser," for he was a "Ph.D. graduate of Dean Acheson's Cowardly College of Communist Containment." Instead of placing such a weak and shortsighted leader in the White House, the American people should elect General Eisenhower, the person the Communists hated and feared the most, because he was "the strongest man to lead the fight for the free world."[48]

In the end, it was the public confidence in Eisenhower's international experience as a military leader that proved to be his greatest asset as a presidential candidate, and he continually expressed his willingness to use this expertise to solve the problem that was uppermost in the public mind in 1952—the Korean War. The general often reiterated his view that the war could have been prevented, although he supported U.S. efforts to bring it to a successful conclusion. He did promise, however, that if elected president there would be "no more Koreas." Eisenhower believed that in the long run it should be our goal to create a situation in Asia whereby American soldiers could be relieved of the duty of fighting in the front lines. He suggested that if further conflict had to take place in that part of the world, it should involve "Asians against Asians, with our support on the side of freedom." For the present, however, the general's primary goal was to end the war as quickly as possible and "lay the foundation for a just and lasting peace." To help achieve this aim, Eisenhower pledged in a dramatic and carefully timed announcement in late October, that if he were elected, he would make a personal trip to Korea.[49]

The response of the Democratic leaders to this Republican critique was to emphasize the positive benefits that had come from twenty years of Democratic control in Washington, coupled with a direct attack on the general as a captive candidate of the Republican Old Guard. Both Stevenson and Truman asserted that Eisenhower's statements on domestic and foreign policy had proven conclusively that he had "surrendered, lock, stock and barrel" to the "reactionaries" in his party. Both men also ridiculed his support of the "liberation" policy. Truman stated that it risked the incitement of uprisings that could only result in the creation of "a new crop of victims" for "the Soviet executioners." Stevenson dismissed the policy as merely a "cynical and transparent attempt, drenched in crocodile tears, to play upon the anxieties of foreign nationality groups" in the United States.[50]

Throughout the campaign, Democratic spokesmen placed a great deal of emphasis upon the Taft-Eisenhower conference at Morningside Heights. That meeting and the subsequent statement released by Taft gave irrefutable evidence, it was asserted, that Eisenhower had adopted the views of the Ohio senator, and had abandoned his allegiance to his earlier principles. To obtain the support of Taft, said Truman, General Eisenhower had "had to swallow the Taft foreign policy hook, line and sinker," which amounted to accepting completely a policy of isolationism. "Every four years," the president added, the Republican party took "their outworn, discredited philosophy," dressed it up "in a new disguise," and attempted to pass it off on the American people. This election, he asserted, they had "tried to clothe it in the shining armor of a national hero." For his part, Stevenson found it particularly deplorable that Eisenhower had accepted Taft's perspective that the "greatest threat to liberty today [was] the cost of our own Federal Government." In Stevenson's opinion, this ignored the greater external danger of international communism.[51]

Stevenson found it ridiculous for Taft to assert that he and the general had only "differences of degree" on foreign policy questions. Either U.S. security was threatened by "world communism" or it was not, and it was "not a question of degree whether we measure our defense by an arbitrary budget or measure our budget by the needs of survival." To follow a policy calling for a "deliberate and systematic weakening of ourselves and our allies" on the grounds that the greatest threat to our security was internal could only have one result: encouraging the "expansion of Soviet power." By accepting this Taftian maxim, said Stevenson,

Eisenhower had changed Theodore Roosevelt's advice from "speak softly and carry a big stick" to "talk tough and carry a twig." The Democratic nominee wondered if the general fully realized the implications of Taft's confident remark that he and Eisenhower only had "differences of degree" on the major international issues. He asked the American people to judge: "Is it a difference of degree to be for or against the North Atlantic Treaty? Is it a difference of degree to blame the Korean War on Stalin or our own President? Is it a difference of degree to be for or against the strengthening of our allies?" In the last analysis, observed Stevenson, "such differences of degree" could very well "turn out to be the difference between success and disaster—between war and peace," and no amount of "tough talk about Communism" would alter that fact or provide the nation with real security.[52]

President Truman also criticized General Eisenhower's willingness to embrace every Republican candidate in the nation regardless of whether the man was "the blackest of reactionaries, a diehard isolationist, or even a moral scoundrel." Eisenhower had endorsed Republican senators William Jenner and Joseph McCarthy, said Truman, even though both had defamed the reputation of Gen. George C. Marshall, the man most responsible for the Republican candidate's rise to fame in the military. Eisenhower had even removed remarks of praise for General Marshall from his speech in Milwaukee, Wisconsin, Truman added, to avoid offending Senator McCarthy. What all of this clearly indicated, asserted the president, was that if Eisenhower were placed in the White House, the real chief executive would be Senator Taft, and at the same time the Old Guard Republicans in the Congress "would push our country into an isolationist foreign policy" irrespective of what the general might attempt to do on his own.[53]

The results of the election of 1952 indicated that the warnings and critiques by Truman and Stevenson did not diminish the credibility or attractiveness of Eisenhower as a presidential candidate. The voting public seemed to accept Eisenhower's contention that the "true issues" in the campaign were "Korea, Communism, corruption and prosperity based on peace." The final tallies gave Eisenhower 55.4 percent of the popular vote and 442 electoral votes, compared to 44.4 percent and 89 electoral votes for Stevenson—a sweeping victory for the general.[54] In retrospect,

Eisenhower's election was illustrative of the personal trust that the general was capable of inspiring among the public at large. His victory was the achievement of an individual, and did not represent an enthusiastic embrace of the Republican party and its principles by the American voter, as later events would make evident. But for a brief period the Republican party did benefit from the general's personal success, narrowly capturing both houses of Congress for the first time in twenty years.

The key issue after 4 November 1952 was how Eisenhower would, as president, reconcile the contradictions in his party's stand on foreign policy and the practical realities he would surely face in formulating the American approach to important international problems. Having won the election, how would he now secure the peace? What would be the future of the "containment" policy that he and his party had so strongly criticized? Would he press the policy of "liberation"? But perhaps the most important question of all was how he would reorder the spending priorities for foreign military and economic aid in such a way as to satisfy the demands of all of the members of his party in the Congress, without undermining American commitments and interests abroad. The general clearly faced the same basic problems with which President Truman had had to struggle, except that Eisenhower also had to deal with additional Republican party dilemmas created by the dynamics of the 1952 presidential campaign. To a large extent, then, Eisenhower's first term was, of necessity, directed toward resolving these fundamental questions of governance theory and practice.

Faced with these circumstances, Eisenhower, as president, did not end the containment policy, but rather extended it to the farthest limits that could have been envisioned for it under the Truman Doctrine, bringing Asia as well as Europe within its scope. Instead of adopting the isolationist and unilateralist perspective of the Republican party's Old Guard on foreign and defense policy, Eisenhower discarded it. Utilizing the technique of the 1952 campaign, Eisenhower adroitly exploited political symbols to advance his policies. Through tactical political gestures such as agreeing with a nonbinding congressional resolution expressing support and concern for "captive peoples" and through public expressions of the virtues of fiscal economy in defense and foreign aid programs, Eisenhower brought a number of congressional Republicans to accept, however grudgingly, a more activist foreign policy. As a consequence, with solid Democratic support for his internationalist approach, Eisenhower helped restore to American foreign policy a strong bipartisan consensus that lasted until it was shattered by the issues of the Vietnam War.

CHAPTER 10

Confronting Cold War Neutralism

The Eisenhower Administration
and Finland, A Case Study

T. Michael Ruddy

Postwar American foreign policy understandably focused on
the global relationship with the Soviet Union. Policymakers
responded to crises throughout the world largely in the context
of their impact on this superpower relationship. As the containment policy evolved and collective security began to figure prominently in American plans, and as the Soviet Union tightened its
grip over its neighbors, Europe divided into rival power blocs. But
some nations remained nonaligned and adopted neutrality to secure their national interests, rejecting ties with these competing
blocs. By the time Dwight D. Eisenhower became president in
1953, neutralism had become an unavoidable component of international affairs, in Third World developing areas as well as in Europe. One of these neutrals was Finland, a nation precariously
poised on the border of the Soviet Union. Finland seldom com-
manded America's primary attention during the 1950s, yet an examination of its relationship with the United States provides a
revealing case study of Eisenhower's foreign policy and its perspective on neutrality. For, contrary to much of the political rhetoric that emanated from the White House, the administration recognized the complexity of the phenomenon of neutrality, the appeal
it held for the smaller nations, and its potential to be exploited by

the Soviet Union. The U.S. response to Finnish neutrality was one important variable that would determine the ultimate success or failure of Finland's effort to preserve its independence.

In the aftermath of World War II, Finnish-U.S. relations were already on a firm footing. After gaining its independence from Russia at the end of World War I, Finland's conscientious dedication to paying its wartime debts and courageous resistance to the Soviet invasion during the 1939–40 Winter War won America's respect and admiration. This was diminished little when the Finns, in what they described as their "Continuation War," allied themselves with the Germans primarily to resist Soviet occupation forces. Nonetheless, at the war's end, Finland was a defeated nation, forced, in June 1944, to accept a harsh armistice imposed by the victorious Soviet Union. Among the provisions of this armistice was the requirement to expel the two hundred thousand Germans stationed in Lapland. As the Germans retreated to Norway, they devastated large areas of Finland in a deliberate scorched-earth policy.[1]

Juro K. Paasikivi, who became Finland's president in 1946, played a key role in determining the direction of his country during the crucial postwar years. For ten years, until his retirement in 1956, he labored to preserve Finland's independence by forging a policy premised on the belief that Soviet interest in Finland was strategic and not ideological. He endeavored to convince the Soviet leadership that his country could be trusted and would in no way compromise Soviet security.[2]

A formal peace treaty signed in 1947 with Great Britain and the Soviet Union and the 1948 Treaty of Friendship, Cooperation, and Mutual Assistance with Moscow underpinned his policy. The peace treaty essentially confirmed the terms of the 1944 armistice. Finland lost 11 percent of its territory, including the Karelian peninsula, the major city of Viipuri, and the Petsamo region on the Arctic Sea; leased the port of Porkkala to the Soviet Union for fifty years; and consented to pay to the USSR reparations of $300 million over six years (later extended to eight). Finland further agreed to legalize the Finnish Communist Party and to punish "war responsibles," officials who had been active in the government between 1939 and 1944, when Finland was at war with the Soviet Union.[3]

At a distinct disadvantage because of the peace terms, the Finns were apprehensive when, shortly after the 1948 Communist coup in Czechoslovakia, Stalin proposed a mutual defense treaty along the lines of those concluded with Hungary and Rumania to guard against possible German attack.[4] However, contrary to their fears, the resulting treaty preserved most of Finland's sovereignty. According to the terms of this ten-year pact, Finland promised to resist an attack on its territory by Germany or any country allied with Germany. Finland agreed that, in the event of an attack, it would consult with the Soviet Union to determine the appropriate response for both nations. The signatories further promised to refrain from joining alliances aimed at each other.[5] By acceding to these treaties, and by declining to participate in the Marshall Plan—although Finland did accept $120 million in United States loans and credits from the World Bank and other agencies— Paasikivi successfully allayed Soviet suspicions that Finland might tie itself more closely to the United States, freeing himself to concentrate on national recovery and fulfilling reparations obligations. Approximately 425,000 citizens who fled the Soviet occupation of the Karelian peninsula were resettled, and Finland's industrial base was expanded and diversified in order to meet reparations requirements, much of which had to be paid in industrial production according to rigid Soviet specifications. By 1952, Finland successfully completed these payments, but at considerable cost. Its economy was weak and heavily dependent on Soviet-bloc trade.[6]

Appraising the situation in Finland, the Truman administration questioned whether Paasikivi's policies could ensure Finnish independence in the long run and was concerned particularly about how Finland's relationship with the Soviet Union would affect American interests. Nevertheless, U.S. policymakers recognized Finland's predicament and accepted its commitments to the Soviet Union as a necessary strategic concession. A 1952 National Security Council report (NSC 121) that defined America's policy toward Finland and Scandinavia remarked that "although the Finns value highly their independence and are intensely anti-Soviet, this country's freedom of action in its foreign relations is drastically curtailed by its proximity to Soviet power and by various treaty obligations."[7]

By 1953, Finland's status had improved considerably. Although Finland's effort to complete its reparation payments had made the nation economically dependent on the USSR, a situation Paasikivi hoped to remedy in the future, the Soviet Union had not interfered in Finland's internal politics. Finland was now in transition. Paasikivi slowly charted a more independent course in the Cold War world. Although Finland preferred closer ties to the United States and the West, preserving its independence required a delicate diplomatic balance between the East and West. Paasikivi was intent on maintaining this balance by avoiding direct involvement in great-power rivalry whenever possible.

The tenor of the political debate during the 1952 presidential election campaign bothered the Finns. Eisenhower and his secretary of state, John Foster Dulles, publicly advocated a more aggressive foreign policy, criticized the Truman administration for its failure to combat Soviet expansion, and urged the rollback of Communist influence in Europe. This may have been only campaign rhetoric, but the Finns felt compelled to distance themselves from a policy that might threaten the balance they were constructing and evoke a hostile response from the Soviets. Even before Eisenhower captured the White House, Urho Kekkonen, then the Finnish prime minister, officially expressed his government's concerns to John Cabot, the U.S. minister to Finland. Kekkonen was "disturbed by some of the comments in the American campaign to the effect that America should aid the Soviet satellites. He said that he did not know exactly what was involved, but please to keep Finland out of any such aid."[8]

As it turned out, such concerns were unwarranted. The new administration recognized Finland's improved situation and tailored its policy accordingly. In 1953, the National Security Council began a reassessment of U.S. policy, which resulted in a 1954 report (NSC 5403) establishing a policy that would remain in place until 1959. While clearly concerned about the spread of communism and Soviet influence, it charted a careful course for policymakers to follow. NSC 5403 paralleled NSC 121 in explicitly recognizing the "delicate balance" in Finnish-Soviet relations. It defined America's objective to be the "continuance of an independent, economically healthy, and democratic Finland, basically oriented to the West (but with no attempt to incorporate Finland in a Western coalition), neither subject to undue reliance on Soviet Bloc trade nor vulnerable to Soviet economic pressures." It noted Finland's strategic importance as a "land buffer" for Scandinavia, as well as its potential for providing the Soviets with advance air defense, early warning systems, and critical naval bases.[9]

NSC 5403, however, was unlike NSC 121 in its more optimistic assessment of Finland's future. Even before Truman left office, State Department officials had begun to recognize that Finland's position was improving.[10] Now in 1954, NSC 5403 was more confident that Paasikivi's policy could succeed in preserving Finland's independence. Although the Communists controlled 22 percent of the seats in the Eduskunta, the Finnish parliament, their party had not participated in the government since 1948. It appeared unlikely that they would become part of the government in the foreseeable future, either by election or coup. Furthermore, since Finland had a traditional animosity toward the Soviet Union, the report predicted that in the event of a general war, Finland would remain neutral, would not willingly give the Soviets military assistance, and would hesitate to permit Soviet troops in Finland. Realistically, NSC 5403 doubted that the USSR would invade Finland "as a cold war move" because it had nothing to gain; but it might pressure Finland for bases and other concessions, especially in the event of West Germany's rearmament.

Finland's economic condition posed the greatest concern. Wartime devastation combined with the demands of reparations obligations left Finland with high industrial production costs, growing unemployment, and difficulties stabilizing and improving the convertibility of its currency. In addition, although Finland preferred strengthening its commercial ties with the West, a significant portion of its trade was with the East, making its economy uncomfortably dependent on the Soviet Union, raising the possibility of Moscow resorting to economic pressure to influence Finnish policy. To illustrate this point, the NSC report cited the example of forest products, Finland's major export to the West. Since 1951, the world demand for, and the price of, these products had been dropping at the same time Finnish trade with the Soviet bloc was rising from 20 percent of its exports in 1950 to 32 percent in 1953.

In the judgment of the authors of NSC 5403, the situation had not reached "crisis proportions," but it warranted "appropriate measures" to increase Finland's Western trade and to address underlying cost and efficiency problems. The report made a number of recommendations: support Finnish requests for loans from the International Bank and for membership in the European Payments Union; take steps to stimulate imports of Finnish products into Great Britain, West Germany, and other Western nations; encourage Finnish government efforts to stabilize its economy; and make available limited U.S. economic assistance.[11]

However clearly and accurately NSC 5403 described Finland's situation and mapped out a course for the United States to follow, implementing such a policy involved reconciling Finland's neutrality with the U.S. government's reliance on collective security to confront the Soviet Union. Neutrality was becoming more pervasive both in Europe and the Third World, and, in essence, it was viewed as contrary to the kind of security manifested in the North Atlantic Treaty and other alliances. The Eisenhower administration's response to neutralism would have a significant influence on America's emerging relationship with Finland.

The administration's public position on neutrality was confusing. Secretary of State John Foster Dulles sounded inflexible when in October 1955 he told an American Legion convention in Miami that "barring exceptional cases, neutrality today is an obsolete conception." Contrary to this unequivocal declaration, at a June 1956 news conference, President Eisenhower appeared to accept neutrality as an option, noting that the United States had been neutral for 150 years, that in 1956 neutrality meant avoiding attachment to military alliances, and that "this does not necessarily mean . . . neutral as between right and wrong or decay and decency." But then he further confused the issue by referring reporters to an upcoming speech Dulles was scheduled to give at Iowa State University. There Dulles asserted that, except under exceptional circumstances, neutrality was an "obsolete," "immoral," and "short-sighted" conception.[12]

Historians have explained these seemingly conflicting statements in different ways. Jurg Martin Gabriel, in *The American Conception of Neutrality After 1941*, emphasized Dulles's tendency to use generalizations. Referring specifically to the secretary's

remarks at Iowa State University that condemned the whole principle of neutrality, Gabriel suggested that "if Dulles had made
specific reference to neutrals like Switzerland or Austria, he might
have made more sense."[13] H. W. Brands, in *The Specter of Neutralism*, identified political forces at work. "The secretary's ser-
monizing was designed to please conservatives, Republicans for
the most part, who distrusted neutralists and continually threatened to block administration initiatives toward countries of the
third world." Brands believed that both Eisenhower and Dulles
recognized the moral dimension of neutralism. But they also understood that great-power politics was essentially amoral, a fact
they could not publicly acknowledge without risking political
repercussions.[14]

In addition to the above possibilities, Eisenhower's and Dulles's
remarks were undoubtedly also a public expression of the
administration's internal efforts to come to grips with postwar
neutralism. As NATO expanded to include Germany in May
1955—a move that increased Soviet-Western tensions—neutralism was an attractive alternative to the collective security approach of that alliance. Nikita Khrushchev, who by 1955 had
emerged as Stalin's successor, embarked on a peace offensive to
exploit neutralism both in Europe and the Third World. In April
1955 the first conference of developing nonaligned nations met
in Bandung, Indonesia, where the delegates endorsed neutralism.
The participants were impressed by Khrushchev's call for "peaceful coexistence." In Europe, Soviet agreement to a peace treaty
that neutralized Austria, Khrushchev's trip to Yugoslavia to heal
the rift with Marshal Tito, and Moscow's return of Porkkala to
Finnish control were concrete manifestations of the Soviet Union's
diplomatic efforts to erode the West's security system. Facing this
turn of international events, the administration realized it had to
address this "third force."

In May 1955 the White House asked the State Department to
prepare a comprehensive report on neutralism in Europe, the Near
East, and Asia. This study was forwarded to the National Security Council in August.[15] The resulting analysis distinguished
between *neutrality*, defined as the "actual status of a nation in
foreign relationships or its governmental policy," and *neutralism*, "essentially . . . an attitude or psychological tendency." The

more "classical" neutralism that had long existed in foreign relations entailed a determination not to take sides in international rivalries, steering clear of emotional or ideological choices between competing forces. However, since the end of World War II, a more problematic "quasi-neutralism" was becoming more prevalent, a "hodge-podge of attitudes and tendencies which, for one reason or another, tend[ed] to impede effective cooperation with other nations." This quasi-neutralism encompassed "any attitude which involve[d] a disinclination to cooperate with U.S. objectives in the cold war and in a possible hot war combined with either a similar disinclination or, at worst, a hesitation to go so far as to cooperate with the USSR objectives."

The study identified a number of factors that explained the expansion of neutralism in Europe: fear of nuclear war, which was "unusually susceptible to exploitation by the Communists"; nationalism; negative reactions to U.S. leadership; a desire to attain security without responsibility; pacifism; selfish pursuit of special interests; and economic motivations. It warned that this trend presented a potential threat but cautioned that heterogeneous tendencies had been lumped together, many of which were not adverse to American interests unless carried to extremes. The latent power of neutralism was great and was growing in certain areas of free Europe, leading to a widespread and deep-seated reluctance to be associated with the United States in military hostilities. Communist strategy could certainly exploit this neutralism, while "the U.S. [stood] to gain more through active and unqualified cooperation with these European nations than it would gain as a result of their assuming a position of neutrality." Hence, the report recommended that policymakers seriously consider measures to check the spread of neutralism and counteract its influence. Still, since there were different forms of neutralism, combating it in certain countries might be counterproductive to American interests.[16]

Finland fell into this latter category. Finland, State Department analysts stressed, had adopted neutrality out of necessity. "Finnish neutralism also rest[ed] on an absence of alternatives to neutrality; despite pro-Western sympathies, most Finns fear[ed] a more active orientation toward the West would lead to swift and painful retribution." The more disturbing neutralism that existed in other countries, such as Finland's Scandinavian neighbors, Denmark and Norway, where neutralist sentiment resisted expanded roles in NATO and tended to be anti-American, was largely absent among the Finnish public. Furthermore, Soviet interests in Finland differed from most other areas of noncommunist Europe. In other regions, the Soviet Union encouraged neutrality because it tended to weaken American influence. But in Finland, where the USSR thought it had an advantage, it discouraged neutralism and promoted "closer political and psychological affinity with the Soviet bloc." The Soviet Union thus was being "essentially pragmatic" in the pursuit of its own national interests.

The State Department analysis concluded that realistically there was little possibility that Finland's nonalliance policy would change in the foreseeable future and that to alter that policy might work against American interests. From Washington's perspective, the litmus test for beneficial neutrality was a strong ideological identification with the West, demonstration of "solid resistance to Communist blandishments," and maintenance of a strong national defense establishment.[17] Finland possessed the first two, and, although its defenses were weak, the precedent of World War II indicated that it would not succumb easily to a Soviet attack.

Underlying this assessment of Finnish neutrality was a recognition that Paasikivi had succeeded in creating a situation whereby Finland was able in the long run to manage its relationship with its Soviet neighbor while at the same time (within limits) fostering closer ties with the West—a situation which certainly benefited American global interests. Based upon this analysis, the United States pursued a dual approach to relations with Finland. Measured economic aid to strengthen the nation's economy and lessen its dependence on East-bloc trade complemented a cautious, essentially hands-off political posture intended to minimize antagonizing the Soviet Union. The United States encouraged the Finns when possible, but for the most part allowed the Finnish government to set its own course. However, this did not prove to be an easy policy to follow.

Although the Eisenhower administration could make a strong argument that economic assistance to Finland, particularly in the form of expanded trade with the West, clearly served American national interests, major obstacles stood in the way of providing that aid. The chief of the international branch of the Bureau of the Budget expressed the problem succinctly in 1956 when he noted that "many countries on the periphery of the Soviet bloc [preferred] to be neutral in the best sense of the word but would welcome aid from the U.S." If these countries did not have to "take sides" to qualify for aid, the Soviets would lose a "propaganda target" in the future, and U.S. aid would be more positively slanted toward peace rather than preparation for war. The same official then lamented the fact that "there [was] still a lot of sentiment within the Executive branch and in Congress to the effect that 'if you are not for us you are against us.' In other words, we would restrict our aid largely to those who [were] willing to stand up and be counted on our side."[18]

This dilemma became abundantly clear when the administration tried to use the Agricultural Trade Development and Assistance Act of 1954 (PL 480) to boost Finland economically. This legislation authorized the sale abroad of surplus agricultural commodities in return for foreign currencies. It stipulated that proceeds from these sales were to be used as loans to promote multilateral trade and economic development.[19] Beginning with a 1955 sale valued at $5.2 million, the program expanded until by June 1957 the U.S. government had accumulated $27.7 million in Finnmarks. The administration wanted to continue this program, but, given the instability of the Finnish currency, it had to dispose of the Finnmarks in a timely fashion before they decreased in value either by inflation or official devaluation.[20] Two options occurred to policymakers: offering other countries aid in Finnmarks rather than dollars to encourage them to purchase Finnish products or simply loaning the Finnmarks back to Helsinki.

Neither option was totally satisfactory. Many nations balked at accepting Finnmarks in place of dollars. Not only was it an unstable currency, but there were few Finnish products that potential trading partners wanted. The high cost of delivery further impeded Finnish competitiveness. In 1957, for instance, the United States offered $12 million in Finnmarks to six Asian nations so that they could purchase small ships. By 1958, only Indonesia had made a firm commitment.[21]

Loaning the funds back to Finland proved even more vexing. The Mutual Defense Assistance Act of 1951, better known as the Battle Act, restricted aid to nations exporting strategic goods to the Communist bloc.²² This legislation threatened to tie the president's hands in his dealings with Finland. Since the end of World War II, Finland's economy had become unavoidably linked to that of the Soviet Union. Even if Finland's trade with the West increased markedly, it would still be dependent to a great extent on Eastern-bloc trade, some of which consisted of prohibited strategic items. The United States was concerned, for example, when in 1955 Finland agreed to build two small tankers for the People's Republic of China. The Finns contended that "vital domestic labor and economic considerations" forced them to seek these markets.²³ Such strategic transfers still conflicted with American security interests.

The administration knew that it could not expect Finland to sever such economic ties, but providing loans would bolster Finland's economy and reduce its vulnerability to Soviet intimidation. On 17 February 1958, Eisenhower, at the recommendation of his National Security Council, signed a presidential determination sanctioning a $14 million loan to Finland on the basis of "overriding foreign policy considerations."²⁴ While this had a beneficial impact, Finland's economy continued to flounder. For this reason, on 24 December 1958 another determination added $5 million more in loans and made Finland eligible for future aid, provided it refrained from shipping Battle Act Category I goods—the most sensitive strategic items—to Communist-bloc nations.²⁵

A cautious, carefully measured, diplomatic stance encouraging Finland's independent course accompanied U.S. economic initiatives. By and large, Helsinki was left to manage its own affairs without American interference. At times, Cold War tensions tested Eisenhower's resolve to continue this course. West Germany's integration into NATO during the spring of 1955 prompted a troublesome response from the Soviet Union, as Khrushchev reacted with his diplomatic offensive, touting "peaceful coexistence."²⁶

American officials distrusted Khrushchev's intentions. Allen Dulles, director of the Central Intelligence Agency, at the 18 January 1956 meeting of the National Security Council worried that the USSR was trying to "use Finland as a lever to create a Scandinavian Federation. The Soviet objective was evidently to get Denmark and Norway out of NATO."[27]

Still, rather than pursue aggressive diplomacy to counter Soviet actions, the United States let Finland fend for itself, while carefully signaling its support. Washington upgraded its legation in Finland to embassy status during the summer of 1955.[28] The State Department also encouraged Finnish efforts to become more involved in the international community. Paasikivi had wanted to join the Nordic Council, a body promoting economic and political cooperation among its member governments, since its founding in 1952. He also had applied for United Nations membership. Taking advantage of Soviet gestures of friendship in 1955, Paasikivi risked Soviet opposition and joined the Nordic Council.[29] Then, with American support, Finland entered the United Nations as part of a "package deal." For more than a year, Moscow had blocked Finnish membership while the United States opposed admission of Eastern European Soviet allies. Ultimately, sixteen new members were admitted, including Bulgaria, Romania, and Hungary along with Finland.[30]

By the time Paasikivi retired in 1956, U.S. policymakers were elated by the strides Finland had made. They were even more encouraged when Juro K. Kekkonen, an old Paasikivi ally, succeeded him. A member of the more conservative Agrarian party, who had served as prime minister in several postwar governments, Kekkonen was committed to following Paasikivi's neutral course. But his brand of neutralism was more outward-oriented. Members of the Operations Coordinating Board (OCB) who monitored U.S.-Finnish relations for the National Security Council were heartened by "the happy state of our relations with Finland and her improved political and economic status." Although Finland was still unavoidably entangled with the Soviet Union, it displayed "greater boldness" in dealing with its neighbor.[31] Not only had Finland expanded its ties with its Nordic neighbors and strengthened its economic links with the West, but Kekkonen's government was now in a sufficiently secure position to criticize the Soviets for their 1956 invasion of Hungary.[32]

America's cautious course had succeeded to this point in part because Finnish neutrality worked to Soviet advantage as well.

In a 1957 visit to Helsinki, Khrushchev praised Finnish-Soviet relations as a prime example of peaceful coexistence and contrasted this relationship with Moscow's relations with the Scandinavian states. However, there were limits to this tolerance. Neutrality was acceptable only as long as it served Moscow's purposes. This became clear in 1958. Finnish parliamentary elections in July precipitated a crisis which Khrushchev described as the advent of a "night-frost" in Soviet-Finnish relations.

Based on the election returns, Kekkonen asked the moderate Social Democrat Karl Fagerholm to form a government. Fagerholm's five-party coalition excluded Communists, despite that party's gains in the elections, and included two conservative Social Democrats who were allies of Väinö Tanner, one of the most notorious "war responsibles" punished under the terms of the 1947 peace treaty and an outspoken anticommunist. Disturbed by these developments, the USSR threatened, among other things, to reduce drastically Finnish-Soviet trade levels if Fagerholm's government stood. Kekkonen bowed to Soviet intimidation. In December, a minority Agrarian Party government was formed with Social Democratic participation.[33]

This uncharacteristically blatant Soviet interference in Finland's internal affairs raised serious concerns among American policymakers. Soon after the parliamentary elections, an OCB report on the progress of U.S. policy in Finland acknowledged that political problems had developed as a result of the elections and that the Communists might benefit. However, it noted that, despite the fact that Communist membership in the Eduskunta had increased from 43 to 50, "the basic political situation [remained] unchanged." The report expected that Khrushchev's policy of "calculated tolerance" of Finnish neutrality would continue.[34]

When John D. Hickerson, U.S. ambassador to Finland, saw a draft of this report, he adamantly disagreed. He was "disturbed by what seem[ed] to be a rather complacent tone to the report," most notably its conclusion that the parliamentary elections left the situation fundamentally unchanged. He not only feared increased Communist influence within the political system, but he argued that ongoing economic problems and recent agreements with the Soviet Union threatened Finnish independence. In his judgment, the situation was deteriorating.[35]

Echoing Hickerson's concerns, a July 1959 OCB report declared that "the Soviet initiative at this time stemmed not only from a decision to exploit a particularly favorable tactical situation in Finland, but probably also from the desire to arrest what they considered to be a general Western gravitation in Finnish policy, both economic and political." Soviet interference in internal Finnish politics was an alarming departure from the past. The report recommended a reassessment of U.S. policy to determine steps "to cope with the changed circumstances regarding Finland."[36]

The National Security Council did revise its recommendations in October 1959 with the issuance of NSC 5914/1. It emphasized Finland's importance as "a buffer against further Soviet encroachment in an area of direct confrontation between the West and Soviet imperialism. "Complete domination of Finland," it predicted, "would be a heavy blow to Western morale and could weaken the resistance of some other small Free World nations to Soviet Bloc pressures." These considerations combined with potential strategic air and naval benefits for the Soviet armed forces made Finland's "continued denial to the USSR . . . both psychologically and militarily important to the West."[37]

Sobered by the events of 1958, policymakers set a more limited goal for American policy. Previously, the United States had ambitiously sought an independent, democratic, and Western-oriented Finland "neither subject to undue reliance on Soviet Bloc trade nor vulnerable to Soviet economic pressures."[38] Khrushchev may have been interested in peaceful coexistence, but as his reaction to the 1958 elections had demonstrated, there were definite limits to what Moscow would tolerate. Likewise, America's capacity to influence the situation in Finland was also limited. Therefore, the new policy revised America's goal to preserving Finland "as free as possible from vulnerability to Soviet pressures."[39]

At the same time that NSC 5914/1 lowered expectations for Finland's future status, it suggested for the first time a potential advantage Finland represented for the United States in its rivalry with the Soviet Union. "If Finland is able to preserve its present neutral status—that of a nation able to maintain its independence despite heavy Soviet pressure—it could serve as an example of what the United States might like to see achieved by the Soviet-dominated nations of Eastern Europe."[40] When the National

Security Council considered this revised policy, Secretary of State Christian Herter questioned the advisability of including this broad goal in a policy specific to Finland. In fact, he wondered if indeed this reflected official thinking.[41] Despite Herter's reservations, that statement remained in the final draft. For although never made part of official U.S. policy, Herter's predecessor, John Foster Dulles, who had publicly supported a rollback of Soviet control over Eastern Europe, had at times envisioned this Finnish solution as an alternative for Eastern Europe.

Dulles had raised this possibility several times in discussions with foreign leaders. During a dinner meeting in April 1954, the secretary of state engaged in a wide-ranging discussion of pressing world issues with Winston Churchill and Anthony Eden. At one point, when the prime minister asserted that European peace was improbable "so long as the satellite countries were held closely under Soviet rule," Dulles proposed that "something like the Finnish relationship might emerge."[42] Later, on 18 July 1955, Dulles suggested it to Soviet diplomats during the Geneva summit. He approached Nikolai A. Bulganin at a state dinner:

> [Dulles] said that US had no desire that USSR "should be ringed by a group of hostile states." In order to avoid this, however, it was not necessary that they be satellites. There was the example of Finland for instance. Bulganin (who visibly froze up at this point) replied in effect that these countries have governments of their own choosing and that our expressed position on this point was not one which could be usefully pressed. This was a situation which could take care of itself with the passage of time.[43]

Dulles may not have truly believed that the Finnish solution could be applied to Eastern Europe. He may have been sparring with the Soviets, trying to seize the diplomatic high ground and weaken the Soviet position. Nevertheless, this was one more advantage the United States derived from the continued independence and neutrality of Finland, and it was stated explicitly in NSC 5914/1.

Whatever the changes in America's policy, the basic pragmatism that had characterized the 1950s remained intact. This realistic policy was due to a complex of factors. To begin with, Finland possessed the dubious advantage of being a relatively unimportant nation in the scheme of Cold War politics. During his April 1954 dinner meeting with Dulles, British Foreign Secretary Anthony Eden had described Finland's international position succinctly when he called Finland "the road to nowhere" when compared with the Eastern European nations which were "the road to somewhere else."[44] This was an apt description of Finland's international status. The small nation often received only scant attention from American policymakers. When Finland did come to the fore in deliberations, it was largely in relation to events transpiring elsewhere in the world.

Benefiting from this neglect, Paasikivi and Kekkonen seized the initiative to shape their country's foreign policy. They maintained a delicate balance between East and West. Despite a preference for closer relations with the West, they refrained from antagonizing their Soviet neighbor. They declined participation in the Marshall Plan and continued to promote trade with the Eastern bloc. Their effort succeeded not only because Finland was not a priority for U.S. policymakers, but also for a time because they could exploit Khrushchev's quest for peaceful coexistence, although, as the events of 1958 revealed, there were limits to Soviet tolerance.

The Eisenhower administration was sensitive to Finland's position, not only because Helsinki had "an absence of alternatives," but also because Finnish neutralism was devoid of anti-American sentiment. In fact, Finnish neutrality was advantageous. Whereas elsewhere the Soviets exploited neutral sympathies to further their own aims, in Finland they tended to discourage neutralism and promote "closer political and psychological affinity with the Soviet bloc."[45] Khrushchev's efforts, beginning in 1955, to portray Finnish neutralism as an element of peaceful coexistence were aberrations in the overall Soviet policy during the 1950s.

Finland's independent neutralism also benefited American global planning in other ways. Although a relatively unimportant nation, its geographic location in the Nordic region complemented European defense needs. A delicate balance evolved after Denmark and particularly Norway joined NATO. Finland and Sweden, neutrals tilting toward the West, stood as buffers, easing somewhat Soviet apprehension at having NATO members so near its border. A reciprocal relationship also developed whereby the continued neutrality of Sweden and Finland depended on and reinforced each other.[46]

Finally, Finland's relationship with the USSR both addressed Soviet security needs and was acceptable to the United States. In fact, to John Foster Dulles and other American policymakers, this Finnish solution was a model that might be emulated in the Eastern European nations along the Soviet border. To "Finlandize" Eastern Europe might defuse this major area of Cold War tensions. Even if this proved unfeasible, at least to have raised the Finnish solution as an alternative would be a propaganda advantage for Washington over Moscow.

In his recent work examining U.S. relations with three nonaligned nations—India, Egypt, and Yugoslavia—H. W. Brands correctly describes American policy under Truman and Eisenhower as essentially flexible and insightful:

> American officials in the Truman and Eisenhower administrations often *spoke* in ideological terms. At a certain level of abstraction they *thought* ideologically. With some exceptions, however, they tended to *act* in a remarkably non-ideological fashion. Understanding what the political market in the United States would bear, they commonly packaged their policies in the wrappings of ideology; but the product they sold reflected primarily a geopolitical interpretation of American strategic, military, diplomatic, and economic interests, and it demonstrated a shrewd weighing of the effects on the international balance of power of the particular activities of specific nonaligned powers.[47]

True, Brands's subjects are Third World nations. Of the three, only Yugoslavia lay within the immediate area of the European superpower blocs. But his characterization holds true in the case of Finland, although Brands underestimates the importance of the ideological rivalry as a component of policymaking.

Finland was a more developed neutral situated precariously on the seam of the two blocs. Although administration actions were often realistic, based on strategic considerations, the ideological rivalry between communism and the capitalist, democratic ideology of the West certainly played a role in shaping American policy. Concerns about communism went beyond political rhetoric; they were an integral part of policy deliberations as well. Seldom was a clear distinction made between the threat emanating from Soviet national power and that from Communist ideology. During a July 1956 meeting of the National Security Council, for example, Vice-President Richard Nixon moved from commenting on the neutral stance of Indian Prime Minister Jawaharlal Nehru to imparting advice on how the United States should confront neutral nations in general. He warned against courting neutrals to the point of "glossing over the difference between the *Communist world* [emphasis added] and the free world." These remarks, in a closed NSC meeting, not in a public forum, mixed the strategic with the ideological components of the Soviet-American rivalry.[48] In another example, Ambassador Hickerson, speaking at a September 1957 conference of Northern European Chiefs of Mission, derided the Finns for regarding "the Russian people rather than Communism as the real menace," suggesting that communism was critical to the equation and that the Finns were naive to discount it.[49] Ideological anxieties were not solely for domestic political consumption. Nevertheless, circumstances in the 1950s dictated that America's response in the case of Finland be measured and cautious, supportive of Finland's neutral, independent course. Even though the Eisenhower administration suspected Soviet intentions, it saw clearly that a flexible policy would best promote American national security interests.

CHAPTER 11

The Unwanted Alliance

Portugal and the United States

J. K. SWEENEY

The Luso-American alliance began as an unlikely juxtaposition of a capitalist democracy inclined by tradition to oppose colonialism and a corporatist autocracy determined to retain the last remnants of a once great empire. It was unnatural in its composition and unwanted by either party. But, as in any marriage of convenience, although neither party sought the union, further considerations merited its consummation and continuation. Yet, if the alliance was unwanted, the relationship between the two nations had its origin in America's earliest days. Lisbon was not only among the first to recognize the new republic on 15 February 1783, but Portugal was also in the first rank among those nations who received diplomatic envoys from the United States.[1] Moreover, Portugal was almost alone among the nations of Europe when it adopted a sympathetic attitude toward the Lincoln administration during the American Civil War.[2] But for a number of reasons, not the least of which were U.S. isolationism and the Portuguese alliance with Britain, contacts between the two nations remained sporadic and relations rather tenuous.[3]

A further complicating factor emerged in 1933 with the establishment of the New State—the authoritarian regime created by Antonio de Oliveira Salazar, whose view of the United States was colored by his belief that the nation was best characterized by Wall Street and California. He believed that the former was irretrievably infected by materialism and that the latter was a pool of immorality. Of course, Salazar was inclined to view most nations outside the Iberian peninsula with considerable skepticism.[4]

Portugal pursued a neutral course during the Second World War to safeguard its independence and national existence. Lisbon did not wish to risk the ignominy produced by its recourse to arms during the Great War. Thus, in 1939, Portugal sought the aura of desirability that an enigmatic neutrality might bring.[5] Such a policy required a delicate touch, to be sure, but it was one which national self-interest appeared to dictate. Nevertheless, Portugal was a small neutral power in a world that despised both small powers and neutrals, a fact of life made exceedingly clear in the months immediately after the fall of France. For one thing, numerous diplomatic posts and international broadcasts revealed that a significant number of Americans supported the preemptive seizure of the Azores. Articles and speeches bore witness to the increased likelihood that the United States might assert itself still further in the North Atlantic.[6] Hence, Lisbon was not altogether surprised when President Franklin Roosevelt informed a radio audience on 27 May 1941 that German control of any of the Atlantic islands imperiled the safety of the Western Hemisphere. Although Secretary of State Cordell Hull quickly disclaimed any aggressive intentions, he did insist that the right of self-defense could involve the occupation of foreign soil.[7] Consequently, Portuguese neutrality faced its first challenge of the war.

It was well that Secretary Hull spoke of an expanded right of self-defense, for plans were soon under development for U.S. occupation of the Azores.[8] President Roosevelt, however, lost interest in the project until his August 1941 meeting with the British prime minister. At that time, Winston Churchill informed the president that the long-awaited German movement against Gibraltar was at hand. The British government was so certain of Gibraltar's fall that it expected to relocate its garrison to the Spanish Canary Islands in September. Churchill asked that the United States secure the Azores until British troops could be spared from the occupation of the Canaries. Roosevelt agreed to the proposal, "no matter what the circumstances requiring it."[9] The German assault on Gibraltar failed to materialize, but Portugal was soon presented with another threat.

The maritime blockade was a traditional mainstay of Britain's approach to war and one of its most effective weapons.[10] Economic warfare, however, requires considerable subtlety and constant adjustment on the part of the blockading power—largely, it must be noted, because any alteration in the conditions of international commerce has the potential to add to the ranks of the enemy. Those states waging economic warfare need to take care, therefore, to ensure that neutral states are not compelled to make too stark an economic choice between the coalitions in conflict. Thus, the British government permitted neutral nations to engage in their normal commercial pursuits, even with Germany, so long as that trade did not exceed prewar levels.

Still, some commodities were of such importance that their export to Axis powers in any quantity was considered dangerous by the British. Unfortunately, many such items were frequently of significant value to the economic health of a particular neutral state. In such cases, the British frequently chose to purchase the materials themselves, thereby denying them to the enemy. As a source of tungsten, wolfram was definitely of strategic value and thus a strong candidate for preemptive purchase. Not surprisingly, inasmuch as the major European supply of the mineral was located in Portugal, Lisbon sought to obtain the maximum benefit from its position as a single-source supplier.[11]

The British were less than pleased by Lisbon's efforts to profit from such wartime exigencies, but they could not see any practical alternative beyond acceptance of the status quo. However, London's unwillingness to challenge the Portuguese over wolfram did not find favor with Washington. The Americans insisted that those neutrals who were more concerned with profits than an end to the war deserved neither sympathy nor consideration.[12] As the war in Europe became more of an American affair, and Washington became less willing to follow the British lead, the Portuguese position on the export of wolfram came under serious attack. Moreover, the issue was not just wolfram exports—Portugal's neutrality was imperiled on two fronts.

Although momentarily eclipsed by Germany's invasion of the Soviet Union and the war in North Africa, the Azores retained their strategic importance. Indeed, Anglo-American planners were soon to aver that an Allied facility in the Azores was crucial to success in the Battle of the Atlantic. Allied aircraft deployed to the islands would also provide additional security once the invasion of German-occupied Europe began.[13] As a result, the British sought naval and air facilities in the Azores. London was confident that it would be "possible to secure Portuguese assent to the use of the bases obtained by the forces of the other" Allies.[14] Unfortunately, the privileges acquired by the British were narrowly defined. This development heightened the U.S. desire to pursue an independent course toward Portugal. By the end of 1943, Washington was committed to a stronger stand on wolfram and the establishment of a separate and equal American presence in the Azores.[15]

But an American air base in the Azores necessitated a diplomatic umbrella to shelter the Portuguese from a seemingly inevitable German wrath. With the Allied campaign in Italy in a stalemate and the strategic bombing campaign little more than a modest success, Salazar would require a compelling reason to move further off the diplomatic fence. Any attempt to persuade Salazar to modify his position on wolfram exports would inevitably focus his attention on the specter of German planes bombing Portuguese cities or sinking Portuguese ships.[16] A Luso-American connection would also be difficult to arrange until both parties were convinced they had the upper hand. Each country would seek to present any concession granted as nothing more than a favor for value received. Furthermore, at least in Portuguese eyes, any concession must be so hedged about with restrictions as to offer scant opportunity for future diplomatic leverage.

Fortunately for the Americans, a bargaining tool existed in the Portuguese colony of East Timor. Japanese forces occupied East Timor in the early months of 1942 as part of their drive on Australia. The Lisbon government protested this action, but the Japanese remained. Salazar was believed to favor the Portuguese liberation of East Timor to ensure that the island returned to Portugal after the war. It seemed reasonable to expect, therefore, that an equitable exchange of favors was in order: the United States would provide the logistical support necessary for Portugal to liberate Timor, and Lisbon would authorize an American air base in the Azores.[17]

Once the negotiations over an Azores base began, the Roosevelt administration pursued a twofold path. The first objective was to obtain permission to begin construction on the island of Santa Maria. If the Portuguese agreed, the completion of the air base would thereby coincide with the conclusion of a diplomatic agreement regarding its use. At the same time, American policymakers sought to fashion an agreement that would allow the establishment of a facility in the Azores with a minimal obligation to support the Portuguese liberation of Timor.

From the outset it was clear that open access to the Azores would not be easy to acquire. Salazar was willing to allow the Americans expanded use of the British facility. He was even amenable to the construction of an airfield, ostensibly for the Portuguese government, which might be assigned to the United States at some point in the indefinite future.[18] However, Salazar also sought to inextricably intertwine the Azores negotiations with the talks about wolfram exports to Germany. It was patently obvious that Salazar preferred to avoid an immediate commitment on either issue by holding a decision on each as hostage to the other. Thus, the American desire for a base in the Azores would insulate Portugal from retaliation for procrastination over ending wolfram shipments to Germany. The Americans would be unwilling to press the British to take a hard line in the wolfram talks lest it jeopardize the acquisition of facilities in the Azores.[19]

Salazar wanted East Timor liberated, and he clearly recognized the controlling influence of the United States in the Pacific theater. Nevertheless, despite some improvement in the Allied military posture, he remained cautious. A declaration of Portuguese belligerency not only risked a German response, it might lead the Japanese to occupy Macao. If Macao were seized, the Chinese would most probably assert their right to liberate the city. The Portuguese had no illusions about the willingness of a postwar Chinese government to return territory obtained from the Ming Dynasty in 1557 by virtue of a disputed lease.[20]

In the minds of most Portuguese, the empire was vital to the nation's existence as a sovereign state. Without the empire, Portugal was little more than a hodgepodge of ethnological remnants strung along a coastal plain. For this reason, the Portuguese were almost pathologically suspicious concerning the empire, and national dismay was the result when even a rumor of foreign annexation was afoot.[21] If Salazar could arrange the liberation of East Timor, and safeguard Macao in the bargain, the consequent prestige would provide valuable assistance to his regime in postwar political battles.

Of course, the American negotiators did not wish to play their final card too quickly, and the Portuguese were determined to extract the best bargain possible. Thus, Washington continued to press the argument that the greatest contribution Portugal could make toward the liberation of Timor would be the construction of an airfield for American use. The actual liberation of Timor, with Portugal's participation, must take second place to that end. Meanwhile, Salazar reminded Roosevelt that the parameters of neutrality were quite narrow. Further, the Portuguese remained unrelenting in their efforts to tie any agreement over the Azores to the continuing wolfram negotiations. Despite considerable pressure from Washington, therefore, Portugal refused to accede to the American request.[22] Instead, Roosevelt was informed that the development of a base in the Azores hinged on the grant of economic benefits equal to those the British government offered Portugal as a condition of their access to the Azores.[23]

Lisbon obviously thought its request reasonable. After all, Salazar still viewed a visible U.S. presence in the Azores as placing Portugal's security at substantial risk. Lisbon was quite astonished when the Americans reacted to the proposal with total outrage. Portugal was informed that it faced a complete curtailment of all economic aid unless it ceased haggling forthwith. Salazar was put on notice that insofar as the U.S. government was concerned, Portuguese feelings "were of secondary importance" with regard to the Azores. It was at this point that Salazar decided upon a tactical retreat.[24]

Once agreement was finally reached concerning Portugal's Southeast Asian colony, the United States was offered control of an air base within the territory of a formerly neutral nation. The American reluctance to make firm commitments regarding Timor involved a great deal more than pique over past Portuguese diplomatic challenges. The proposed agreement concerning East Timor would commit U.S. policymakers to a military operation which was, at that stage of the Pacific campaign, quite unnecessary.

Furthermore, once operational plans for the liberation of the colony were developed, the Portuguese might well insist on their implementation. The War Department would then face logistical demands in support of an activity which would hamper, rather than contribute to, the defeat of Japan.

For their part, the Portuguese were equally adamant that planning go forward for the liberation of Timor and the operation itself be viewed as anything but pro forma. The Portuguese confessed they were profoundly disinterested in whether such plans were implemented, announcing that it was unlikely the United States would be involved in the liberation of Timor; but protocol must be observed. Quite obviously, the form and the symbols of alliance were more important than the substance. Ultimately, Lisbon gave way on the first point of contention, the question of operations, and the United States conceded the second, the question of plans. Certain other minor issues remained to be resolved, but Portugal was bereft of further significant reasons for delay. On 28 November 1944, the necessary documents were exchanged in Lisbon, and the United States and Portugal were well beyond the courtship stage.[25]

In this encounter, the United States reaped greater rewards from Portugal than did the British—despite the benefits afforded the latter by their ancient alliance. Britain was required to undertake extensive commitments and furnish substantial aid, whereas America was able to construct an extensive facility on the basis of a nebulous promise to be redeemed in an uncertain future. Admittedly, a considerable U.S. investment was lost after the war when the Portuguese required the use of the older facility on Terceira rather than the base on Santa Maria. Moreover, the U.S. air base intended for use prior to the invasion of Europe was not completed until well after D-Day.[26] Still, if the war in the Pacific had lasted, as anticipated, into 1946, the deployment of forces from the European theater would have justified the expense of constructing the Santa Maria facility.

The path of the neutral in time of war is not an easy one. Those nations which find themselves expending lives and treasure are inclined to view noncombatants with a jaundiced eye. It is quite likely that most Americans in the course of World War II judged neutrals to be, at best, enemy sympathizers and most probably traitors to the human community.[27] Portugal suffered an additional onus in that it was commonly lumped with Spain as a Fascist state. The degree of Portugal's commitment to fascism was, of course, somewhat suspect. Salazar, along with Eamon De Valera of Ireland, found much that was attractive in the Corporatist philosophy that emerged between the two world wars. Still, for all its superficial similarities, corporatism was not, and is not, fascism.[28]

Whether Portugal was a Fascist state was, however, quite irrelevant. Spain would most assuredly face punishment for its prewar associations and its wartime decisions; and, so long as it was sympathetic to the government of Francisco Franco, the Salazar regime would be caught in the fallout. The domestic opponents of Salazar were confident that an international campaign in support of a new government in Portugal would definitely be a feature of the postwar world. Opposition leaders could not conceive that a world so critical of Spain would not wish to support political reform in Portugal.[29] They took heart from the United Nation's refusal to entertain Portugal's application for membership. But all attempts by anti-Salazar forces to secure anything other than informal support from the United States foundered on the rock of aviation technology.

So long as the ability of military aircraft to cross the Atlantic remained limited, the Azores were crucial to the defense of the United States.[30] Although some few of those responsible for the drafting of the North Atlantic Treaty might have wished to exclude Lisbon from participation in the new alliance, such a decision was inconceivable.[31] While Portugal might be perceived as ideologically affiliated with international pariahs such as Spain and Argentina, the fortunes of geography and the historical accident of maritime exploration combined to render Portugal relatively immune to serious criticism.[32] American policymakers even encouraged Lisbon to continue its application for admission to the United Nations.[33]

The Luso-American alliance was based on several instruments. The Santa Maria and Timor agreements, as well as the Air Transport Agreement of 1945, laid the foundation. The North Atlantic Treaty and the Azores Treaty of 1951 further codified the Luso-American connection by creating a permanent U.S. presence in the Azores.[34] The 1951 treaty was unique in that it did not involve an annual rent paid to the host country. Rather, the United States agreed to furnish military aid sufficient to allow Portugal to satisfy its obligations under the Atlantic Alliance. The Portuguese used the Azores as a bargaining chip to gain entry into NATO and then persuaded the United States to supply the necessary equipment/training so that Portugal might appear to be a credible member of the alliance.

Lisbon viewed the Luso-American connection as a limited partnership at best. Portugal would deal with the United States as a theoretical equal, and any concessions granted would be on a strictly quid pro quo basis. But Lisbon would make every effort to ensure that the Portuguese quid would far exceed the American quo. Salazar perceived the Luso-American connection as a shield against the vicissitudes of the Cold War. If forced to choose between the United States and the Soviet Union, Portugal would select the former. Nevertheless, Portugal would prefer to defer the decision and eschew any connection beyond that demanded by "immediate and practical urgency."[35] Salazar remained suspicious of the benefits to be gained from irrevocable commitments to one Cold War camp in an increasingly interdependent world. Indeed, his initial response to the plan for European economic cooperation proposed by Secretary of State George Marshall was to offer unilateral aid to those European countries devastated by the war.[36]

Thus, the Truman administration's avowed policy of encouraging Portuguese participation in the integration of Western Europe and assisting Lisbon's development of its African colonies was largely thwarted. Even so, the Azores were of such importance that all other aspects of American policy must proceed "along lines best calculated to serve our interest in the undisturbed development of this [U.S.-Portuguese] relationship."[37] Unfortunately, this pattern of diplomacy allowed the Portuguese to secure an important favor.

American policymakers preferred to see themselves as espousing the cause of anticolonialism. As postwar movements for self-determination gathered steam, this historic American position was a potentially valuable foreign policy tool. Nonetheless, in the years after the Second World War, the nation's anticolonial posture was often more rhetorical than real. The anticolonial impulse was perforce circumscribed by the apparent demands of the emerging Cold War. Anticolonialism proved to be a device whose utility was limited by the degree to which Washington found it necessary to rely on imperial nations for assistance in its struggle to contain the Soviet Union.[38]

Therefore, the 1951 agreement with Portugal included an exchange of letters whereby the United States promised it would not object if arms supplied to defend metropolitan Portugal were transferred to a Portuguese colony.[39] The Department of State, motivated by an equal mixture of conviction and diplomatic calculation, continued to mouth fervent phrases of support for those who would lift the yoke of colonialism. But the American position was consistently undermined by its diplomatic cooperation with an imperial nation exceptional in its unregenerate attitude. Needless to say, those people in the midst of nationalist struggles saw no reason to view the United States as an ally.[40] This attitude did not change through the 1950s, as Washington and Lisbon remained locked in their Cold War embrace.

The administration of the first president born in the twentieth century appeared to offer unparalleled opportunities to explore new diplomatic initiatives. Indeed, the administration of John F. Kennedy did inaugurate a substantive shift in the American stance on colonial activities in Africa: the Mozambican Liberation Movement (FRELIMO) and the National Liberation Front of Angola (FNLA) found themselves in receipt of American aid; in the UN Security Council, the United States publicly attacked Portuguese colonial activities; and Congress enacted an arms embargo against Portugal in response to international criticism of Lisbon's African polices. Each of the foregoing actions was probably related to a perception, shared even within the Portuguese army, that FRELIMO and the FNLA were gaining strength. But that opinion was not shared by the one person most able to effect a change in Portugal's African policy.[41]

Antonio Salazar remained obdurate on the matter of Portugal's empire. Indeed, the successive challenges to Portuguese sovereignty led Salazar to undertake a stubborn effort to shore up his nation's colonial claims. He began by refusing to negotiate a renewal of the 1957 Supplementary Defense Agreement defining U.S. rights to facilities in the Azores. In order to demonstrate the extent of his displeasure, Salazar waited until 30 December (the agreement was scheduled to end on 31 December) before agreeing to extend the American presence in the Azores until 1 January 1964. The Portuguese government also mobilized the usual suspects to remind President Kennedy that the islands had lost none of their strategic importance in the last decade.[42]

The entire affair was definitely a learning experience for the new president. Afterward, John Kennedy determined that the expedient course of action was twofold. The United States would quietly support the anticolonial activities of certain nationalist groups in Portugal's African colonies as well as attempt to persuade Lisbon to implement "basic . . . reforms in Portuguese colonial policy." Such activities, however, would be conducted in such a manner as to "minimize the possibility of losing the Azores" and thus avoid the "grave military consequences which would attend such a loss."[43] The Johnson administration continued this cautious policy with respect to Portugal's African colonies, most especially when the war in Vietnam became the lodestone of American foreign policy.[44]

During the Cold War, not a few Americans questioned the need to concern themselves with the fate of Portugal or the future of her colonial empire when the whole of Western civilization was presumably at stake. A nation thoroughly convinced of the overweening importance of its own interests found it difficult to recognize the needs of another, or attempt to understand the complexities of others' internal political situations.[45] But Portugal's geostrategic importance allowed Lisbon to extract significant concessions from the United States. The Portuguese were also able to induce their ally to assist in the continuing maintenance of the empire. This commitment exposed Washington to critical commentary which, in the course of time, diminished the credibility of the nation's opposition to colonialism.[46]

Still, the United States continued its policy of forbearance, save for a brief contretemps during the Yom Kippur War. In early October 1973, in view of the enormous equipment losses suffered by the Israeli Defense Force, the Nixon administration initiated an emergency resupply operation via the Azores. The Portuguese government promptly suggested that the use of a NATO facility for non-NATO activity warranted additional treaty concessions. The American response was uncharacteristically short. The secretary of state refused to consider Portugal's suggestion. Furthermore, Henry Kissinger indicated the United States would adopt a more rigorous and demanding stance with respect to Portugal's colonial policies in Africa if Lisbon persisted. Portugal gave way. However, the Portuguese discovered, much to their surprise, that acceptance of the American ultimatum brought support from an unexpected quarter. Those American organizations supporting Israel added Portugal to their list of favored causes.[47] But before Lisbon could reap an immediate reward for an act of diplomatic necessity, a coup d'état installed a new government in Lisbon on 25 April 1974.[48]

Questions about the future of European colonialism and the need to confront an apparently aggressive Soviet Union posed an insuperable dilemma for the United States in the postwar decades. Precedent and ideological consistency mandated a national response that condemned colonialism in all its manifestations. Nonetheless, most influential policymakers believed that the dead hand of the past must not be allowed to endanger interallied relations or the security of potential overseas bases. As a result, the United States sought to balance contradictory goals by assuming a rhetorical anticolonial posture while underwriting the colonial aspirations of its European allies. This effort to split the difference between the dreams of indigenous peoples and the interests of colonial powers was extremely frustrating, but seemingly necessary.[49]

The Portuguese government installed in 1974 was inclined toward colonial disengagement. Yet, no sooner did Portugal, and its erstwhile ally, escape from one colonial morass than another imbroglio appeared. New developments bid fair to place Washington in an unenviable position between two parties—each of whom was deemed strategically crucial and deserving of special consideration. May 1974 saw the emergence of three political movements in East Timor, representing the plausible options facing the colony: union with Indonesia, continuation of colonial status, and independence. Independence was easily the most popular alternative, with the status quo and union with Indonesia a distant second and third. Despite Lisbon's reservations, the Portuguese governor was authorized to open negotiations with the contending factions. The talks were disrupted, however, when the party favoring union with Indonesia launched an armed rebellion. The ensuing civil war saw the defeat of the pro-Indonesian faction and the victory of the group seeking independence. On 28 November 1975 came the establishment of the Democratic Republic of East Timor.[50]

But the life of the new nation was of short duration. In the early hours of 7 December 1975, Indonesian armed forces invaded and drove what passed for a Timorese army into the hills. In July 1976, despite an international chorus of disapproval, East Timor was annexed by Indonesia.[51] Portugal and Indonesia were thus at odds, and each expected the United States to favor its cause. In this instance, the Azores finally met their match. Landing privileges were important, but the movement of submerged submarines was far more crucial.[52] Shipments of arms and other forms of aid to Indonesia continued unabated, and the American representative to the United Nations made his own contribution toward allowing that organization to place East Timor in diplomatic limbo.[53]

The United States did not suffer the public opprobrium in Portugal that attended the fall of authoritarian regimes in Greece and Spain. It was no secret that neither party to the Luso-American connection was especially pleased with the ideology or the actions of the other. In this way, the United States profited from Salazar's obvious disdain and was seldom viewed as a bulwark of the regime.[54] That Washington was the recipient of a significant reservoir of goodwill became readily apparent as a different Portugal emerged from the debris of the New State. Even so, the new Luso-American relationship was not without new difficulties.

Revolutions seldom pursue a straight path. They lurch from crisis to catastrophe as incremental reformers vie with cataclysmic reconstructionists for the allegiance of the moderate majority. But if the course of the Portuguese revolution was confused and uneven, the American response was equally tortuous and contradictory. As scenes of ideological discord passed across the Portuguese stage, Washington listened carefully for the sound of falling dominoes that would herald the emergence of a Communist state in southern Europe.[55]

Washington despaired of the possibility of a democratic denoue-ment in Portugal, and many of those party to the revolutionary process waited expectantly for an American-inspired counterrevo-lution. President Gerald Ford's assertion that the composition of Portugal's government precluded the nation's continued mem-bership in NATO sent shock waves through Lisbon. After all, the Nixon administration saw fit to overthrow the government of Salvador Allende for its political misdeeds, and the diplomatic connection between Chile and Washington was relatively minor. What would America do if faced with a major assault on the doc-trinal purity of the Atlantic Alliance at the very moment when the imminent demise of Francisco Franco jeopardized Spain's political orthodoxy?[56] Fortunately for Portugal, Richard Nixon and his peripatetic secretary of state were deeply involved with af-fairs Middle Eastern and Soviet; further, the Watergate dilemma diverted the president's attention, and some time passed before Gerald Ford firmly grasped the levers of presidential power. Then came the 25 November 1975 revolt of the moderates, and the days of the radical left in the Portuguese government were over.[57]

By 1979, with Lisbon clearly inclined toward an "anti-totali-tarian Atlantic" posture, the Carter administration requested an expansion of the Azores facilities as well as access to locations on the mainland—especially an air base in Beja then used by West Germany. This request produced an exchange of notes in Decem-ber 1983 (the Lajes Agreement) and another exchange in March 1984 (the GEODSS Agreement). Washington offered a significant increase in financial aid, while Lisbon agreed to prolong the Ameri-can presence in the Azores and provide access to sites on the mainland.[58] Neither nation was altogether pleased with the 1983 accord, which perhaps explains why, in American eyes at least, Portugal is anything but a loyal ally and steadfast friend. Portugal refused transit rights for Egyptian aircraft purchased from the United States in 1983 and joined with the other nations of the European Community to refuse overflight privileges when the Reagan administration sent aircraft to bomb Libya in 1986.[59]

The United States no longer takes Portugal for granted, and Portugal is no longer certain of the stability of its relationship with Washington. As a democratic nation freed from responsibil-ity for a colonial empire and a member of the European Commu-nity, Portugal is not the same country Henry Kissinger addressed with "unusual abruptness" in 1974. The American response to the Portuguese revolution was characterized as one of "oscillations, contradictions, uncertainties, unexplained shifts in policy, and . . . a lack of understanding."[60] That appraisal is, needless to say, all too true of the whole of the Luso-American experience since 1940, if not an accurate indictment of the American approach to the world. Nevertheless, although love was never a factor, honor was observed more in the breach, and obedience was foreign to both parties, the marriage of convenience between Portugal and the United States remains a touchstone of each nation's policy planning.

Notes

Works by Lawrence S. Kaplan are referred to by their abbreviated title only following the first full citation.

Introduction

1. *Akron Beacon Journal*, 2 March 1986.
2. Interview with Lawrence S. Kaplan, 8 October 1994, by Scott L. Bills and E. Timothy Smith. Unless otherwise indicated, all subsequent quotes come from this interview.
3. "This is Kent, Ohio," vertical file F.7.5.1., American History Research Center, Kent State University Archives, Kent, Ohio.
4. P. Scott Corbett to Scott L. Bills, 15 December 1994.
5. Kaplan was early on a supporter of the American effort in Vietnam, until, as he says, he came to study it more thoroughly. He also remarked, during the Bills/Smith interview, "If I were a student in the sixties . . . I would have been opposed to the war, I'm sure of it."
6. Peter Novick, *That Noble Dream: The "Objectivity Question" and the American Historical Profession* (Cambridge, Eng.: Cambridge University Press, 1988), 415, 417.
7. See John Lewis Gaddis, "The Emerging Post-Revisionist Synthesis on the Origins of the Cold War," *Diplomatic History* 7, no. 3 (Summer 1983): 171–90, and the responses that followed by Lloyd C. Gardner, Lawrence S. Kaplan, Warren F. Kimball, and Bruce R. Kuniholm. The original paper and responses were based on a session at the annual meeting of the Organization of American Historians, 8 April 1983. Kaplan

does regret one remark in particular: his assertion that, in effect, a group of historians who did not directly experience World War II and the emergence of the Cold War could not really understand the fear and volatility of the period (see ibid., 194). In his interview for this volume, he characterized the claim as a "a stupid thing to say because historians can't live through everything—how could we write [about] the past? But that's the mood I was in at that moment." The remark did draw the attention of Peter Novick in his *Noble Dream* (p. 452).

8. Kaplan was jokingly referring to Warren Kimball's remark, commenting on Gaddis's essay: "I would argue that postrevisionism is, at best, just what Gaddis fears we will call it, orthodoxy plus archives. Postrevisionism may serve to designate those histories that have been written recently and that avoid the kind of paranoiac name-calling of a decade ago, but they are still the same genus, if not species, as the realists—a geopolitical view of the Cold War in which the main philosophical content is little more than a vague but overarching pessimism about human nature and the use of force." See "Responses to John Lewis Gaddis," *Diplomatic History* 7, no. 3 (Summer 1983): 198–99.

1. Perspectives on the Early Republic

1. See Samuel F. Bemis, *Jay's Treaty: A Study in Commerce and Diplomacy* (New York: Macmillan, 1923), and his *John Quincy Adams and the Foundations of American Foreign Policy* (New York: Knopf, 1949).

2. Lawrence S. Kaplan, "The Philosophes and the American Revolution," *Social Science* 31 (January 1956): 31–36.

3. Idem, *Jefferson and France: An Essay on Politics and Political Ideas* (New Haven: Yale University Press, 1967).

4. For Kaplan's bibliographical insights, see his "The American Revolution in an International Perspective: Views from Bicentennial Symposia," *International History Review* 1 (July 1979): 408–26, and "The Treaty of Paris, 1783: A Historiographical Challenge," in ibid. 5 (August 1983): 431–42.

5. Lawrence S. Kaplan, *Entangling Alliances with None: American Foreign Policy in the Age of Jefferson* (Kent, Ohio: Kent State University Press, 1987), viii, xii.

6. Idem, *Colonies into Nation: American Diplomacy, 1763–1801* (New York: Macmillan, 1972).

7. See the following works by Max H. Savelle: "Colonial Origins of American Diplomatic Principles," *Pacific Historical Review* 3 (September 1934): 334–50; "The Appearance of an American Attitude toward External Affairs, 1750–1775," *American Historical Review* 52 (July 1947): 655–66; and *The Origins of American Diplomacy: The International History of Angloamerica 1492–1763* (New York: Macmillan, 1967).

8. *Colonies into Nation,* 10–11.

9. Ibid., xii.

10. Ibid., 111.

11. Kaplan, "The Founding Fathers and the Two Confederations: The United States and the United Provinces of the Netherlands, 1783–1789," in *Entangling Alliances with None,* 46–47. This essay was published originally as "The Founding Fathers and the Two Conferations: The U.S. of America and the United Provinces of

the Netherlands, 1783–89," in *A Bilateral Bicentennial: A History of Dutch-American Relations, 1782–1982*, ed. J. W. Schulte Nordholt and Robert P. Swierenga (Meulenhoff, Amsterdam: Octagon Books, 1982).

12. See idem, "The Treaties of Paris and Washington, 1778 and 1949: Reflections on Entangling Alliances," in *Diplomacy and Revolution: The Franco-American Alliance of 1778*, ed. Ronald Hoffman and Peter J. Albert (Charlottesville: University Press of Virginia, 1981), 154, 162.

13. Lawrence S. Kaplan, "Toward Isolationism: The Rise and Fall of the Franco-American Alliance, 1775–1801," in *The American Revolution and "A Candid World,"* ed. Kaplan (Kent, Ohio: Kent State University Press, 1977), 150. Part of this essay appeared as "Toward Isolationism: The Jefferson Republicans and the Franco-American Alliance of 1778," in *Historical Reflections/Reflexions Historiques* 3 (Summer 1976): 69–81.

14. *American Revolution*, 145, 146.

15. See, for example, Lawrence S. Kaplan, "Reflections on Jefferson as Francophile," in the *South Atlantic Quarterly* 79 (January 1980): 38–50; reprinted in *Entangling Alliances with None*, 24–34.

16. *Jefferson and France*, 9.

17. Kaplan, "Jefferson as Francophile," in *Entangling Alliances With None*, 34.

18. *Jefferson and France*, 14.

19. Kaplan, "Consensus of 1789: Jefferson and Hamilton on American Foreign Policy," in *Entangling Alliances with None*, 77, published originally in the *South Atlantic Quarterly* 71 (January 1972): 91–106.

20. Lawrence S. Kaplan, "The Neocolonial Impulse: The United States and Great Britain, 1783–1823," in Morrell Heald and Lawrence S. Kaplan, *Culture and Diplomacy: The American Experience* (Westport, Conn.: Greenwood, 1977), 54.

21. "Consensus of 1789," 73.

22. *Jefferson and France*, 36, 73.

23. "Toward Isolationism," 69–81.

24. *Colonies into Nation*, 219.

25. Ibid., 219, 251.

26. Ibid., 247; "Toward Isolationism," 152.

27. "Treaties of Paris and Washington," 176.

28. Lawrence S. Kaplan, "Thomas Jefferson: The Idealist as Realist" in *Makers of American Diplomacy*, ed. Frank J. Merli and Theodore A. Wilson, 2 vols. (New York: Scribner's, 1974), 1:59.

29. Idem, "Jefferson and the Constitution: The View from Paris, 1786–1789," *Diplomatic History* 2 (Fall 1987): 323.

30. Ibid., 326.

31. "Neocolonial Impulse," 57; Kaplan, "Jefferson, the Napoleonic Wars and the Balance of Power," in *Entangling Alliances with None*, 114. The "Jefferson, Napoleonic Wars" essay was published originally in *William and Mary Quarterly* 15 (April 1957): 196–218.

32. Kaplan, "France and Madison's Decision for War, 1812," in *Entangling Alliances with None*, 128, published originally in the *Mississippi Valley Historical Review* 50 (March 1964): 652–71.

33. Kaplan, "Jefferson's Foreign Policy and Napoleon's Ideologues," in *Entangling Alliances with None*, 100, published originally in *William and Mary Quarterly* 19 (July 1962): 344–59.

34. "Jefferson and Balance of Power," 117.

35. "Jefferson: Idealist as Realist," 57; Louis M. Sears, *Jefferson and the Embargo* (Durham, N.C.: Duke University Press, 1927).

36. Kaplan, "France and the War of 1812," in *Entangling Alliances with None*, 245, 151, published originally in *Journal of American History* 57 (June 1970): 36–47.

37. "Decision for War," 140–41.

38. "Jefferson and Balance of Power," 121.

39. Lawrence S. Kaplan, "Jefferson as Anglophile: Sagacity or Senility in the Era of Good Feelings?" *Diplomatic History* 16 (Summer 1992): 493.

40. See the following works by Kaplan: *Jefferson and France*, 141; "Jefferson and Balance of Power" (p. 123), and "The Paris Mission of William Harris Crawford, 1813–1815" (p. 152), both in *Entangling Alliances with None*. The latter essay was originally published in the *Georgia Historical Quarterly* 60 (Spring 1976): 9–23.

41. Kaplan, "The Independence of Latin America: North American Ambivalence, 1800–1820," in *Culture and Diplomacy*, 90, 70.

42. "Jefferson: Idealist as Realist," 53.

2. NATO and the United States:
An Essay in Kaplanesque History

1. See, for instance, the following works by Lawrence S. Kaplan: "The Cold War and European Revisionism," *Diplomatic History* 11 (Spring 1987): 143–56; "L'impact de Spoutnik sur la politique extérieure américaine" [The impact of Sputnik on American foreign policy], *Relations Internationales* 71 (Autumn 1992): 327–38; and the translations of several conference papers.

2. For example, "The United States and the Origins of NATO, 1946–1949," *Review of Politics* 31 (April 1969): 210–22, is included in "The United States and the Atlantic Alliance: The First Generation," in *Twentieth-Century American Foreign Policy*, ed. John Braeman, Robert H. Bremner, and David Brody (Columbus: Ohio State University Press, 1971), 294–342.

3. For instance, Lawrence S. Kaplan's "NATO and Its Commentators: The First Five Years," *International Organization* 8 (November 1954): 447–67; "The Korean War and U.S. Foreign Relations: The Case of NATO," in *The Korean War: A 25-Year Perspective*, ed. Francis H. Heller (Lawrence: Regents Press of Kansas, 1977), 36–75; "Isolationism, the United Nations, and the Cold War," chap. 9 in Morrell Heald and Lawrence S. Kaplan, *Culture and Diplomacy: The American Experience* (Westport, Conn.: Greenwood, 1977), 215–41; "Toward the Brussels Pact," *Prologue* 12 (Summer 1980): 73–86; and "The Treaties of Paris and Washington, 1778 and 1949," in *Diplomacy and Revolution*, ed. Ronald Hoffman and Peter J. Albert (Charlottesville: University Press of Virginia, 1981), 151–94, are all included in *The United States and NATO: The Formative Years* (Lexington: University Press of Kentucky, 1984).

4. Four, to be precise: *NATO After Thirty Years*, ed. Lawrence S. Kaplan and Robert W. Clawson (Wilmington, Del.: Scholarly Resources, 1981); *NATO and the Medi-*

terranean, ed. Lawrence S. Kaplan, Robert W. Clawson, and Raimondo Luraghi (Wilmington, Del.: Scholarly Resources, 1984); *Dien Bien Phu and the Crisis of Franco-American Relations, 1954–1955,* ed. Lawrence S. Kaplan, Denise Artaud, and Mark R. Rubin (Wilmington, Del.: Scholarly Resources, 1990); and *NATO After Forty Years,* ed. Lawrence S. Kaplan et al. (Wilmington, Del.: Scholarly Resources, 1990).

5. The encyclopedic entry is another manifestation of Kaplan's stature as America's preeminent NATO historian. "North Atlantic Treaty Organization," in *The Harry S. Truman Encyclopedia,* ed. Richard S. Kirkendall (Boston: G. K. Hall, 1989), 258–61.

6. "The Cold War and European Revisionism," 143.

7. Lawrence S. Kaplan, "After Twenty-Five Years: NATO as a Research Field," American Historical Association *Newsletter* 12 (November 1974): 6–7.

8. Idem, *A Community of Interests: NATO and the Military Assistance Program, 1948–1951* (Washington, D.C.: Historical Office, Office of the Secretary of Defense, 1980), 181.

9. See "Commentary on 'The Emerging Post-Revisionist Synthesis on the Origins of the Cold War,'" *Diplomatic History* 7 (Summer 1983): 194–97.

10. Cf. works by Kaplan: "NATO and its Commentators," 447; "NATO and the Language of Isolationism," *South Atlantic Quarterly* 57 (April 1958): 205; "The United States and the Atlantic Alliance," 301; and "The United States and the Origins of NATO, 1946–49," *Review of Politics* 31 (April 1969): 213.

11. Lawrence S. Kaplan, "Western Europe in 'The American Century': A Retrospective View," *Diplomatic History* 6 (Spring 1982): 113–15.

12. "The Korean War and U.S. Foreign Relations," 70.

13. Geir Lundestad, "Empire by Invitation? The United States and Western Europe, 1945–1952," SHAFR *Newsletter* 15 (September 1984): 1–21, and idem, "Empire by Invitation? The United States and Western Europe, 1945–1952," *Journal of Peace Research* 23 (September 1986): 263–77.

14. Lawrence S. Kaplan, *The End of the Alliance: Lessons of the 1960s* (Washington, D.C.: Woodrow Wilson International Center for Scholars, 1990), 3, 7, 17.

15. Cf. works by Kaplan: "NATO and its Commentators," 449–50, and "Collective Security and the Case of NATO," in *The Origins of NATO,* ed. Joseph Smith (Exeter, U.K.: University of Exeter Press, 1990), 101.

16. Lawrence S. Kaplan, "NATO after 33 Years: Records and Their Classification," SHAFR *Newsletter* 13 (December 1982): 9–10.

17. Cf. works by Kaplan: "Treaties of Paris and Washington"; "The Monroe Doctrine and the Truman Doctrine: The Case of Greece," *Journal of the Early American Republic* 13 (Spring 1993): 1–21; *The End of the Alliance,* and "The INF Treaty and the Future of NATO: Lessons from the 1960s," in *American Historians and the Atlantic Alliance,* ed. Lawrence S. Kaplan (Kent, Ohio: Kent State University Press, 1991), 135–53.

18. *A Community of Interests,* 169.

19. Cf. Warren F. Kuehl, Colin Gordon, Robert Spencer, and Martin I. Elzy in, respectively, *American Historical Review* 86 (1981): 816–17; *International Affairs* 57 (1981): 323–24; *Annals of the American Academy of Political Science* 458 (November 1981): 192–93; and *Journal of American History* 70 (June 1983): 196.

20. *The United States and NATO,* ix.

21. See Steven L. Rearden in *Journal of American History* 72 (September 1985): 453–54. Cf. also the reviews by Peter G. Boyle, Robert J. McMahon, Richard S. Kirkendall, and John Lewis Gaddis, respectively, in *History* 70 (October 1985): 475; *International History Review* 8 (August 1986): 446–48; *American Historical Review* 90 (December 1985): 1298; and *Pacific Historical Review* 55 (November 1986): 650–51.

22. For the importance of Western Union, see especially Lawrence S. Kaplan, "An Unequal Triad: The United States, Western Union, and NATO," in *Western Security, The Formative Years: European and Atlantic Defence, 1947–1953*, ed. Olav Riste (Oslo: Universitetsforlaget, 1985), 107–27; and idem, "Die Westunion und die militärische Integration Europas 1948–1950. Eine Darstellung aus amerikanischer Sicht" [Western Union and European military integration 1948–1950. An American perspective], in *Die westliche Sicherheitsgemeinschaft, 1948–1950: Gemeinsame Probleme und gegensätzliche Nationalinteressen in der Gründungs phase der Nordatlantische Allianz*, ed. Norbert Wiggershaus and Roland G. Foerster (Boppard am Rhein: Harald Boldt Verlag, 1988), 37–56.

23. Cees Wiebes and Bert Zeeman, "Het ontstaan van de NAVO" [The birth of NATO], *Intermediair* 21 (13 December 1985): 67–71.

24. In 1991, he added a sixth milestone: the INF Treaty of 1987. See *American Historians and the Atlantic Alliance*, 3.

25. Lawrence S. Kaplan, *NATO and the United States* (Boston: Twayne, 1988), 184. Cf. reviews by Jonathan M. Nielson and Hans L. Trefousse, respectively, in *International History Review* 11 (February 1989): 190–93, and *Journal of American History* 76 (June 1989): 312–13. For some comments on the revised edition of *NATO and the United States*, see section V of this essay.

26. "NATO and the Language of Isolationism," 204–15.

27. "The United States and the Origins of NATO," 211.

28. In a later contribution, Kaplan uses "nonentanglement" instead of "isolationism"; see "North Atlantic Treaty Organization," 258.

29. "The United States and the Origins of NATO," 220–21. Cf. "The Korean War and U.S. Foreign Relations," 68, in which Kaplan considers the Korean War the real watershed.

30. "Western Europe in 'The American Century,'" 112, 120.

31. Lawrence S. Kaplan, "NATO Retrospect," *Review of Politics* 23 (October 1961): 447–58.

32. "The United States and the Atlantic Alliance," 310–11. For Kaplan's later use of the phrases "a spindly bridge," "sluggish pace," "air of illusion," and "fragile," see "The Korean War and U.S. Foreign Relations," 47–49.

33. At a later stage, Kaplan added a fourth consequence of the Korean War: a "massive increase in military assistance"; see "North Atlantic Treaty Organization," 260.

34. "The Korean War and U.S. Foreign Relations," 60.

35. Ibid., 58. See also "The United States and the Atlantic Alliance," 320. The theme of cunning Europeans (in this case, the French) manipulating well-intentioned and credulous Americans returns later in Kaplan's career when he evaluates the precursor of NATO, the Western Union (concluded by Britain, France, and the Benelux countries on 17 March 1948). In his opinion, the Western Union was "an elaborate device to entangle the United States," a successful ploy to manipulate the Truman

administration into accepting the Atlantic alliance. In his efforts to gratify the Old World, however, Kaplan overlooks serious differences of agreement between the Western Union countries themselves as to the need for an alliance with the United States and possible alternatives. Although the conclusion of "an elaborate device" may hold ground for the British and Dutch governments, as far as the French and Belgians were concerned Western Europe was in need of armaments and emergency planning instead of paper guarantees. See Cees Wiebes and Bert Zeeman, "Belgium, the Netherlands and Alliances, 1940–1949" (Ph.D. diss., Leyden University, 1993).

36. "NATO Retrospect," 450–51.

37. Lawrence S. Kaplan, "NATO After 20 Years—an American Perspective," *NATO Letter* 18 (June 1970): 14–18, and "The United States and the Atlantic Alliance," 342.

38. "The United States and the Origins of NATO," 210.

39. Lawrence S. Kaplan, "NATO and the Nixon Doctrine: Ten Years Later," *Orbis* 24 (Spring 1980): 149–64, and idem, "NATO: The Second Generation," in *NATO After Thirty Years*, 3.

40. *NATO After Thirty Years*, 4.

41. "NATO and the Nixon Doctrine Ten Years Later," 159.

42. Ibid., 164; see also "NATO: The Second Generation," 27–29.

43. "NATO and its Commentators," 455.

44. *American Historians and the Atlantic Alliance*, 8.

45. Lawrence S. Kaplan, *NATO and the United States: The Enduring Alliance* (Boston: Twayne, 1994), 162–84.

3. Diplomacy without Armaments, 1945–1950

1. Robert H. Ferrell, *Choosing Truman: The Chicago Convention of 1944* (Columbia: University of Missouri Press, 1994).

2. Walker diary, 15 April 1945, Walker Papers, Hesburgh Library, University of Notre Dame, South Bend, Ind.

3. Stettinius: "Mr. President, do you really believe that you can do this thing and put Byrnes in without its appearing publicly like a kick in the pants for me?" President Truman: "I sincerely believe it can be done that way." Stettinius diary, 25 June 1945, "Calendar Notes . . . ," Box 245, Stettinius Papers, University of Virginia Library, Charlottesville.

4. Robert L. Messer, *The End of an Alliance: James F. Byrnes, Roosevelt, Truman, and the Origins of the Cold War* (Chapel Hill: University of North Carolina Press, 1982), 53–64.

5. Omar N. Bradley and Clay Blair, *A General's Life: An Autobiography* (New York: Simon & Schuster, 1983), 474.

6. Ibid., 474.

7. Tang Tsou, "Civil Strife and Armed Intervention: Marshall's China Policy," *Orbis* 6 (1962): 89–90.

8. David A. Rosenberg, "U.S. Nuclear Stockpile 1945 to 1950," *Bulletin of the Atomic Scientists*, May 1982, 27–29.

9. Robert H. Ferrell, ed., *Truman in the White House: The Diary of Eben A. Ayers* (Columbia: University of Missouri Press, 1991), 161, entry of 14 October 1946; Ferrell,

ed., "A Visit to the White House, 1947: The Diary of Vic H. Housholder," *Missouri Historical Review* 78, no. 3 (April 1984): 329; Gregg Herken, *The Winning Weapon: The Atomic Bomb in the Cold War, 1945–1950* (New York: Knopf, 1980), 196–97.

10. Samuel R. Williamson, Jr., and Steven L. Rearden, *The Origins of U.S. Nuclear Strategy: 1945–1953* (New York: St. Martin's, 1993), 125. The purpose of Soviet investigation of radar jamming could also have been to confuse SAC's targeting that was based on synthetic radar images. Rearden to the author, 27 September 1993.

11. Harry R. Borowski, *A Hollow Threat: Strategic Air Power and Containment before Korea* (Westport, Conn.: Greenwood, 1982).

12. Verne W. Newton, *The Cambridge Spies: The Untold Story of Maclean, Philby, and Burgess in America* (Lanham, Md.: Madison Books, 1991).

4. "Answering the Call":
The First Inaugural Addresses of Thomas Jefferson
and William Jefferson Clinton

The author wishes to thank Harry W. Fritz, William W. Weeks, and—as always—Lawrence S. Kaplan for helpful comments on a draft of this essay.

1. *Daily Progress* (Charlottesville, Va.), 18 January 1993, A-1.

2. "American Renewal: We Must Care for One Another," 20 January 1993, *Vital Speeches of the Day* 59 (15 February 1993): 258–59. All quotations from Clinton, unless noted otherwise, are from this text.

3. *Daily Progress,* 18 January 1993, A-6.

4. "Let us resolve to make our Government a place for what Franklin Roosevelt called bold, persistent experimentation, a Government for our tomorrows, not our yesterdays."

5. Philip Hamburger, "The Inauguration," *New Yorker,* 8 February 1993, 76.

6. Marshall Ingwerson, "Clinton Posts Renewal as Theme for Presidency," *Christian Science Monitor,* 22 January 1993, A-1.

7. Ibid., A4. Ingwerson credits the "jeremiad" comparison to Professor Craig Allen Smith. See Smith, "The Jeremiadic Logic of Bill Clinton's Policy Speeches" in Stephen A. Smith, ed., *Bill Clinton on Stump, Style, and Stage: The Rhetorical Road to the White House* (Fayetteville: University of Arkansas Press, 1994), 73–100.

8. Ibid. Dan Balz, writing for the *Washington Post,* suggested that Clinton's speech was also similar to George Bush's, especially Clinton's borrowing of the image of an "American Renewal"—the title of Bush's economic program. Balz, "A Recasting of Themes: Campaign Ideas Echo Succinctly in Speech," *Washington Post,* 21 January 1993.

9. "Two words—'at home'—out of a text of nearly fourteen hundred: that was the total treatment of domestic policy in John F. Kennedy's Inaugural Address." "Comment: Two Speeches," *New Yorker,* 1 February 1993, 5–6.

10. Jeffrey H. Birnbaum and Michael K. Frisby, "Asking His Generation to Accept Responsibility For Governing, Clinton Becomes 42nd President," *Wall Street Journal,* 21 January 1993.

11. Christopher Hitchens, "Minority Report: What I Saw at the Instauration," *Nation,* 15 February 1993, 186.

12. William Safire, "Inaugural Nitpicks," *New York Times Magazine*, 7 February 1993, 12.

13. "For the *CHRONICLE*, Old South—No. XXX. 'On President JEFFERSON'S Speech,'" *Independent Chronicle & Universal Advertiser* (Boston), 16–19 March 1801. See also "Political Miscellany. FOR THE CHRONICLE. The *SIGNS OF THE TIMES*— No. VI. *Addressed to the Men who call themselves FEDERALISTS*," ibid., 23–26 March 1801; and "Political Miscellany," 2–6 April 1801.

14. The *Columbian Sentinel/Massachusetts Federalist* (Boston) printed the address twice, on 14 and 18 March 1801. By way of contrast, the *Maryland Gazette* (Annapolis) did not print the first inaugural at all. The second inaugural appears, without comment, in the 14 March 1805 edition.

15. "The VISION OF HYPERION; *Taken from his own mouth, and published at the desire of his hearers*," Connecticut Courant (Hartford), 31 August 1801.

16. "*From the Commercial Advertiser*, No. 2. To the President of the United States," *Connecticut Courant*, 2 November 1801. See also "*Communication*. PRESIDENTIAL INFLUENCE," ibid., 19 October 1801.

17. Dumas Malone, *Thomas Jefferson and His Times*, 6 vols. (Boston: Little, Brown, 1948–81), 4:28, 17, 18.

18. Merrill Peterson, *Thomas Jefferson and the New Nation: A Biography* (New York: Oxford University Press, 1970), 655.

19. "Comment: Two Speeches," *New Yorker*, 1 February 1993, 6.

20. This term is borrowed from the classic account of "insider Washington," because in 1801 everyone lived in boarding houses. See James Sterling Young, *The Washington Community, 1800–1826* (New York: Harcourt, Brace and World, 1966).

21. "Thomas Jefferson: First Inaugural Address in Washington, D.C., Wednesday, March 4, 1801," *Inaugural Addresses of the Presidents of the United States from George Washington, 1789, to George Bush, 1989* (Washington, D.C.: GPO, 1989), 13–17. All quotations from Jefferson, unless noted otherwise, are from this text.

22. The *Connecticut Courant*, 9 November 1801, no. IV, demeaned this passage with the words: "If by that power you mean the Supreme God, I heartily unite with you, for we have great and pressing occasion for his assistance."

23. Merrill D. Peterson, ed., *The Portable Thomas Jefferson* (New York: Viking, 1975), 252.

24. William Peden, ed., *Notes on the State of Virginia* (Chapel Hill: University of North Carolina Press, 1954), 159. For a rebuttal, see *Connecticut Courant*, 9 November 1801, no. III.

25. It is interesting to note that Jefferson used a variation of this scripture, taken from 2 Thessalonians, in a letter to Edward Coles, 25 August 1814, in Andrew A. Lipscomb and Albert E. Bergh, eds., *The Writings of Thomas Jefferson*, 20 vols. (Washington, D.C.: Thomas Jefferson Memorial Association, 1903–5), 11:419–20.

26. In the words of Merrill Peterson, "Nine-tenths of the American people professed this creed, in Jefferson's opinion. . . . The old polarities of liberty and power, rights and duties, individual enterprise and national purpose, the state and the central governments—these were swept away as the new President identified the principles of the federal union with the principles of republican freedom." *Thomas Jefferson and the New Nation*, 656.

27. Jefferson to Spencer Roane, 6 September 1819, in Peterson, *Portable Thomas Jefferson*, 562.

28. "Draft of Instructions to the Virginia Delegates in the Continental Congress (MS Text of *A Summary View, &c*)," in Julian Boyd et al., eds., *The Papers of Thomas Jefferson*, 24 vols. to date (Princeton: Princeton University Press, 1950–), 1:122.

29. Peden, *Notes*, 164–65.

30. Ibid., 175; Drew McCoy, *The Elusive Republic: Political Economy in Jeffersonian America* (Chapel Hill: University of North Carolina Press, 1980), esp. chap. 8.

31. Lawrence S. Kaplan, *Colonies into Nation: American Diplomacy, 1763–1801* (New York: Macmillan, 1972), chap. 10.

32. Lawrence S. Kaplan, "Jefferson and the Constitution," *Diplomatic History* 11 (Fall 1987): 321–35. See also "Thomas Jefferson: The Idealist as Realist," in Kaplan's *Entangling Alliances with None* (Kent, Ohio: Kent State University Press, 1987), 3–23.

33. "Washington's Final Manuscript of the Farewell Address, Dated September 19, 1796," in Felix Gilbert, *To the Farewell Address: Ideas of Early American Foreign Policy* (Princeton: Princeton University Press, 1961), 145. See also Kaplan, "The Consensus of 1789: Jefferson and Hamilton on American Foreign Policy," in *Entangling Alliances*, 67–78.

34. "Draft Remarks of President-Elect Bill Clinton to the Diplomatic Corps, Georgetown University, January 18, 1993"; text provided by the White House.

35. Ibid. This reference to "human rights" is significantly different from President Jimmy Carter's use of that phrase. See Walter LaFeber, "From Confusion to Cold War: The Memoirs of the Carter Administration," *Diplomatic History* 8 (Winter 1984): 1–12.

36. "Draft Remarks of President-Elect Bill Clinton."

37. See especially N. Gordon Levin, Jr., *Woodrow Wilson and World Politics: America's Response to War and Revolution* (New York: Oxford University Press, 1968), and Lloyd E. Ambrosius, *Wilsonian Statecraft: Theory and Practice of Liberal Internationalism during World War I* (Wilmington, Del.: Scholarly Resources, 1991).

38. "An Enemy to Persecution," *Trenton Federalist*, 2 July 1801, as reprinted in the *Connecticut Courant*, 27 July 1801. See also *Columbian Sentinel/Massachusetts Federalist* (Boston), 5 and 29 August 1801. For a discussion of Jefferson's partisan removals, see Carl E. Prince, "The Passing of the Aristocracy: Jefferson's Removal of the Federalists, 1801–1805," *Journal of American History* 57 (December 1970): 563–75.

39. Fawn M. Brodie, *Thomas Jefferson: An Intimate History* (New York: W. W. Norton, 1974), 337. Garry Wills argues that Abraham Lincoln's "Gettysburg Address" accomplished what Jefferson's words envisioned; see his *Lincoln at Gettysburg: The Words that Remade America* (New York: Simon & Schuster, 1992).

40. Ronald L. Hatzenbuehler, "Thomas Jefferson," in William C. Spragens, ed., *Popular Images of American Presidents* (Westport, Conn.: Greenwood, 1988), 27–45.

41. "A Dawn of Promise," *New York Times*, 21 January 1993, p. A-24.

5. Internationalism and the Republican Era

The author wishes to acknowledge the research contribution made by the late Warren Kuehl. This chapter summarizes a portion of a fuller account, coauthored by Dunn and Kuehl, titled *Keeping the Covenant: American Internationalists and the League of Nations, 1920–1939*, forthcoming from the Kent State University Press.

1. "Hope Wilson Will Resubmit Treaty," *New York Times*, 4 November 1920.

2. William A. Williams, *The Tragedy of American Diplomacy* (New York: Dell, 1972); Joan Hoff-Wilson, *American Business & Foreign Policy, 1920–1933* (Lexington: University Press of Kentucky, 1971); Carl P. Parini, *Heir to Empire: United States Economic Diplomacy, 1916–1923* (Pittsburgh: University of Pittsburgh Press, 1969); Michael J. Hogan, *Informal Entente: The Private Structure of Cooperation in Anglo-American Diplomacy, 1918–1928* (Columbia: University of Missouri Press, 1977); Melvin P. Leffler, *The Elusive Quest: America's Pursuit of European Stability and French Security, 1919–1933* (Chapel Hill: University of North Carolina Press, 1979); Frank Costigliola, *Awkward Dominion: American Political, Economic, and Cultural Relations with Europe, 1919–1933* (Ithaca: Cornell University Press, 1984); Emily S. Rosenberg, *Spreading the American Dream: American Economic and Cultural Expansion, 1890–1945* (New York: Hill and Wang, 1982).

3. Warren F. Kuehl, *Seeking World Order: The United States and International Organization to 1920* (Nashville: Vanderbilt University Press, 1969); Charles Chatfield, *For Peace and Justice: Pacifism in America 1914–1941* (Knoxville: University of Tennessee Press, 1971); Sondra R. Herman, *Eleven Against War: Studies in American Internationalist Thought, 1898–1921* (Stanford: Hoover Institution Press, 1969); Charles DeBenedetti, *Origins of the Modern American Peace Movement, 1915–1929* (Millwood: KTO Press, 1978); Robert A. Divine, *Second Chance: The Triumph of Internationalism in America During World War II* (New York: Atheneum, 1967).

4. As historians approach a post-postrevisionist synthesis of the era, this marginalization is likely to intensify. By marginalization, I refer to the tendency of each group to ignore the work of the others. Revisionist historians write about those who supported a policy of increased economic internationalist activity, without reference to those who claimed the internationalist label and sought more than "independent internationalism." Equally, historians of internationalism refer to the opposition solely as isolationists. Although somewhat unwieldy, the term "post-postrevisionist" appears in Ernest May, ed., *American Cold War Strategy: Interpreting NSC 68* (New York: St. Martin's, 1993).

5. See, for example, "The Two Conventions," *New York Times*, 30 May 1920.

6. Definitions of opinion makers and the attentive public are provided by Melvin Small, who asserts that "there are several publics in the United States whose members shift from issue to issue. At the top of the apex of a pyramid that might represent all citizens are the opinion makers, a very small coterie of government officials, respected national leaders and celebrities, editors, and journalists. Below them is a group called the attentive public that might be as large as 25 percent on some issues. The well-educated and well-read people tend to pay attention to international politics and influence others around them"; see Small, "Public Opinion" in Michael J. Hogan and Thomas G. Paterson, eds., *Explaining the History of American Foreign Relations* (Cambridge, Eng.: Cambridge University Press, 1991), 165–76.

7. Morrell Heald and Lawrence S. Kaplan, *Culture and Diplomacy: The American Experience* (Westport, Conn.: Greenwood, 1977), ix.

8. Historians have recognized this diversity, analyzing the groups within a variety of categories. Warren Kuehl developed such labels as generalists, arbitrationists, legalists, federationists, world government supporters, and sanctionists to define the

groups. Other historians have marked the division between polity internationalists and community thinkers, or between internationalists and peace advocates. Kuehl, *Seeking World Order*, viii. For other divisions, see "Internationalists as a Current in the Peace Movement: A Symposium," in Charles Chatfield, ed., *Peace Movements in America* (New York: Schoken, 1973), 171-91.

9. This analysis is in near agreement with that advanced by Manfred Jonas, in that Jonas sees the denigration of nationalism, "at the very least a rejection of the idea of absolute national sovereignty" as key to any discussion of internationalism. However, whereas he asserts that there never was a community of American internationalists, but only those who supported a geographically expanded nationalism, this chapter posits that there was such a group but that they failed to address this basic issue. See Jonas, untitled contribution to "Internationalism as a Current in the Peace Movement: A Symposium," ibid., 174-79.

10. See Ralph Stone, *The Irreconcilables: The Fight Against the League of Nations* (New York: W. W. Norton, 1970); Manfred Jonas, *Isolationism in America 1935-1941* (Ithaca: Cornell University Press, 1969). For a review of isolationist writings, see Justus D. Doenecke, ed., *The Literature of Isolationism: A Guide to Non-Interventionist Scholarship, 1930-1972* (Colorado Springs: Myles, 1972).

11. *New York Evening Post*, 31 March 1923; Lodge to George Harvey, 23 December 1921, Lodge Papers, Massachusetts Historical Society, Boston, Mass. For expositions on the complexities, see Selig Adler, *The Isolationist Impulse: Its Twentieth-Century Reaction* (New York: Abelard-Schuman, 1957), who lists hyphenate voters, 83-84, 88-89, 291-92; conservatives, 298-99, 311; liberals, 167-70; nationalists, 179-83; and what he calls progressive isolationists, 170-75. Stone, *The Irreconcilables*, also notes the surprising diversity among the opponents of the League in 1919-20.

12. Borah to Manley Hudson, 15 November 1924, Hudson Papers; *Wallace (Idaho) Miner*, 10 April 1924; Sweetser Diary, 12 December 1922 entry, Arthur Sweetser Papers, Library of Congress, Washington, D.C.

13. Edward Nelson Dingley, *The League of Nations* (n.p., n.d.), pamphlet, Holt Papers; *New York Times*, 15 May, 21 July 1923; William N. Brigance, "The Bible of the Isolationists," *Independent* 118 (19 February 1927): 213-15; "Queer Fish in the League of Nations Pool," *Literary Digest* 79 (24 November 1924): 38-40, 42. See also Beth McKillen's analysis, which suggests that labor and immigrant groups opposed the League because

> at home, the war boards centralized certain kinds of economic and foreign policymaking powers at the executive level and placed them in the hands of a few nonelected officials and civilian elites. Similarly, the league was designed to place some diplomatic powers that were previously reserved for individual states in the hands of a few prominent world leaders who would occupy five permanent positions on the influential executive council. Thus the league, like the war boards, would centralize certain types of policymaking and diminish the influence of democratic forces in constituent countries.

Beth McKillen, "The Corporatist Model, World War I, and the Public Debate over the League of Nations," *Diplomatic History* 15 (Spring 1991): 188.

14. "The Peace Treaty versus Politics," *World Tomorrow* 3 (February 1920): 40; "Germany, France and European Peace," *New Republic* 43 (3 June 1925): 31–35; "Last Gasp from Versailles," *New Republic* 82 (13 February 1935): 4–5; Jordan to P. M. Matthieff, 8 November 1922, to Ethel Barr, 20 March 1923, David Starr Jordan Papers, Hoover Institution on War & Peace, Stanford University, Calif.; Michael Wrezin, *Oswald Garrison Villard: Pacifist at War* (Bloomington: Indiana University Press, 1965),186; Harry Elmer Barnes, "National Self-Determination and the Problems of the Small States," in *The League of Nations: The Principles and the Practice*, ed. Stephen Duggan (Boston: Atlantic Monthly Press, 1919), 173–79; Frederick G. Howe, "Where are the Pre-War Radicals?" *The Survey* 56 (1 April 1926): 50–52.

15. Norman Thomas, the party's regular presidential candidate, noted in 1930 that while he now supported membership, he could not forget that the League had failed to achieve a truly interdependent world. It had accomplished positive work, extended its usefulness, and thus could be considered worthwhile despite its limitations. Bernard K. Johnpoll, *Pacifist's Progress: Norman Thomas and the Decline of American Socialism* (Chicago: Quadrangle Books, 1970), 51–52; Thomas, "Now I am for the League," *World Tomorrow* 13 (April 1930): 176–78.

16. "Geneva—a League Onward," *Independent* 119 (8 October 1927): 349; E. B. Reed, "Common Sense and the League," *Yale Review* 13 (January 1924): 276–88; Frank H. Simonds, "From Geneva to Washington," *Review of Reviews* 74 (October 1926): 405–8; idem, "League of Nations Not Real Factor in Big Problems," *Boston Sunday Herald*, 13 April 1924; Philip Marshall Brown, "The League of Nations at Work," *Independent* 107 (17 December 1921): 284–85; idem, *International Society: Its Nature and Interests* (New York: Macmillan, 1923), 114–22.

17. "Senator Pepper and the League of Nations," *Outlook* 133 (18 April 1923): 697; *Philadelphia Public Ledger*, 10 April 1923; "The Evolving League," *Independent* 110 (28 April 1923): 278–79.

18. H. H. Powers, "Independence and Isolation," *Atlantic Monthly* 141 (February 1928): 258–71; Frank Lowden to Mrs. Blaine, 16 April 1923, Blaine Papers.

19. "The League on Its Merits," *Independent* 110 (14 April 1923): 242–43; "Mr. Hughes' Apologia," ibid. 111 (15 September 1923): 100–101.

20. Interestingly, Hamilton Holt was also a member of this group of liberals, although he clearly became much more a supporter than his fellows. League of Free Nations Association to Wilson (copy of cablegram), 19 June 1919, McDonald to David Starr Jordan, 6 August 1919, McDonald to Members, 28 November, 20 December 1919, Jordan Papers; Hull to Hoover, 9 April 1920, Hull Papers; *New York Times*, 10 May 1920; Adler, *The Isolationist Impulse*, 52–53, 61, 128.

21. Chatfield, *For Peace and Justice*, 40, 96, 101; "The Peace Treaty versus Politics," *World Tomorrow* 3 (February 1920): 40; "Why We Do Not Support the League," ibid. (November 1920): 340–41; "The League Assembly," ibid. 4 (January 1921): 6; "The League and Disarmament," ibid. 4 (August 1921): 227–28; Sara Lyman Patrick, "Internationalism and Emotional Loyalty," ibid. 8 (October 1925): 305–6; "As We See It: Behind Peace Programs," ibid. 9 (April 1926): 122; "The League-Locarno Muddle," ibid. 9 (April 1926): 123; "Rebellion at Geneva," ibid. 10 (October 1927): 389.

22. James L. Tryon, "An American Idea of a League of Nations," *Advocate of Peace* 82 (April 1920): 122-27; Calvin DeArmond David, *The United States and the Second Hague Peace Conference: American Diplomacy and International Organization, 1899– 1914* (Durham, N.C.: Duke University Press, 1976), 356-58.

23. The most prominent of the signatories were Lyman Abbott, former editor of *The Outlook* magazine, philosopher and educator Nicholas Murray Butler, New York City attorney Paul D. Cravath, President William H. P. Faunce of Brown University, President John C. Hibben of Princeton, Herbert Hoover, Charles Evans Hughes, President Ernest M. Hopkins of Dartmouth College, Columbia professor of Political Science Samuel McCune Lindsay, A. Lawrence Lowell, Elihu Root, recently retired president of Cornell University Jacob Gould Schurman, Henry Stimson, former Secretary of Commerce and Labor Oscar Straus, William Allen White, and former Attorney General George Wickersham.

24. *New York Times*, 29 June 1920; Kurt Wimer, "Woodrow Wilson and a Third Nomination," *Pennsylvania History* 29 (April 1962): 209-10.

25. Minutes, Committee of Management, 6 May 1920, Straus Papers; Lowell to Edward Cummings, 18 November 1920, Lowell Papers; Eben W. Martin to Taft, 7 March 1921, Taft to Walter A. Payne (unsent letter), 13 December 1920, Taft Papers.

26. Taft used this appointment to buttress his arguments for caution, arguing that Hughes might accomplish "our ultimate purpose." Lowell to Taft, 9 March 1921, Taft to Lowell, 12 March 1921, Lowell Papers; Taft to Caspar Yost, 16 April 1921, Taft Papers.

27. Lowell to Taft, 19 February, Short to Taft, 15 April 1921, Taft Papers; Minutes of Executive Committee, 23 April 1921, Shailer Mathews Papers, University of Chicago; Ruhl J. Bartlett, *League to Enforce Peace* (Chapel Hill: University of North Carolina, 1944), 200.

28. Statement of Special Committee on Program and Resolution, 30 April 1921, Marburg to Short (copy), 2 May 1921, Lowell Papers.

29. Clark to Short, 4 May 1921, League to Enforce Peace Papers; Taft to Lowell, 5 May 1921, Taft Papers; Taft to Marburg, 5, 8 May 1921; Lowell to Marburg, 5 May 1921, Marburg to Taft, 6 May 1921, Marburg to Short, 7 May 1921, in Theodore Marburg, *Development of the League of Nations Idea*, ed. John H. Latane (New York: Macmillan, 1932), 2:687-90; Parsons to Herbert S. Houston, 23 May 1921, Parsons Papers; Taft to Parsons, 26 April 1921, Taft Papers.

30. Short to Taft, 10 March 1921, Taft to Houston, 23 April 1921, Houston to Taft, 23 June 1921, Taft Papers; Report of Secretary in Minutes of Executive Committee, 21 April 1921, Taft Papers.

31. Marburg to Taft, 22 June 1921, Short to Taft, 24 June 1921, Taft Papers; Lowell to Marburg, 24 June 1921, Lowell to Short, 1 July 1921, Lowell Papers.

32. Adler, *Isolationist Impulse*, 149-50; Minutes of Executive Committee, 19 October, and Minutes of Committee, National Conference and Program, 28 October 1921, Lowell Papers; *New York Times*, 21 October 1921; John Chalmers Vinson, *The Parchment Peace: The United States Senate and the Washington Conference, 1921– 1922* (Athens: University of Georgia Press, 1955), 72-74, 76-77, 98, 140-48.

33. Wickersham to Short, 27 December 1921, Short to Lowell, 14 September 1923, Short Papers; Wickersham to Lowell, 21 March 1922, Wickersham to Lowell, 8 April 1922, Irving Fisher to Lowell, 19 August 1922, Lowell Papers.

34. Fisher to Lowell, 20 July 1921, Lowell Papers.

35. Holt's speech can be found in the Box 13, Series 9, Wilson Papers; *Boston Globe*, 2 December 1921. Because its drive competed with that of the Woodrow Wilson Foundation, the Woodrow Wilson Club was the least successful of the three organizations focusing on Wilson's name.

36. Holt to Fisher, 15 April 1921, Fisher Papers; Schuyler N. Warren to Short, 28 April 1921, Short Papers; Warren to John R. Bolling, 6 July, 22 December 1921, 2 March 1922, Bolling to Warren, 7 July, 11, 14 October, 7 November 1921, Wilson Papers; *New York Times*, 23 October 1921; *Boston Globe*, 5 November 1921; Warren Kuehl, *Hamilton Holt: Journalist, Internationalist, Educator* (Gainesville: University of Florida Press, 1960), 158–59.

37. Hull to Wilson, 5 May 1922, Wilson to Hull, 6 May 1922, Wilson Papers; Kuehl, *Holt*, 160; Warren Kuehl's interview with Schuyler N. Warren, 3 August 1952, New York City. Warren served as treasurer of the Woodrow Wilson Democracy.

38. Fosdick to Sweetser, 20 March 1922, Sweetser Papers; Hudson to Sweetser, 19, 20 March, 26 April, 12 October 1922, Hudson Papers.

39. Minutes, Committee for Treaty Ratification, 1 June 1922, Box R1573, League of Nations Archives. Participants included Charles Macfarland, Stephen P. Duggan, Harriet Laidlaw, John Foster Dulles, Sidney Gulick, Charles R. Levermore, John H. Finley, and Fisher. Charles S. Macfarland, *Across the Years* (New York: Macmillan, 1936), 178. The group originated from a meeting at the Yale Club, 27 December 1921, which had been called to develop support for the Washington Disarmament Conference. It was followed by meetings 9 and 17 February 1922. Wickersham to Lowell, 10 February 1922, Lowell Papers.

40. "America and the Next War," *New Republic* 35 (8 August 1923): 274–75; "American Isolation and European Dissensions," *New Republic* 30 (1 March 1922): 4–6; "The League and the Conference," ibid. 28 (5 October 1921): 149–50; "The Future of the League of Nations," ibid. 31 (7 June 1922): 29–31.

41. Chatfield, *For Peace and Justice*, 106, 109, 112, 297. A brief description of the council's structure and work and a list of cooperating groups can be found in Edith E. Ware, ed., *The Study of International Relations in the United States: Survey for 1934* (New York: Columbia University Press, 1934): 356–57. Its neutrality position is noted in "With the Organizations," *Living Age* 354 (March 1938): 93.

42. Sweetser Diary, 29–30 November, 7–8 December 1922, Sweetser Papers; Parsons to Schuyler N. Warren, Jr., 19 December 1922, Parsons Papers; Hoyt L. Warner, *The Life of Mr. Justice Clarke: A Testament of the Power of Liberal Dissent in America* (Cleveland: Western Reserve University Press, 1959), 128–29.

43. Two days later, Clarke met with Wickersham, and in ensuing meetings the planners agreed on details for the merger. The Clarke committee opened offices in New York City on 14 December, and the next day Holt disclosed the names of 112 sponsors. These national leaders in business, religion, education, journalism, and politics had long been associated with campaigns to involve their nation in international affairs. Minutes of the meeting, 5 December 1922, Hudson Papers; *New York Times*, 15, 16 December 1922; Wickersham to Stimson, 28 December 1922, Stimson Papers; Warner, *Clarke*, 129–30.

44. A subcommittee of Holt, Colby, Charles H. Strong, and Charles H. Levermore had resolved the question of who would lead the group. Clarke would be president,

Wickersham could head the council, and Colby would chair the executive committee. Minute Book, LNNPA, 14 January 1923, Clark M. Eichelberger Papers, New York Public Library.

45. Report of the Secretary of the New York Peace Society for 1922, NYPS Papers; Minutes of Executive Committee, 27 January 1923, Hudson Papers.

46. Minutes of Executive Committee, 8, 16 February 1923, Eichelberger Papers; Kuehl, *Holt,* 168–69.

47. Warner, *Clarke,* 140–41; Minutes of Executive Committee, 7 June 1923, Eichelberger Papers; Holt to Short, 31 March 1925, Short Papers; Bauer to Butler, 6 December 1930, Butler Papers.

48. Colby and Short to Lowell, 8 April 1924, Clarke to Lowell, 19 April 1924, Lowell Papers; Short to Fosdick, 11 April 1924, Fosdick Papers; Colby to Hudson, 27 May 1924, Hudson Papers; Minutes of Executive Committee, 9 April 1923, Eichelberger Papers; "Now Is The Time," *League of Nations Herald,* 15 May 1924, 1–2; Mrs. James Lees Laidlaw, "Definite Political Work," ibid., 1 September 1924, 1–2; William H. Short, "Our Non-Partisan Political Campaign," *League of Nations Herald,* 1 October 1924, 4–5.

49. Newton Baker took the floor to warn against this innocuous statement. As he appealed to the ideals and memory of Woodrow Wilson and pleaded for a substitute statement committing the party to membership, many delegates and reporters wept. They then ignored Baker by adopting the original plank 742 to 353. Fred L. Israel, *Nevada's Key Pittman* (Lincoln: University of Nebraska Press, 1963), 52–53; C. H. Cramer, *Newton D. Baker: A Biography* (Cleveland: World, 1961), 217–20; "The League as a Campaign Issue," *Literary Digest* 82 (12 July 1924): 10; *New York Times,* 28, 29 June 1924.

50. "League as a Campaign Issue," 10–11; "The Week," *New Republic* 39 (9 July 1924): 167–68; "Memorandum of Referendum Provision," in David Hunter Miller Papers, Library of Congress; Review *of Reviews* 70 (August 1924): 118–19. The third candidate in the election of 1924, Robert M. La Follette of the Progressive ticket, opposed League membership.

51. William H. Short, "Election and League," *League of Nations Herald* 2 (December 1924), 1–2.

52. Fosdick to Baker, 5 November 1924, Baker Papers.

53. W. M. Davis to Hughes, 10 April 1923, State Department file 500C/161, National Archives; Report of First Ten Months, 12 November 1927, Eichelberger to Mrs. Blaine, 27 December 1930, Meeting of League of Nations Non Partisan Association of Illinois, 19 April 1928, Blaine Papers.

54. Colby to Mrs. Blaine, 11 July 1924, Blaine Papers; *New York Times,* 11, 19 January, 16 February 1926. The association published the *League of National Bulletin* (March–September 1923); the *League of Nations Herald* (September 1923–June 1925); *League of Nations News* (July 1925–April 1932); and *League of Nations Chronicle* (May 1932–March 1935). For several years it also supported the annual yearbooks on the League of Nations.

55. Quarterly Report of the Chairman [Colby], Executive Committee, n.d. [1 June 1923], Hudson Papers; Kuehl, *Holt,* 169. Fisher spent eight months on one tour. *League of Nations Herald,* 1 January 1925, 3.

56. *New York Times,* 16 April, 10 June 1926, 27 April 1928, 5 May 1930; Bauer to Mrs. Blaine, 12 March 1928, Colby to Mrs. Blaine, 11 July 1924, Bauer to Mrs. Blaine, 22 July 1926, Report of Activities by Bauer to LNNPA of Illinois, 19 April 1928, Blaine Papers.

57. *League of Nations Herald,* 15 June 1924, 4; *New York Times,* 5 June 1930.

58. Bauer to Mrs. Blaine, 2 April 1931, 6 November 1929, 19 November 1930, Blaine Papers.

59. Minutes of Executive Committee, 17 July 1923, Hudson Papers; Minutes of Board of Directors, 10 December 1924, Eichelberger Papers; Minutes of Executive Committee, 27 January 1925, Blaine Papers; *New York Times,* 3 May 1927; "Political Program" adopted by Executive Committee, 12 April 1927, Blaine Papers; "Steps Toward Peace," *Independent* 118 (28 May 1927): 549–50.

60. Cramer, *Baker,* 223–24; *New York Times,* 19 August 1928; *Hartford Courant,* 20 August 1928; N. H. Davis to Sweetser, 23 July 1928, Sweetser Papers.

61. *New York Times,* 17 December 1928; By-Laws, December–January, 1929, Lowell Papers; Hudson to James T. Shotwell, 9 March 1929; Shotwell to Hudson, 11 March 1929, James T. Shotwell Papers, Columbia University.

62. For discussion of many of these groups, see Warren Kuehl, "Webs of Common Interest Revisited: Nationalism, Internationalism and Historians of American Foreign Relations," *Diplomatic History* 10 (Spring 1986): 107–20.

6. Public History Serves the Nation:
The Historical Service Board, 1943–1945

1. See Robert Kelley, "Public History: Its Origins, Nature, and Prospects," *Public Historian* 1 (Fall 1978): 16–28; Richard G. Hewlett, "The Practice of History in the Federal Government," ibid., 29–36; David S. Trask, "The State of Public History in the Washington Area," ibid., 37–41; George T. Mazuzan, "Official Government Historians and Standards for Scholarship," *Government Publications Review* 15 (1988): 225–29; Stetson Conn, "The Army's World War II History and Related Publications," in Robin D. S. Higham, ed., *Official Histories: Essays and Bibliographies from Around the World* (Manhattan: Kansas State University Library, 1970), 553–64; Shepard Clough, *The Life I've Lived: The Formation, Career, and Retirement of an Historian* (Washington, D.C.: University Press of America, 1981); *New York Times,* 10 September 1944; *New York Herald Tribune,* 10, 12 September 1944; *Christian Science Monitor,* 18 September 1944; Luther Huston, "Round Table for GI's," *New York Times Magazine,* 1 October 1944.

2. John D. Millette, *The Organization and Role of the Army Service Forces,* vol. 10 of *The United States Army in World War II* (Washington, D.C.: GPO, 1954).

3. "Col. Spaulding's Report to the Executive Committee of the AHA," 2 September 1943, Box 384, Papers of the American Historical Association, Manuscript Division, Library of Congress (hereafter cited as AHA Papers).

4. Ibid.

5. Ibid. .

6. Continuous surveys documented the tenth-grade-level factor. See, for example, Report C-91, Box 1003, Research Division, Surveys of Troop Attitudes, 1942–June

1955, RG 330 (hereafter cited as RG followed by number), Records of the Secretary of Defense, Assistant Secretary of Defense, Manpower, Personnel and Reserve, Military Reference Branch, National Archives (hereafter cited as MRB).

7. "Col. Spaulding's Report," AHA Papers; Abstract of Minutes of Executive Committee Meeting, 2 September 1943, ibid.; *Annual Report of the American Historical Association, 1943* (Washington, D.C., 1944), 1:3–6; Osborn to Henry Wallace, 7 December 1944, Box 400, Chief of Staff, U.S. Army, Chief of Information, Troop Information and Education Division, Decimal File, 1943–48, 370.1, RG 319, Records of the Army Staff, MRB.

8. *AHA Annual Report, 1943* 1:6–7, 8.

9. See copy of contract in Box 383, AHA Papers.

10. Complete manuscripts and related correspondence for each pamphlet are located in the Historical Service Board files in the AHA Papers.

11. Blegen to authors, n.d.; Spaulding to Blegen, 18 November 1943, Box 383, AHA Papers.

12. "Guide for Discussion Leaders," Education Manual (EM-1), Box 388, AHA Papers.

13. "Historical Service Board Record of Current Progress," 2 July 1945, Box 383, and manuscripts of pamphlets, Boxes 388–401, AHA Papers; M. F. Mochau to Spaulding, "Information-Education Program During Personnel Readjustment Period," 21 October 1945, p. 5, Chief of Staff, U.S. Army, Chief of Information, Troop Information and Education Division, Decimal File 1943–48, 370.1, RG 319, MRB.

14. Blegen to Goodrich, 18 January 1944; memo of conversation, Blegen and Goodrich, 24 January 1944; "Report of T. C. Blegen," 22 August 1944, Box 383, all in AHA Papers.

15. "Report of T. C. Blegen," 22 August 1944, Box 383, AHA Papers.

16. Ford to Spaulding, 20 June 1945, ibid.; *Annual Report of the American Historical Association, 1944* (Washington, D.C., 1945), 1:21–22.

17. Osborn to Blegen, 3 August 1944; "Report of T. C. Blegen," 22 August 1944, Box 383, AHA Papers.

18. Taylor to Blegen, 21 October 1944, "Lend-Lease," Box 391; Ford to Colegrove, 15 December 1944, 19 January 1945, Colegrove to Ford, 10 January, 23 August 1945; "What Shall be Done About Japan After Victory?" Box 392, Ford to Sellin, 1 August 1945, "Can We Avoid a Postwar Crime Wave?" Box 388, AHA Papers.

19. Manuscript, "Shall We have Universal Military Training?" Box 394, AHA Papers.

20. Wilson to Blegen, 19 January 1944; Blegen to Kirk, 15, 22 January, 3, 12, 16, 17, 26 February 1944; Kirk to Blegen, 26 January, 8, 16, 19 February 1944, Box 394, AHA Papers.

21. Report B-177, "Attitude Toward Universal Military Training," Box 993, Research Division, Surveys of Troop Attitudes, 1942–June 1955, RG 330, MRB; Report C-97, Box 1003; Report C-133, Report C-135, Box 1004, ibid.; Karl W. Marks to Blegen, 27 April 1944, memo, Blegen to Ford, n.d., Ford to Blegen, 1 April 1944, Box 394, AHA Papers.

22. Blegen to Goodrich, 4 April 1944, AHA Papers.

23. Memo of conversation, Blegen and Spaulding, 29 April 1944; Blegen to Kirk, 16 June 1944, ibid.

24. "Report of T. C. Blegen," 22 August 1944; HSB, Record of Current Progress, Exhibit B, 2 July 1945, Box 383, ibid.

25. Edward R. Stettinius to Henry L. Stimson, 26 December 1944, U.S. Army Adjutant General Decimal File 300.7, RG 407, Records of the Adjutant General's Office, MRB; Thomas Ford to Guy Stanton Ford, 2 July 1945; Spaulding to G. S. Ford, 10 October 1945; G. S. Ford to Spaulding, 9 November 1945, Box 383, AHA Papers; *Annual Report of the American Historical Association, 1945* (Washington, D.C., 1947), 1:6.

26. Osborn to George Marshall, 6 August 1945, Chief of Staff, U.S. Army, Chief of Information, Troop Information and Education Division, Decimal File 1943–48, 319.1, RG 319, MRB.

27. Report No. ETO 15, *Report on Attitudes of Enlisted Men Toward Army Talks,* January 1944, Box 1015; Report C-91, "Miscellaneous Reports on E. M. Attitudes in North Atlantic Division, Air Transport Command," 15 November 1944, Box 1003, RG330, MRB.

28. Report No. ETO-14, "Survey of Soldiers on Suggested Topics for Army Talks," 25 January 1944, Box 1015, RG 330, MRB.

29. See Robert Kelley, "Public History: Its Origins, Nature, and Prospects," *Public Historian* 1 (Fall 1978): 16–28.

7. The African Sojourn of the Council of Foreign Ministers: Transnational Planning and Anglo-American Diplomacy, 1945–1948

1. The phrases come, respectively, from "Charity Begins at Home," 14 June 1917, in V. I. Lenin, *The National Liberation Movement in the East* (Moscow: Foreign Languages Publishing House, 1962), 198; and "The Foreign Policy of the Russian Revolution," 27 June 1917, ibid., 200. The opening sentence, of course, borrows a phrase from William A. Williams, *Empire as a Way of Life* (New York: Oxford University Press, 1980), with his emphasis on American "imperial self-deception," that is, desiring the gains of empire without acknowledging its existence (p. ix).

2. See Michael W. Doyle, *Empires* (Ithaca: Cornell University Press, 1986), passim, for a full discussion and analysis of the various influences upon the character of imperial relationships. Regarding the value of pericentric analysis, Doyle contended, "It accounts for who imperialized whom. It thus distinguishes effective resistance and dependency from imperialism" (p. 229). Doyle's overall viewpoint, however, is that pericentric analysis must be combined with systemic and metrocentric perspectives for a full understanding of the "complex character of empires" (p. 231).

3. Powell Spring to Stettinius, 9 January 1945, 740.00119 EW/1-1945, Decimal Files, RG 59, Department of State records, National Archives and Records Administration, Washington, D.C. (hereafter cited as DSNA). For examples of State Department planning papers, see Harry N. Howard, Division of Special Research (SR), "Italy: Foreign Policy, 1919–1940," 10 December 1942, Document T-179, Postwar Planning Folder, Box 88C, Lot 122, RG 353, DSNA; David Harris (SR), "The Italian Empire: Political Considerations," 29 December 1942, T-202, ibid.; and Shepard B. Clough (SR), "The Italian Empire: Its Relations to the Italian Economy," 18 December 1942, T-191, ibid. See Luigi Sturzo, *Italy and the New World Order,* trans. Barbara B. Carter

(London: MacDonald, 1944), 69, 117, 182, 237, 252. The American edition of Sturzo's book appeared under the title *Italy and the Coming World*, trans. Barbara B. Carter (New York: Roy Publishers, 1945). It was a bit updated and offered additional appendixes. The Sicilian-born Sturzo was ordained as a priest in 1894 and taught political science and philosophy for the Seminary of Caltagirone (Sicily) before becoming active in antifascist politics. He fled Italy in 1924, living in Paris, then London.

4. Eden statement from House of Commons, *Parliamentary Debates* 377 (1942): cols. 77–78, quoted in Majid Khadduri, *Modern Libya: A Study in Political Development* (Baltimore: Johns Hopkins Press, 1963), 35. The oft-cited source for the history of the Sanusi confraternity is E. E. Evans-Pritchard, *The Sanusi of Cyrenaica* (London: Oxford University Press, 1949), who traces Sanusi-inspired nationalism through rudimentary expressions under Ottoman rule, followed by widespread guerrilla struggle against Italian occupation during 1911–17 and 1923–32, and then to a final stage of transformation to a political movement comprised of both rural Bedouin and townspeople during World War II. For a brief summary of his themes, see Evans-Pritchard, "The Sanusi of Cyrenaica," *Africa* 15 (1945): 61–79. See Scott L. Bills, *Empire and Cold War: The Roots of US–Third World Antagonism, 1945–47* (New York: St. Martin's, 1990), chap. 4, for a discussion of Foreign Office planning and Bevin's strategic concerns. The notion of a Greater Somalia was more beloved in the Colonial Office and by some military officers than it was in the Foreign Office. Briefly, the proposal would have created a unified ethnic Somali state, combining the territories of British Somaliland, Italian Somaliland, and the Ogaden region of Ethiopia. Opposition from Addis Ababa and the lack of support from any other big power doomed the proposal. For a good summary of the Greater Somalia ideal, see Philip E. Mitchell, "Policy for Italian East Africa," 15 August 1941, enclosure with Mitchell to Oliver Stanley, Colonial Office, 5 February 1945, file FO 371/50788, item U2619/51/70, PRO (hereafter cited file/item); for a discussion that focuses upon Colonial Office planning, see William Roger Louis, *The British Empire in the Middle East, 1945–1951: Arab Nationalism, the United States, and Postwar Imperialism* (New York: Oxford University Press, 1984), chap. 7.

5. See Bills, *Empire and Cold War*, 105–16, for a summary of CFM proceedings regarding the Italian colonies. Alan Bullock, *Ernest Bevin: Foreign Secretary, 1945–1951* (New York: W. W. Norton, 1983), 261, has pointed out that Communist political strength in France provided a "strong incentive" for Georges Bidault to play the role of mediator in the CFM's second session. For American thinking on detailed agreements, see "Draft Trusteeship Agreement for Libya," 5 April 1946, Box 263, Lot File: Records of the Deputies for the Former Italian Colonies (hereafter Lot File: Deputies), RG 43, DSNA.

6. Carlo Sforza, "The Near East in World Politics," in *The Near East: Problems and Prospects*, ed. Philip W. Ireland (Chicago: University of Chicago Press, 1942), 3–30; quotes from pp. 6, 13, 15.

7. Ivanoe Bonomi to Truman, 8 May 1945, FW740.0019 EW/5-1945, RG 59, DSNA; Ferruccio Parri (president, Italian Council of Ministers) to Truman, 22 August 1945, U.S. Department of State, *Foreign Relations of the United States, 1945* (Washington, D.C.: GPO, 1968), 4:1022–24 (hereafter cited as *FRUS* followed by the appropriate year and volume number); Alcide de Gasperi (foreign minister) to secretary of state,

22 August 1945, *FRUS, 1945* 4:1024–29; "Summary of Italian Views for an Equitable Solution of the Principal Questions Which May be Discussed at the London Peace Conference," 4 September 1945, *FRUS, 1945* 2:106–8.

8. Byrnes to De Gasperi, 4 September 1945, *FRUS, 1945* 4:1032–33.

9. See "Treaty of Peace with Italy," *Treaties and Other International Agreements of the United States of America, 1776–1949*, vol. 4, *Multilateral, 1946–1949*, comp. Charles I. Bevans (Washington, D.C.: GPO, 1970), 311–402; see pp. 322 (Article 23) and 385–86 (Annex XI). The treaty and its seventeen annexes also dealt, inter alia, with boundary adjustments, the establishment of the free state of Trieste, limits on Italian armed forces, and reparations.

10. Sayyid Idris to Ronald Campbell, Foreign Office, 24 July 1946, FO 371/57186/U6748, PRO; Warner minute, 29 August 1946, FO 371/57187/U7082, PRO; Cumming (CCAO) to Gen. A. V. Anderson, Director Civil Affairs (DCA), received in War Office 30 August 1946, enclosure in FO 371/57187/U6995, PRO.

11. "Disposal of Italian Colonies," meeting minutes, secretary of state's office, Paris, 6 September 1946, FO 371/57187/U7083, PRO. Regarding the other Italian colonies, Bevin favored ceding Eritrea to Ethiopia and organizing Somalia as either an Italian or UN trusteeship. He was concerned that too much attention was being directed toward the Libyan territories. While Bevin felt that Ethiopian incorporation of the ex-colony was not the best solution from the Eritrean perspective, it made sense for Britain. "If the Italians were to come back [to Eritrea], and to go Communist," remarked Bevin, "they would be another thorn in our side."

12. An excellent summary of the strategic importance of Cyrenaica was supplied by Brigadier R. D. H. Arundell, who was chief civil affairs officer for the Middle East during 1944–45. Cyrenaica, he wrote, "must be regarded as the western bastion of the Middle East. The Power which controls this territory sits astride the sea lanes of the Eastern Mediterranean, and can threaten the Nile Valley by land and air." He contended that a careful and thoughtful tutelage could lay the groundwork "for an easy transition from a B.M.A. [British Military Administration] to an Arab State with an Emir and a British Resident." See Arundell, "Future Policy in Cyrenaica: Note by C.C.A.O.," 13 November 1944, Appendix B of ORC [Overseas Reconstruction Committee] (45)9, 13 July 1945, FO371/50790/U5520, PRO. In an update of July 1945, Arundell observed that Cyrenaica remained vitally important. He argued that British strategic interests in Tripolitania were "entirely negative": the area need not be administered by Britain, but it must be denied to a hostile power. See "Future of Cyrenaica and Tripolitania: Note by Chief Civil Affairs Officer, Middle East," 10 July 1945, DC (45)7 (Revised), Appendix 1: "Cyrenaica" and Appendix 2: "Tripolitania," FO371/50790/U5577, PRO.

13. Scott Fox to Gen. A. V. Anderson, 29 October 1946, FO 371/53520/J4492, PRO.

14. Reilly to Bellenger, secretary of state for war, 27 January 1947, FO 1015/87, PRO. See also Bellenger to Reilly, 21 November 1946, FO 371/53521/J5012 and FO 1015/1, PRO; "Terms of Reference," n.d., ibid. Other designated members of the Working Party were John A. de C. Hamilton, with experience in the Sudan and Middle East service; F. C. Newton of the Treasury; and Denis A. Greenhill, of the Foreign Office, as the group's secretary. Herbert R. Stewart was later appointed to the party as an agricultural expert, and Lt. Col. J. S. Crum replaced Greenhill for the Tripolitania tour.

15. "Report by the War Office Working Party on Cyrenaica, December 1946–January 1947," Cairo, 27 January 1947, FO 1015/87, PRO; "Cyrenaica," Bellenger memorandum, 11 April 1947, CP(47)126, PRO.

16. "Report by the War Office Working Party on Tripolitania," 8 March 1947, FO 1015/129, PRO. While not asked to advise the British government about the future status of Tripolitania, the Working Party offered a final chapter expressing concerns about the fate of such a heterogeneous state. Whatever trusteeship formula was chosen, an independent Tripolitania would face difficult times with its lack of natural resources and its agriculture and livestock-raising "at the mercy of a capricious rainfall." Hence, the future "does not justify much optimism."

17. Louis, *British Empire in the Middle East*, 265.

18. See Herbert R. Stewart, "Notes and Future Developments of Agriculture in Tripolitania," 10 March 1947, FO 1015/129, PRO. This was a companion study to the Working Party's report; Stewart was a member of the party and wrote much of its report on the agrarian economy of Tripolitania.

19. Charles (Rome) to Bevin, 12 February 1947, FO371/63190/J1627, PRO; see also Charles to Bevin, 25 February 1947, FO 371/67808/Z2308, PRO. S. J. Woolf, "The Rebirth of Italy, 1943–50," in *The Rebirth of Italy 1943–50*, ed. Woolf (London: Longman, 1972), contended that the loss of colonies aroused "remarkably little public feeling" in Italy (p. 228). However, most other authors have characterized the African colonies as a live issue well stoked by partisanship and press reports; see C. Grove Haines, "Problem of the Italian Colonies," *Middle East Journal* 1 (October 1947): 430; "Italy's Former Colonies," *Economist*, 28 June 1947, 1014–15; and G. K. N. Trevaskis, *Eritrea: A Colony in Transition: 1941–52* (New York: Oxford University Press, 1960), 78–79. Christopher Seton-Watson, "Italy's Imperial Hangover," *Journal of Contemporary History* 15 (1980): 169, does say, however, that because Italy's modern empire was "one of the smallest and shortest lived," its "imperial hangover was therefore less severe than those of other imperial powers." Antonio Varsori, "De Gasperi, Nenni, Sforza and their role in Post-War Italian Foreign Policy," in *Power in Europe? Great Britain, France, Italy, and Germany in a Postwar World, 1945–1950*, ed. Josef Becker and Franz Knipping (New York: Walter de Gruyter, 1986), points to the De Gasperi-Sforza effort to build close ties with the United States as the key element in reestablishing Italian sovereignty (p. 102)—overestimating, however, in the process, U.S. support for Italy's international claims (p. 106).

20. Attlee to Charles, 29 March 1947, FO 371/63190/J1627,PRO; Hoyer Millar minute, 10 March 1947, ibid. See also Hoyer Millar's separate minute of 10 March 1947 in FO 371/67808/Z2308, PRO.

21. Utter report, 5 June 1946, Box 5, Lot File: Records of the Division of African Affairs, RG 59, DSNA.

22. Utter, "Interview with Sayid Idriss El Senussi," 27 March 1946, enclosure in S. Pinkney Tuck (Cairo legation) to secretary of state, 4 April 1946, Box 150, Post Files: Cairo Legation & Embassy, 1936–55, RG 84, DSNA, Suitland Reference Branch.

23. Ibid.

24. Utter, "Report on Tripolitania," 26 February–8 March 1946, enclosure in S. Pinkney Tuck (Cairo) to secretary of state, 8 April 1946, 865C.00/4-846, Decimal Files, RG 59, DSNA. Interestingly, Utter recorded local reservations about collective

trusteeship—fears that it might introduce big-power rivalry into Tripolitania at the moment when its peoples needed calm, practical planning. See also Utter, "The Fezzan, Why It Should Not Be Separated from Tripolitania," enclosure in Tuck to secretary of state, 12 April 1946, 865C.00/4-1246, RG 59, DSNA.

25. Haines, "Problem of the Italian Colonies," 418–19, 430, 431.

26. Chargé in the U.K. (Clark) to secretary of state, 13 August 1947, 865.014/8-1347, RG 59, DSNA; Bevin remarks, "Informal Notes of a Meeting Held in the Foreign Office," 25 September 1947, FO 371/63197/J4662, PRO; Henderson to Lovett, 28 August 1947, Country and Area Files: Europe 1947–48, Lot File: Policy Planning Staff, RG 59, DSNA.

27. Instructions from the deputies, London, 21 October 1947, CFM/D/L/47/IC/25, *FRUS, 1947* 3:609–11; "Time-Table of the Conference of Deputies and of the Commission of Investigation," 21 October 1947, CFM/D/L/47/IC/27, ibid., 612; "Procedure for Hearing 'Other Interested Governments' and the Governments of Italy and Egypt," 21 October 1947, CFM/D/L/47/IC/29, ibid., 613–14. The commission would keep the following records: meeting summaries; interview transcripts; summaries of investigations conducted on the spot; and an index of documentary material acquired. The nineteen "other interested governments" approved were Australia, Belgium, Brazil, Byelorussia, Canada, China, Czechoslovakia, Egypt, Ethiopia, Greece, India, Italy, the Netherlands, New Zealand, Pakistan, Poland, South Africa, the Ukraine, and Yugoslavia. During its investigation, the commission was empowered to confer with anyone or any group in the colonies. The COI would coordinate timetables, local itineraries, and technical arrangements with the British Military Administration in each territory. While in the field, the COI's chairmanship rotated among the delegations every seven days, as it did with the deputies.

28. Scott Fox minute, 4 February 1947, FO 371/63188/J755, PRO; Stafford, "Note on Cyrenaica," 9 February 1947, FO 1015/149, PRO. Similarly, Christopher L. S. Cope, in a minute of 7 February 1947, FO 371/63187/J517, PRO, contended that the British government must "ensure that the terms of reference of the investigating commission should be strictly defined and their powers carefully circumscribed." The term *safari* was used frequently by Kenyon C. Bolton, Division of International Conferences (IC), as he sought to deal with COI logistics; see his memorandums of 10, 16, 20 October 1947, Box 235, Lot File: Deputies, RG 43, DSNA.

29. "Subject: Disposition of the Italian Colonies," JCS memorandum, transmitted in SWNCC to State Department, 8 July 1947, *FRUS, 1947* 3:592–94. Further, the JCS doubted that Italy had sufficient military forces to maintain order in overseas territories; and, even if Italian troops were installed, armed conflict between Italian and Arab forces "would threaten world peace."

30. Central Intelligence Group, "Significant Considerations Regarding the Disposition of the Italian African Colonies," ORE 39, 25 July 1947, Box 254, President's Secretary's Files, Truman Papers, Harry S. Truman Library, Independence, Mo.

31. Michael H. Hunt, *Ideology and U.S. Foreign Policy* (New Haven: Yale University Press, 1987), 17–18, 107, 117, 124, 127, 138, 153, 159; "Italy's Former Colonies," 1014–15.

32. Utter (Asmara) to secretary of state, received 25 November 1947, 865.014/11-2547, RG 59, DSNA; Utter (Asmara) to secretary of state, received 10 December 1947,

865.014/12-1147, RG 59, DSNA; Utter (Asmara) to Lewis Douglas (London), 17 December 1947, Box 235, Lot File: Deputies, RG 43, DSNA. Frank E. Stafford, "The Ex-Italian Colonies," *International Affairs* 25 (January 1949): 47–55, recalled that the COI's progress through Eritrea was accompanied by "noisy, but generally good-tempered, crowds with organized parades and side-shows" (p. 48). The commission, he reported, was confronted by such "curiosities" as an old man from one village who claimed to represent forty thousand dead people whom he had seen in his dreams (pp. 48–49).

33. Utter (Asmara) to Joseph Palmer (Division of African Affairs, hereafter AF), 28 December 1947, Box 235, Lot File: Deputies, RG 43, DSNA; Alfred E. Wellons (AF) to Joseph Palmer (AF), 5 January 1948, Box 3, Lot File: African Affairs, RG 59, DSNA, with a summary report on the Eritrea hearings. Both Utter and Stafford believed that the French and the Soviet commissioners deliberately sought a distorted report.

34. Lascelles minute, 25 November 1947, FO 371/69327/J6, PRO. Regarding the matter of higher-level Anglo-French talks on cooperation in Africa, see, for example, minutes of a meeting involving Colonial and Foreign Office analysts, 16 December 1947, FO 371/67699/Z11160, PRO.

35. *New York Times*, 13, 14 January 1948. Grabbing much bigger headlines was a U.S.-U.K. agreement to reopen Mellaha field to military transport flights.

36. Brig. J. F. Benoy to Gen. D. C. Cumming, 28 January 1948, FO 1015/3B, PRO. Benoy wrote, "From our recent experiences I suppose we must expect that the political temperature in Tripoli will rise considerably during the weeks immediately preceding the Commissions arrival." See also the comments of Brig. T. R. Blackley, Tripoli, 17 March 1948, before the COI, Box 237, Lot File: Deputies, RG 43, DSNA.

37. See Mallet (Rome) to Foreign Office, 10 February 1948, FO 1015/5, PRO; Mallet to Foreign Office, 17 February 1948, telegram nos. 297–99, FO 1015/13, PRO.

38. Sforza to Bevin, 25 February 1948, FO 371/69330/J1939, PRO.

39. Cumming, "Notes on Cyrenaica," n.d., attachment, William S. Moore, military attaché, Cairo legation, to War Department, 23 September 1943, Box 5, Lot File: African Affairs, RG 59, DSNA.

40. Louis, *British Empire in the Middle East*, 20–21.

41. "British Military Administration, Cyrenaica," attached to E. A. V. de Candole, acting chief administrator, to CCAO, GHQ, MELF, 31 December 1947, FO 1015/143, PRO; Cyrenaican petition, "Our National Demands," 7 May 1946, attached to Lt. Col. A. Sillery, acting CCAO, to DCA, 31 May 1946, FO 1015/4, PRO. The latter petition was forwarded at the request of Sayyid Idris and included about five hundred signatures.

42. Khadduri, *Modern Libya*, 88–95; memorandum, Umar al-Mukhtar Club to "Various Parties in Tripolitania," 19 September 1947, FO 1015/4, PRO (for a description of the "club," see Khadduri, *Modern Libya*, 62–65); Kirkbride to Cumming, 21 February 1948, FO 1015/5, PRO, contains the quote about Sayyid Idris.

43. Sadawi to Deputies, 6 October 1947, with Penney (Cairo) to Scott Fox (Egyptian Department), 11 October 1947, FO 1015/4, PRO; Penney to Scott Fox, 20 March 1948, FO 1015/5, PRO. The Tripoli BMA's Monthly Intelligence Report No. 28, March 1948, affirmed that Sadawi had been very successful in spreading his ideas through-

out the territory and noted that he had assured the BMA full cooperation in avoiding disorders, a promise he "faithfully fulfilled." FO 1015/36, PRO. Stafford, 8 April 1948, FO 1015/94, PRO, also reported the great success of Sadawi:

> The programme has swept the whole country and although among the uneducated the degree of understanding of the three points is not great, there is no doubt that the people of Tripolitania have expressed to us their desire for independence. The influence of religion on the acceptance of the programme is strongly marked and probably over-riding and the further away from towns the Working Groups went, the clearer it appeared that the driving power is more the banner of Islam than local Arab nationalism.

Utter agreed; see his dispatch of 10 April 1948, 865.014/4-1048, RG 59, DSNA.

44. COI communiqué to the press, 7 March 1948, Tripoli, CFM/D/L/47/I.C.COM 55, Box 236, Lot File: Deputies, RG 43, DSNA (communiqués with similar phrasing were issued for each territory visited); "Questions to be asked . . . ," CFM/D/L/47/ I.C.COM 60, ibid.

45. The phrase is from a remark by the French deputy, Massigli, who said during a discussion of the Eritrea report, "I do not believe that we can achieve a sound solution from a battle of statistics. They are deceptive, especially in such territories." U.K. verbatim minutes, 34th meeting, DEPITCOL, 10 August 1948, FO 1086/127, PRO.

46. COI, 5th hearing, Cyrenaica, 1 May 1948, National Congress, Box 237, Lot File: Deputies, RG 43, DSNA.

47. COI, 2d hearing, Tripoli, 21 March 1948, United National Front, Box 237, Lot File: Deputies, RG 43, DSNA; COI, 3d hearing, Tripoli, 21 March 1948, National Party, ibid.; COI, 4th hearing, Tripoli, 21 March 1948, Free National Bloc, ibid.

48. COI, 4th hearing, Tripoli, 21 March 1948, Free National Bloc, Box 237, Lot File: Deputies, RG 43, DSNA; see also similar comments by Sadawi, 9th hearing, 23 March 1948, ibid., and by a spokesman for the Cyrenaican National Congress, 1 May 1948, ibid.

49. Utter (Tripoli) to secretary of state, 15 April 1948, 865.014/4-1548, RG 59, DSNA.

50. James E. Miller, "Taking Off the Gloves: The United States and the Italian Elections of 1948," *Diplomatic History* 7 (Winter 1983): 35–36. American intervention in Italian politics in 1948, wrote Miller, marked a "watershed in the development of U.S. foreign policy." E. Timothy Smith, "U.S. Security and Italy: The Extension of NATO to the Mediterranean, 1945–49," in *NATO and the Mediterranean,* ed. Lawrence S. Kaplan et al. (Wilmington, Del.: Scholarly Resources, 1985), pointed out, "Despite the moderate public goals of the PCI, U.S. officials perceived the party as a potential revolutionary force and as a tool of Soviet foreign policy" (p. 138). See also Smith's *The United States, Italy and NATO, 1947–52* (New York: St. Martin's, 1991), chaps. 1–2.

51. COI, *Report on Libya,* pt. 1 (Tripolitania), 1–94 passim, Box 237, Lot File: Deputies, RG 43, DSNA; the Libya report is also available in file FO 1015/104, PRO.

52. COI, *Report on Libya,* pt. 2 (Fezzan), 1–51 passim, Box 237, Lot File: Deputies, RG 43, DSNA. For discussion of dissatisfaction within the COI about the Fezzan visit, see U.K. verbatim minutes, 167th meeting, COI, 26 June 1948, FO 1086/125, PRO.

53. COI, *Report on Libya*, pt. 3 (Cyrenaica), 1–68 passim, Box 237, Lot File: Deputies, RG 43, DSNA. Utter later reported that the only purpose served by the visit to Italy "was to placate Italian authorities and refugees by registering the latter's views"; Utter's comments in Caffery (Paris) to secretary of state, 28 May 1948, *FRUS, 1948* 3:911–12. The COI reports on Eritrea and Somalia are also in Box 237, Lot File: Deputies, RG 43, DSNA.

54. U.S. verbatim minutes, 28th meeting, DEPITCOL, 16 June 1948, Box 235, Lot File: Deputies, RG 43, DSNA. The American minutes show John Utter as chair (not Philip Bagby, as indicated in the U.K. minutes), and this is supported by the official "Record of Decisions." At the 29th meeting, Saksin complained again about the delays, saying: "It would be very strange if the Deputies could not complete their work within a year and leave to the Ministers only a few days to make their decision." U.S. verbatim minutes, 29th meeting, DEPITCOL, 6 July 1948, ibid.

55. Bevin memorandum, "The Czechoslovak Crisis," 3 March 1948, CP(48)71, CAB 129/25, PRO; Bevin memorandum, "The Threat to Western Civilisation," 3 March 1948, CP(48)72, CAB 129/25, PRO. For a full analysis of the evolution of Bevin's thinking about rebuilding Western Europe and snagging the United States as an active partner, see Alan Bullock, *Ernest Bevin: Foreign Secretary, 1945–1951* (New York: W. W. Norton, 1983), chap. 13; also John Baylis, *The Diplomacy of Pragmatism: Britain and the Formation of NATO, 1942–1949* (Kent, Ohio: Kent State University Press, 1993).

56. On the other hand, some State Department analysts believed that the Italian elections obscured broader political principles. Joseph Palmer of the Division of African Affairs, for example, worried that U.S. policy toward the colonies would be made "piecemeal" through a series of "gradual steps" rather than "on the basis of the *whole* story." Such a turn was, in fact, quite possible, since Palmer had already seen this happen with America's Indochina policy, forged through cumulative ad hoc decisions made by the Joint Chiefs of Staff as the State Department waited in vain for FDR and then Truman to take the lead. "Every day that passes," wrote Palmer, "enhances the possibility of a decision being made primarily in the light of the political situation in Italy as brought out by the telegrams from Europe. . . . AF remains convinced that the net logical balance is weighted against a return of these colonies to Italy." In this argument, at least, Palmer had the support of the Joint Chiefs, who continued to prefer a British guiding hand in the eastern Mediterranean and Red Sea regions. Palmer (AF) to Loy Henderson (Office of Near Eastern and African Affairs [NEA]), 5 March 1948, 865.014/3-548, RG 59, DSNA; JCS memorandum, 18 March 1948, *FRUS, 1948* 3:906–7. For a pertinent discussion of the formulation of U.S. Indochina policy, see Bills, *Empire and Cold War*, chap. 5. For the views of the British Chiefs of Staff, see Anderson to Bevin, 31 March 1948, FO 371/69330/J2350, PRO; Bevin to Anderson, 15 April 1948, ibid.

57. Secretary of state to Gallman (London), 30 April 1948, *FRUS, 1948* 3:908.

58. For British verbatim minutes of the Deputies' meetings, see FO 1086/127; for U.S. records, see Box 235, Lot File: Deputies, RG 43, DSNA. In the midst of such discussions, on 23 July, Truman approved NSC 19/1 as the basic guideline for American negotiators. This document signaled the formal abandonment of any U.S. desire for collective administration of the ex-colonies. Rather, the State Department had "informally and secretly acquiesced in the British desire for a trusteeship over

Cyrenaica." See "Disposition of the Former Italian Colonies in Africa," NSC 19/1, 21 July 1948, Box 203, President's Secretary's File, Truman Papers, Truman Library; secretary of state to London embassy, 23 July 1948, *FRUS, 1948* 3:923–24, for a summary.

59. See "Recommendations by the Deputies," 31 August 1948, *FRUS, 1948* 3: 942–48.

60. Scott Fox minute, 24 May 1948, FO 371/69335/J3840, PRO; Clutton minute, 28 May 1948, ibid.; Bell meeting summary, Bevin's room, 2 July 1948, FO 371/69338/ J4629, PRO.

61. Secretary of state to Ambassador Douglas (London), 8 July 1948, 865.014/7-748, RG 59, DSNA. See also H. E. Allen (IC) to Warren Kelchner, 8 July 1948, Box 235, Lot File: Deputies, RG 43, DSNA, concerning the colonial issue, noting the department "is following the policy already established of attempting to avoid any Four Power discussions at the top level on this or other current problems."

62. Bevin to Oliver Franks (Washington), 10 July 1948, FO 371/69338/J4732, PRO; Douglas to secretary of state, 15 July 1948, *FRUS, 1948* 3:919–21; secretary of state to London embassy, 15 July 1948, *FRUS, 1948* 3:921.

63. For instance, the Cyrenaican National Congress had proclaimed independence earlier in the year, petitioning the BMA, the Four Powers, and other Arab governments for recognition of its claim that Italian renunciation of sovereignty in 1947 signified an end to external occupation. While Sayyid Idris had promised to moderate the Congress's drive, the amir himself was becoming less cooperative. See National Congress memorandum, 14 January 1948, enclosure in S. Pinkney Tuck (Cairo) to secretary of state, 8 April 1948, 865.014/4-848, RG 59, DSNA; National Congress resolution of 7 February 1948, in Tuck (Cairo) to secretary of state, 17 March 1948, 865.014/3-1748, RG 59, DSNA; summaries of Scott Fox conversations with Sayyid Idris, 23–25 February 1948, FO 371/69329/J1455, PRO. For events in Tripolitania, see Orray Taft, Jr. (consul, Tripoli) to secretary of state, 10 June 1948, 865C.00/6-1048, RG 59, DSNA; BMA Cyrenaica, Monthly Political Report No. 30, 7 July 1948, FO 1015/36, PRO; BMA Tripolitania, Monthly Political Intelligence Report No. 32, July 1948, FO 1015/36, PRO; Sadawi-sponsored petition, 9 August 1948, FO 1015/4, PRO; BMA Tripolitania, Monthly Intelligence Report No. 33, August 1948, FO 1015/36, PRO. Taft (Tripoli) to secretary of state, 19 August 1948, 865C.00/8-1948, RG 59, DSNA, pointed out that there were "recurrent rumors" of Arab agitation in Tripoli. "There is no question but that the increasing political activities and maneuvers among the Arab leaders are attracting considerable attention and that they will build up to a crescendo around September 15," wrote Taft. The U.S. consulate in Tripoli had been reopened on 4 June 1948; for the department's instructions that Taft keep a low profile, see Loy Henderson to Taft, 14 May 1948, Box 5, Lot File: African Affairs, RG 59, DSNA.

64. U.K. verbatim minutes, 1st meeting, CFM, 13 September 1948, Paris, FO 1086/128, PRO. The exchange caused Douglas to wire the State Department and request some kind of official confirmation: "As [the] whole session may turn on this issue, I should appreciate receiving early tomorrow morning specific statement, in name of [the] President if possible, that I am fully authorized to take decision on behalf of the US Government regarding the disposal of the former Italian colonies, in implementation of the treaty of peace with Italy." Douglas (London) to secretary

of state, 13 September 1948, 865.014/9-1348, RG 59, DSNA. The official "Record of Decisions," 13–15 September 1948, is in Box 261, Lot File: Deputies, RG 43, DSNA.

65. U.K. verbatim minutes, 2d meeting, CFM, 14 September 1948, 11:00 A.M., Paris, FO 1086/128, PRO.

66. U.K. verbatim minutes, 3d meeting, CFM, 14 September 1948, 3:30 P.M., Paris, FO 1086/128, PRO.

67. U.K. verbatim minutes, 4th meeting, CFM, 14 September 1948, 11:30 P.M., Paris, FO 1086/128, PRO; U.K. verbatim minutes, 5th meeting, CFM, 15 September 1948, noon, ibid.

68. Louis, *British Empire in the Middle East*, 53; Bruce R. Kuniholm, *The Origins of the Cold War in the Near East: Great Power Conflict and Diplomacy in Iran, Turkey, and Greece* (Princeton: Princeton University Press, 1980), xvii–xviii, xx–xxi, and passim; Lawrence S. Wittner, *American Intervention in Greece, 1943–1949* (New York: Columbia University Press, 1982), 307–8.

69. Benjamin Rivlin, "Unity and Nationalism in Libya," *Middle East Journal* 3 (1949): 41.

70. H. W. Brands, "Fractal History, or Clio and the Chaotics," *Diplomatic History* 16 (Fall 1992): 500.

71. "Italy's Former Colonies," 1014–15; Trevaskis, *Eritrea*, 83.

8. Beyond the Water's Edge: Liberal Internationalist and Pacifist Opposition to NATO

1. Ralph B. Levering, *The Public and American Foreign Policy, 1918–1978* (New York: Morrow, 1978), 104–5. For an analysis of this consensus and its breakdown, see Ole R. Holsti and James N. Rosenau, *American Leadership in World Affairs: Vietnam and the Breakdown of Consensus* (Boston: Allen and Unwin, 1984). On the emergence of the anti-Vietnam War movement from the 1950s peace movement, see Charles DeBenedetti and Charles Chatfield, *An American Ordeal: The Antiwar Movement of the Vietnam Era* (Syracuse: Syracuse University Press, 1990). The consensus had an impact far beyond foreign policy. For its effects on the family, see Allan C. Carlson, "Foreign Policy, 'the American War,' and the Passing of the Post-War Consensus," *This World*, no. 5 (Spring-Summer 1983): 18–54; and Elaine Tyler May, *Homeward Bound: American Families in the Cold War Era* (New York: Basic Books, 1988).

2. Lawrence S. Kaplan, "After Forty Years: Reflections on NATO as a Research Field," in *NATO: The Founding of the Atlantic Alliance and the Integration of Europe*, ed. Francis H. Heller and John R. Gillingham (New York: St. Martin's, 1992), 17–19.

3. Thomas G. Paterson, *Meeting the Communist Threat: Truman to Reagan* (New York: Oxford University Press, 1988), 95.

4. Although he focuses on isolationists, see Justus D. Doenecke, *Not to the Swift: The Old Isolationists in the Cold War Era* (Lewisburg, Pa.: Bucknell University Press, 1979), 244–45, for the impact of Cold War critics on historical revisionism in the 1960s. For an overview of the influence of the early Cold War critics on later peace movements, see Robert Kleidman, *Organizing for Peace: Neutrality, the Test Ban, and the Freeze* (Syracuse: Syracuse University Press, 1993).

5. Vandenberg quoted in Cecil Van Meter Crabb, Jr., *Bipartisan Foreign Policy, Myth or Reality?* (White Plains: Roe, Peterson, 1957), 161.

6. On the effort to assure U.S. participation in the United Nations, see Robert A. Divine, *Second Chance: The Triumph of Internationalism in America During World War II* (New York: Atheneum, 1967).

7. See Mary Sperling McAuliffe, *Crisis on the Left: Cold War Politics and American Liberals 1947–1954* (Amherst: University of Massachusetts Press, 1978), 63, 70, 146–47.

8. Lawrence S. Kaplan, "Collective Security and the Case of NATO," in *The Origins of NATO*, ed. Joseph Smith (Exeter, U.K.: University of Exeter Press, 1990), 97. On the concept of "new internationalism," see also Divine, *Second Chance*, 183. For a discussion of postwar isolationism, see Doenecke, *Not to the Swift*, and Ted Galen Carpenter, "The Dissenters: American Isolationists and Foreign Policy, 1945–1954" (Ph.D. diss., University of Texas at Austin, 1980). Carpenter notes that the main theme of "traditional" isolationism was support for a "unilateral foreign policy" (p. 6). For a discussion of internationalism and the peace movement, see "Internationalism as a Current in the Peace Movement: A Symposium," in *Peace Movements in America*, ed. Charles Chatfield (New York: Schocken, 1973), 171–91.

9. See Harold Josephson, "The Search for Lasting Peace: Internationalism and American Foreign Policy, 1920–1950," in *Peace Movements and Political Cultures*, ed. Charles Chatfield and Peter van den Dungen (Knoxville: University of Tennessee Press, 1988), 215; and Charles Chatfield, *The American Peace Movement: Ideals and Activism* (New York: Twayne, 1992), 97–98.

10. Paterson, *Meeting the Communist Threat*, 101.

11. Chatfield, *American Peace Movement*, 91.

12. An example of the changed attitudes toward the United Nations can be seen in both the War Resisters League and the National Council for Prevention of War. In 1945, both organizations opposed the UNO. Frederick Libby, the executive secretary of the National Council went so far as to say, "Cooperation without entanglements would be my slogan." By 1949, however, both organizations, while rejecting the Atlantic Pact, supported strengthening the United Nations. For opposition to the United Nations, see U.S. Congress, Senate, *The Charter of the United Nations: Hearings Before the Committee on Foreign Relations*, 79th Cong., 1st sess., 1945, 396–97 and 712–14. For support for the UNO and opposition to the North Atlantic Treaty, see Frederick Libby, "Doubts Assail the Pact Supporters," *Peace Action*, May 1949, National Council for Prevention of War, DG 23, Box 430, North Atlantic Treaty File, Swarthmore College Peace Collection, Swarthmore, Pa., and "Statement on the North Atlantic Defense Pact by the War Resisters League," 4 April 1949, War Resisters League, Document Group 46 (hereafter DG), Box 26, Atlantic Pact File, Swarthmore College Peace Collection (hereafter cited as SCPC).

13. Josephson, "The Search for Lasting Peace," 215–16; and Chatfield, *American Peace Movement*, 99. On anticommunism and the labor movement, see Richard M. Fried, *Nightmare in Red: The McCarthy Era in Perspective* (New York: Oxford University Press, 1990); Federico Romero, *The United States and the European Trade Union Movement, 1944–1951*, trans. Harvey Fergusson II (Chapel Hill: University of North Carolina Press, 1992); and Ronald Filippelli, *American Labor and Postwar Italy, 1943–1953* (Stanford, Calif.: Stanford University Press, 1989).

14. Fried, *Nightmare in Red*, 87.

15. McAuliffe, *Crisis on the Left*, 7, 5.

16. Charles DeBenedetti, "Introduction," in DeBenedetti, *Peace Heroes in Twentieth-Century America* (Bloomington: Indiana University Press, 1986), 11.

17. Harriet Hyman Alonso, *Peace as a Women's Issue; A History of the U.S. Movement for World Peace and Women's Rights* (Syracuse: Syracuse University Press, 1993), 170. The American section of the WILPF was founded in 1920.

18. The National Council for Prevention of War was a clearinghouse for the American peace movement. Founded in 1921, the NCPW reached its peak of strength in the mid-1930s. Libby to Connally, 4 May 1949, Papers of the National Council for the Prevention of War, DG 23, Box 430, North Atlantic Treaty File, SCPC. Dennis, because he was under indictment for conspiring to overthrow the U.S. government, did not appear before the committee, sending only a printed statement. See Joan Lee Bryniarski, "Against the Tide: Senate Opposition to the Internationalist Foreign Policy of Presidents Franklin D. Roosevelt and Harry S. Truman, 1943–1949" (Ph.D. diss., University of Maryland, 1972), 263–64.

19. Taylor, *Congressional Record*, 12 March 1948, 94, pt. 2:2684.

20. Cass Canfield, 12 May 1949, U.S. Congress, Senate, *North Atlantic Treaty: Hearings before the Committee on Foreign Relations*, 81st Cong., 1st sess., 1949, 3:841–42 (hereafter referred to as *North Atlantic Treaty* followed by volume and page). According to Milton Katz, the United World Federalists gradually grew more conservative, supporting both the cold war consensus and efforts to establish world government. See Milton Katz, *Ban the Bomb: A History of SANE, The Committee for a Sane Nuclear Policy, 1957–1985* (Westport, Conn.: Greenwood, 1986), 6–7.

21. William C. Berman, "James Paul Warburg: An Establishment Maverick Challenges Truman's Policy Toward Germany," in *Cold War Critics: Alternatives to American Foreign Policy in the Truman Years*, ed. Thomas G. Paterson (Chicago: Quadrangle, 1971), 55–56; and James P. Warburg, *Last Call for Common Sense* (New York: Harcourt, Brace, 1949), 7–8. A recent book on the Warburg family is Ron Chernow, *The Warburgs: The Twentieth Century Odyssey of a Remarkable Jewish Family* (New York: Random House, 1993).

22. On the Vandenberg Resolution, see Lawrence S. Kaplan, *NATO and the United States: The Enduring Alliance* (Boston: Twayne, 1988), 21–24.

23. F. Ross Peterson, *Prophet Without Honor: Glen H. Taylor and the Fight for American Liberalism* (Lexington: University of Kentucky Press, 1974), 78–79.

24. Gerald Horne, *Black and Red: W. E. B. Du Bois and the Afro-American Response to the Cold War, 1944–1963* (Albany: State University of New York Press, 1986), 22–23, 64; Thomas Borstelmann, *Apartheid's Reluctant Uncle: The United States and Southern Africa in the Early Cold War* (New York: Oxford University Press, 1993), 116, 67; and Mark Soloman, "Black Critics of Colonialism and the Cold War," in Paterson, ed., *Cold War Critics*, 207–8, 213.

25. See National Committee for Peaceful Alternatives, CDG-A, SCPC.

26. Charles DeBenedetti, *Peace Reform in American History* (Bloomington: Indiana University Press, 1980), 153.

27. Bred Andersen, Abraham Kaufman, and Frances Ross Ransom to Muste, 3 June 1947, WRL, DG 46, Box 26, Atlantic Pact File, SCPC.

28. James Finucane, "Forty Faults Flaw Atlantic Pact," *Peace Action*, February 1949, National Council for the Prevention of War, DG 23, Box 430, North Atlantic Treaty File, SCPC.

29. "Statement on the North Atlantic Defense Pact by the War Resisters League," 4 April 1949, WRL, DG 40, Series B, Box 26, Atlantic Pact File, SCPC.

30. The National Peace Conference was formed in 1933 to unify and coordinate efforts of various organizations interested in peace. Minutes of the National Peace Conference Special Meeting on the North Atlantic Treaty, 4 April 1949, WRL, DG 40, Series B, Box 12, National Peace Conference File, SCPC.

31. Taylor, *Congressional Record*, 20 July 1949, 95, pt. 7:9783.

32. The text of the North Atlantic Treaty can be found in Kaplan, *NATO and the United States*, 219–21.

33. Thomas M. Campbell, Jr., "NATO and the United Nations in American Foreign Policy: Building a Framework for Power," in *NATO After Thirty Years*, ed. Lawrence S. Kaplan and Robert W. Clawson (Wilmington, Del.: Scholarly Resources, 1981), 133, 146–47.

34. Alan K. Henrikson, "The North Atlantic Alliance as a Form of World Order," in *Negotiating World Order: The Artisanship and Architecture of Global Diplomacy*, ed. Hendrikson (Wilmington, Del.: Scholarly Resources, 1986), 116–17; Roland Stromberg, *Collective Security and American Foreign Policy: From the League of Nations to NATO* (New York: Frederick A. Praeger, 1963), 193–94; and Lawrence S. Kaplan, *The United States and NATO: The Formative Years* (Lexington: University of Kentucky Press, 1984), 32, 40.

35. Claude Pepper, *Congressional Record*, 15 July 1949, 95, pt. 7:9602–3. Other hesitant supporters expressed similar points of view before the Senate Foreign Relations Committee during the hearings on the pact. They included Norman Thomas, head of the U.S. Socialist party; Mrs. Clifford Bender of the Women's Division of Christian Service of the Methodist Church; and Stephen M. Schwebel, national chairman of the Collegiate Council for the UN. See *North Atlantic Treaty* 2:730–42, 653–57, 3:1007–12.

36. E. Raymond Wilson and Barbara S. Grant, "Some Questions and Comments About the North Atlantic Treaty and the Accompanying Rearmament Program," 25 April 1949, Friends Committee on National Legislation, DG 47, Series H, Box 20, North Atlantic Pact File, SCPC.

37. Mrs. Alexander (Annalee) Stewart, 13 May 1949, *North Atlantic Treaty* 3:429–31. See also "Proposed Principles and Policies to be presented for consideration and action to the Annual Meeting 1949," Women's International League for Peace and Freedom, DG 43, Series A, Microfilm Reel 130.13, SCPC.

38. Charles F. Boss, Jr., 16 May 1949, *North Atlantic Treaty* 3:988, 990, 996, and 997.

39. Glen Taylor, *Congressional Record*, 8 April 1949, 95, pt.3:4141, and ibid., 20 July 1949, 95, pt. 7:9783, 9787.

40. "The Atlantic Pact is a Suicide Pact," statement by the executive committee of the FOR, March 1949, copy in possession of the author.

41. Sayre to Wagner, 16 May 1949, Sayre Papers, DG 117, Series E, Box 3, North Atlantic Pact File, SCPC.

42. Wallace, 5 May 1949, *North Atlantic Treaty* 2:418, 431; Wallace to Herman Wright, 24 March 1949, Reel 45, Henry A. Wallace Papers, University of Iowa Libraries, Iowa City; Ronald Radosh and Leonard P. Liggio, "Henry A. Wallace and the Open Door," in Paterson, ed., *Cold War Critics*, 104.

43. Edward Richards, 17 May 1949, *North Atlantic Treaty* 3:1081; Frederick Libby, 12 May 1949, ibid., 896; Dudley Burr, 10 May 1949, ibid. 2:708–9; Richard Morford, 11 May 1949, ibid. 2:805; and Lee Howe, 16 May 1949, ibid. 3:1042.

44. Mrs. Clifford Bender, 16 May 1949, *North Atlantic Treaty* 3:1005–6, and Henry Cadbury, ibid., 11 May 1949, 2:762.

45. Taylor, *Congressional Record*, 20 July 1949, 95, pt. 7:9785; ibid., 8 April 1949, 95, pt. 3:4142, and Wherry, *Congressional Record*, 20 July 1949, 95, pt. 7:9100.

46. James Warburg, *The Long Road Home: The Autobiography of a Maverick* (Garden City, N.Y.: Doubleday, 1964), 256; idem, 10 May 1949, *North Atlantic Treaty* 2:674.

47. Warburg, *Last Call*, 208–9, 217.

48. James Warburg, 10 May 1949, *North Atlantic Treaty* 2:672, 683–84, 691, 693.

49. Arthur A. Ekirch, Jr., *The Civilian and the Military* (New York: Oxford University Press, 1956), 273–75, 277.

50. George Hartman (WRL) to senators, 6 May 1949, WRL, DG 46, Box 26, Atlantic Pact File, SCPC; Richards, 17 May 1949, *North Atlantic Treaty* 3:1082–83; and annual meeting resolutions, 5–8 May 1949, WILPF, DG 43, Series A, Reel 130.13, SCPC.

51. Press Release, Brethren Service Commission, 25 March 1949, Church of the Brethren, CDG-A, Brethren Service Commission File, SCPC; and Curry, 12 May 1949, *North Atlantic Treaty* 3:835–36.

52. "Shall the Generals Run Our Foreign Policy?" *Christian Century*, 23 February 1949.

53. Taylor, *Congressional Record*, 8 April 1949, 95, pt. 3:4141.

54. Scott L. Bills, "The United States, NATO, and the Third World: Dominoes, Imbroglios, and Agonizing Appraisals," in *NATO After Forty Years*, ed. Lawrence S. Kaplan, S. Victor Papacosma, Mark R. Rubin, and Ruth V. Young (Wilmington, Del.: Scholarly Resources, 1990), 154; Bills, "The United States, NATO and the Colonial World," in *NATO After Thirty Years*, ed. Kaplan and Clawson, 158; and Thomas J. Noer, *Cold War and Black Liberation: The United States and White Rule in Africa, 1948–1968* (Columbia: University of Missouri Press, 1985), 6. See also Borstelmann, *Apartheid's Reluctant Uncle*, 99–100, and the chapter by J. K. Sweeney in this volume.

55. See the text of the NAT in Kaplan, *NATO and the United States*, 220.

56. Wilson and Grant, "Some Questions and Comments About the North Atlantic Treaty and the Accompanying Rearmament Program," 25 April 1949, Friends Committee on National Legislation, DG 47, Series H, Box 20, North Atlantic Pact File, SCPC; and Dobbs, 5 May 1949, *North Atlantic Treaty* 2:483.

57. Thomas, 13 May 1949, *North Atlantic Treaty* 3:968, and Hunton, 13 May 1949, ibid. 3:965.

58. Stewart, 16 May 1949, *North Atlantic Treaty* 3:1049–50; Walls, 16 May 1949, ibid. 3:1024–25; and Hunton, 13 May 1949, ibid. 3:964.

59. James Warburg, "The Atlantic Defense Pact and the Proposal to Rearm Western Europe," 10–11; James Warburg, CDG-A, SCPC.

60. For such a recent interpretation, see John Lewis Gaddis, "Presidential Address: The Tragedy of Cold War History," *Diplomatic History* 17 (Winter 1993): 1–16.

61. James Finucane, "How to Deal with the Devil," *Peace Action*, April 1950, NCPW, DG 23, Box 487, Releases 1950 File, SCPC.

62. Wallace, 5 May 1948, *North Atlantic Treaty* 2:432.

63. Taylor, *Congressional Record*, 20 July 1949, 95, pt. 7:9785.

64. Wilson and Grant, "Some Questions and Comments About the North Atlantic Treaty and the Accompanying Rearmament Program,"25 April 1949, Friends Committee on National Legislation, DG 47, Series H, Box 20, North Atlantic Pact File, SCPC; and Wilson to Graham, 7 July 1949, ibid.

65. "Draft letter to Senators for Endorsement by Individuals," 24 June 1949, Committee for Peaceful Alternatives to the North Atlantic Pact, CDG-A, SCPC; and Stewart, 13 May 1949, *North Atlantic Treaty* 3:937.

66. A. J. Muste, *A Pacifist Program—1949* (New York: Fellowship Publications, 1949).

67. "The Atlantic Pact is a Suicide Pact," statement by the executive committee of the FOR, March 1949, copy in possession of the author.

68. Kaplan, *United States and NATO*, 46. An indication of the small size of the opposition can be found in the Gallup Polls taken during the debate on ratification of the NAT. Polls published in May and July 1949 revealed that 67 percent of the American public surveyed supported ratification of the pact, while opposition was limited to 12–15 percent. See George Gallup, *The Gallup Poll: Public Opinion 1935–71*, 3 vols. (New York: Random House, 1972), 2:815, 829–30.

69. Lawrence S. Wittner, *Rebels Against War: The American Peace Movement, 1941–1960* (New York: Columbia University Press, 1969), 201–2, 213. See also Thomas Paterson, "Introduction: American Critics of the Cold War and Their Alternatives," in Paterson, ed., *Cold War Critics*, 14.

70. Richard Falk, "Lifting the Curse of Bipartisanship,"*World Policy Journal* 1 (Winter 1983): 127; and Paterson, *Meeting the Communist Threat*, 101, 104.

71. DeBenedetti and Chatfield, *An American Ordeal*, 13, 21.

72. Falk, "Lifting the Curse of Bipartisanship," 129–30.

9. Republican Party Politics, Foreign Policy, and the Election of 1952

1. A fine survey of Republican Party history and politics is George H. Mayer, *The Republican Party 1954–1966* (New York: Oxford University Press, 1967). Also useful for a chronology of the election of 1952 and key details relating to both major parties is Barton J. Bernstein's chapter on this election in Arthur M. Schlesinger, Jr., ed., *History of American Presidential Elections, 1789–1968*, 4 vols. (New York: Chelsea House, 1971), 4:3215–37.

2. The best scholarly biography of Taft is James T. Patterson, *Mr. Republican: A Biography of Robert A. Taft* (Boston: Houghton Mifflin, 1972); an earlier and highly sympathetic account is William S. White, *The Taft Story* (New York: Harper and Brothers, 1954).

3. Robert A. Taft to Benjamin S. Hubbell, 17 August 1951, Box 944, Robert A. Taft Papers, Library of Congress, Washington, D.C.; Robert A. Taft to Paul Shafer, 5 November 1951, ibid.; Robert A. Taft to Miller Freeman, 4 January 1952, Box 876, ibid.; *New York Times*, 23 March 1952.

4. *New York Times*, 3, 12, 16, 23, 29 February 1952.

5. Ibid., 27 March, 13 June 1952.

6. In anticipation of his quest for the presidency in 1952, Taft had written a short book, released late in the fall of 1951 entitled *A Foreign Policy for Americans* (Garden City, N.Y.: Doubleday, 1951), in which he summarized the basic views on foreign policy he had expressed in piecemeal fashion in numerous earlier speeches. Most of the speeches Taft gave on foreign policy in 1952 derived from this book. See *New York Times*, 23 February, 19 March 1952.

7. *New York Times*, 7 April, 13 June 1952.

8. Ibid., 29 April, 6, 26, 30 June 1952.

9. Ibid., 17 February, 25 June 1952.

10. Paul T. David et al., *Presidential Nominating Politics in 1952*, 5 vols. (Baltimore: Johns Hopkins University Press, 1954), 1:25–26.

11. Lodge made these remarks in a conversation with Eisenhower on 4 September 1951. See David, *Presidential Nominating Politics*, 27; Dwight D. Eisenhower, *Mandate for Change 1953–1956* (Garden City, N.Y.: Doubleday, 1963), 16–18; Dwight D. Eisenhower interview, 20 July 1967, Dwight D. Eisenhower Oral History, OH#11, 17–18, Dwight D. Eisenhower Library, Abilene, Kans.

12. Eisenhower, *Mandate for Change*, 18; Dwight D. Eisenhower, *At Ease: Stories I Tell to Friends* (Garden City, N.Y.: Doubleday, 1967), 370–71; Eisenhower interview, OH#11, 11–12, Eisenhower Library. The Eisenhower-Taft meeting took place on approximately 1 February 1951 during a period when Eisenhower had returned to Washington from SHAPE in Paris.

13. Eisenhower interview, OH#11, 11–15, Eisenhower Library; Eisenhower, *At Ease*, 371–72.

14. Eisenhower was particularly impressed by the sentiment expressed in his favor at a large indoor rally, held 8 February 1952 at New York's Madison Square Garden; see Eisenhower, *Mandate for Change*, 19–21; Eisenhower interview, OH#11, 19, Eisenhower Library. In a long private conversation with *New York Times* correspondent C. L. Sulzberger on 11 December 1951, Eisenhower stated that he did not want to seek the presidency, nor would he in any way attempt to assist the political leaders who were attempting to draft him. He would only run for the office if the American people drafted him as a candidate, but he hoped that this would not happen. Sulzberger, *A Long Row of Candles: Memoirs and Diaries 1934–1954* (Toronto: Macmillan, 1969), 699–705. Eisenhower's biographer, Stephen E. Ambrose, aptly concludes that the general's real dilemma was that he "wanted to be nominated by acclamation," a posture his close friends knew was untenable in the circumstances. Ambrose, *Eisenhower: Soldier, General of the Army, President-Elect 1890–1952*, 2 vols. (New York: Simon & Schuster, 1983), 1:518.

15. Gen. Lucius D. Clay interview, 20 February 1967, 7–8, Columbia University Oral History Project, Columbia University, New York, N.Y.; Eisenhower, *Mandate for Change*, 21–23. Eisenhower recalled that in this meeting he "tentatively agreed" to return to the United States as soon as he finished "his duties in Europe." He added that "if nominated at the convention," he "would campaign for the Presidency." In his own mind, however, Eisenhower was committed "to run if nominated, but not to seek the nomination."

16. Memorandum of Donald Cook conversation with Gen. Lucius D. Clay in London, 17 February 1952, Box 1, William E. Robinson Collection, Eisenhower Library.

17. Sulzberger, *A Long Row of Candles,* 616–17, 646, 693–94, 702; the private luncheon was held in Paris on 6 March 1951. The Chiang Kai-shek remark was made on 12 March 1951; the China comment was made on 27 June 1951; and the statement on the value of Taft's pledge on NATO was made on 13 November 1951.

18. Eisenhower to George A. Sloan, 29 January 1952, Box 1, William E. Robinson Collection, Eisenhower Library; Eisenhower to George Whitney, 29 January 1952, ibid.

19. Eisenhower to J. Earl Shaefer, 27 December 1951, Box 1, J. Earl Shaefer Papers, Eisenhower Library.

20. Herbert Brownell interview, 5 March 1965, 20–21, Dulles Oral History Collection, Princeton University, Princeton, N.J.; Everett McKinley Dirksen interview, 19 July 1966, 4–5, ibid.

21. Eisenhower to John Foster Dulles, 15 April 1952, Box 483, John Foster Dulles Papers, Princeton University, Princeton, N.J.; Dulles to Eisenhower, 20 May 1952, ibid.; Gen. Lucius D. Clay interview, 12 March 1965, 9–10, Dulles Oral History, Princeton University.

22. Eisenhower, *Mandate for Change,* 41; *New York Times,* 13, 22 June 1952; Donald Bruce Johnson, *National Party Platforms 1840–1956,* 2 vols., rev. ed. (Urbana: University of Illinois Press, 1978), 1:496–505.

23. Johnson, *National Party Platforms,* 498–99. The concept of "liberation" of captive peoples and the attack on containment were clearly contributions of Dulles. See his earlier expression of these views in John Foster Dulles, "A Policy of Boldness," *Life,* 19 May 1952, 146–60. See also Louis L. Gerson, *John Foster Dulles* (New York: Cooper Square, 1967), 70–76.

24. *New York Times,* 5 June 1952.

25. Ibid., 6, 8, 24, 27 June 1952.

26. Ibid., 5, 6, 24 June 1952.

27. Ibid., 6, 13, 20, 22, 25 June 1952. Taft chastised the general on one occasion for choosing to contend with "a straw man in the form of an isolationist, presumably a Republican" rather than deal with the substantive issue—the "complete failure" of the Truman administration's foreign policy. Ibid., 25 June 1952.

28. Taft's biographer concludes that the personal appeal of Eisenhower and the slogan "Taft Can't Win," "hurt Taft badly" during the campaign for the nomination; see Patterson, *Mr. Republican,* 560–62; Schlesinger, *History of Presidential Elections* 4:3231.

29. Patterson, *Mr. Republican,* 559–60. For a summary of the delegate challenges and procedural controversies see ibid.,551–58. Also see Schlesinger, *History of Presidential Elections* 4:3229–30. The total number of votes for Eisenhower after delegations had completed their switch to him on the first ballot was 845, compared with 280 for Senator Taft. Prior to changes in the original tallies of the delegations, Eisenhower received 595 votes to Taft's 500. Gov. Earl Warren of California had received 81, Harold Stassen of Minnesota 20, and Gen. Douglas MacArthur 10. After the changes were made, Governor Warren still retained 77 votes and General MacArthur 4.

30. Eisenhower, *Mandate for Change,* 46; *New York Times,* 12 July 1952; Sherman Adams, *Firsthand Report: The Story of the Eisenhower Administration* (New York:

Harper and Brothers, 1961), 34–36. Both Eisenhower and Adams stated that Nixon was at the top of the general's list of prospects for vice-president. Nixon's strongest advocate among Eisenhower's close advisers was Herbert Brownell, later to serve as attorney general during Eisenhower's first term as president.

31. Sen. H. Alexander Smith interview, 1962, 282–86, Columbia Oral History Project, Columbia University. For other examples of the bitterness over Eisenhower's nomination by Taft and his friends, see Patterson, *Mr. Republican,* 570–73.

32. Eisenhower to Taft, 17 July 1952, Box 990, Taft Papers, Library of Congress; "Advice to Eisenhower" memo, Box 1178, ibid.; "Memorandum on General Eisenhower," Box 990, ibid.

33. "Advice to Eisenhower" memo, Box 1178, ibid.

34. Taft to Everett Dirksen, 6 August 1952, Box 1054, ibid.

35. Taft to Wallace F. Bennett, Taft to Arthur V. Watkins, Taft to Hugh Butler, all 13 August 1952, ibid. Governor Stevenson was nominated to the presidency by the Democrats on 24 July 1952.

36. Patterson, *Mr. Republican,* 576–77; Eisenhower, *Mandate for Change,* 64. The meeting was held at the general's home at Morningside Heights in New York City near Columbia University.

37. "Agenda" of Robert A. Taft, Box 1178, Taft Papers, Library of Congress. This is Taft's own handwritten outline of points to discuss with General Eisenhower at the Morningside Heights meeting.

38. Ibid.; *New York Times,* 13 September 1952.

39. Draft of Taft press statement of 12 September 1952, with handwritten corrections by the senator, Box 1178, Taft Papers, Library of Congress.

40. Press statement of Robert A. Taft of 12 September 1952, reprinted in Schlesinger, *History of Presidential Elections,* 4:3311–13.

41. Ibid.

42. *New York Times,* 6, 13, 21, 23, 26 August 1952; 3, 9, 13 September 1952.

43. Ibid., 9 August 1952. For Stevenson's commitments to the New Deal and Fair Deal programs, see his speeches of 26 July 1952 and 28 August 1952, reprinted in Adlai E. Stevenson, *Major Campaign Speeches of Adlai E. Stevenson 1952* (New York: Random House, 1953), 7–10, 23–29.

44. Thruston B. Morton interview, 9 February 1966, 2–5, Dulles Oral History, Princeton University; Dulles, "Notes for Foreign Policy Discussion," 21 August 1952, Box 483, Dulles Papers, Princeton University; *New York Times,* 14, 25, 28 August, 4, 5, 27 September, 21 October, all 1952.

45. *New York Times,* 26 August, 6, 26 September, 22, 23 October 1952.

46. Ibid., 5, 10 September, 15, 16 October 1952.

47. Ibid., 16, 21, 27 September, 3, 4, 31 October 1952.

48. Ibid., 18, 19 September, 9, 10, 15, 17, 22 October 1952.

49. Ibid., 27 September, 3, 9, 14, 15 October 1952; Eisenhower speech of 25 October 1952, reprinted in Schlesinger, *History of Presidential Elections* 4:3325–30.

50. Stevenson, *Campaign Speeches,* 128, 170, 211; *Public Papers of the Presidents of the United States: Harry S. Truman, 1952–53* (Washington, D.C.: Office of the Federal Register,* National Archives and Records Administration, 1966), 551, 639, 686.

51. *Public Papers of the Presidents, Harry S. Truman, 1952–53*, 678, 682, 685–86, 693, 706, 724; Stevenson, *Campaign Speeches*, 141, 170, 186, 187, 193, 250, 270.

52. Stevenson, *Campaign Speeches*, 186–87.

53. *Public Papers of the Presidents 1952–53*, 569, 739–40, 831–32, 955–56, 959. Stevenson concurred with Truman's remarks and added that Eisenhower's acceptance of the Old Guard line after winning the position as Republican standard-bearer illustrated that the reactionary wing of that party had "lost the nomination but won the nominee"; Stevenson, *Campaign Speeches*, 269–70.

54. *New York Times*, 1 November 1952; Louis Harris, *Is There a Republican Majority?* (New York: Harper and Row, 1954), 23–27; Samuel Lubell, *The Revolt of the Moderates* (New York: Harper and Row, 1956), 39; Schlesinger, *History of Presidential Elections* 4:3258.

10. Confronting Cold War Neutralism:
The Eisenhower Administration and Finland, A Case Study

1. Roy Allison, *Finland's Relations with the Soviet Union* (New York: St. Martin's, 1985), 12–16; Keith W. Olson, "Finland: Between East and West," *Wilson Quarterly* 10 (Autumn 1986): 56–58.

2. Allison, *Finland's Relations with the Soviet Union*, 17–18; John Vloyantes, "Finland," in *Europe's Neutral and Nonaligned States: Between NATO and the Warsaw Pact*, ed. S. Victor Papacosma and Mark R. Rubin (Wilmington, Del.: Scholarly Resources, 1989), 143–44.

3. Allison, *Finland's Relations with the Soviet Union*, 171–73.

4. Ibid., 20–21; Pekka K. Hamalainen, "The Finnish Solution," *Wilson Quarterly* 10 (Autumn 1986): 68.

5. Allison, *Finland's Relations with the Soviet Union*, 21–25, 174–75.

6. Ibid., 113; Arthur Spencer, "Finland Maintains Democracy," *Foreign Affairs* 31 (January 1953): 301–9.

7. National Security Council, "The Position of the United States with Respect to Scandinavia and Finland," Report 121 (hereafter NSC followed by report number), 8 January 1952, Folder: NSC Meeting No. 111, 16 January 1952, Box 216, President's Secretary's File, Papers of Harry S. Truman, Harry S. Truman Library, Independence, Mo.

8. John Cabot, Memorandum of Conversation, 17 September 1952, RG 84, Box 4, Finland Classified General Records: 1950–52, National Archives, Suitland, Maryland (hereafter NA).

9. NSC, Report 5403, "U.S. Policy Toward Finland" (hereafter NSC 5403), 12 January 1954, Folder: NSC 5403-US Policy Toward Finland (1), Box 8, Policy Papers Subseries, National Security Council Series, White House Office (hereafter WHO): Office of Special Assistant for National Security Affairs, Dwight D. Eisenhower Library, Abilene, Kans. (hereafter DDEL). President Eisenhower formally approved this policy on 25 January 1954; see memorandum by James S. Lay, Executive Secretary, NSC, 25 January 1954, Folder: OCB 091 Finland (File #1) (1) (cont.), Box 29, OCB Central Files, WHO: National Security Council Staff Papers, 1948–61, DDEL.

10. Report from American Legation in Helsinki, "Diminishing of Soviet Pressure on Finland," 10 April 1952, Box 4, Finland Classified General Records: 1950–52, RG 84, NA.

11. NSC 5403.

12. *New York Times,* 11 October 1955, 10 June 1956; U.S. Government, *Public Papers of the Presidents of the United States: Dwight D. Eisenhower, 1956* (Washington, D.C.: GPO, 1958), 554–55.

13. Jurg Martin Gabriel, *The American Conception of Neutrality After 1941* (New York: St. Martin's, 1988), 186, 262n91.

14. H. W. Brands, *The Specter of Neutralism: The United States and the Emergence of the Third World, 1947–1960* (New York: Columbia University Press, 1989), 307.

15. Robert Murphy to Nelson A. Rockefeller, 19 August 1955, Folder: #9 Bandung (1), Box 2, Planning Coordinating Group Series, WHO: NSC Staff Papers, DDEL.

16. "Neutralism in Europe, Summary Report," Folder: #9 Bandung (2), ibid.

17. Ibid.; "Neutralism in Finland," 13 June 1955, Folder: #9 Bandung (3), ibid.

18. Memorandum from the chief of the International Branch, Bureau of the Budget (Marcy), to the director of the Bureau (Brundage), 4 September 1956, U.S., Department of State, *Foreign Relations of the United States: 1955–57* (Washington, D.C.: GPO, 1989), 10:103 (hereafter *FRUS* followed by the appropriate year and volume).

19. Public Law 480, *Agricultural Trade Development and Assistance Act of 1954, U.S. Statutes at Large* 68, pt. 1 (1954): 454–59.

20. NSC, Operations Coordinating Board (hereafter OCB), Progress Report, NSC 5403, 2 January 1958, Folder: NSC 5403-Policy Toward Finland (1), Box 8, Policy Papers Subseries, NSC Series, WHO: Office of Special Advisor for National Security Affairs Records, 1952–1961, DDEL. American fears were realized in 1957 when the Finnmark was devalued from 230 to 320 to the dollar, reducing the fund by 28 percent. Although the devaluation made Finnish exports more attractive, it was costly for the United States.

21. Ibid.; OCB, "Problems in Developing Uses for Finnmarks," 12 June 1957, Folder: OCB 091 Finland (File #2) (8), Box 30, OCB Central Files, WHO: NSC Staff Papers, 1948–61, DDEL. Besides the ships, other items encouraged for purchase included $7 million for prefabricated housing for air force family housing in Europe and $1 million for paper products to Korea.

22. Public Law 213, *Mutual Defense Assistance Control Act of 1951, U.S. Statutes at Large* 65 (1951): 644–47.

23. Daily Intelligence Abstract #488, 1 November 1955, File: OCB 350.05 (File #2) (9), Box 111, OCB Central Files Series, December 1954–February 1956, WHO: NSC Staff Papers, DDEL; Intelligence Notes, 15 August 1956, File: OCB 350.05 (File #3) (6), February-October 1956, ibid. By mid-1956, concern still existed that the Finns continued to trade with "Red China," but there was some consolation that it included no more tankers; see minutes of NSC Meeting, 19 July 1956, Folder: 291st Meeting, Box 8, NSC Series, Ann Whitman File, DDEL; Jack K. McFall, Oral History Interview, Truman Library.

24. NSC, OCB, Progress Report, 2 January 1958, DDEL; C. Douglas Dillon to President, 11 February 1958, DDEL; memorandum for the secretary of state from Dwight D. Eisenhower, 15 February 1958, DDEL.

25. C. Douglas Dillon, under secretary of state for economic affairs, to Gen. C. P. Cabell, acting director, Central Intelligence Agency, 19 September 1958, Folder: Chronological File, September 1958 (1), Box 5, Papers of Christian A. Herter, DDEL; NSC Report 5914/1, U.S. Policy Toward Finland, Financial Appendix, 14 October 1959, Folder: NSC 5914/1, U.S. Policy Toward Finland, Box 27, NSC Series, Policy Papers Subseries, WHO: Office of Special Assistant for National Security Affairs, DDEL.

26. Allison, *Finland's Relations with the Soviet Union*, 38–39 and 104–5; Gabriel, *The American Conception of Neutrality after 1941*, 179–80.

27. Memorandum of discussion, 273d NSC Meeting, 18 January 1956, *FRUS, 1955–57* 10:67; see also, ibid. 27:484–85.

28. NSC, OCB, Progress Report on United States Policy Toward Finland, 23 November 1955, Folder: OCB 091 Finland (File #2) (1), Box 29, OCB Central Files, WHO: NSC Staff Papers, 1948–61, DDEL. John Foster Dulles had strongly recommended embassy status as early as July 1954, specifically to counter growing Soviet efforts to enhance its prestige there; see J. F. Dulles, memorandum for the president, 18 July 1954, Folder: Finland, Box 9, International Series, Ann Whitman File, DDEL.

29. For a brief discussion of the U.S. position on Finnish membership in the Nordic Council, see NSC, OCB, Progress Report, 23 November 1955, Folder: OCB 091 Finland (File #2) (1), Box 29, OCB Central Files, WHO: NSC Staff Papers, 1948–61, DDEL.

30. *FRUS, 1955–57* 11, documents some of the negotiations leading to this "package deal."

31. D. W. Gladney to Elmer B. Staats, 28 November 1956, Folder: OCB 091 Finland (File #2) (6) (cont.), Box 30, OCB Central Files, WHO: NSC Staff Papers, 1948–61, DDEL.

32. NSC, OCB, Progress Report on NSC 5403, 12 June 1957, Folder: NSC 5403-Policy Toward Finland (1), Box 8, Policy Papers Subseries, NSC Series, WHO: Office of the Special Assistant for National Security Affairs Records, 1952–61, DDEL.

33. John P. Vloyantes, *Silk Glove Hegemony: Finnish-Soviet Relations, 1944–1974* (Kent, Ohio: Kent State University Press, 1975), 92–108; Allison, *Finland's Relations with the Soviet Union*, 138–40.

34. NSC, OCB, Progress Report on NSC 5403, 9 July 1958, Folder: NSC 5403-Policy Toward Finland (1), Box 8, Policy Papers Subseries, NSC Series, WHO: Office of the Special Assistant for National Security Affairs Records, 1952–61, DDEL.

35. John D. Hickerson to Jeremiah O'Connor, operations coordinator, office of the under secretary, Department of State, 15 September 1958, Folder: U.S. Policy Toward Finland, Box 8, Briefing Notes Subseries, NSC Series, ibid.

36. NSC, OCB, Report on U.S. Policy Toward Finland, 1 July 1959, Folder: NSC 5403-Policy Toward Finland (1), Box 8, Policy Papers Subseries, NSC Series, ibid.

37. NSC, Report 5914/1, "U.S. Policy Toward Finland," 14 October 1959, Folder: NSC 5914/1-U.S. Policy Toward Finland, Box 27, ibid.

38. NSC 5403.

39. NSC 5914/1.

40. Ibid.

41. Minutes of NSC meeting, 1 October 1959, Folder: 420th Meeting, Box 8, NSC Series, Ann Whitman File, DDEL.

42. John Foster Dulles, Memorandum of Dinner with Sir Winston Churchill, 12 April 1954, Folder: Meetings with President (4), Box 1, White House Memorandum Series, Papers of John Foster Dulles, DDEL; see also, John L. Gaddis, "The Unexpected John Foster Dulles: Nuclear Weapons, Communism, and the Russians," in *John Foster Dulles and the Diplomacy of the Cold War*, ed. Richard H. Immerman (Princeton: Princeton University Press, 1990), 67–68.

43. Memorandum for Record of the President's State Dinner, Geneva, 18 July 1955, *FRUS, 1955–57* 5:372–73; see also, Memorandum of Conversations at President's Dinner, Geneva, 18 July 1955, ibid., 5:377.

44. Dulles, Memorandum of Dinner with Churchill, 12 April 1954, Folder: Meetings with President (4), Box 1, White House Memorandum Series, Papers of John Foster Dulles, DDEL.

45. "Neutralism in Europe, Summary Report," Folder: #9 Bandung (1), Box 2, Planning Coordinating Group Series, WHO: NSC Staff Papers, DDEL.

46. NSC, Report 6006/1, "U.S. Policy Toward Scandinavia (Denmark, Norway, and Sweden)," 6 April 1960, Folder: NSC 6006/1-Scandinavia (Denmark, Norway, Sweden), Box 28, Policy Papers Subseries, NSC Series, WHO: Office of the Special Assistant for National Security Affairs Records, 1952–61, DDEL; Northern European Chiefs of Mission Conference, London, 19–21 September 1957, Ambassador White's appraisal of Swedish position, *FRUS, 1955–57* 4:624–25.

47. Brands, *Specter of Neutralism*, 9.

48. Memorandum of discussion, 290th NSC Meeting, 12 July 1956, *FRUS, 1955–57* 10:82–83.

49. See for example, Hickerson's remarks, Northern European Chiefs of Mission Conference, London, 19–21 September 1957, summary of proceedings, *FRUS, 1955–57* 4:619–20.

11. The Unwanted Alliance:
Portugal and the United States

1. José Calvet de Magalhães, "An Historical Outline of Portuguese-American Relations," in *Portugal: An Atlantic Paradox*, ed. de Magalhães (Lisbon: Institute for Strategic and International Studies, 1991), 15. David Humphreys presented his credentials to the Portuguese authorities on 13 May 1791; see Richardson Dougall and Mary Patricia Chapman, *United States Chiefs of Mission, 1778–1973* (Washington, D.C.: GPO, 1973), 125.

2. de Magalhães, "An Historical Outline," 37.

3. The first formal treaty of alliance between Britain and Portugal was signed in 1386, but that connection was preceded by the 1373 Treaty of Peace and Friendship. Although both countries saw Spanish aggression as the focus of the alliance, the extensive, albeit diminished, Portuguese colonial empire soon became of primary importance; see Robert G. Caldwell, "The Anglo-Portuguese Alliance Today," *Foreign Affairs* 21 (October 1942): 149. Portugal was exceedingly capable at playing the great powers off against another, but the British alliance was especially valuable in disputes with France or Germany; Fernando J. Andresen Guimarães, "The Collapse of the New State and the Emergence of the Angolan Civil War," *Camões Center Quarterly* 5 (Winter 1993–94): 16.

4. Salazar was impressed by Germany's opposition to communism, but the barbaric nature of the Nazi regime disturbed him. He wondered if the German appetite would be satisfied short of world domination. As for the British, Salazar's political opponents were strong supporters of Britain and thus the friend of his enemies was also damned. Moreover, the Anglo-Russian alliance caused him to question London's commitment to the anticommunist cause; see George Kennan to Secretary Hull, 4 February 1943, 853.00/1064, Decimal Files, RG 59, Department of State Records, National Archives, Washington, D.C. (hereafter cited as DSNA). Ambassador Norweb believed this dispatch to be a most important and revealing communication. Indeed, he repeatedly insisted that it contained the key to the success of the negotiations for a base in the Azores. R. Henry Norweb, personal interview, 23 January 1970, Cleveland, Ohio.

5. Portugal sought to escape the "disdain of both successful suitor and rejected swain." Lisbon to State Department, 6 October 1944 (#1041), 740.0011 EW 1939/10-644, RG 59, DSNA.

6. Katharine Duff, "Neutrals and Non-Belligerent Allies: Portugal," in *Survey of International Affairs, 1939–1946: The War and the Neutrals*, ed. Arnold J. Toynbee (London: Oxford University Press, 1956), 318; *New York Herald Tribune*, 18 March 1941; *Christian Science Monitor*, 15 May 1941, and *New York Times*, 7, 17 May 1941. The *Monitor* also published an editorial cartoon showing a Nazi jackboot descending upon the Azores with Uncle Sam announcing, "That's too close for comfort." Sen. Claude Pepper and Robert R. McCormick (of the *Chicago Tribune*) were presented as favoring the protective occupation of the islands. *Congressional Record*, 77th Cong., 1st sess., 1941, 87, pt. 12: A3379; Lisbon to State Department, 16 April 1941, 853B.014/11, RG 59, DSNA; Lisbon to State Department, 15 November 1941, 853.00/1029, RG 59, DSNA; State Department to Lisbon legation, 9 May 1941, U.S. Department of State, *Foreign Relations of the United States 1941* (Washington, D.C.: GPO, 1959), 2:841–42 (hereafter cited as *FRUS* followed by the appropriate year and volume number); and Hugh Kay, *Salazar and Modern Portugal* (New York: Hawthorn, 1970), 160–62. The White House announced the establishment of a "neutrality patrol" in the North Atlantic by the U.S. Navy on 6 September 1939; see Patrick Abbaza, *Mr. Roosevelt's Navy: The Private War of the U.S. Atlantic Fleet, 1939–1942* (Annapolis: Naval Institute Press, 1975), 62.

7. Portuguese legation to secretary of state, 30 May 1941, *FRUS, 1941* 2:844–47.

8. President Roosevelt directed the secretaries of war and navy on 22 May 1941 to prepare to occupy the Azores in one month's time. For details, consult Stetson Conn and Byron Fairchild, *The Framework of Hemisphere Defense* (Washington, D.C.: GPO, 1960); Mark S. Watson, *Chief of Staff: Prewar Plans and Preparations* (Washington, D.C.: GPO, 1950); Richard M. Leighton and Robert W. Coakley, *Global Logistics and Strategy, 1940–1943* (Washington, D.C.: GPO, 1955); and Stetson Conn, Rose C. Engleman, and Byron Fairchild, *Guarding the United States and Its Outposts* (Washington, D.C.: GPO, 1964).

9. Joint Planning Committee to Joint Board, 23 September 1941, JB #325, Serial 694-1, RG 225, War Department records, National Archives, Washington, D.C.; memo of conversation (Welles and Bianchi), 24 December 1941, *FRUS, 1941* 2:856–57; Forrest C. Pogue, *George C. Marshall: Ordeal and Hope, 1939–1942* (New York: Viking, 1966), 306; Theodore A. Wilson, *The First Summit: Roosevelt and Churchill at Placentia*

Bay (New York: Houghton Mifflin, 1969), 150; memo of conversation (FDR and Churchill), 11 August 1941, *FRUS, 1941* 1:356; Conn, *Framework of Hemisphere Defense,* 139–40; and Kay, *Salazar,* 164.

10. W. N. Medlicott, *The Economic Blockade,* 2 vols. (London: Her Majesty's Stationery Office, 1952–59), 1:63–133.

11. The major supplier of wolfram was China, but those supplies were lost to European acquisition with the closing of the Trans-Siberian railroad to commercial traffic following the German invasion of the USSR. Efforts to restrict the sale of wolfram to the Axis powers ran afoul of Salazar's reluctance to deny Germany the output of mines owned by German nationals. When the free sale of wolfram produced an inflationary situation that violated Salazar's economic orthodoxy, he decreed that all purchases would take place in a government-controlled marketplace with specified percentages going to the respective belligerents; see J. K. Sweeney, "The Portuguese Wolfram Embargo: A Study in Economic Warfare," *Military Affairs* 38 (February 1974): 24. See also Douglas Wheeler, "The Price of Neutrality: Portugal, the Wolfram Question and World War II," *Luso-Brazilian Review* 23 (Summer and Winter 1986): 107–27, 97–111; John Kemler, "The Struggle for Wolfram in the Iberian Peninsula, June 1942–June 1944" (Ph.D. diss., University of Chicago, 1949).

12. Cordell Hull remarked, "If we are divided, we are ineffective." *Vital Speeches* 10 (9 April 1944): 388; and Cordell Hull, *Memoirs of Cordell Hull,* 2 vols. (New York: Macmillan, 1948), 2:1339–40.

13. Maurice Matloff, *Strategic Planning for Coalition Warfare, 1943–1944* (Washington, D.C.: GPO, 1959), 131; Anthony Eden, *The Reckoning* (Boston: Houghton Mifflin, 1965), 453; Winston S. Churchill, *The Hinge of Fate* (Boston: Houghton Mifflin, 1950), 789; Samuel Eliot Morison, *The Atlantic Battle Won, May 1943–May 1945,* vol. 10 in the *History of United States Naval Operations in World War II* (Boston: Little, Brown, 1959), 44; FDR to Churchill, 6 October 1943, *FRUS, 1943* 2:547–48; R. Henry Norweb, personal interview, 23 January 1970.

14. Although a diplomatic approach was successful, the first item on the Anglo-American agenda was the forcible occupation of the Azores. "Joint War Plans Committee," J.W.P.C. 32, 16 May 1943, Leahy File, Combined Chiefs of Staff No. 381, Azores (5-7-43) Sec. 1, RG 218, National Archives; "Joint Chiefs of Staff 83rd Meeting," 17 May 1943, Leahy File, Combined Chiefs of Staff No. 318, Azores (5-7-43) Sec. 1, ibid. The plan was scrapped after opposition from Anthony Eden and Clement Attlee as well as a lack of logistical capability; Winant to secretary of state, 29 June 1943, *FRUS, 1943* 2:535.

15. Elements of the U.S. Navy and Marine Corps were stationed in the Azores during the Great War. President Roosevelt, in his capacity as under secretary of the navy, later asserted he personally supervised the dismantling of those American facilities; George F. Kennan, *Memoirs: 1925–1945* (Boston: Little, Brown, 1967), 161. Kennan was the chargé d'affaires when the American minister (Bert Fish) died and thus the senior American diplomat in Portugal. The decision to acquire an American base in the Azores produced some interesting consequences for Kennan and nearly ended the negotiations before they began; Kennan, *Memoirs,* 142–63. The Portuguese offer to allow greater use of the existing British facilities was not acceptable to the Americans. The Army Air Force believed that attempting to operate from only one

airfield in the Azores was too dangerous. Equipment and lives would surely be lost in lieu of a suitable alternate field for use during bad weather. Moreover, the existing British facilities could not be expanded to handle any increase in air traffic incident to the invasion of Europe. Finally, another airfield was deemed essential even if the war in Europe were concluded, since the fastest route to East Asia was through the Azores. The negotiations were in the hands of R. Henry Norweb, a newly assigned career diplomat who enjoyed a reputation as a troubleshooter. The tall, aristocratic Norweb established a personal relationship with Salazar which proved exceedingly useful; R. Henry Norweb, personal interview, 23 January 1970.

16. A German submarine harassed a Portuguese ship *(Serpa Pinto)* on the high seas in May 1944 and two persons drowned. Although Salazar was more annoyed than intimidated at the time, the episode does indicate that his fears in at least one respect were not unfounded. Medlicott, *Economic Blockade* 2:605; and Lisbon to State Department, 31 May 1944, 711.53/46, RG 59, DSNA.

17. Norweb to secretary of state, 24 November 1943, *FRUS, 1943* 2:570; Duff, "Neutrals," 341–44; Lisbon to State Department, 19 February 1943, 740.0011 EW 1939/38174, RG 59, DSNA; R. Henry Norweb, personal interview, 23 January 1970; Lisbon to State Department, 26 November 1943, 811.34553b/33, RG59, DSNA.

18. Norweb to secretary of state, 2 December 1943, *FRUS, 1943* 2:573–76.

19. Lisbon to State Department, 21 April 1944, 711.53/36, RG 59, DSNA; Lisbon to State Department, 22 January 1944, 811.34553b/61, RG 59, DSNA; and Lisbon legation to State Department, 4 March 1944, *FRUS, 1944* 4:19–20. The use of the Azores as the last card in any negotiation proved a recurring theme in relations between the United States and Portugal. See naval attaché, Lisbon, to chief of naval operations, 19 August 1944, OPD 350.05 Portugal, Decimal Files 1942–45, RG 165, War Department Records, National Archives; and "Salazar's Current Prospects," Central Intelligence Agency Memo No. 9-64, 8 June 1964, National Security File, Country File, Portugal, vol. 1, Lyndon B. Johnson Library, Austin, Tex.

20. A. H. de Oliveira Marques, *History of Portugal,* 2 vols. (New York: Columbia University Press, 1975), 1:234. Although virtually surrounded by the Japanese early in the China campaign, Macao remained a neutral outpost in a sea of belligerency. Duff, "Neutrals," 341.

21. Lisbon to Department of State, 19 February 1943, 740.0011 EW 1939/28173, RG 59, DSNA. Insofar as the New State was concerned, the loss of the colonies meant the end of the regime; Guimarões, "Collapse of the New State," 9.

22. Portugal was threatened with the alienation of its Pacific colonies if it did not act quickly. But Lisbon was confident the American need for a facility in the Azores was so absolute that it could drive a hard bargain. The Portuguese were aware of an article by Arthur Krock indicating that a base in the Azores was important to postwar American security; *New York Times,* 13 October 1943. This appraisal anticipated an official judgment that the facility was "required for defense of the Western Hemisphere" in the postwar world; see "U.S. Requirements for Post-War Air Bases," JCS 570/1, 15 November 1943, MR Naval Aide's File (A-42 Air Routes), Franklin D. Roosevelt Library, Hyde Park, N.Y.; State Department to Lisbon, 11 July 1944 (#1959), 811.20 Def. (M) Portugal/7-744, RG 59, DSNA; Lisbon to State Department, 12 July 1944 (#2144), 811.20 Def. (M) Portugal/7-1244, RG 59, DSNA;

Lisbon to State Department, 11 July 1944 (#2137), 811.34553b/7-1144, RG 59, DSNA; Norweb to secretary of state, 19 May 1944, and secretary of state to Norweb and reply, 10–13 July, *FRUS, 1944* 4:25, 46–49; R. Henry Norweb, personal interview, 23 January 1970; Lisbon to State Department, 14 June 1944, 711.53/55 RG 59, DSNA; and State Department to Lisbon, 16 June 1944, 711.53/33, RG 59, DSNA.

23. Lisbon to State Department, 2 October 1944 (#3045), 811.34553b/10-244, RG 59, DSNA; and Norweb to secretary of state, 3 October 1944, *FRUS, 1944* 4:73–75.

24. Secretary of State to Norweb, 6 October 1944, *FRUS, 1944* 4:76–78; memorandum of conversations, 6 October 1944, 811.34553b/10-644, RG 59, DSNA; Lisbon to State Department, summary of discussions with Salazar, 811.34553b/11-1144, RG 59, DSNA. Salazar even authorized construction of the Santa Maria air base although no agreement yet existed regarding Timor. R. Henry Norweb promised, on his own authority, to obtain War Department approval for the Portuguese liberation of Timor; R. Henry Norweb, personal interview, 23 January 1970. See also U.S. military attaché (Lisbon) to War Department, 24 September 1944 (#445), RG 165, NA; Lisbon to State Department, 11 July 1944 (#2137), State Department to Lisbon, 11 July 1944 (#1959), and Lisbon to State Department, 12 July 1944 (#2144), 811.20 Def. (M) Portugal/7-7441, RG 59, DSNA; and Norweb to secretary of state, 13 July 1944, *FRUS, 1944* 4:48–49. Portugal agreed to embargo wolfram on 6 June 1944, but the news of the invasion of northern France overshadowed the Portuguese announcement. Thus, neither Salazar nor Portugal received full credit for a blatant violation of the established standards governing the actions of neutral states; Norweb to secretary of state, 12 October 1944, and Norweb to secretary of state, 6 June 1944, *FRUS, 1944* 4:82, 127; Lisbon to State Department, 13 October 1944 (#3138), 811.34553b/10-1344, RG 59, DSNA; State Department to Lisbon, 19 October 1944 (#2757), 811.34553b/10-1944, RG 59, DSNA; Lisbon to State Department, 19 October 1944 (#3189) 753.94/10-1944, RG 59, DSNA; Lisbon to State Department, 25 October 1944 (#3252) 811.34553b/10-44, RG 59, DSNA; and U.S. military attaché (Lisbon) to War Department, 24 October 1944 (#494), Map Room—Spain, Portugal, Azores (2) Sec. 1, Roosevelt Library.

25. Lisbon to State Department, 29 October 1944 (#3291), 811.34553b/10-2944, RG 59, DSNA; State Department to Lisbon, 27 October 1944 (#2827), 811.34553b/10-2744, RG 59, DSNA; Lisbon to State Department, 10 November 1944 (#3981), 811.34553b/11-1044, RG 59, DSNA; and State Department to Lisbon, 14 November 1944 (#2943), 811.34553b/11-1444, RG 59, DSNA.

26. Portugal paid $859,000 for a facility and equipment worth an estimated $2,200,000; *New York Times*, 25 September 1946. Furthermore, once the United States was formally obligated to assist Portugal in the liberation of East Timor, that pledge became a bargaining counter in future negotiations. The question of the liberation of Timor was a prominent feature during the conclusion of a Portuguese-American air transport agreement on 6 December 1945. See Lisbon to State Department, 21 July 1945 (#1568), 753.94/7-2145, RG 59, DSNA; and *Treaties and Other International Agreements of the United States of America, 1776–1949*, 5 vols. (Washington, D.C.: GPO, 1974), 2:351–55.

27. This observation is attributed to Dean Acheson; Urs Schwarz, *The Eye of the Hurricane: Switzerland in World War Two* (Boulder, Colo.: Westview, 1980), 155.

28. Corporatism in its most simplistic form involves the establishment of a system of state-licensed monopoly capitalism supported by an authoritarian/democratic political system. The state is thus theoretically run by representatives of all occupations for the coordinated good of the whole community. Still, although often confused with fascism, corporatism is different. Fascism involves a leadership principle, a mass political party, and an aggressive foreign policy that are not characteristic of corporatism. Furthermore, as with Stalin, Salazar was the master of the official governmental ideology, not its servant. He controlled an authoritarian state in which only a portion of the population determined what was right for the rest. In point of fact, he is reliably reported to have characterized his fellows as a "cursed race, half of whom wouldn't do anything without a whip." See Tom Gallagher, *Portugal: A Twentieth-Century Interpretation* (Manchester, Eng.: Manchester University Press, 1983), 149.

29. Spain's postwar ostracism began with the Potsdam declaration that barred the nation from membership in the United Nations and climaxed with a 4 March 1946 joint statement by Britain, France, and the United States calling upon the Spanish people to overthrow the regime of Francisco Franco. Hence, opening the Azores to Allied aircraft brought a public reminder that Portugal was in the same ideological camp as Spain; "Tarring with the Fascist Brush," *The Commonweal* 34 (29 October 1943): 27. The campaign to reform Portugal did not, however, attain the heights reached by the international critics of Spain. This was perchance a consequence of the guilt the victorious allies assumed in consequence of their actions during the Spanish Civil War. Despite considerable motivation to the contrary, Salazar continued publicly to support the Franco regime. He championed Spain's entry into NATO despite the problems that proposal created with regard to Portugal's own entry into the alliance; Lawrence S. Kaplan, *The United States and NATO* (Lexington: University Press of Kentucky, 1984), 109.

30. Stephen S. Kaplan, "The Utility of U.S. Military Bases in Spain and Portugal," *Military Review* (April 1977): 51. An alternative route by way of Newfoundland and England was considered less desirable by virtue of erratic weather patterns. As a result, attempts by Portuguese opposition groups to secure American backing went unrewarded; Chester Bowles to Harry Truman, 17 June 1948 and reply dated 21 June 1948, Official File, Harry S. Truman Library, Independence, Mo. Even after the advent of in-flight refueling, the Azores retained their importance.

31. Albano Nogueira, "The Pull of the Continent," in *NATO's Anxious Birth: The Prophetic Vision of the 1940s*, ed. Nicholas Sherwen (New York: St. Martin's, 1985), 68, 70. The United States took a strong position in support of Portugal as a founding member of the alliance. When the issue of the dictatorial nature of the Portuguese government was raised in an executive session of the U.S. Senate, a State Department representative responded that "if it is a dictatorship, it is because the people freely voted for it." This exercise in self-deception was undoubtedly more effective in that Portugal—along with Norway, Denmark, Italy, and Iceland—was viewed as a peripheral member added to the alliance to perform a specific function. The Portuguese accepted this role willingly and refrained from involvement in the politics of policy making; see Kaplan, *The United States and NATO*, 109–10, 128, 141. Canada was the

only charter signatory to offer consistent opposition to Portugal's membership; Mark Stenhouse and Bruce George, "Defense Policy and Strategic Importance: The Western Perspective," in *Portuguese Defense and Foreign Policy Since Democratization*, ed. Kenneth Maxwell (New York: Camões Center, 1991), 31.

32. Portugal, for its part, was concerned about membership in an organization that excluded neighboring Spain—most particularly inasmuch as Portugal and Spain were diplomatically intertwined. In point of fact, Salazar frequently spoke in favor of bringing Spain into the alliance as a founding member; Kaplan, *United States and NATO*, 83, 109.

33. Kay, *Salazar*, 182–83; and De Oliveira Marques, *History of Portugal* 2:217–19. General opposition to Portugal's admission to the United Nations was slight by 1947; in fact, it was only the negative votes of the USSR that kept it out of the organization until 1955.

34. The Azores treaty provided the United States with a base in the islands for a five-year period ending 1 September 1956; *United States Treaties and International Agreements*, 5 vols. (Washington, D.C.: GPO, 1956), 3:2264–67.

35. MacVeagh to secretary of state, 30 November 1948, *FRUS, 1948* 3:1012–16.

36. Àlvaro de Vasconcelos, "Portuguese/US Relations in the Field of Security," in *Portugal: An Atlantic Paradox*, 54. Salazar once defined the goals of any government as the establishment of a "political, economic and social nationalism, controlled by the unquestionable sovereignty of the strong state." Such goals were antithetical to the cooperation envisaged by the Organization for European Economic Cooperation. Portugal was ultimately a participant, but a reluctant one at best; De Oliveira Marques, *History of Portugal* 2:181.

37. "Policy Statement—Relations of the U.S. with Portugal," 20 October 1950, *FRUS, 1950* 3:1540, 1546.

38. Robert J. McMahon, *Colonialism and Cold War: the United States and the Struggle for Indonesian Independence, 1945–49* (Ithaca: Cornell University Press, 1981), 305. The policy of the United States was consistently antagonistic toward the aspirations of the Indonesian nationalists until the point when the Dutch effort to retain the colony imperiled American objectives elsewhere. This was another instance in which American officialdom spoke, and possibly thought, in ideological terms, yet acted in a contrary fashion with respect to the emerging Third World; see H. W. Brands, *The Specter of Neutralism: The United States and the Emergence of the Third World, 1947–1960* (New York: Columbia University Press, 1989), 9. The United States was not alone in this approach; despite the obvious propaganda value, the principle of self-determination was seldom acknowledged or widely applied by the USSR before the mid-1950s; see Scott L. Bills, *Empire and Cold War: The Roots of US–Third World Antagonism, 1945–47* (New York: St. Martin's, 1990), 203–4.

39. Richard D. Mahoney, *JFK: Ordeal in Africa* (New York: Oxford University Press, 1983), 196, and John Seiler, "The Azores as an Issue in U.S.-Portuguese Relations, 1961–1993" (Paper presented to the International Conference Group on Modern Portugal, University of New Hampshire, 21 June 1979), 3. The letters are dated 5 January 1951.

40. Robert Herrick, "United States Foreign Policy and Portugal: A Reevaluation," *The New Scholar* 3, no. 2 (1971): 130.

41. The State Department split over whether to support a security council resolution calling for self-determination in Angola, but President Kennedy accepted Dean Rusk's advice to vote in favor of the motion; Thomas J. Schoenbaum, *Waging Peace and War* (New York: Simon & Schuster, 1988), 375–76. The Portuguese felt betrayed by the American support of the Angolan resolution. During a plenary debate on Angola in 1962, Ambassador Adlai Stevenson confirmed that any diversion of NATO-designated equipment to Africa would be treated as a violation of the defense agreement with Portugal; see Stenhouse and George, "Defense Policy and Strategic Importance," 33. The Portuguese defense minister told Salazar that resistance to the FNLA would launch the army on "a suicide mission in which we could not succeed"; Douglas Porch, *The Portuguese Armed Forces and the Revolution* (Stanford: Hoover Institution Press, 1977), 37. By the middle of the decade the assessment changed to reflect an understanding that Portugal would remain in control of Angola and Mozambique indefinitely; Piero Gleijeses, "The United States, Mercenaries, and the Congo," *Diplomatic History* 18, no. 2 (Spring 1994): 208–9 n.5.

42. De Magalhães, "An Historical Outline," 49. A further year's prorogation to the agreement was later granted, but an American presence in the Azores was very much at the whim of the Portuguese government. Portuguese efforts to influence the U.S. government, particularly Congress, led to an investigation and legislation to limit foreign lobbying efforts; Kenneth Maxwell, "Portuguese Defense and Foreign Policy: An Overview," in *Portuguese Defense and Foreign Policy Since Democratization*, 6.

43. Seiler, *Azores*, 6. See Mahoney, *JFK*, 186–222, for a careful examination of the Luso-American connection during the Kennedy administration.

44. "Portuguese African Territories," 15 February 1964, National Security File, Country File, Portugal, Vol. 1, Johnson Library, and Maxwell, "Portuguese Defense and Foreign Policy," 6.

45. Henry Kissinger's summary dismissal of postrevolutionary Portugal as a "lost cause" with Mário Soares cast as a Portuguese Kerensky is a case in point. Kissinger is the ultimate bogeyman for his blatant and unwarranted support, in Portuguese eyes, of an independent nation in the Azores; De Vasconcelos, "Portuguese/US Relations," 62–63, and Walter Isaacson, *Kissinger* (New York: Simon & Schuster, 1992), 673–74.

46. Robert A. Diamond and David Fouguet, "Portugal and the United States: Atlantic Islands and European Strategy as Pawns in African Wars," *Africa Report* 15, no. 5 (May 1970): 15–17, and Robert Herrick, "United States Foreign Policy and Portugal: A Reevaluation," *The New Scholar* 3, no. 2 (1971): 125–63, serve as representative examples.

47. Maxwell, "Portuguese Defense and Foreign Policy," 6; and De Vasconcelos, "Portuguese/US Relations," 55. Kissinger mentioned the episode in his memoirs, but simply noted that he sent a letter of "unusual abruptness" to the Portuguese prime minister; *Years of Upheaval* (Boston: Little, Brown, 1982), 520. It should be noted that Portugal, which depended on the Middle East for 85 percent of its oil imports, was also subjected to the retaliatory oil embargo by OPEC imposed on 21 October.

48. Salazar suffered a brain hemorrhage during an operation to remove a blood clot and was replaced as prime minister by Marcelo Caetano on 26 September 1968. Caetano preserved the main outlines of the old regime and was overthrown in a bloodless action by the Armed Forces Movement; De Oliveira Marques, *History of*

Portugal 2:224, 264–65. In retrospect, Portugal's politics and its economy outgrew that structure of authority so carefully devised and so lovingly maintained by Antonio Salazar. Marcelo Caetano promised reform, but could not, in the time available, satisfy the rising expectations of the Portuguese people; see Guismarães, "Collapse of the New State," 10.

49. Robert J. McMahon, "Anglo-American Diplomacy and the Reoccupation of the Netherlands East Indies," *Diplomatic History* 2, no. 1 (Winter 1978): 21. This policy proved more effective in the Dutch East Indies than in French Indochina. In the process of walking the straight and narrow, however, on occasion the United States found itself inclined to one side. In January 1970, for example, the United States enunciated a policy in support of white racist regimes in Rhodesia and South Africa. The United States also sought to sustain Portuguese efforts to contain the nationalist forces in Angola and Mozambique—thereby creating a protective belt to shield South Africa. In accord with this policy, despite an official embargo, the United States transferred substantial quantities of dual-use equipment to Portugal for use in its colonial campaigns. This policy was known within the Nixon administration inner circle by the quite remarkable nickname, "Tar Baby!" as outlined in option 2 of NSSM-39, 19 December 1969; see Tad Szulc, *The Illusion of Peace* (New York: Viking, 1978), 220–24. Despite its public protestations to the contrary, the United States pursued a course which was anything but neutral in Southern Africa.

50. For the most recent works on this subject, see J. K. Sweeney, "East Timor Declares Independence But is Annexed by Indonesia," in *Great Events from History II: Human Rights*, ed. Frank N. Magill (Pasadena, Calif.: Salem, 1992), 1835–38; Ian Rowland, *Timor* (Santa Barbara: Clio, 1992); and John G. Taylor, *The Indonesian Occupation of East Timor, 1974–1989: A Chronology* (London: Catholic Institute for International Relations, 1990).

51. A number of Timorese lost their lives in the course of resisting the Indonesian occupation. The extent of the losses among the inhabitants of East Timor is very much in dispute—as is just about everything else about this tragic affair. Kenneth M. Quinn, "East Timor, Indonesia and U.S. Policy," *U.S. Department of State Dispatch* 3 (16 March 1992): 213–16, and John W. Bartlett, "Blood on Our Hands," *On the Issues* (Winter 1992): 38–41, 55–57, are representative examples of the two extremes. Portugal immediately broke diplomatic relations with Indonesia and asked for UN sanctions and assistance in returning Timor to its preinvasion status. The matter reappears on the UNO's agenda on an annual basis, and both Portugal and Indonesia carefully note which nations abstain and which support the resolution. The United States traditionally abstains from the issue.

52. American submarines passing through the Straits of Malacca from the Indian to Pacific Oceans must surface and are, therefore, capable of detection by satellite surveillance. An alternate route south of Australia would increase reaction time and reduce on-station time for units deploying into the Indian ocean. The Malacca straits are also too shallow for the large tankers moving oil into the Pacific. William L. Scully, "Indonesia and the U.S.," *Heritage Foundation Backgrounder*, 12 October 1982, 7–8.

53. Noam Chomsky, "A Curtain of Ignorance," *Southeast Asia Chronicle* 74 (August 1980): 4, and John Pilger "The West's Dirty Wink," *Manchester Guardian*, 12 February 1994. President Gerald Ford, accompanied by Henry Kissinger, visited Jakarta

on 5–7 December 1975. Indonesian communications intercepted by American intelligence organizations revealed that President Suharto was concerned that an invasion of East Timor might jeopardize American military aid. According to Central Intelligence Agency and Defense Intelligence Agency reports, Suharto wished to look Ford and Kissinger "in the eye" and obtain their approval of the invasion. Both Ford and Kissinger were in Jakarta and met with Suharto the day before the invasion began. Kissinger later publicly suspended arms shipments to Indonesia but ordered them secretly resumed shortly thereafter; see Allan Nairn, "Tragedy in East Timor: A Roundtable Discussion," *Camões Center Quarterly* 4 (Autumn and Winter 1992–93): 15, and Isaacson, *Kissinger*, 681. The United Nations continues to recognize Portugal as the "legal administrator" of East Timor, which might irritate Indonesia but does nothing to reverse its act of annexation; *The Economist*, 28 November 1992. When the Netherlands raised the issue of human rights violations in East Timor in 1992, the Indonesian response was to reject, with the approval of the World Bank, any further Dutch aid. Portugal was able to veto a new ASEAN-EC agreement because of East Timor, but most EC countries view the issue as a bilateral problem and conduct business as usual with ASEAN; Bilahari Kausikan, "Asia's Different Standard," *Foreign Policy* 92 (Fall 1993): 29.

54. In point of fact, the strongest anti-American feelings are to be found in those segments of Portuguese society that suffered the most from the effects of the overthrow of the old regime; De Vasconcelos, "Portuguese/US Relations," 56. Moreover, by far the largest percentage of those members of the military establishment who left the country for training purposes in support of Portugal's NATO activities were naval officers. And if the Armed Forces Movement (MFA) was "the vanguard of the revolution, the navy was the vanguard of the MFA." The Portuguese navy was very much a factor in the creation of the First Republic in 1910 and continued its liberal political tradition throughout the Salazar years. Porch, *Portuguese Armed Forces*, 145–47.

55. Tad Szulc, "Lisbon & Washington: Behind the Portuguese Revolution," *Foreign Policy* 21 (Winter 1974–75): 4. The gains for the USSR in such an eventuality would have been manifold: operational Atlantic bases for the Soviet fleet; use of the most important shipyard in Western Europe and a potential threat to the American nuclear submarine base at Rota, Spain; see ibid., 45.

56. The involvement of the United States in the coup which destroyed the government of Salvador Allende in 1970 was widely suspected and later confirmed by a congressional investigation. Henry Kissinger briefly considered various counter-revolutionary options in Portugal but was eventually persuaded to pursue a more supportive role. The U.S. embassy under Ambassador Frank Carlucci undertook a successful campaign against the antidemocratic elements in Portugal and the wild men in Washington; Maxwell, "Portuguese Defense and Foreign Policy," 7. Carlucci had a reputation for toughness in difficult situations as well as a fluent command of the Portuguese language. He was also able to secure, in the person of Herbert Okun, a deputy with similar linguistic skills; Szulc, "Lisbon & Washington: Behind the Portuguese Revolution," 34. Kissinger did not authorize paramilitary operations in postrevolutionary Portugal, but he did support secret aid for those factions within Angola who lost the struggle for power that followed Portugal's withdrawal; Gaddis Smith, *Morality, Reason and Power* (New York: Hill and Wang, 1986), 138. A valuable introduction

to American policy toward Angola may be found in Gerald J. Bender, "Angola, the Cubans, and American Anxieties," *Foreign Policy* 31 (Summer 1978): 3–30. See also Gerald J. Bender, "Angola: Left, Right, and Wrong," ibid. 43 (Summer 1981): 53–69; and Wayne S. Smith, "A Trap in Angola," ibid. 62 (Spring 1986): 61–74. The Central Intelligence Agency was involved in Portugal but not to a major degree, and its role was far from decisive; Szulc, "Lisbon & Washington," 10–13, 56.

57. Douglas Porch, *The Portuguese Armed Forces and the Revolution*, 222–29. The Portuguese were virtually excluded from most NATO activities for much of 1974–75. They did not complain and in fact seemed to prefer that state of affairs; Szulc, "Lisbon & Washington," 46. Secretary Kissinger was criticized for crying wolf about the dangers of a Communist victory in Portugal, but it must be noted that, as with Waterloo, it may have been a near run. Most of those members of the Portuguese military involved in the November confrontation believed the nation to be on the brink of civil war; Maxwell, "Portuguese Defense and Foreign Policy," 2.

58. The United States obtained implicit agreement for the use of the Azores when the security of certain Arab nations was at issue. The second exchange of notes involved the establishment of a satellite tracking station (GEODSS) as well as the possible placement of pre-positioned vessels at Porto Santo, Madeira; see Maxwell, "Portuguese Defense and Foreign Policy," 7; and De Vasconcelos, "Portuguese/US Relations," 61, 72–74. Coincident with the opening of negotiations over the Azores, Portugal installed its first resident ambassador in Israel. It is speculated that Lisbon hoped to use the goodwill created by the Yom Kippur War resupply to persuade Israel to employ its good offices in support of the Portuguese position; Maxwell, "Portuguese Defense and Foreign Policy," 9. In 1988, the Reagan administration sought to shift the emphasis in Portuguese relations from leasing base facilities to NATO anti-submarine warfare activities by the Portuguese navy; Stenhouse and George, Defense Policy and Strategic Importance," 39.

59. The Egyptian aircraft decision was specifically designed to express Portuguese displeasure with the low level of financial assistance furnished by the United States; De Vasconcelos, "Portuguese/US Relations," 65.

60. Szulc, "Lisbon & Washington," 60.

Select Bibliography

Works by Lawrence S. Kaplan

"The Philosophes and the American Revolution," *Social Science* 31 (January 1956): 31–36.

"Jefferson, the Napoleonic Wars, and the Balance of Power," *William and Mary Quarterly* 14 (April 1957): 196–218. Reprinted in *Essays on the Early Republic, 1789–1815*, ed. Leonard W. Levy (Hinsdale, Ill.: Dryden Press, 1974), and in Lawrence S. Kaplan, *Entangling Alliances with None: American Foreign Policy in the Age of Jefferson* (Kent, Ohio: Kent State University Press, 1987).

"Jefferson's Foreign Policy and Napoleon's Ideologues," *William and Mary Quarterly* 19 (July 1962): 344–59. Reprinted in Lawrence S. Kaplan, *Entangling Alliances with None: American Foreign Policy in the Age of Jefferson* (Kent, Ohio: Kent State University Press, 1987).

"France and Madison's Decision for War, 1812," *Mississippi Valley Historical Review* 50 (March 1964): 652–71. Reprinted in Lawrence S. Kaplan, *Entangling Alliances with None: American Foreign Policy in the Age of Jefferson* (Kent, Ohio: Kent State University Press, 1987).

[Editor]. "A New Englander Defends the War of 1812: Senator Varnum to Judge Thatcher," *Mid-America* 46 (October 1964): 269–80.

"Decline and Fall of Federalism: Historic Necessity?" in *Main Problems in American History*, ed. Howard Quint et al. (Homewood, Ill.: Dorsey Press, 1964). Reprinted in *The Federalists: Realists or Ideologues*, ed. George Billias (Boston: D. C. Heath, 1970), 99–105.

[Editor]. "Jonathan Russell and the Capture of the Guerriere" (unpublished poem), *William and Mary Quarterly* 24 (April 1967): 284–87.

Jefferson and France: An Essay on Politics and Political Ideas (New Haven: Yale University Press, 1967). Chapter 5 reprinted in *The Critical Years: American Foreign Policy, 1793–1823*, ed. Patrick C. T. White (New York: Wiley, 1970), and in *Major Problems in American Foreign Policy*, ed. Thomas G. Paterson (Lexington, Mass.: D. C. Heath, 1978). The book was reprinted in full by Greenwood Press, 1980.

"France and the War of 1812," *Journal of American History* 57 (June 1970): 36–47. Reprinted in Lawrence S. Kaplan, *Entangling Alliances with None: American Foreign Policy in the Age of Jefferson* (Kent, Ohio: Kent State University Press, 1987).

"The Consensus of 1789: Jefferson and Hamilton on American Foreign Policy," *South Atlantic Quarterly* 71 (January 1972): 91–105. Reprinted in Lawrence S. Kaplan, *Entangling Alliances with None: American Foreign Policy in the Age of Jefferson* (Kent, Ohio: Kent State University Press, 1987).

Colonies into Nation: American Diplomacy, 1783–1801 (New York: Macmillan, 1972).

"Thomas Jefferson: The Idealist as Realist," in *Makers of American Diplomacy*, ed. Frank J. Merli and Theodore A. Wilson, 2 vols. (New York: Scribner's, 1974), 1:53–79. Reprinted in *Major Problems in American Foreign Policy*, ed. Thomas G. Paterson (Lexington, Mass.: D. C. Heath, 1978 [also included in the 1995 edition]). Reprinted in Lawrence S. Kaplan, *Entangling Alliances with None: American Foreign Policy in the Age of Jefferson* (Kent, Ohio: Kent State University Press, 1987).

"Jefferson et la France," *Informations et Documents* 348 (December 1974-January 1975): 27–33.

"Founding Fathers on the Founding Fathers: Reflections on Three Generations of American Diplomatic Historians," Society for Historians of American Foreign Relations *Newsletter* 6 (December 1975): 1–8.

"The Paris Mission of William Harris Crawford, 1813–1815," *Georgia Historical Quarterly* 60 (Spring 1976): 9–23. Reprinted in Lawrence S. Kaplan, *Entangling Alliances with None: American Foreign Policy in the Age of Jefferson* (Kent, Ohio: Kent State University Press, 1987).

"Toward Isolationism: The Jeffersonian Republicans and the Franco-American Alliance of 1778," *Historical Reflections/Réflexions Historiques* 3 (Summer 1976): 69–81.

"Toward Isolationism: The Rise and Fall of the Franco-American Alliance, 1775–1801," in *The American Revolution and 'A Candid World,'* ed. Lawrence S. Kaplan (Kent, Ohio: Kent State University Press, 1977),

134–60. Reprinted in Lawrence S. Kaplan, *Entangling Alliances with None: American Foreign Policy in the Age of Jefferson* (Kent, Ohio: Kent State University Press, 1987).

"The Diplomacy of the American Revolution: The Perspective from France," *Reviews in American History* 4 (September 1976): 385–90.

[Editor and contributor]. *The American Revolution and "A Candid World"* (Kent, Ohio: Kent State University Press, 1977).

"The American Revolution in Its Bicentennial Perspective: The View from Bicentennial Symposia," *International History Review* 1 (July 1979): 408–26.

"Reflections on Jefferson as a Francophile," *South Atlantic Quarterly* 79 (Winter 1980): 38–50. Also published in *La Revolution Amèricaine et Europe* (Paris: CNRS, 1979), 399–412. Reprinted in Lawrence S. Kaplan, *Entangling Alliances with None: American Foreign Policy in the Age of Jefferson* (Kent, Ohio: Kent State University Press, 1987).

"The Treaties of Paris and Washington, 1778 and 1949: Reflections on Entangling Alliances," in *Diplomacy and Revolution: The Franco-American Alliance of 1778*, ed. Ronald Hoffman and Peter J. Albert (Charlottesville: University Press of Virginia, 1981), 151–94.

"Paranoia and American Revolutionary Diplomacy," *Reviews in American History* 9 (June 1981): 166–71.

"The Founding Fathers and the Two Confederations: The United States of America and the United Provinces of the Netherlands, 1783–89," in *A Bilateral Bicentennial: A History of Dutch-American Relations, 1782–1982*, ed. J. W. Schulte Nordholt and Robert P. Swierenga (New York: Octagon Books, 1982), 33–48. Reprinted in Lawrence S. Kaplan, *Entangling Alliances with None: American Foreign Policy in the Age of Jefferson* (Kent, Ohio: Kent State University Press, 1987).

[Contributing editor]. "Colonial and Imperial Diplomacy to 1774," in *Guide to American Foreign Relations Since 1700*, ed. Richard D. Burns (Santa Barbara, Calif.: Clio Press, 1982), 85–109.

"The Treaty of Paris, 1783: A Historiographical Challenge," *International History Review* 5 (August 1983): 431–42.

"Thomas Jefferson and Foreign Relations," in *Thomas Jefferson: A Reference Biography*, ed. Merrill A. Peterson (New York: Scribners, 1986), 311–30.

Entangling Alliances with None: American Foreign Policy in the Age of Jefferson (Kent, Ohio: Kent State University Press, 1987).

"Jefferson and the Constitution: The View from Paris, 1786–1789," *Diplomatic History* 11 (Fall 1987): 321–35.

"Jefferson as Anglophile: Sagacity or Senility in the Era of Good Feelings?" *Diplomatic History* 16 (Summer 1992): 487–94.

"The Monroe Doctrine and the Truman Doctrine: The Case of Greece," *Journal of the Early Republic* 3 (Spring 1993): 1–21.

American Diplomacy—NATO and the Cold War

"NATO and Its Commentators: The First Five Years," *International Organization* 8 (November 1954): 447–67.
"NATO and the Language of Isolationism," *South Atlantic Quarterly* 57 (April 1958): 204–18.
"NATO Retrospect," *Review of Politics* 23 (October 1961): 447–58.
"NATO and Adenauer's Germany: Uneasy Partnership," *International Organization* 15 (November 1961): 618–30.
"The United States, Belgium, and the Congo Crisis of 1960," *Review of Politics* 29 (April 1967): 239–56.
[Editor]. *Recent American Foreign Policy: Conflicting Interpretations* (Homewood, Ill.: Dorsey Press, 1968). Revised edition, 1972.
[Editor]. *NATO and the Policy of Containment* (Boston: D. C. Heath, 1968).
"The United States and the Origins of NATO, 1946–1949," *Review of Politics* 29 (April 1969): 239–56.
"The United States, The NATO Treaty, and the UN Charter," *NATO Letter*, May 1969, 22–26.
"NATO After Twenty Years: An American Perspective," *NATO Letter*, June 1970, 14–18.
"The United States and the Atlantic Alliance: The First Generation," in *Twentieth-Century American Foreign Policy*, ed. John Braeman, Robert H. Bremer, and David Brody (Columbus: Ohio State University Press, 1971), 294–342.
"The Yom Kippur War of 1973," pamphlet (Cleveland, Ohio: Cleveland Jewish Federation, 1974).
"After Twenty-five Years: NATO as a Research Field," American Historical Association *Newsletter* 12 (November 1974): 6–7.
"Toward the Atlantic Alliance: The Military Assistance Program and Western Europe, 1947–1949," *Proceedings of the Conference on War and Diplomacy* (Charleston, S.C.: The Citadel, 1976), 88–95.
"The Korean War and U.S. Foreign Relations: The Case of NATO," in *The Korean War: A 25-Year Perspective*, ed. Francis H. Heller (Lawrence: Regents Press of Kansas, 1977), 36–75.
"NATO and the Nixon Doctrine: Ten Years Later," *Orbis* 24 (Spring 1980): 149–64.
"Toward the Brussels Pact," *Prologue* 12 (Summer 1980): 73–86.
"NATO in the Second Generation," *NATO Review*, October 1980, 1–7.

*A Community of Interests: NATO and the Military Assistance Program,
1948–1951* (Washington, D.C.: Office of the Secretary of Defense,
Historical Office, 1980).

"Israel and American Public Opinion, Continuity and Change," *International Insight* 1 (Winter 1981): 1–6.

"The Political Perspective," in *The American-European Balance Since
1939*, ed. J. R. Greenway (Norwich, Eng.: University of East Anglia,
1980), 13–24.

[Coeditor and contributor]. *NATO After Thirty Years* (Wilmington, Del.:
Scholarly Resources, 1981).

[Coeditor and contributor]. *The Warsaw Pact: Political Purpose & Military Means* (Wilmington, Del.: Scholarly Resources, 1982).

"Western Europe in 'The American Century': A Retrospective View,"
Diplomatic History 6 (Spring 1982): 111–23.

"NATO After 33 Years: Records and Their Classification," Society for
Historians of American Foreign Relations (SHAFR) *Newsletter* 13,
no. 5 (December 1982): 9–11.

"Commentary on 'The Emerging Post-Revisionist Synthesis on the Origin of the Cold War,'" *Diplomatic History* 7 (Summer 1983): 194–98.

"Richard Coudenhove-Kalergi," in *Biographical Dictionary of Internationalists*, ed. Warren F. Kuehl (Westport, Conn.: Greenwood, 1983),
172–74.

The United States and NATO: The Formative Years (Lexington: University Press of Kentucky, 1984).

"La Sicurezza Collettiva e La NATO Nella Prospettiva Americana," *La
Revista Italiana Di Strategia Globale*, Nuova Serie No. 4, 2 Semestre
(1984): 333–67.

[Coeditor and contributor]. *NATO and the Mediterranean* (Wilmington,
Del.: Scholarly Resources, 1985).

"An Unequal Triad: The United States, Western Union, and NATO," in
Western Security, The Formative Years: European and Atlantic Defense, 1947–1953, ed. Olav Riste (Oslo: Universitetsvarlaget, 1985),
107–27.

"The United States, NATO, and the Third World: Security Issues in Historical Perspective," in *East-West Rivalry in the Third World*, ed. Robert W. Clawson (Wilmington, Del.: Scholarly Resources, 1986), 3–22.

"The Cold War and European Revisionism," *Diplomatic History* 11
(Spring 1987): 143–56.

[Coauthored with Kathleen Kellner]. "Lemnitzer: Surviving the French
Military Withdrawal," in *Generals in Politics: NATO's Supreme
Allied Commander*, ed. Robert S. Jordan (Lexington: University Press
of Kentucky, 1987), 93–121.

[Coeditor and contributor]. *Dien Bien Phu and the Crisis of Franco-American Relations, 1954–1955* (Wilmington, Del.: Scholarly Resources, 1990).

"The 'Atlantic' Component of NATO," in *Transatlantic Relations on the Eve of the XXI Century*, ed. José Enes (Ponta Delgada: CEIRE, 1989), 61–69.

[Coeditor]. *NATO After Forty Years* (Wilmington, Del.: Scholarly Resources, 1990).

"Collective Security and the Case of NATO," in *The Origins of NATO*, ed. Joseph Smith (Exeter, U.K.: University of Exeter Press, 1990), 95–112.

"Lyman L. Lemnitzer," in *Historical Dictionary of the Korean War*, ed. James I. Matray (New York: Greenwood Press, 1991), 246–47.

American Historians and the Atlantic Alliance (Kent, Ohio: Kent State University Press, 1991).

"European Security Without the Soviet Union: Implications for the United States," *Arms Control* 12 (December 1991): 139–45.

"After Forty Years: Reflections on NATO as a Research Field," in *NATO: The Founding of the Atlantic Alliance and the Integration of Europe*, ed. Francis H. Heller and John R. Gillingham (New York: St. Martin's, 1992), 15–23.

"Cold Warriors: Wise, Prudent, and Foolish," *Reviews in American History* 10 (September 1992): 411–15.

[Coeditor]. "Fingerprints on History: The NATO Memoirs of Theodore C. Achilles," *Occasional Papers*, no. 1 (Kent, Ohio: Lyman L. Lemnitzer Center for NATO and European Community Studies, 1992).

"Western Union and European Military Integration 1948–1950—An American Perspective," in *The Western Security Community, 1948–1950*, ed. Norbert Wiggershaus and Roland G. Foerster (Providence, R.I.: Berg Publishers, 1993), 45–67. The same article appeared earlier in *Die Westliche Sicherheitsgemeinschaft, 1948–1950*, ed. Norbert Wiggershaus and Roland G. Foerster (Boppard am Rhein: H. Boldt, 1988), 37–56.

"Dean Acheson and the Atlantic Community," in *Dean Acheson and the Making of U.S. Foreign Policy*, ed. Douglas Brinkley (New York: St. Martin's, 1993), 28–54.

"NATO in the 1990s: An American Perspective," *Paradigms* 7 (Winter 1993–94): 1–21.

"The U.S. and NATO in the Johnson Years," in *The Johnson Years: LBJ at Home and Abroad*, ed. Robert A. Divine (Lawrence: University Press of Kansas, 1994), 119–49.

NATO and the United States: The Enduring Alliance (1988; updated ed., Boston: Twayne, 1994).

American History — General

"Frederick Jackson Turner and Imperialism," *Social Science* 27 (January 1952): 12–16.

"A Fulbright Scholar's Appreciation of Lincoln," *The Funnel* [The United States Educational Commission in the Federal Republic of Germany] 5 (November 1959): 8–11.

"Der Kolonialismus in der Geschichte der Vereinigten Staaten von America," *Frankfurter Hefte* 15 (October 1960): 705–14.

[Coauthor]. *The Frontier in American History and Literature: Essays and Interpretation* (Frankfurt-Main: Verlag Moritz Diesterweg, 1960).

"A European Legacy," *The Serif* 3 (September 1966): 3–8.

"The Brahmin as Diplomat in Nineteenth Century America: Everett Bancroft Motley Lowell," *Civil War History* 19 (March 1973): 5–28.

[Coauthor, with Morrell Heald]. *Culture and Diplomacy: The American Experience* (Westport, Conn.: Greenwood Press, 1977). "The Neocolonial Impulse: The United States and Great Britain, 1783–1823," and "The Independence of Latin America: North American Ambivalence, 1800–1820," were reprinted in Lawrence S. Kaplan, *Entangling Alliances with None: American Foreign Policy in the Age of Jefferson* (Kent, Ohio: Kent State University Press, 1987).

"May 4, 1970: The Perspective from Europe," *Left Review* 4 (Spring 1980): 15–18. Reprinted in *Kent State/May 4: Echoes Through a Decade*, ed. Scott L. Bills (Kent, Ohio: Kent State University Press, 1982), 105–11.

"The Development of American Nationalism in the Nineteenth Century," in *German-American Interrelations, Heritage, and Challenge*, ed. James F. Harris (Tubingen: Attempto, 1985), 95–102.

"The Decade of the 1970s," in *A Book of Memories: Kent State University 1910–1992*, ed. William H. Hildebrand, Dean H. Keller, and Anita D. Herington (Kent, Ohio: Kent State University Press, 1993), 185–89.

Works in Progress

"History of the Office of Secretary of Defense: The Early McNamara Years, 1961–65."

"Jefferson as Federalist, 1799–1803."

Master's Theses and Doctoral Dissertations Directed by Lawrence S. Kaplan

(The list includes only those for which Kaplan was the principal director.)

Master's Theses

STUDENT'S NAME	THESIS TITLE	YEAR
Glenn Jacobsen	"Pennsylvania and the Federal Constitution of 1787: Radical Versus Conservatism in a Democratic State"	1957
Patricia A. McCardel	"The British Role in the Indian Wars in Ohio, 1792–1795"	1957
Robert F. Miller	"The Stimson Doctrine as a Force in U.S.-Japanese Relations, 1931–1941"	1960
Aloha P. Broadwater	"Rufus King and American Foreign Policy: Minister to England in the Administrations of George Washington, John Adams, and Thomas Jefferson, 1796–1803"	1961

Carlton B. Smith	"The Susquehanna Valley's Reaction to Federalist Foreign Policy, 1790–1800"	1962
Joe Segraves	"American Prisoners of War in the American Revolution"	1962
Arthur W. Gosling	"Jonathan Russell and the War of 1812: The Tactics of Diplomacy in Crisis"	1964
Edmund B. Thomas, Jr.	"The Wyoming Land Dispute: A Study of Mediation in Early America"	1964
Leanne Tucker Corbi	"The Public Life of John Armstrong"	1965
Twila Z. Linville	"The Dissolution of an Alliance—A Study of Franco-Russian Relations, 1797–1801"	1965
Leonard C. Schlup	"Diplomacy and the Presidential Election of 1844"	1967
Robert Derry	"Soviet and Chinese Relations with the Democratic Republic of Viet-Nam, 1947–1955"	1968
Judith Woehrmann	"Civil Rights and the Negro in the Press of the Old Northwest 1954–1962"	1968
David K. McQuilkin	"Evidences of German Opinion and the Treaty of Björko"	1968
Paul Summers	"Soviet Economic Penetration and Influence in Rumania, 1944–1953"	1968
Ronald L. Hatzenbuehler	"The Election of 1812"	1969
Emily J. Yang	"Yalta and China"	1971
Khosrow Foroughi	"NATO: Battle Ground of Personalities, DeGaulle vs. Kennedy"	1972
Michael F. Lazarus	"Albert Gallatin and France, 1816–1823"	1972

Frank Yeropoli	"Francis James Jackson in America, 1809–1810"	1972
Douglas Dykstra	"The Richard Rush Ministry to Great Britain, 1818–1825"	1972
William J. Marshall	"Reuben G. Beasley in London, American Consul and Agent for Prisoners, 1811–1815"	1972
Charles P. Wilkins	"George F. Kennan and The Cold War in Europe"	1973
John A. Lamont	"The Atom Bomb: Diplomacy and the War in the Pacific"	1974
A. Gregory Moore	"The Preservation of Friendship: Roosevelt and the Japanese, 1905–1908"	1974
Frank E. Norwalk	"United States, Great Britain and Emerging India, 1941–1947"	1974
Scott L. Bills	"Along the Hegemonial Periphery: Globalism and the Politics of U.S. Policy Formation Toward Indochina, 1945–1948"	1976
Colleen M. Schroer	"From Ostracism to Rapprochement: American Diplomatic Relations with Spain 1945–1950"	1977
Lynne Jurkovic [Dunn]	"The United States and the Brussels Pact: The Creation of Western Unity"	1977
E. Timothy Smith	"The Cold War in Italy: Italian-American Relations, 1945–49"	1977
Joan F. Reiss	"America's 'Last' Chance in China? The Marshall Mission Reconsidered"	1977
Charles Jeffrey Waite	"The Impact of the Cold War on the Western Hemisphere Alliance System"	1978

Louis F. DiCola	"Anglo American Press Opinion During the Korean War"	1981
Timothy S. Evans	"The Reality and Rhetoric of Liberation: A Study of Liberation as a Major Objective of U.S. Foreign Policy, 1953–56"	1982
Russell Van Wyk	"The United States and the Integration of the Federal Republic: The German Election of 1953"	1982
Patricia Casey	"NATO, Greece, and Turkey, 1949–1952"	1983
Richard Markwardt	"A Policy of Pragmatism: U.S. Diplomatic Relations with Spain"	1983
Elizabeth Benedetto	"Eighteenth Century Diplomatic History: American Benjamin Franklin and the Diplomatic Game"	1984
Victor Rosenberg	"The United States and the Geneva Conference on Indochina"	1986
Doris (Zbornik) Fiebiger	"Spain's Reaction to Portugal's Entry into NATO"	1988
Gweneth Burton	"The Big Three and the European Defense Community: American, French, and British Perspectives"	1989
James F. Talbot	"The Canadian Role in the Formation of NATO"	1991
Robert P. Batchelor	"The Delicate Balance: The Brussels Pact, NATO, and the United States, 1948–1951"	1993
Michael Hoover	"Pariah to Partner: U.S.-Spanish Relations, 1947–1953"	1993

Doctoral Dissertations

STUDENT'S NAME	DISSERTATION TITLE	YEAR
Paul J. Woehrmann	"Fort Wayne, Indiana Territory, 1794–1819: A Study of a Frontier Post"	1967

Thomas G. DeCola	"Roosevelt and Mussolini: The Critical Years—1938–1941"	1967
Joseph May	"John Foster Dulles and the European Defense Community"	1969
George T. Mazuzan	"Warren R. Austin: The Liberal Internationalist and U.S. Foreign Policy"	1969
Emmett E. Panzella	"The Atlantic Union Committee: Political Action Organization for the Federation of NATO"	1969
William J. Furdell	"Cordell Hull and the London Economic Conference of 1933"	1970
Jerry K. Sweeney	Portuguese-American Diplomatic Relations During the Second World War	1970
Reed R. Eaton	"The Public Career of Stephen Girard"	1971
Twila M. Linville	"The Public Life of Jonathan Russell"	1971
Ronald L. Hatzenbuehler	"Foreign Policy Voting in the United States Congress, 1808–1812"	1972
T. Michael Ruddy	"Charles E. Bohlen and the Soviet Union"	1973
Richard F. Grimmett	"The Politics of Containment: The President, the Senate and American Foreign Policy, 1947–1956"	1973
Christopher Williams	"United States' Relations with Liberia, 1940–1960"	1976
Shlomo Moskovits	"The United States' Recognition of Israel in the Context of the Cold War, 1945–1948"	1976
A. Gregory Moore	"Theodore Roosevelt and China, 1901–1909"	1978
Steven P. Sapp	"America's Role in the Rebirth of France: Jefferson Caffery and American-French Relations, 1944–1949"	1978

Leo J. Mahoney	"A History of the War Department Scientific Intelligence Mission (ALSOS), 1943–1945"	1981
E. Timothy Smith	"The United States, Italy and NATO: A Study of Italian-American Relations, 1948–1952"	1981
Scott L. Bills	"The United States, NATO, and the Politics of Colonialism, 1945–1949"	1981
Lynne Jurkovic [Dunn]	"The Life and Diplomatic Career of Eleanor Lansing Dulles"	1982
Hakon Ostholm	"The First Year of the Korean War: The Road Toward Armistice"	1982
Anna H. Rubin	"Sholom Aleichem: The Author as Social Historian"	1982
Marshall Kuehl	"Philip C. Jessup: From America First to Cold War Interventionist"	1985
John C. Kessler	"Spruille Braden as a Good Neighbor: The Latin American Policy of the U.S., 1930–1947"	1985
Steve Henstridge	"The United States, The Soviet Union, and the North Atlantic Treaty, 1948–1949"	1986
Kathleen Kellner	"Broker of Power: General Lyman Lemnitzer, 1946–1969"	1987
Victor R. Rosenberg	"When the Weather Clears: Soviet-American Relations, 1953–1955"	1990
Sidney R. Snyder	"The Role of the International Working Group in the Creation of the North Atlantic Treaty: December 1947–April 1949"	1992
Anna W. True [Co-Adviser]	NATO After All! Konrad Adenauer's Diplomatic Efforts to Rearm Western Germany, 1954–1955"	1993

Contributors

SCOTT L. BILLS is professor of history at Stephen F. Austin State University, Texas. His dissertation, "Cold War Rimlands: The United States, NATO, and the Politics of Colonialism, 1945–1949," was completed in 1981. His publications include *Kent State/May 4: Echoes Through a Decade* (1982, rev. ed. 1988), *Empire and Cold War* (1990), and *The Libyan Arena* (Kent State University Press, 1995). He served as coexecutive editor of the journal *Peace & Change* during 1994–97.

ALEXANDER DECONDE, professor of history emeritus, University of California, Santa Barbara, is the author of a number of articles and three books on the early national period. These volumes deal with the politics and diplomacy of the Franco-American Alliance, the Quasi-War with France, and the Louisiana Purchase. His most recent book, *Ethnicity, Race, and American Foreign Policy* (1992), includes a chapter on the early republic.

LYNNE K. DUNN is associate professor of history at Winthrop University, Rock Hill, South Carolina. Her dissertation, completed in 1982, combined her interests in diplomatic and women's history by focusing on the diplomatic career of Eleanor Lansing Dulles. She is currently completing work on a full-length biography of Eleanor Dulles and has coauthored (with the late Warren Kuehl) the book *Keeping the Covenant: American Internationalists and the League of Nations, 1920–1939* (forthcoming from the Kent State University Press).

ROBERT H. FERRELL has taught for many years at Indiana University in Bloomington. He is author of numerous works on American diplomacy, including a textbook that has gone through four editions. In recent years, he has written much about the presidency of Harry S. Truman, and his ninth book on the subject, *Harry S. Truman—A Life*, appeared in 1994.

RICHARD F. GRIMMETT is specialist in national defense with the Foreign Affairs and National Defense Division, Congressional Research Service, at the Library of Congress. For over twenty-two years, he has served as an adviser to the U.S. Congress on international security policy issues, and is author of numerous congressional reports dealing with such matters. He received his Ph.D. from Kent State in 1973 after completing a dissertation titled, "The Politics of Containment: The President, the Senate and American Foreign Policy, 1947–1956."

RONALD L. HATZENBUEHLER teaches at Idaho State University. His dissertation, "Foreign Policy Voting in the United States Congress, 1808–1812," was completed in 1972. He is coauthor (with Robert L. Ivie) of *Congress Declares War: Rhetoric, Leadership, and Partisanship in the Early Republic* (Kent State University Press, 1983).

GEORGE T. MAZUZAN is executive associate in the Office of Legislative and Public Affairs at the National Science Foundation in Washington, D.C. He also serves as the foundation's Historian. From 1978 to 1986, he was historian at the United States Nuclear Regulatory Commission. He has published widely in the field of recent U.S. history and is author of *Warren R. Austin at the U.N., 1946–1953* (1977), coeditor of *The Hoover Presidency: A Reappraisal* (1974), and coauthor of *Controlling the Atom: The Beginnings of Nuclear Regulation, 1946–1962* (1984).

T. MICHAEL RUDDY is professor of history at St. Louis University. He received his Ph.D. from Kent State in 1973 after completing a dissertation titled, "Charles Bohlen and the Soviet Union." His publications include *The Cautious Diplomat: Charles E. Bohlen and the Soviet Union* (Kent State University Press, 1986) and a number of articles on U.S. Cold War foreign policy. In addition to working on a manuscript examining U.S.-Finnish relations after 1945, he is currently researching NATO relations with nonmember states between 1949 and 1956.

E. TIMOTHY SMITH is professor of history at Barry University in Miami Shores, Florida. He completed his doctorate at Kent State University in 1981. In addition to several articles on the topic of U.S.-Italian relations, his expanded dissertation was published as *The United States, Italy and NATO, 1947–52* (1991). He is currently researching the pacifist and internationalist opposition to the foreign policy of the Truman administration.

J. K. SWEENEY is professor of history at South Dakota State University. His dissertation was titled "Portuguese-American Diplomatic Relations During the Second World War." He is coauthor of *A Handbook of American Diplomatic History* (1993) and editor/coauthor of *A Handbook of American Military History* (1996).

CEES WIEBES is a lecturer in international relations at the Department of International Relations and Public International Law of the University of Amsterdam. He received his Ph.D. from Leyden University. He is the author of numerous books and articles on postwar international relations and intelligence. He is coeditor of the *Yearbook* for the history of Dutch foreign policy.

BERT ZEEMAN is reference and acquisitions librarian for political science and history at the University Library of the University of Amsterdam. He earned his doctorate from Leyden University. He has published widely in the field of postwar international relations, especially on the Cold War. He is coeditor of the *Yearbook* for the history of Dutch foreign policy.

Index

Scott L. Bills is professor of history at
Stephen F. Austin State University in
Nacogdoches, Texas. He edited *Kent
State/May 4: Echoes through a Decade*
and has authored *Empire and Cold War*
and *The Libyan Arena: The United
States, Britain, and the Council of For-
eign Ministers, 1945–1948*. He served as
co-executive editor of the journal *Peace &
Change* from 1994–97.

E. Timothy Smith is professor of history
and chair of the Department of History
and Political Science at Barry University.
He is the author of *The United States,
Italy, and NATO, 1947–1952*.